Living
Options
in World
Philosophy

Living
Options
in World
Philosophy

John A. Hutchison

The University Press of Hawaii and
The Research Corporation of the University of Hawaii
Honolulu

Manufactured in the United States of America

Library of Congress Cataloging in Publication Data

Hutchison, John Alexander, 1912–
  Living options in world philosophy.

  Bibliography: p.
  Includes index.
  1. Philosophy.   2. Philosophy, Comparative.
  3. Philosophy and religion.   I. Title.
B74.H85   190   76-46489
ISBN 0-8248-0455-4

Contents

1
Toward
Global
Philosophy

DURING THE WEEK of July 20, 1969, the people of the world were given a momentary vision of global unity. During this week the Apollo XI astronauts made man's first successful moon landing and return to earth. For a brief moment humankind seemed drawn together by a common enthusiasm. Both literally and figuratively man had a view of spaceship earth from outer space, and there was a momentary sense of global unity transcending all differences. But the vision faded as quickly as it appeared, and human beings quickly resumed the fratricidal divisions and conflicts that have been the chronic lot of humanity, and which now constitute our acute contemporary predicament.

The vision of one world is by no means new. Seers and sages throughout human history have dreamed this dream. The great prophets of Israel broke through the tribalism and nationalism of Israel's earlier history, and proclaimed a message of one God who was creator and lord of all. One God, therefore one mankind, was the logic of their vision. In a later century of intense nationalism, Jesus of Nazareth reached back and laid hold of this faith of the prophets in the one universal God and gave it new and eloquent meaning in his Kingdom of God, where, he said, people would gather from all parts of the earth. The Stoic philosophers of Greece and Rome spoke of the world as *kosmopolis*, the city of the world. In other faiths and philosophies of the world, there have been analogous images and ideas of a single human community.

Yet, it has been the historic significance of modern natural science and science's brawny child technology to give material substance to what had previously been an apocalyptic vision of last things. For of all the forms and movements of human thought, natural science is the one inherently universal in outlook. It is so in the precise sense that scientific knowledge consists of impersonal generalizations transcending all particular circumstances, such as individual personality, race, and nationality. Furthermore, those who pursue and embody science constitute a genuinely universal human community. What is even more important, the impact and consequences of science and technology have thrust humankind into an existent unity for good or evil from which there is no turning back.

Yet here too ambiguity persists. For, from scientific technology have come alike the new instrumentalities that have brought the people of the earth together as never before, and the deadly instrumentalities of nuclear warfare that make the suicide of mankind a literal possibility. The same scientific and technical instrumentalities may be used equally for genuine communication and community or for ideological conflict, propaganda, and nuclear warfare.

These facts are so well known that it is today virtually a cliché to declare that we shall have one world or none. Nevertheless, these familiar words do define a crisis in human history, whose reality and significance are hard to overstate. For crises of comparable significance we shall have to go far back in human history to the period approximately 4000 to 3000 B.C., when several of the folk cultures of the Eurasian landmass from Greece and Egypt in the west to China in the east were transformed into archaic civilizations; and what we have since learned to call humanity was set on its way. Since this movement was characterized by the emergence of cities, it has been labeled the ancient "urban revolution." Several features that distinguish the newly emergent civilized societies of the urban revolution from precivilized folk societies may be mentioned: (1) increased size, (2) accumulation of capital, with the accompanying institution of taxation, (3) monumental public works, (4) writing, (5) the beginnings of exact sciences, (6) division of labor, (7) a privileged ruling class, (8) the state, and (9) standing armies and the institutionalization of warfare.[1]

Some millennia later, in another period of history which Karl Jaspers and others have termed the Axis Age (approximately 700 to 400 B.C.), strong individuals in these archaic city-state civilizations pushed away the tight embrace of ancient society and dared to assert their individual human selfhood.[2] The defining feature of the Axis Age was thus the historic emergence of individual human selfhood. With individual selfhood came revolutionary new possibilities for social change, for it brought to mankind enormously greater flexibility of response. Some of the great individuals who produced this age were religious founders or reformers, such as the prophets of Israel, Zoroaster of ancient Iran, and the unknown author of the Bhagavad

Gita in India. Others were philosophers, from Thales in Greece to Confucius in China.

Our contemporary crisis, which is of comparable magnitude and significance to these two ancient ages, consists of the fact that now, as the consequence of many complex causes, humankind has effectively become one. As a result, we human beings are now either partners together in a common doom or inheritors of a common human promise. In either case, our destiny is one. Where it will lead us, along what paths, to face whatever new perils and problems, no one can now say. In any event, this book is written in the conviction that as we move into this unknown future we humans shall need philosophy as our guide.

I daresay not many philosophers, professional or amateur, would quarrel with these judgments. Yet the odd fact is that today academic philosophy seems very largely confined within the narrow limits of what would more properly be labeled modern Western philosophy. In current philosophizing there is some concern with ancient and medieval philosophy, yet these sources are seldom decisive or even influential in our philosophic discussion.

What is even more serious is that concern for the philosophy of the non-Western cultures is still peripheral or nonexistent. Many philosophers who would be ashamed of ignorance in other fields continue to pass over the non-Western world (which is both historically and geographically most of mankind) without a glance or a twinge of conscience. This situation can be judged only as a continuation of the arrogant provincialism that has characterized the long tradition of Western dealings with the peoples of Africa and Asia. I write in the modest hope of challenging these attitudes as unworthy of philosophy.

Philosophy has contributed significantly to bringing mankind to its present unity. Historically, philosophy has characteristically been the foe of narrowness, bigotry, and intolerance. When it has been alive and awake to its task, it has held that nothing human is alien to its inclusive vision. True, there have existed many systems of philosophy devoted to rationalizing the status quo; in the currently popular phrase, there have been philosophies and philosophers of every establishment that has exercised dominion over men's minds and lives. However, the task of challenging and criticizing these establishments has also been philosophical. I believe that philosophy is called again to the double task of criticism and guidance in humanity's present time of need. The real question is whether our philosophy is today sufficiently vital and vigorous to be able to hear and heed this call.

There are both similarities and differences to philosophy in the issues that relate our theme of global unity to mankind's historic religions. We have already alluded to the vision of universal humanity which is embedded in several of these faiths. The universal religions are those which dare to address man as human, rather than as Japanese, American, Eskimo, or Andaman Islander. In these terms, it is a historical fact that many of mankind's religions have not been universal, but inherently local in nature and significance; and even those that profess universality have often reverted in practice to localism or provincialism.

Speaking in most general terms, we may characterize the religious vision as that of a trans-human absolute, variously expressed and characterized in the symbols of different traditions. The religious object is variously characterized as God, Brahman, Nirvana or Shunya, the One, Heaven—and as we shall presently see—much else. However formulated, it has served man as a kind of Archimedean point above the common world of nature and society. When humanity has served this vision with integrity of heart and mind, it has been the source of such virtues as wisdom, faith, and love. Mankind desperately needs these virtues today, whatever their source or the symbolic forms in which they find expression.

Yet, a crucial problem is what may be termed the pathology of this vision of a trans-human absolute. This pathology consists in the persistent human tendency not to serve it, but to make it serve man's egotistical purposes. Reinhold Niebuhr wrote mordantly of man's tendency to "absolutize" his relative concerns, whether individual or collective, of people, class, or nation. Man does this in a variety of ways, characterizing these concerns as divine, absolute, or otherwise final, and hence above criticism. The consequences of this tendency are summarized in Niebuhr's trenchant epigram: When man plays God, he becomes the devil to his fellowman.

This same issue can be expressed in terms of the attitude of conviction that lies at the center of what traditional religions have called faith. Authentic conviction or faith inclusively unifies the self, and hence makes possible the freedom and love in which human selfhood finds fulfillment. But it is as easy as it is tragic for this attitude of conviction or faith to become exclusive, rigid, defensive, and hence irrational. When this happens it produces all the vices charged to traditional religion by its critics. Religions then harden into systems of intolerance and fanaticism, which produce not unity but disunity and conflict. Hence the biblical text, by their fruits you shall know them, seems particularly pertinent today for the judgment of mankind's traditional religions. Furthermore, one of philosophy's functions in many times and places in human history has been this critical appraisal and evaluation of religion.

Indeed, the relation of philosophy to religion is an issue which will be with us throughout the pages that follow. The ethical or moral criticism of religion has just been alluded to. In the next chapter we shall argue more generally that the origin or source of philosophical thinking lies in the questioning of a religious tradition. To be sure, once a philosophy has come into being it goes its own way and lives its own independent life, related to some or all of the many facets of human culture. Of these, the exposition and/or criticism of religion is only one. Yet, a glance at our table of contents will show how many of the world's philosophical options bear some continuing relation to religion.

This issue is one on which many contemporary Western philosophers will disagree with the viewpoint of our study. Speaking out of the staunchly secular viewpoint that has won the field in contemporary Western philosophy, these philosophers look with both disagreement and disapproval at what appears to them an unjustified and obsolete preoccupation with religion (or perhaps even with prescientific superstition). At this point in our study we can only reply that we must take philosophy where we find it. And we sometimes find it in strange, unlikely places. We can also ask the reader to withhold judgment on this issue until the pertinent facts are before him.

My central aim in the chapters that follow is a modest one. It is to draw the living philosophies of the world together into a common arena of discussion. I seek to draw them close enough together so that each will know of the others' existence. The first modest step toward philosophizing in global context is to be aware of the options. Hence, we shall attempt to lay out the living options in world philosophy as fully and fairly as possible. Then, in the last chapter, we shall attempt to trace the path of the options at least a short distance into the human future.

In this connection it is pleasant to acknowledge the pioneering work in this field accomplished over the past half-century at the University of Hawaii, in sponsoring conferences of Asian and Western philosophers, in holding seminars, in publishing books and periodicals, and surely not least of all, in discussions in the classrooms and studies of its philosophy and religion departments. The result of these labors has been at least a beginning of acquaintance, both intellectual and personal, between philosophers of Asia and the West. In passing, it is a puzzling question as to why this work has not had a wider impact than has been the case.

It is well to be aware from the outset of the problems and perils of the method we shall follow. For one thing, the philosophies discussed here are by no means the simple and discrete entities that the chapter titles may suggest. There is more often than not a significant overlap among them; common issues and problems run like weavers' shuttles back and forth across them. Perhaps a more illuminating metaphor, especially for the Western philosophies to be considered, is that of style. Our philosophies are not so much systematic types as they are different styles of philosophical thinking. Or, indeed, they are keys in which, like musical composition, philosophies are composed. Again, it must be frankly conceded that a different author might well have drawn the boundary lines between philosophies in ways very different from mine.

Yet, perhaps the most important limitation of all is that of sheer space. Any one of the philosophies considered might easily have occupied the entire book. Indeed, every single idea and person considered is worthy of far more detailed treatment than possible here. For this limitation, I can only plead the nature of my project as a whole. The first reading of any philosophy is bound to be superficial; but there must be a first reading!

Of the chapters that follow, chapter 2 deals with the nature and method of philosophical thinking, and chapter 15 returns to the theme of philosophy in a global context. Concerning chapter 2, some friendly critics have suggested it would come better at the end than at the beginning of the book, after the method has been practiced and illustrated. I can only say that it deals with methods and tools of study which I have found essential to the study of the chapters that follow. Hence, I have persisted in its present location. But having raised this issue, I am content to let each reader deal with it as he wishes.

The intervening chapters, namely 3 through 14, deal respectively with the "living options" of our title. They may be read in any order that the reader's interest may determine, as there is no cumulative or sequential order among them.

Any book is addressed by the author to the reader; it is in other words literally an essay in communication. My book is no exception to this rule. It will perhaps facilitate communication to say what sort of readers I have had in mind as these pages have taken shape. First and most important is the thoughtful general reader, concerned as I am for the problem of global unity, interested to know what goes on in philosophy around the world, and wanting to see how philosophy may make a contribution, however modest, to the problem of global unity.

But I have also had in mind professional colleagues whose education has to date left blank the field of non-Western philosophy. Let me say that this book has grown out of study and travel over several years, aimed at filling this blank in my own mind and life. I have sought to place the main forms of living non-Western as well as Western philosophy within the single arena of contemporary philosophic discussion.

For the sake of those who may wish to know my sources, I have included notes, which however, in order not to encumber the general reader, have been placed at the end of the book. I have also included after each chapter a selection of books that I have found essential, and which readers may find helpful in further study.

This book is an introduction in still a further sense. It is a bare beginning in a line of thought that must be developed further if mankind is to have a future. Hence, it is my expectation that others, readers of this book hopefully among them, will push onward with ideas that here receive at most an initial statement.

II
What
Philosophy
Is and Does

BEFORE WE CAN PROCEED with our study of the world's living philosophic options, we must pause to consider the question of what philosophy is and does. Among the many reasons for this is that an inescapable aspect of philosophic thinking is reflection on its own nature. Some forms of human thinking and practice may be done—and even done better—without conscious attention to what they are and do. However, this is not true of philosophy. There is, as we shall have repeated occasions to point out, such a thing as unconscious philosophy. In this chapter we shall argue that philosophy may be defined in terms of the horizon of widest generality around all human thought and culture; and it is a fact that this horizon may or may not be consciously recognized. However, *unconscious* necessarily means uncriticized and uncritical, for we cannot criticize that of which we are unconscious. Hence, we will philosophize well only when we are clearly aware of what we are doing.

Philosophy is today enjoying a period of vigorous life in many parts of the world, yet there is little or no agreement among contemporary philosophers concerning the nature and function of philosophy. Quite the contrary, wherever philosophers gather for discussion, there is widespread controversy and conflict on this key question. Thus, any answer that can be given here must be understood to be controversial, and hence open to further discussion. The answer here will be this author's own, and the reader is encouraged to respond with his own way of philosophizing. For, as we shall presently argue, each man must ultimately be his own philosopher. Furthermore, the emphases of this chapter are aimed at the project before us, namely, that of beginning to philosophize in a global context.

The world greatly needs philosophy today, for, as the preceding chapter asserted, the present is an age of radical revolution, when humanity has struck tents and is moving into an unknown future. One of the historic roles of philosophy has been guidance for such a time as this. Yet, the world needs philosophy—let it be added—only if philosophy can rise to this historic occasion.

In this chapter we shall consider very briefly three questions: first, what philosophy is; second, how it goes about its work; and third, what it will and will not do for us. We shall also sketch with equal brevity some main, recurring themes of the philosophies of the succeeding chapters.

What Philosophy Is

First, it is important to say as emphatically as possible that philosophy is a way of thinking before it is a system of conclusions neatly packaged in a system. True, whenever successful thinking occurs, there will be conclusions, but they will invariably be tentative, forever subject to revision. "Not philosophy but to philosophize" is an ancient Greek maxim worthy of following wherever man aspires to think philosophically. It must be accounted an occupational hazard of professional philosophers that the conclusions of certain great philosophers of the past are gathered into systems which soon become the isms of the textbooks.

This constitutes a warning for a study of the world's philosophies that proceeds by types. As argued in chapter 1, these types must be understood as ways or indeed styles of philosophizing rather than as systems, closed and complete. Clearly, no one lives within a system of philosophy as a family resides in a house. Nineteenth century philosophers constructed philosophical systems as nineteenth century gentlemen built stately mansions. The twentieth century has bulldozed both the mansions and the systems to rubble, to make room for highways, parking lots, and other putatively useful facilities.

Yet while philosophy is thinking, not all thinking is philosophical thinking—even though philosophy in one of its aspects is a dimension of the mind's whole life. What then is distinctive of philosophical thinking?

The contrast between natural science and philosophy may serve us as a point of departure. Science and philosophy have so many similarities that some philosophers seek to extend the scientific method to their own discipline. Yet, there is at least one fundamental contrast. Scientific thinking occurs within a definite domain, usually delineated by the basic definitions and primary categories of the particular science. Thus, for example, mechanics deals with matter in motion, chemistry with the composition of matter, and so on. While the boundaries of a given science change significantly with time, at any given moment they are definite.

This definite domain is an indispensable feature of scientific thinking, for it makes possible a decisive judgment whether a given issue is relevant or irrelevant, that is, inside or outside the field in question. Hence, in a word, the scientist knows where to look—and where not to look—in order to test his hypothesis or theory. From this it follows that scientific statements are susceptible of decisive testing, that is, of verification or disproof.

If, on the other hand, the scientist were told to look to the entire universe (defined as the scheme-of-things-entire, or the absolute totality of all things whatsoever) as his domain, no such decisive test would be possible. We argue that this is precisely philosophy's predicament. From the possibility of decisive testing within a definite domain follows in turn the cumulative or progressive character of scientific knowledge—a trait not shared by knowledge in the humanities, including philosophy—and many would add, also not shared by the social sciences.

Philosophical thinking appears preeminently to lack such a definite domain. It is man's attempt to say something true—and to think something true—whose referent is absolutely everything. More precisely, it is his effort to think within the widest context that his mind is capable of envisaging. It is the effort of his mind to place himself and all his experience within this widest possible totality, in order to orient himself to the scheme-of-things-entire. Thus, while the sciences deal with limited totalities, such as all bodies, all elements and compounds of matter, all living organisms, and so on, philosophy seeks to deal with that completely unlimited totality which mankind sometimes calls the universe.

Readers familiar with current philosophical discussion will recognize this definition of philosophy's nature and task as similar to that of traditional metaphysics, against which a half-century of antimetaphysical criticism and polemics have been waged. It is significant therefore to quote in support of this view the definition of philosophy's task given by one of the most consistently antimetaphysical philosophers of the past generation, the late G. E. Moore. In *Some Main Problems of Philosophy* he characterized philosophy's task in the following words:

> To begin with then, it seems to me that the most important and interesting thing which philosophers have tried to do is no less than this; namely: To give a general description of the whole of the Universe, mentioning all the most important kinds of things which we *know* to be in it, considering how far it is likely that there are in it important kinds of things which we do not absolutely

know to be in it, and also considering the most important ways in which these various kinds of things are related to one another. I will call all this for short "Giving a general description of the whole Universe" and hence will say that the first and most important problem of philosophy is: To give a general description of the *whole* Universe.[1]

To Moore may also be added the example of Wittgenstein's *Tractatus Logico-Philosophicus*, which begins with definition of *world* as "everything that is the case." Returning to the same theme, Wittgenstein asserts, "the totality of existent atomic facts is the world" (2.04), and again, "the total reality is the world." (2.063).[2] To be sure, Wittgenstein does not give an inventory of this unique class or set, but rather asserts its logical structure. That is to say, he approaches it intensionally rather than extensionally. One need not agree with Wittgenstein's characterization of the world (and I for one would disagree with such aspects as his rigid separation of fact from value) in order to see in this concept of the world a formulation of the distinctive philosophic or metaphysical notion of all-inclusive totality.

This concept of all-inclusive totality has recently been accorded logical formulation by Alvin Plantinga in *Possible Worlds* and *God, Freedom and Evil*.[3] Plantinga begins with a correlation between propositions and states of affairs. Thus a proposition *p* corresponds to a state of affairs *s*, if it is impossible that *p* be true and *s* fail to obtain, and conversely if it is impossible that *s* obtain and *p* fail to be true. From this it follows that some states of affairs "obtain," and others do not; and among the latter some are possible and others impossible.

Plantinga then defines a world as a state of affairs large enough to be "maximal" or "complete." These latter terms are defined in turn by means of the logical relation of inclusion and its negative, preclusion. Inclusion, we are told, is the relation between states of affairs analogous to the logical relation of entailment among propositions. Corresponding to each possible world, there is a set of propositions which Plantinga calls its "book." A book is "a *maximally consistent set* (italics by Plantinga) or propositions," so large that the addition of another proposition will yield an "explicitly inconsistent set."[4] In these terms every "possible world" is said to have its "book." From this Plantinga draws the following conclusion:

> It should be obvious that exactly one possible world is actual. At *least* one must be, since the set of two propositions is a maximally consistent set, and hence a book. But when it corresponds to a possible world, and the possible world corresponding to this set of propositions (since it's a set of *true* propositions) will be actual. On the other hand there is at *most* one actual world. For suppose

there were two: W and W'. These worlds cannot include all the same states of affairs, if they did they would be the very same world. So there must be at least one state of affairs S such that W includes S and W' does not. But a possible world is maximal; W' therefore includes the complement, $\bar{S}$ of S. So if both W and W' were actual, as we have supposed, then both S and $\bar{S}$ would be actual—which is impossible. So there can't be more than one possible world that is actual.[5]

This view of the nature of philosophy, along with the contrast between science and philosophy that follows from it, may be confirmed by noting the presence in any representative sample of philosophic discourse of some very odd words. The list begins with such terms as *Reality*, *Being*, or *Being-as-such*, *Nature*, or *Universe*. (This last word as used in philosophy differs sharply from its meaning in the natural sciences. In the latter it means the physical universe, which is a definite, determinate, and hence a scientific concept, whereas in philosophy it has the meaning of an absolutely inclusive totality.) As we have seen, the list also includes such words as *world*, or its Greek analogue, *kosmos*. As we will presently see, Asian philosophy will add such terms as *Brahman*, *Shunya*, and the Chinese *T'ai Chi* (the Great Ultimate).

The queer behavior of these words will become clear if we try to treat them as terms in ordinary discourse, claiming reference to identifiable features within human experience. I may call the paper on which I write, white, and the pencil marks, gray, with some presumption that the reader will know what is meant and how to test these claims to meaning and truth. But suppose I claim the paper to be "real" or a part of "reality," or even go on to assert metaphysically or ontologically that it is part of a single system of Reality. How then will these words be defined or these statements tested? We shall return presently to some proposed answers to these questions. Here we note the distinctive and different use of words generated by the philosophic concept of all-inclusive totality.

This distinctive character of philosophy generates also a very different relation between the expert and the common man, the professional and the amateur, from that which prevails in many other fields. Philosophy contrasts with such fields as natural science, medicine, or law where the authority of the expert is well-nigh absolute. If I want the answer to a scientific question I ask a scientist. So analogously in legal or medical questions, my reliance on expert knowledge is virtually total.

The relation is different in a field like philosophy, where perforce each man must do his own thinking if it is to have any validity for him, and where the professional philosopher is at most a guide who leads the way over a trail which each person must walk for himself. Some activities one can and should delegate to others, but other activities are inescapably the individual's own prerogative. The range of the latter is from commonplace activities like eating one's own dinner to being born or dying. They include making up one's own mind, making one's own important choices or decisions. Doing one's own philosophizing falls into this class. Another person can no more do my philosophizing for me than he can eat my dinner and have it nourish me. This being the case, the relation of the professional philosopher to the amateur, or in other words, to Everyman as philosopher, is limited to criticism, suggestion, and guidance. For again, each man must ultimately do his own philosophizing.

This feature of philosophy is often forgotten by professional philosophers. Like any other academic discipline, philosophy has developed its own technical problems and language. These are genuine problems, and it is well that some people are professionally concerned with them. However, they bear the same relation to the whole of philosophy that the producers' goods industry bears to the whole economy. Just as the economy exists to satisfy material needs, so philosophy exists to cultivate wisdom. Accordingly, any philosophy that forgets this goal in its exclusive preoccupation with the professional problems of philosophers has sold its humane birthright for a mess of technical verbiage.

Some of us who work in philosophy departments sometimes wonder how far this sellout has gone. Not only does humane philosophizing occur in other departments; we also wonder how much, if any, still goes on in our department. Abraham Kaplan has mordantly and aptly remarked that in the love of wisdom, as in other forms of love, the professionals sometimes know least about it.

Philosophic Method

The unique context of all-inclusive totality generates the distinctive features of philosophic method. From the preceding paragraphs, several conclusions about method follow logically. The most pervasive and most important feature is that philosophy is an activity; it is one of the kinds of actions that men do—withal a highly distinctive form of doing. Beyond this generic character as an action or activity there are four specific traits of philosophical method, namely, (1) its analogical or metaphorical nature, (2) its presuppositional character, (3) the relation of critical to constructive philosophy, and (4) its relation to historical tradition. We shall consider them briefly in order.

(1) The first feature, already alluded to, has to do with the use of words

for the distinctive philosophic function. Language comes into being for the primary purpose of guiding man's behavior in the world of objects that environs him. How then can it be reshaped for this new function, pointing to something beyond, transcending the common world, or at least different from the common world? Concerning the terms *transcendence* and *transcend*, a logical whole taken as an integral configuration (in German a *Gestalt*) may be said to transcend any specific one or any numerable group of its parts. In this sense, the world or universe may be said to "transcend" the kind of finite human experience that gives birth to and primarily engages language. In passing, there are other uses of the word *transcend*; for example, the traditional monotheistic God is said in another and different sense to transcend the world.

The question concerning the relation of language to this new function is a fair one to which, at least in some quarters, considerable thought has been devoted. To answer in a summary word, this novel philosophic use may be characterized as metaphorical or analogical projection.

Approaching any new object, man first characterizes it as like *a* or *b*, which he already knows, perhaps adding other similes and even indicating ways in which the new entity is also unlike familiar objects. Presently *like* falls away, and simile becomes metaphor. Gradually the metaphor becomes familiar, and is accepted as a literal predicate. It has been accurately observed that such a dead metaphor lies at the base of many words now deemed to have literal or nonmetaphorical meaning. The question is at what point metaphor dies, becoming an ordinary literal predicate.

Adequately understood, as such writers as Philip Wheelwright and Paul Ricoeur have instructed us, metaphor is not simply the "implied comparison" of the textbooks of grammar and linguistics.[6] Rather it is a basic strategy of the human mind in laying hold of its world. For we must not assume the finality of any one way of gathering the innumerable particulars of experience into the conventional groupings of words. On the contrary, we must assert the possibility of ever new and different ways of making these groupings. In this context (if we may define metaphor by means of a metaphor) we may say that metaphor runs a sword through the fullness of experience, impaling together some new or striking group of particulars, effecting some novel classification of particulars. As such it is a basic device of the human mind and tongue.

In a way similar to metaphor, the human mind lays hold upon the unique totality that is the defining feature of philosophic thinking. It is "like this" or "like that" entity within the world of people and things. Stephen Pepper's *World Hypotheses* studies this situation, though it unduly restricts the range of metaphors available for metaphysical predication.[7] For our present viewpoint, any metaphor that man has used to characterize the scheme-of-things-entire takes on metaphysical significance. The problem consists of making a reasoned judgment concerning its adequacy for this function.

The traditional Thomist concept of analogy is useful in this connection. The Greek term, *analogia*, originally meant *proportion*, in the mathematical sense of the word. Thus if we assert $a : b : : c : d$, and if we know the values of three of these symbols we can solve for the fourth. Thus, mathematically we may say that $2 : 4 : : 8 : x$, and solve for x, which in this case is 16. In the application of analogy to metaphysical thinking, the first symbol, *(a)* stands for the context of man's everyday experience; the second, *(b)*, for the meaning of the term or word in question in this ordinary context; the third term, *(c)*, stands for what we have called the unique concept of all-inclusive totality, and the fourth, *(d)*, for which we seek to solve, will be the analogical projection of the second term into this new context. Thus, for example, we may wish to speak of the universe as either mechanistic or mental. Analogical reasoning begins with *(a)*, ordinary human experience, and *(b)*, the literal meaning of either of these adjectives in this context. The third term, *(c)*, is the universe or all-inclusive totality of which we wish analogically to predicate, *(d)*, the adjectives in question.

Many contemporary philosophers would question or reject the third term of this analogy and, with two undefined terms, would conclude that the proposition is insoluble. We reply that we have fixed the meaning of the third term by stating its function in our mind's life, namely, that of all-inclusive totality. It forms the horizon of all-inclusive totality around man's world. Hence, the fourth term becomes determinate.

An additional feature of considerable importance concerning metaphysical terms, though seldom recognized, is that they are also very often powerful expressive symbols. As such they function in human discourse in ways similar to the key words or images of a poem. This dimension of metaphysical terms also points significantly to the fact that they are vehicles for the expression of attitude or states of feelings. Still we seek not just any images or symbols, but well-founded, rationally explicable and defensible ones. The student of philosophy asks on what rational ground he may be led to accept or reject any or all of the images or analogical symbols that are proposed as candidates for metaphysical predication.

The answer in most general form is that we seek terms and statements most adequate to the facts of existence. Each of the words of this last sentence cries out for more detailed explanation than is here possible. Yet, we must at least sketch a line of explanation and exposition. A statement is ideally adequate if it conflicts with no factual evidence, satisfies the widest field of pertinent evidence, and leaves no areas unexplained. Some such formulation of the idea of adequate explanation, incidentally, holds good not only for philosophy but for all kinds of explanation over the whole wide field of human thought.

A key word here is *fact*, and as many readers well know, recent and contemporary philosophy has given much attention to what a fact is. Perhaps the simplest and readiest definition of a fact is that it is the referent of a true singular proposition. Modern logic has classified propositions as singular (those which refer to *this* or *that*, to *John* or *Mary*) and general (those which refer to groups of *this's* or *that's*, *Johns* or *Marys*). Whether the world to which our statements refer is made up of individual facts waiting like berries on a bush to be picked is a matter on which we need not commit ourselves. For, in any case, this is the character of the language and logic by which we cope with this world. Accordingly, we here characterize a fact functionally by the way we catch it in the net of language, namely by means of singular statements that pass our tests for meaning and truth. The process of determining the truth or falsehood of such statements, while it has significant overall or general features, also in other respects has a specific matter that varies from one region of experience to another. It will differ in, say, biology and history, as the methods of those disciplines differ from each other.

We return to the key problem for philosophic method and language, namely the unlimited domain of philosophical thinking and discourse. One traditional definition of philosophy is that it is the discipline for which *all* facts are relevant. How shall we cope with this unique and odd situation? First we shall readily concede that conclusive verification or proof for any philosophical statement is not possible. With Hume we must say that here (as indeed in all matters of factual knowledge) probability is the guide of life. But how can we even achieve probability, particularly on the larger issues of philosophic concern? The answer in all candor is that we must seek those views that are supported by the weight of evidence, or in alternative formulation, those that cohere with the wider, more extensive fields of facts. Then we must leave the issue open for further exploration. Philosophic questions, unlike some scientific questions, seem never to be definitely and fully answered and done with. Hence, any individual person's most basic intellectual commitment is properly not to any particular conclusion but to the whole unending corporate process of critical inquiry.

Two further observations may also be added. First, if the conclusions of section (3) below are correct, then philosophical questions constitute what William James called forced options. Hence, the question is never, philosophy or no philosophy, but rather, *which* philosophy will I have? Further, in the face of what we have called philosophy's infinite domain, we proceed methodologically by systematic extrapolation from specifically delineated or defined areas of experience, seeking always the most widely coherent or adequate extrapolation.

(2) Second, we have alluded to unconscious philosophizing, namely to philosophical ideas and attitudes of which the holder is unconscious, but which can be shown to have consequences in his thought and action. Such elements frequently function as unconscious assumptions or postulates of thought. Hence, as a second feature of its method, the task of philosophy is to draw these into the open where they may be critically appraised. In other words, philosophy proceeds by what may be called a presuppositional method.

In recent philosophy R. G. Collingwood is well-known for his view that metaphysics consists of the ''absolute presuppositions'' that lie unconscious at the foundations of the mind of an individual or a culture. There is important truth here, but in Collingwood it suffers from ambiguous and distorted formulation.[8] For one thing, Collingwood never tells us clearly what he means by *presupposing*, and indeed, the logical analysis of this word is still a significant agenda for philosophy. What are the defining features of a presupposition?[9] More importantly, Collingwood argues that metaphysics consists necessarily of unconscious presuppositions, and that to dig out such assumptions, or presuppositions, and exhibit them to the light of day in effect kills them. Hence, in Collingwood's view, philosophers become the archaeologists of the dead presuppositions, which is to say, of the dead metaphysical systems of past ages. It is important to point out that in Collingwood's view a man can never become aware of his own deepest presuppositions. Certainly he cannot both be aware of them and still hold them. In this view the act of awareness destroys its presuppositional status, shifting the activity of presupposing to some other preassumption, which at the moment of being presupposed lies unconscious at the very bottom of one's mind.

Our first response to Collingwood is to agree generally with the view that an important part of the work of philosophy consists of drawing such unconscious and half-conscious assumptions into the light of day and subjecting them to critical scrutiny. Surely this is never easy and never altogether certain in its findings; and when one's own deepest assumptions are involved, it is sometimes as painful as it is difficult—as psychoanalysis has amply shown. However, to deny in advance the possibility of such self-analysis underestimates what we may call the reflexive power of the mind, namely its capacity to turn analysis back upon itself. That none of us ever achieves more than partial success in this activity is no excuse for evading or avoiding the attempt, for this is a very important area of experience—too important to leave unexamined and uncriticized. To do this analysis while still holding these assumptions may perhaps be compared to the task of working on an electric power line without turning off the power—a dangerous but important operation.

(3) The preceding paragraph leads us to a third related aspect of philosophical method, namely, its correlation of critical to constructive thinking, or as some would prefer, of analytic to synthetic thinking. The former is frequently defined as the rigorous and comprehensive criticism of other people's philosophies, while the latter is defined as the constructing of one's own philosophic system—building one's mansion or pitching one's tent, as the case may be. Often it is assumed that these two activities are separable, that the first can be carried on independent of the second. In other fields of thought, as for example, natural science, it does appear possible to criticize one theory without presupposing an alternative theory of one's own. In such fields as science it is possible to stand clear of all hypotheses or theories. It is precisely this detachment from all theories, and mutual separability of theories, that seem impossible in philosophy. In this region of the mind's life, if I criticize one theory I do so on the basis of some other, which consciously or unconsciously I assume and hold. Apparently it is not possible for the human mind to divest itself of all philosophic assumptions or presuppositions. When a person tries to do this, he simply makes one more philosophy out of the vain attempt to hold no philosophy. This issue is by no means merely verbal. Rather, the philosophic function of one's mind continues to operate, and hence is driven underground, where it continues to influence his thought and action in ways of which he is unaware. Hence, the unconscious philosophizing, to which we have alluded.

This is an impasse that is avoidable if we assume that criticism and construction, analysis and synthesis, are dual aspects of the integral task of philosophic thinking. One may be emphasized and the other deemphasized, one may be done well and the other ill, but clearly neither occurs entirely apart from the other. The critical aspect of philosophy is simply every person's rigorous critical reflection carried on within the wide context of Reality. All criticism tends to become philosophical just in the measure that its context widens to include all Reality.

Philosophical construction or synthesis, by contrast, defies easy description. As we have argued, metaphysical system-building in the fashion of much traditional nineteenth century philosophy is a crude parody of constructive philosophizing. Construction is properly that activity of thinking by which a person, consciously acknowledging what we have termed all-inclusive totality, seeks terms by which to cope with it, orients himself to it, and hence finds guidance for his human journey. Indeed it will be more accurately descriptive of this philosophic activity to drop the metaphor of construction for that of orientation, or for that of guidance along a path. Thus what we have termed constructive philosophizing will consist of orienting oneself on the map of Reality and then plotting one's journey by means of this map.

(4) From our assertion that every man is his own philosopher, it might be concluded that solitary individualism, even solipsism, is the final word in philosophy. Actually, just the opposite is the case. Each of us does his own philosophizing, to be sure, but he does so within a community and a tradition.

It is not the case that human selves first develop, Robinson Crusoe fashion, as self-sufficient individuals who then subsequently assemble together to constitute society. Rather is it true that individual selves are brought into being, nourished, sustained, molded, and guided by an environing society. The existent reality is always selves-in-community. Such concrete communities or cultures may be defined as societies of people drawn together around certain unifying valuations that define and guide their common life. Tradition, as the term is used here, is simply the culture or community in its transmissive aspects, passing on its basic valuations from one generation to the next.

The writer and most readers of this book are members of that culture or civilization that historians have labeled as the West. We live, and hence we philosophize, within this tradition. This means that we do our philosophical thinking with Plato, Aristotle, and others of this Western philosophical tradition, looking over our shoulders. By this I mean that our philosophizing takes place within this historical tradition, and is informed and guided by the ideas and values of this tradition. Furthermore, this is true whether we consciously acknowledge it or not.

The term, *philosophy*, is, of course, Greek in origin, and at least one contemporary philosopher, Martin Heidegger, has proposed to reform philosophy by turning back to its earliest, pre-Platonic Greek sources.[10] To this somewhat extreme conclusion, it may be replied that a more adequate historical view of the situation will acknowledge that, while the sources of Western philosophy do indeed lie in certain limpid springs in ancient Greece, nevertheless the stream that has its source there has flowed like a river through many territories, both influencing and being influenced by surrounding landscapes. The stream of Western philosophy has also been fed by many other ancillary sources and streams, from ancient Christianity to modern natural science.

John Herman Randall has made a similar assertion concerning Western philosophy, by means of a different metaphor. Philosophy, he suggests, may be compared to a courtesan who has from age to age lived with different men.[11] *Philosophia* cohabited first with certain ancient Greek inquirers and teachers. Later she lived for a time with early Christian ascetics and theologians such as Origen and Augustine. Still later she paused for a time with a scholastic doctor and monk named Aquinas, then with a heretical monk and mystic named Eckhart. More recently her favors have fallen to scientists, and to students of history and politics.

Whatever one's preference in metaphors, the point is clear that philosophical thinking is inescapably historical in character. It is an activity taking place in time, both being influenced by what has gone before in the tradition and influencing what follows. If this trait is not always perceptible in the small problems of philosophy, it does become visible in the larger problems. This implies that the history of philosophy is logically related to present-day philosophizing in ways in which the history of natural science is not related to contemporary scientific work. One can learn a natural science with only incidental glances at the history of science; in philosophy this independence of the past is not the case.

The relation of the individual to his culture and tradition has an additional and all-important implication for this book. We are concerned with global philosophy. If it is true that Western man philosophizes in a historical tradition, this is equally true of others as well, of East Indians, Chinese, and Japanese. Hence, if we are to have any chance to understand their philosophies, we shall have to look at the different civilized traditions in which they occur and of which they are parts. These reflections raise also the further enormously difficult question of whether there is or ever will be a global culture and tradition—an issue which we defer until the closing chapter of our study.

Uses and Limits of Philosophy

What will philosophy do for us—and what won't it do? What are the aims or goals of philosophical thinking? What is its chief end or summum bonum?

(1) First of all, it is important to say, loud and clear, that it will not give us arcane or esoteric knowledge. Especially at the beginning of this study this must be said against a succession of Western students of the Orient, from

Madame Blavatsky and Annie Besant to Allen Ginsberg, who invest the mysterious East with mysteries past all rational finding out. In passing, this must also be asserted against those Western philosophies such as some nineteenth century idealisms, which claim to penetrate beyond the door that never opens or the veil that is never lifted.

Against all such views, philosophies of common sense and common language argue validly that philosophy has no access to any knowledge not equally accessible to the common man, to man as man. This is both true and significant, but it is a truth that cuts two ways. It denies arcane knowledge. However, if it limits philosophy to the vision of the common man, it also calls attention to philosophic issues that are embedded in our common humanity. And these are most of the truly significant issues of what the previous section termed constructive philosophy.

Contemporary analytic philosophy has argued long and intensely that most of the business of philosophy consists of clarifying the muddles and snarls of traditional philosophy. We readily concede the conclusion that there have been much muddling and gabbling in traditional philosophy. Therefore, the critical task of clarification is a labor of major proportions and significance. But it is not the whole task of philosophy. Whitehead wrote in characteristic epigram: "It is written that man shall not live by bread alone; how much more is it true that he shall not live by disinfectant alone."[12]

(2) A further good or goal of equal magnitude with clarification is that of perspective. If it be true that philosophy consists of inquiry into the widest, most general categories applicable to experience and reality, then it follows that one benefit to be derived from this activity is perspective—the perspective of seeing oneself as a part of the scheme-of-things-entire, as a member of the universe. In an age of intense preoccupation with the here-and-now, such a perspective of the wide horizon and the long look is a great and precious good.

Yet, the qualification must immediately be added that the good of perspective is more a by-product than a direct result of philosophic thinking. One does not engage in philosophy in order to achieve perspective, but rather because one is interested in philosophic problems. Yet, it is the testimony of many wise persons that the balanced vision which sees life steadily and whole accrues as a by-product of work in this field of study.

(3) The motto of the Phi Beta Kappa society inscribed in Greek on its seal and key is *Philosophia Biou Kybernetes*, "philosophy the guide of life." For many past generations of people, philosophy performed this function—with widely varying degrees of success. But the more urgent question is whether and how it can perform this role in today's world.

If there is any single question or problem that surfaces in thoughtful minds all over the contemporary world, it is simply and plainly how to be human. In the face of so many powerful forces, internal and external, that depersonalize and dehumanize, this question is intensely and existentially real. In such a world as this, what are the humanizing values? By what means and in what terms may we lay hold upon them and sustain them in our individual and common life? In today's world no questions have more terrifying urgency than these. Hence, they constitute a kind of standing challenge to all the world's faiths and philosophies to give a convincing answer. A primary task of contemporary philosophy consists, then, of the articulation and appraisal of the values that define and sustain our humanity.

The contemporary global integration of mankind again places new demands on our philosophies in this issue. For, in this new context we see that there is not just one humanism, but several. Indeed, there are as many humanisms as there are civilized cultures and traditions. What has often passed as humanism must now wear the label, Western humanism. For there also exist Indian humanism, Chinese and Japanese humanism, and doubtless many more as well, each with its own answer to the human question: What must I do and be to become human and civilized? To this question we shall return in the next section.

Some Main Themes of Philosophy

As we have argued, no man ever lives completely within a single system of philosophy. This is true, among other reasons, because recurring themes or issues move like weavers' shuttles back and forth across our types or options of philosophy. These themes range from the nature of cause, or of knowledge, to the nature and status of human value. Here we select for brief exposition three such recurring themes that combine intrinsic interest with pertinence to the project of this book.

(1) The first such theme is the question of our preceding section, namely, the status and significance of human nature. Most of the world's philosophies deal in their respective ways with such issues as the puzzling combination of freedom and necessity that characterizes man's relation to his world, and with what philosophy calls man's chief good or summum bonum. The latter issue is sometimes formulated in contemporary philosophy as the problem of value, including the relation of value to fact. Hence, most of the ways of philosophy that follow in this book yield some distinctive view of man. In many cases this view will be explicit and clear, in other cases the reader will have to draw out lines of implication to make explicit and clear a view of the human situation.

This aspect of philosophy has particular pertinence to our situation in the second half of the twentieth century. For ours is a time in which all the traditional values that have given shape and meaning to personality and culture are being rudely and radically challenged. Hence, to put this question and to help man achieve answers is a central part of philosophy's contemporary task.

As we shall see in chapter 5, existentialism is a philosophy that has taken the question, What is man?, and placed it in the center of philosophic inquiry. The details of existentialism will have to wait until chapter 5. Here, however, we can note that the existential question itself is part of the human situation. In other words, man is the creature who asks, who am I?, and what must I do and be to be genuinely human?

For such questions there seem to be no parallels in animal life. If the dog asks the question, what must I do and be to be genuinely canine? he keeps it a secret from us. The case is similar for the cow, the horse, and other creatures. The dog's caninity, the cow's bovinity, and the horse's equinity appear to human observation to be given facts of nature, not at all problematic to these respective creatures.

With man the situation is radically different. His essence, namely his humanity (however this may be defined or described) *is* a problem for him. He does ask what his humanity is or consists of. So it is that man's humanity is not just a fate to be endured, but an ideal to be aspired to, to be won or lost on the playing field of human existence. For it must also be noted that man not only asks this question, he lives out his answer. This is not the kind of question that can be answered in a classroom or in a book of philosophy, but rather in man's whole active life.

To visualize the significance of this existential question for the world's philosophies which we seek to study, I propose an allegory or parable. Let the reader imagine a circle at the center of which stands a little fellow who is apparently talking to himself. Some observers assert that he is babbling incoherently, yet if we listen carefully we shall hear from his lips precisely the questions we are concerned with, who am I?, why am I alive? The little man in the center of the circle is, of course, Everyman.

Around the circumference of the circle stands a large and varied group of people who appear to be calling their answers to his questions. They speak in many different languages, and behave in various ways toward the man in the middle and toward each other. Some appear unaware of the existence of others. Some quarrel with their neighbors, and make threatening gestures toward others and toward the man in the middle. Still others take an opposite tack, whispering so quietly that they appear to be silent. Some appear to be talking nonsense. A few seem to speak plainly and forthrightly.

These people gathered around the circumference of the circle represent the faiths and philosophies of mankind, the functioning value systems that offer answers to the human question. Among their various answers, the man in the middle must make his choice and live his life. Our task in this study will be, in effect, to observe, to report, and to appraise this extraordinary conversation.

(2) Our second theme is the relation of philosophy to religion, and to its opposite: namely, nonreligion or secularity. This issue lies across our path in most of the chapters that follow. It raises its head at every meeting of East-West philosophers. For, as we have seen, modern Western philosophy, since the Renaissance and particularly during the past half-century, has undergone as thoroughgoing a secularization as any cultural form in all of human history. Contemporary Western philosophers, proud of this newly-achieved freedom of secularity, are often baffled and distressed to find their opposite numbers from Asian cultures still significantly related to traditional religions. Again, it is puzzling for the Occidental student to learn such lessons as that Indian philosophy and culture never had an eighteenth century enlightenment.

Involved in this perplexity are several tangled issues, perhaps the most important of which is a working definition of religion, and by implication, an adequate working conception of secularity. We shall need a definition of religion broad enough to cover the wide variety of religious phenomena, particularly those of the non-Western world, and objective enough to maintain neutrality among their conflicting claims.

Within present limits of space it must suffice to define a religion as "an existent system of holy forms,"[13] or more precisely "an existent system of symbolic forms which elicits from a man or group of men the emotion of the holy."[14] By *holy* we mean, with Rudolph Otto, that unique affection or emotion which is most readily characterized by saying that it is like a combination of wonder, awe, fear, and mystery. The symbolic forms that constitute a religion may be forms of feeling, belief or practice, or a combination of all three. They may be public or private, individual or social, or a combination of all of these. Most religions involve all these elements, and do so in a baffling variety of ways. The Western student must also be prepared for surprising new forms as he journeys to the non-Western world. For example, few if any of the Asian religions have such elements as God and congregational worship; rather do they have a puzzling variety of religious objects, and of forms of celebration. In the wide world and the long course of human history the variety of religious forms seems infinite.

Yet, it is the presence of the holy that constitutes any existent system of forms as a religion; and contrariwise, the absence of the holy is what distinctively characterizes the secular areas or regions of personality and culture. (It is interesting to note in passing that *religion* has two negatives, *nonreligion* and *irreligion*. The secular seems more accurately indicated by the former than the latter.)

Perhaps the most illuminating approach to the holy is to indicate that it occurs as the emotive accompaniment of acts of allegiance, commitment, or valuation, or as Paul Tillich put the matter, of "ultimate concern."[15] And it does so significantly whether these are officially designated as religious or not. For example, the rituals of the flag and patriotism frequently elicit such a holy response, sometimes more lively than officially sacred or holy ceremonies. So too does allegiance to family. In contrast to Tillich's ultimate concern, I would prefer the slightly variant formulation of "ultimate valuation," meaning by "ultimate" simply that valuation which has top priority in the life of a person or a culture. Again, such attitudes and actions have as their emotive or affective accompaniment the holy. And once in being, this emotion readily attaches itself to the symbolic forms that have called it into being.

One advantage of this approach to the subject is that it makes clear to us that the human contents, the human raw material, by which all religions are constituted, are the values men live by. If now these values are conjoined with their distinctive affective accompaniment, which we have called the holy (as in human existence these elements are joined together), the result is sacred value, which is, once again, the human content or substance of religion.

A further significant feature of the religions of the world is the powerful symbols in terms of which they are expressed and communicated. By the term, *symbol*, we mean not simply or primarily the visible symbols like the cross, or the star and crescent, or even symbolic actions like bowing or crossing oneself. Rather, we mean the most basic terms, verbal and otherwise, in which the respective faiths find articulation. In this sense, the Judeo-Christian term, *God*, is a primary symbol. So too is Buddhist *Nirvana* or the Hindu *Brahman*. Furthermore, these basic symbols of any particular religion —Christianity, Hinduism, or Buddhism—have an altogether particular and concrete character. They are not just any available symbols, but rather precisely this or that unique cluster of symbols and no other.

To see the importance of symbol to faith, we need only point to the different and contrasting viewpoints of observer and participant, or, stated metaphorically, to the difference between the viewpoints of the grandstand and the playing field. As students of these issues, our viewpoint is properly that of observers, and our language reflects this detached, objective viewpoint. As in the present discussion, we speak in such terms as religion, values, symbols, and similar concepts. But if or when we move from grandstand to playing field, that is, from being observers to being participants, our language changes accordingly. As participants we speak now in the concrete and powerful symbolic language of the community of faith in which we participate. As the late H. Richard Niebuhr once remarked, "men do not live and die for values, but for God, for country, and for Yale."[16] In this new context value becomes the faith which nourishes and sustains personality and community.

In this process of symbolic expression which the religious experience seems to demand for itself, we also see an all-important transformation, namely, that of religious experience becoming a religion. At precisely this point we see the adjective, *religious*, becoming the noun or substantive, *religion*. For a religion is simply a concrete historic community of ultimate valuation, with its own unique and distinctive symbol-system, whether Buddhist, Muslim, Christian, Marxist, or whatever.

Two aspects of symbolism, in particular, call for comment in relation to philosophy, namely, myth and ritual. Symbols come in many sizes, shapes, and kinds. Words, actions, objects—virtually anything—can take on symbolic quality. Of these innumerable forms, myth and ritual assume primary significance as symbolic word and symbolic act. R. R. Marett once remarked that the meaning of life is sung out and danced out before it is thought out. The dance, or more generally, the symbolic action, may be taken as our characterization of ritual or ceremony, the contents of which are the values that give meaning to life.

Among the verbal symbols that are sung or recited, some may be observed to have narrative form. These become sacred stories or myths. The religious significance of the myths of any people is, again, that of a symbolic, narrative statement of their fundamental values. Therefore, learning the myth of one's society is a basic form of moral and religious transmission and instruction.

Myth has several notable characteristics. Its form is poetic. Hence, Santayana once remarked that poetry is myth that we no longer believe, and Reinhold Niebuhr replied that myth is poetry we *do* believe.[17] However, the language of concrete images that myth speaks involves a serious problem. Mythical statements can easily be mistaken for literal commonsense statements or statements of science. As has been said, myth tells many little lies in the interest of one great truth. The failure to distinguish between these types of concern and statement results in what Gilbert Ryle calls a category mistake, that is, a confusion between different types and uses of language.

Incidentally, Ryle has taken this feature or problem of myth as a definition. Myth, he writes in *The Concept of Mind*, is a category mistake.[18] From the viewpoint of the present study, Ryle's assertion is a mistake, but an understandable one, for myths frequently do involve such confusion of categories.

These features of myth are of basic importance to philosophy, for the good reason that philosophy originates in the process of critical reflection upon myth. When men turn their critical analysis upon myth, asking, Why? How? Is it so?, philosophy is born. We may witness the process of birth in societies as different as ancient Greece, India, China, and medieval and modern Europe. In all of these societies philosophy is born out of critical reflection on myth. To be sure, once in existence, philosophy goes its own way and lives its own life; our statement is an assertion about genesis, not about philosophy's whole nature and functioning.

We have defined religion in terms of the holy. Accordingly, those regions of experience in personality and culture where the holy is absent are properly termed secular. Speaking factually, in the most sacred person or culture, it is possible to find at least a few secular concerns; and conversely, the holy has a way of asserting itself sometimes in unconscious ways in the lives of persons and societies that claim to be totally and completely secular.

These characterizations take on significance as they are applied to real persons and real situations. Thus, to cite a few examples, it is true to say that classical China was a more secular, less sacral culture, than India; that Erasmus was a more secular person than Bernard of Clairvaux; and that Benjamin Franklin was more secular than Cotton Mather. Movements of secularization are observable in societies from Greece and Mesopotamia to China and Japan. Sometimes, too, we find, as in the early medieval period of Europe, movements in the opposite or sacralizing direction; out of a previously secular society emerge new sacral forms.

Probably the most massive and remarkable movement of secularization in human history is that of the modern or post-Renaissance West. Since the influence of the West has become worldwide, the terms, *secularization*, *Westernization*, and *modernization* are often taken as virtually synonymous in the non-Western world, where they still constitute a challenge to many traditional cultures and religions.

In the tendency or trend to secularization it will be useful to note at least three stages, which thus also become three distinguishable and contrasting meanings of the terms, *secular* and *secularizing*. First and most basically, these words mean freedom from ecclesiastical control. In this sense, such concerns as art, politics, and economics achieved secularization during the early modern period of the West. A second meaning consists of giving due recognition to secular concerns on the life of persons and culture. In this meaning, the Protestant Reformation may be said to have had a secularizing effect on European and American society. Secular concerns are asserted in their own right, asking and needing no justification in institutionally religious terms. Still a third stage and meaning may be characterized as a total assertion of secular concerns, with the correlative implication that religious concerns no longer have any valid existence whatsoever. This last may be taken as the meaning of the contemporary term, *secularism*. A great deal of current discussion of the secular is confused by an ambiguous moving back and forth among these three distinguishable concepts, which in historic fact seem to operate relatively independently of each other. It is sufficient for our purpose simply to take account of these issues. Sacral societies and people have their distinctive problems, as also do their secular opposites. We need not take sides in the current controversies which swirl about these issues in many quarters.

Contemporary Western philosophy is staunchly secular in outlook, but we must also recognize that in other times and places other attitudes have prevailed. It is the part of common sense and even of wisdom to say that philosophy is where you find it—whether under a monk's cowl, in an eighteenth century drawing room, in a Buddhist meditation hall, in a mud hut on some remote island, or indeed, even at times at meetings of the American Philosophical Association. Our task is to understand it wherever it occurs, and to press on with its work.

(3) A third and last theme which will recur repeatedly through the following pages turns upon the vexed words, *mystical* and *mysticism*. In current popular uasge, these terms may well appear ambiguous past the point of possible salvage. Spiritualist seances, psychic phenomena—and now more recently hippie leaders and their communes—all lay claim to the terms, *mystic* or *mystical*. Small wonder that many contemporary philosophers use them as synonyms for unreason. In this currently popular philosophical usage, the mystical and the rational function as contradictory opposites. Does not the mystic claim esoteric and bizarre forms of knowledge, inherently incapable of rational tests and appraisal? Does not reason dispel such fog? Yes, answer many contemporary Western philosophers to this question, and seek thereby to close the discussion.

For this unhappy situation William James must bear a substantial share of blame. In his *Varieties of Religious Experience* he deliberately emphasized extreme, bizarre, and pathological forms of religious experience, and implicitly but clearly rejected the canons of traditional rational theology.[19] He also placed a highly questionable equals sign between religious experience and mystical experience. In *Varieties* and other writings he also employed the profoundly problematic conception of "over belief" in defense of religion. This is to say, where argument, pro and con, hangs in the balance, one is justified in appealing pragmatically to consequences to defend such an over belief. Few thoughtful believers would willingly accept any such defense of their views.

While clearly there is no single or common use of the terms, *mystic* and *mysticism*, there are significant historical traditions in the West and in other civilized cultures, whose canons of interpretation will establish a few highly important critical norms and rules that will provide guidance, at least for those who will take the trouble to read history. As we shall soon see, mysticism stands for both a form of experience and of thought, and in both cases there are at our disposal historical bodies of highly disciplined and reasoned experience. In this historical context three uses of these terms may be identified.

(a) *Mystical* is often taken to designate any form of religious experience (or more broadly, any form of value experience) in which immediacy is a prominent or highly significant element. By *immediacy* is meant the direct, unmediated, or intuitive quality of the experience. In this case, the object, however understood or interpreted, appears directly to the person rather than being manifested through the mediation of anything else, whether Bible, church, or human reason. Perhaps the adjective, *mystical*, is more appropriate for this wide usage than is the substantive, *mysticism*.

Beyond this first use, the noun or substantive, *mysticism*, is applied to two sharply contrasting types of experience and thought. One is frequently characterized as the mysticism of communion, and the other as the mysticism of ontological union or absorption. Mystics speak characteristically of "union" with the object of mystical experience. Yet the term *union* possesses at least two contrasting meanings. There can be union or harmony between two friends, though they maintain their separate existences. On the other hand, there is a union of absorption in which all separate individual existence disappears. Rivers flow into the ocean, the drop of water is absorbed in the great ocean of Being. The difference between these two types of mystical experience will turn out to be extremely important in several of the traditions we shall study in this book.

(b) The mysticism of communion emphasizes a direct or unmediated relation to the religious object, which is often (though by no means always) known as God. The direct person-person relation of human friendship or love is taken as defining man's relation to God or Ultimate Reality. Often

this claim to direct communion with God has quickened and vitalized a
religion previously in the grip of pedantry or institutionalism. The mystic
with his claim to direct experience is scornful of the authority of church or
rabbinical tradition, or indeed any other form of mediation. His is the claim
to direct experience that carries its own authority. We shall encounter this
pattern of mysticism in Christianity, Judaism, and Islam. In contemporary
thought Martin Buber is probably its most distinguished exponent, and his
book *I and Thou* its clearest exposition. Quaker thought and life in Christianity, devotional theism in the tradition of the *Bhagavad Gita*, and the
philosophy of Islamic Sufism, Pure Land Buddhism, and of Ramanuja in
Hinduism, all illustrate the mysticism of communion.

(c) The mysticism of absorption or ontological union is regarded by many
writers as the sole legitimate use of the word. Such is the usage of W. T.
Stace's notable *Mysticism and Philosophy*.[20] This form of experience occurs
when the seeker is absorbed, or claims total absorption, in the object. Some
writers characterize this experience as one of unitive consciousness or cosmic
consciousness transcending all plurality or duality. It posits a single reality,
ontological union with which constitutes the highest form of human fulfillment, and separation from which is asserted to be both evil and illusory. As
we shall see in subsequent chapters, the way in which this experience is said
to be achieved and the ways in which it is understood and interpreted vary
from tradition to tradition, from Advaita Vedanta in India to Zen Buddhism
in Japan, or from Plotinus to Eckhart in the West.

The monistic type of mysticism has the further implication of bringing into being a distinctive philosophical outlook that has great importance among
the world's systems of philosophy. Mysticism as we have characterized it is
primarily a type of experience. Yet once this experience occurs, it demands
categories of understanding and communication. This latter development
brings into being a distinctive kind of philosophy. Neoplatonism as articulated by Plotinus stands in the West as a model for such mystical
philosophy. However, the Vedanta philosophy of Hinduism, various types
of Buddhist philosophy, Ibn Arabi's philosophy in Islam as well as modern
Western philosophic idealism, all provide examples of what we may appropriately call the philosophy of mysticism. It is of course important to
realize in all the occurrences of this philosophy that, while it springs from the
experience of mystical vision and devotion, once this monistic philosophic
view of the world emerges, it goes its own way and lives its own independent
life. In modern Western philosophy both Spinoza and Hegel come to mind
in this connection. Their philosophic systems have their respective sources in
Jewish and Christian traditions of mystical devotion and thought, but they
make their claims to truth in their own independent philosophic terms.

It will be noted that both the mysticism of communion and of union claim a transcendent object. Both are therefore involved (along with other types of metaphysical thinking as discussed in the previous section of this chapter) in some serious and highly significant problems of language. How can we speak, and much more, how can we think, critically concerning a transcendent object? All that was said earlier concerning metaphysical thinking must be repeated here. Actually some of the mystics and philosophers of mysticism have been very much aware of this problem, and have labored productively at its solution. Here a summary word must suffice. The language of the mystics begins in a silence that distinguishes it once for all from literal predication. From this point onward, it proceeds through a combination of metaphor, negation, and paradox to characterize its transcendent referent. We may also add that it also ends in silence, namely in the silent contemplation of, and absorption in, its object. In addition to those general features, let it be added that each of the world's philosophic and religious traditions has its own distinctive system of symbols for the expression of mystical experience.

SUGGESTIONS FOR FURTHER READING

As many of these works are classics that have appeared in numerous editions, only the most accessible publication is indicated.

Ayer, A. J. *Language, Truth and Logic*. New York: Dover Publications, 1952.
Broad, C. D. *Scientific Thought*. New York: Harcourt Brace, 1923.
Buber, M. *I and Thou*. New York: Scribners, 1958.
Carnap, Rudolph. *The Logical Structure of the World*. Berkeley: University of California Press, 1967.
Cassirer, E. *An Essay on Man*. New Haven: Yale University Press, 1944.
Cohen, Morris. *Reason and Nature*. Glencoe: Free Press, 1953.
Collingwood, R. *An Essay on Philosophic Method*. Oxford: Clarendon Press, 1933.
———. *An Essay on Metaphysics*. Oxford: Clarendon Press, 1948.
Dewey, J. *Reconstruction in Philosophy*. New York: New American Library, 1950.
———. *Experience and Nature*. Chicago: Open Court, 1958.
Emmet, D. *The Nature of Metaphysical Thinking*. London: Macmillan, 1945.
Heidegger, M. *Introduction to Metaphysics*. New Haven: Yale University Press, 1959.
———. *What is Called Thinking*. New York: Harper, 1968.
James, W. *The Varieties of Religious Experience*. New York: Longmans, 1902.
———. *Pragmatism*. New York: Longmans, 1946.
Langer, S. *Philosophy in a New Key*. Cambridge: Harvard University Press, 1957.
Moore, G. E. *Some Main Problems of Philosophy*. London: Macmillan, 1953.

Nagel, Ernest. *Sovereign Reason*. Glencoe: Free Press, 1954.

————. *Logic Without Metaphysics*. Glencoe: Free Press, 1957.

Otto, Rudolph. *The Idea of the Holy*. New York: Oxford University Press, 1950.

————. *Mysticism East and West*. New York: Mendran Books, 1957.

Pepper, S. *World Hypotheses*. Berkeley: University of California Press, 1942.

Randall, J. H. *The Career of Philosophy*. New York: Columbia University Press, 1962.

Russell, B. *Mysticism and Logic*. London: Allen & Unwin, 1949.

————. *Introduction to Mathematical Philosophy*. New York: Macmillan, 1963.

Ryle, G. *The Concept of Mind*. New York: Barnes & Noble, 1959.

Sartre, J. P. *Existentialism*. New York: Philosophical Library, 1947.

Stace, W. T. *Mysticism and Philosophy*. Philadelphia: Lippincott, 1960.

————, ed. *The Teachings of the Mystics*. New York: New American Library, 1960.

Whitehead, A. N. *Science and the Modern World*. New York: Macmillan, 1925.

Wittgenstein, L. *Tractatus Logico-Philosophicus*. London: Routledge & Kegan Paul, 1922.

————. *Philosophical Investigations*. New York: Macmillan, 1959.

III
Instrumental
Naturalism

WE BEGIN OUR JOURNEY among contemporary philosophies in familiar landscape, with the well-known scenes and shapes of American pragmatism, or instrumental naturalism. Among American students the main ideas and persons of this philosophy as well as its leading concerns are generally well-known. It is true that younger philosophers have moved on to new issues, but this is in part because many of those constituting pragmatism or instrumental naturalism can today be taken for granted. Yet to this we must immediately add that if some major aspects of this philosophy may be assumed as secure achievements, some other aspects already seem dated and even obsolete. In some important ways, this is a philosophy of the recent past rather than the present.

As in the case of any large movement in philosophy, labels tend to be arbitrary and misleading. Hence, it is an open question whether with William James and C. S. Peirce we should call this philosophy pragmatism, or follow John Dewey's nomenclature of instrumental naturalism. As we shall soon see, both labels point to important aspects of the philosophy. The appellation of James and Peirce is more widely familiar, but in many respects Dewey was much the most influential and important figure. Hence, we use his label.

In any case a word of caution is pertinent against overestimating the substantive significance of labels. What is important is not the label but the content of thought. Indeed, as we begin our journey among contemporary philosophies it is well again to underscore this warning, and to extend it in advance to all the philosophies we shall study. Labels have their indispensable use in the kind of study on which we are embarking. But they have their dangers as well. If philosophy consists of the kind of thinking described in the last chapter, then to characterize it in terms of the standardized isms of the textbooks is to reify abstractions or to fall into what Whitehead termed the fallacy of misplaced concretion.

In the formulation and nomenclature of either James and Peirce or of Dewey, here is a philosophy that has had widespread influence not only in America but in Europe and Asia as well. Dewey's lectures in Russia, Japan, and China influenced both philosophy and education around the world. Under the title, pragmatism, this philosophy has often been characterized by Europeans (quite erroneously as we shall soon argue) as the distinctively American philosophy, or even as the ideology of the American businessman. Concern with what James liked to call "cash values," that is, successful consequences, carries an altogether different meaning for philosophical pragmatists and for business tycoons.

Pragmatism or instrumental naturalism has its source in the work of Charles Sanders Peirce (1838–1914), William James (1842–1910), and John Dewey (1859–1952). The original impetus was an article of Peirce's published in *Popular Science Monthly* in 1878 entitled, "How to Make Our Ideas Clear," pointing to differences in practical consequences as the primary means of clarification.[1] However, it was not until 1898 that James picked up the suggestion of Peirce's pragmatism (or "pragmaticism" as Peirce was subsequently led to rebaptize his view), in a lecture at the University of California. In 1907 James published a book entitled *Pragmatism: A New Name for Some Old Ways of Thinking*.[2] Dewey, while influenced by Peirce and James, nevertheless found his own way independently to similar conclusions. By the early decades of the present century pragmatism had emerged as full-fledged philosophic movement. While James died in 1910 and Peirce in 1914, Dewey's vigorous leadership continued through the entire first half of the twentieth century.

A native of Vermont, Dewey did his graduate study in philosophy not in Europe, but at the newly-founded Johns Hopkins Graduate School. He taught at the University of Michigan from 1884 to 1889, and at the newly-founded University of Chicago from 1894 to 1904. At Chicago Dewey participated actively in Jane Addams' Hull House and in a wide variety of other social and civic causes. Most important of all, he was instrumental in founding the famous laboratory school, often labeled the "Dewey School," which served as a place to apply and test his developing educational philosophy.

Dewey left Chicago for Columbia in 1904, remaining there until his retirement in 1930, producing a great volume of books, articles, and lectures in which his philosophy found full articulation as well as application to the problems of America and the world. He continued his interest and leadership in social causes and in active philosophic work until his death at the age of ninety-two. Under his leadership instrumental naturalism became not only a vigorous movement among American philosophers but also a philosophic synthesis whose influence extended into virtually every aspect of American culture.

From its inception, instrumental naturalism has consistently sought to be a critical philosophy, whose characteristic stance is one of attack upon all vested interests or establishments, philosophical, social, and every other sort. It is ironical that in more recent years, instrumental naturalism has been the position of the older established members of the philosophic community, often at first attacked then ignored by younger men interested in other issues. For, in its early days it was a critical protest in the name of a new and vigorous liberalism against a sterile nineteenth century philosophic and cultural establishment scornfully called by Santayana "the genteel tradition." But as the movement developed, Dewey and his colleagues turned their fire on established ideas in education, religion, politics, economics—in virtually every aspect of human life and society. They demanded not only that philosophic ideas make a difference but that they make a humane difference. In this demand Dewey and his colleagues became an important part of the American liberal tradition. In their demand that philosophy play a real part in decreasing human misery and in increasing the sum total of human happiness and satisfaction, Dewey and his associates and followers found their way into virtually every important social and intellectual controversy in the first half of twentieth century America.

Of these many concerns, the reconstruction, or rather the reconception, of America's public educational system may well stand as the greatest single achievement of Dewey's philosophy. Dewey never held any post other than professor of philosophy, so he worked by the power of ideas. Yet it may be said that his ideas penetrated America's educational enterprise wherever educators were able and willing to think about what they were doing. It is fashionable, a half-century later, to point to defects and shortcomings in Dewey's educational philosophy. We shall do so, too. It is even fashionable among people who have never read a line of Dewey's philosophy to make him the scapegoat for educational ills and problems of every sort. Yet, clearly, Dewey's massive achievement in liberalizing and humanizing America's schools will stand long after his petty detractors have returned to their proper oblivion.

If instrumental naturalism is a fighting philosophy, it is pertinent to ask what are its weapons and what are the issues of its warfare. To answer these questions will reveal some of its underlying affirmations, thus verifying the previous chapter's assertion that no philosophy can be critical without at the same time being constructive as well. Actually, instrumental naturalism has never sought to hide its constructive aspect. Stated in summary fashion this philosophy has claimed to be: (1) pragmatic, (2) naturalist, (3) humanist, and (4) liberal. Let us examine these adjectives in turn. To underscore our polemic against isms in philosophy, we shall keep these terms in adjectival rather than substantive form—a procedure that all three founders of this philosophy would have approved.

Pragmatist

As already noted, pragmatism began with Peirce, who launched it as a theory concerning the meaning of ideas, and by implication, concerning the meaning of the statements in which those ideas occur. Question: how shall we make our ideas clear? Answer: by noting their consequences, by pointing to the differences they make in overt behavior. Such was Peirce's initial suggestion. In passing, we note that it is similar to proposals made by other philosophies and philosophers. For example, years later P. W. Bridgman proposed the hypothesis of operationalism in physics, asserting that the meaning of physical concepts consists in the operations that they lead physicists to perform.[3] Similar also is the verification principle of the logical positivists (to be discussed in the next chapter) which asserts that the meaning of a statement consists of the procedures necessary to verify it.

James and Dewey in their respective ways expanded the pragmatic theory of meaning, making it a theory of truth as well as of meaning, covering the whole field of knowledge, and asserting that truth and falsehood are to be defined and interpreted in terms of successful or unsuccessful consequences. It must be frankly conceded that neither man was free of ambiguity, which has misled both friends and enemies. For example, success in strictly intellectual consequences, as against the broader human consequences of one's thought, would seem to constitute an indispensable distinction, yet neither James nor Dewey made or observed such a distinction with any degree of rigor.

In defense of James and Dewey, two judgments—one negative and one affirmative—may be ventured. The first is that neither man ever stated or intimated a view of successful consequences even remotely similar to success in the popular sense, for example, of a business enterprise. Indeed, James lashed out at Americans who worship "the bitch goddess Success," and equally caustic remarks are strewn through Dewey's pages. At least this misunderstanding of pragmatism is without foundation and without excuse.

The second judgment is that the model for successful knowledge for both

James and Dewey continued to be the natural sciences, in which the aim of knowledge is prediction and control of the subject matter. Indeed, the aim of science may be said to be the continuing reconstruction of scientific knowledge itself, and through this knowledge the reconstruction of those portions of the world to which it refers. Hence, it may be safely asserted that when James and Dewey speak of the successful readjustment effected by knowledge, they have in mind the kind of success enjoyed by a scientific hypothesis or theory. In Dewey's formulation it is in this sense that ideas are to be understood as instrumental.

At least three important lines of historical influence converge upon this pragmatic view of meaning and truth. (1) Probably the strongest is in the title essay of one of Dewey's early books, *The Influence of Darwin on Philosophy*.[4] Focusing attention upon the living, responsive, evolving human organism, which seeks, as do all organisms, to respond in ways promoting survival, Dewey asked for the meaning of mind or mental behavior. Replying in this context, he asserted that mind emerges as a new device to guide organic behavior. This approach was asserted both as a view of the origin and of the function of mentality. As to the former, while all organisms respond to present stimuli, some acquire the capacity to respond on the basis of past experience to expected or future stimuli. It is precisely this capacity to respond to expected or future conditions that constitutes mind or intelligence. At the level of animal life, this constitutes both the origin and the meaning of mental behavior. It is also in this context that intelligence acquires the meaning of problem-solving. This is to say, problems in the relation of organism to environment are solved in ways promoting organic survival.

At the emergent human level the crucial questions are precisely what is meant by the terms, *life, problem, solution,* and *adjustment.* Clearly the term, *life,* assumes new emergent meanings at the human level. Hence, one might conclude that new meanings accrue to the other terms as well. Thus, the terms, *problem* and *solution,* are not to be interpreted in the new context in a purely organic or reductively biological sense. The meaning of the word, *adjustment,* at the new level is of crucial importance, for it raises the question: adjustment to what? There is little doubt that Dewey intended the new emergent human level of meaning for all his basic terms. Yet it must be frankly conceded that his writings never overcame a certain looseness or ambiguity that permitted some of his less gifted followers and—what is perhaps more important—his enemies to attach other, reductive meanings to his words. Such are the uses and misuses of ambiguity in philosophy.

(2) As already noted, James and Dewey carried on their philosophical

work in close relation to psychology and the social sciences. Both men made distinguished contributions to these studies. Hence, it is natural to find in their philosophies a strong influence from the new sciences of man and society. They sought to construct philosophic views of mind and knowing, drawn from these sources and pertinent to these concerns. If preconceived philosophic ideas disagree, so much the worse for them. If such ideas block the path of scientific advance, they must be pushed out of the way. There must, furthermore, be no gaps or gulfs, no dualism, between natural science and social science. What the natural sciences have already accomplished in their fields will soon be achieved by the sciences of man. Such at least was the confident prediction. Science, both natural and social, aims at prediction and control; indeed, it aims at nothing less than a continuing and total reconstruction of knowledge and experience. It cannot be repeated too many times that for both James and Dewey it is this model that underlies the pragmatic interpretation of mind and its characteristic activity of knowing, with respect both to those successful actions which thus claim title to truth, and to those unsuccessful cognitive actions which thus constitute falsehood.

(3) Still a third line of thought influential in pragmatism is the emphasis upon action. In traditional philosophy, voluntarism or volitionalism is the view that asserts the primacy of the will or volition in either or both the human self and the world. Pragmatism stands in this voluntarist tradition, though its significance is to bring voluntarism down to earth, giving it tough-minded, empirical interpretation. For pragmatism, will or volition is not some unearthly transcendental or metaphysical entity, but simply the total living, responsive, active human organism. And pragmatism has never doubted that the tools of social science and psychology are sufficient for the understanding and control of this subject matter.

What now may be said in critical appraisal of this pragmatic approach to meaning and truth? In a famous paper entitled "The Thirteen Pragmatisms" A. O. Lovejoy called attention to the many different and sometimes incompatible meanings of *pragmatism* in the writings of James and Dewey.[5] He argued that its theory of meaning must be distinguished from its theory of truth. Yet, even as a theory of meaning, pragmatism can hardly be the whole story, for if we had no prior intimation of meaning we would not know how to draw out its consequences for subsequent pragmatic appraisal or testing.

The failure of pragmatism to distinguish purely intellectual consequences from the broader human and social consequences, lies at the base of Morris Cohen's drastic criticism in his essay, "In Dispraise of Life, Experience and Reality," in which pragmatism is charged with encouraging anti-intellectualism and sentimental romanticism.[6] It does so by its ambiguous refusal to distinguish intellectual consequences from other kinds, and by its consequent understatement and confusion of the role of logic and the intellect with other human concerns.

Whitehead once perceptively distinguished what he called the reason of the foxes and the reason of the gods, the former being animal intelligence, which is aimed at the goal of biological survival, while the latter is the exercise of an intrinsic and distinctive human function.[7] It must be said that pragmatism has never seen the force of this distinction, and thus has often fallen into views of the mind's life which are narrow and shallow, failing to do justice to that full emergent life of human reason which Whitehead called the reason of the gods.

Naturalist

Dewey and his followers have expounded the pragmatic view of mind in close relation to a metaphysics or ontology which carries the label, naturalism. What is meant by metaphysical naturalism? How adequate or inadequate is this metaphysics? The question of what Dewey and his followers have meant by naturalism is by no means unequivocally clear. However, their various answers seem always to combine two elements: first, the approach to nature as the domain or object-matter of scientific knowing; and second, a claim either implicit or explicit for the final validity of scientific intelligence as a way of knowing nature.

From the already noted emphasis of pragmatism on science, it is only a step to the assertion that science alone constitutes genuinely reliable knowledge. Dewey took that step, asserting that scientific intelligence alone makes good the claim to constitute valid and true knowledge. Other competing claims are found on critical analysis to be empty, or to miss the mark, or indeed, to be reducible to science.[8]

More affirmatively, it is asserted that scientific intelligence is competent for the purposes of understanding and control in all areas of man's experience of the world. Few convictions are more central or more important to this philosophy than the competence, indeed the omnicompetence, of the scientific method for acquiring and communicating knowledge. In the view of instrumental naturalists, the scientific method is man's best and strongest resource in the struggle to achieve a good life. For it is precisely by means of this method that man acquires knowledge of the causes of things and is thus able to eliminate evils and stabilize the existence of goods that give meaning to human life.

As to the nature of scientific knowing, it is nothing more or less than the refinement, sharpening, and full development of ordinary human intelligence. So, for example, when there appeared a textbook entitled *Introduction to Logic and Scientific Method*, Dewey is said to have quipped, "Why the 'and'?"[9] For there are no cleavages in the life and function of the mind. There is simply human intelligence brought to bear upon the various regions of man's experience of the world, and brought to its highest fulfillment in scientific knowing.

Throughout naturalist writing runs a sharp polemic against all forms of dualism. To be sure, experience sometimes exhibits dual or even multiple aspects; but on closer scrutiny and on further experience, the massive fact is not discontinuity but continuity—continuity and unity over the whole vast field of Nature or Reality. It is a continuity perceptible to those who view the world through the eyes of modern science. So it is that Science and Nature taken together constitute the first word and the last word on man's understanding of himself and his world.

If we ask the meaning of the nature implied in naturalism, several answers are forthcoming from philosophic naturalists, none of them identical, and some in apparent conflict with one another. One is that Nature is the object-matter of science, and since science is the sole form of reliable knowledge, it follows that Nature is reality, total and complete.

In many writings Dewey used the term, *Nature*, explicitly as what chapter 2 of this book has called an all-inclusive totality word. The Greeks used the term *Being* or *Being-as-such*, nineteenth century idealists spoke of *Reality* or *Ultimate Reality*, but the present age prefers the term, *Nature*, as its characteristic designation of the *scheme-of-things-entire*. So at least the term, *Nature*, seems to function in the writings of contemporary naturalists.

If we press the question of what implications are involved in this idea, several responses are forthcoming from Dewey and his followers. Perhaps first and most critically, naturalism means nonsupernaturalism or even antisupernaturalism. Once more, it asserts that Nature is the whole of Reality, saying in effect: "Nature is all there is; there isn't any more, and if anybody says there is, he is talking nonsense."

This doctrine sets itself squarely against all two-story views of the universe, such as those expressed or implied in traditional Christian theology and popular religion, and in many forms of idealist philosophy. Naturalists assert that such two-story models are without basis in fact. There is simply no good reason to assume that any such supernature exists, and many good reasons to conclude the opposite. Further, naturalism sees the origin of such ideas in man's desire for escape from the grim world of reality or as compensation for its all-too-evident evils. Bluntly stated, naturalism denies the existence of the God of traditional Western religion. As Sidney Hook has written, naturalists disbelieve in God for the same reason that they disbelieve in leprechauns, fairies, and witches.[10]

With equal vigor, however, Dewey's naturalism sets itself against the reductive naturalism or materialism of the nineteenth century, with its assertions that only the atoms and molecules of matter "really exist"—all else being "mere appearance." Against all such views, contemporary naturalism affirms that nature includes as real existents, man and the human spirit in all its varied life. Especially must it be emphasized that human values are included as components of nature, as "real" as atoms, organisms, or any other entities that might be specified.

To deny real existence to these emergent aspects of man's life, or to assert that man is "nothing but" an organism or a chunk of matter is to commit the fallacy of reductionism, or the "nothing but" fallacy. Rather, human experience is what it is, namely, what it shows itself to be to the eyes of intelligent observation. So it is that instrumental naturalism is committed to a two-front warfare against supernaturalism on the one hand and against reductive naturalism or materialism on the other.

Involved in this two-front warfare is naturalism's distinctive approach to human values. Against reductive naturalism, Dewey and his fellow-adherents of instrumental naturalism have argued long and insistently that the values which humanize men are as real as atoms, stars, and any other kinds of existence. Furthermore, values are what they appear to be in the public experience of mankind. Against idealists and supernaturalists, on the other hand, they have urged the natural character of these values. By this at least two things are intended, first that there are no fundamental cleavages between fact and value or matter and spirit, which would place value in a realm of its own apart from the rest of existence. Second, values are accessible and amenable to scientific understanding and control. By means of scientific intelligence, values may be understood, cultivated, and stabilized in existence. Once again, science turns out to be man's most powerful resource in the struggle for a good life, if men will only have the good sense and the self-sufficient courage to use it.

Instrumental naturalist metaphysics has not lacked vigorous critics. One line of critical attack has alleged a curious logical circle between the assertion of the omnicompetence of scientific method and characterization of nature, the object-matter of science, as the whole of reality. Do not naturalists put the rabbit in the hat with the first assertion, and take it out with an attitude of surprised discovery in their second assertion?

Other logically minded critics point to an alleged self-contradiction in the assertion that science is the sole reliable form of knowledge. What, they ask, of *that* assertion? Clearly, it is not a part of any recognized science; therefore if it is true, its truth falsifies itself. Some naturalists reply to this that they want just enough metaphysical philosophy to provide a justification and defense of science against its enemies.

Other critics point out that no existing natural science claims for itself exclusive or final validity. Indeed, if one is to observe modern scientific method factually, it shows itself very powerful in some regions of experience but inept and powerless in others. In the field of moral values, scientific method has been less successful than, say, in the nature of matter. A closely related criticism turns upon the distinction between science and philosophy as different forms of thought. For example, our last chapter pointed to some basic differences between science and philosophy. Against such views naturalists have tended to argue that philosophy may and must use scientific methods, and that hence there is little or no difference between scientific and philosophical methods of knowing. Their critics disagree.

Humanist

Another key word of this philosophy is *humanist*. Yet this term is itself so multivalued that we shall have to unpack a few of its many meanings to see which ones are applicable to Dewey and his followers. In addition to its many traditional meanings, humanism has served in the nineteenth and twentieth centuries as a label (self-applied) for the religious views of persons who, unable in this modern, scientific age to believe in God, still resolve to believe in Man or Humanity. This is the definition invoked by members of the American Humanist Association and its fellow travelers throughout the world.[11] It has been an observable fact that many adherents of instrumental naturalism have found their way into such organizations. Such a humanism is also undoubtedly the tacit credo of many more people than the numbers of its conscious adherents. The humanist credo affirms either explicitly or implicitly the autonomy and self-sufficiency of Man armed with modern science.

Yet, the label humanism also points to other accents and emphases of the instrumental naturalist philosophy. We noted in the last section the contention of this philosophy that emergent human concerns possess a reality and significance irreducible to organic or material terms. Humanism is often a label for this antireductionist view of man. Again, in an age of burgeoning science and technology, an ever-present question is whether man is the master or slave of his technology. Scientific humanism may be described as the view which argues that science and technology ought always to serve human well-being.

In this context Dewey added his own distinctive philosophical account of what human values are, how they come into existence, and how they may be cultivated and stabilized, or, in other words, his own value theory or axiology. It begins by pointing to the natural facts of enjoyment or satisfaction, and their opposites of pain and dissatisfaction. All such experiences are what they are, that is, what they are perceived or directly experienced to be. Yet, in their natural occurrences such enjoyments or satisfactions are unstable or fugitive. However, once they occur, it is possible for us to focus attention upon them—to make them, in other words, objects of conscious choice or decision. At the moment when some experience of enjoyment or satisfaction is made the object of deliberate choice or decision, it becomes a value. In other words, value is born of choice or decision deployed upon the field of human satisfaction. Thereafter it becomes a matter of conscious cultivation by means of human intelligence.

From this point onward, scientific intelligence is concerned with the experience of value in its manifold aspect, noting qualities and relations, and not least of all studying the causes and conditions of values in order that their existence may be nurtured and controlled. In this cultivation of values, according to Dewey, the sciences of man have a very significant contribution to make. By pointing to causes and conditions, they provide the possibility of control and stabilization.

Critics of humanistic naturalism frequently attack this view of value as seriously defective. If values are what Dewey describes them to be, have we not eliminated the momentous difference between good and evil, between valid and invalid values? By letting go any transcendent source and standard have we not abandoned ourselves to a hopeless relativism where *my* values are what *I* like or desire, and *yours* are what *you* like or desire, with no way of choosing between us?

The response of instrumental naturalists is to deny both the necessity and utility of such a transcendent source and standard. Men neither have nor need a heavenly yardstick to measure their values by. Indeed, replies the naturalist, some who have claimed such a standard of value have conducted their actual human value-relations with great evil, that is, with great damage to persons and values.

What is often called value relativism points to nothing more threatening than the great variety of values observable in the wide world and the long course of history. That such variety exists, is an observable fact, asserts the naturalist to his traditionalist critic. The situation is like a garden where there are many kinds of plants and flowers—and some weeds, too. In this situation it is, once more, the function of human intelligence to discriminate among the species, to study the conditions that provide for the cultivation of attractive and useful plants in this human garden. Dewey and his followers have never doubted the efficiency and sufficiency of intelligence for this task. This confidence is an integral part of the humanism of this philosophy. It constitutes humanism's rejoinder to the charge of relativism.[12]

Values, as has been said, are of many kinds. Yet, two kinds especially demand attention, namely esthetic and moral, the former constituting the subject matter of art, and the latter, of morality and ethics. We shall consider Dewey's view of morality and ethics in the next section. Meanwhile, esthetic value for Dewey is that which is characterized by immediacy or intuitive quality. However, this means simply that it is the leading edge of the mind's encounter with nature or world. Far from being cooped up in the privacy of a single subject, or being secret, private, or transcendental, such esthetic values are widely shared. What is even more important, they are malleable and hence educable. They may be reshaped or reformed, hence guided by intelligence to stable cultivation and deliberate fulfillment. This is precisely what happens in experience of the arts.

The appearance of Dewey's *Art as Experience* in 1934 caught many readers by surprise.[13] For they had supposed that Dewey and his philosophy were so preoccupied with urgent issues of moral and social valuation as to have literally no time for art. A more careful reading of Dewey's previous philosophical work might have avoided this surprise. For esthetic value was for him a lifelong concern. The role of art in human life is the deliberate, systematic cultivation of man's natural capacity for immediate enjoyment, or direct satisfaction of the world in all its manifold aspects.

Liberal

As attention turns from esthetic to moral and social valuation, we come face to face with the professed liberalism of the philosophy we are seeking to characterize. But, again, in the terms, *liberal* and *liberalism*, we face multivalued words which have been seriously applied to social viewpoints ranging from W. E. Gladstone to Franklin Roosevelt, from Herbert Hoover to John Dewey, or more recently from the Kennedy brothers to Barry Goldwater. Here, clearly, is the word which wins the prize for greatest ambiguity in the whole field of social philosophy—an achievement as great as it is dubious. Our present use of the term derives very largely from the usage fixed in American social thought by James and Dewey themselves. A liberal, James argues, is a meliorist standing between standpat conservatism on the one hand and nihilistic radicalism on the other.[14] Dewey, too, held a lifelong hostility to the extremes of both right and left. He articulated a social philosophy of the continual reshaping or reconstructing of experience by the instrumentality of intelligence. His stance, like that of James, was neither that of the conservative nor of the radical, but of the liberal reformer, in the literal sense of reshaping old forms. As such, his social philosophy finds an important place in the continuing tradition of American liberal social thought.[15]

Dewey's ethics, or theory of moral valuation, is of a piece with the rest of his philosophy. First, it is mordantly critical of traditional ethics with its ideas of fixed goods or goals of human striving and its equally rigid transcendent principles of right and wrong. Here, as elsewhere, preconceived traditional ideas are in need of drastic criticism in order to bring them into living relation to the present experience of men. So Dewey abandoned what he regarded as sterile and remote absolutes for concern with what he termed the situation, which is to say, the actual living situations where conflicts of value occur, and choices, hopefully intelligent choices, must be made. From this viewpoint, traditional principles must be regarded as so many hypotheses to be tested factually, and to be continually reformed and reshaped in the light of ongoing experience. If many traditional ethical principles flunk this test, so much the worse for them. Dewey's emphasis upon the actual situation of moral choice led to the labels of situationalism or contextualism for his ethics. Critics have charged a relativity or relativism of contexts or situations, but proponents of this view have continued to respond that the reference to context or situation keeps moral thought living and relevant—in contrast, once more, to the sterility of traditional ethical theory. In all of this we see again Dewey's view of the function of human intelligence looking back over past experience, appraising alternatives and guiding choices to satisfying future goals as they come into view.

This philosophy vigorously denies that either ethical theory or moral practice may be cooped up in any limited area of experience or thought. Rather, it is the case that the continuing reshaping and redirection, literally the reforming of the whole human experience, constitutes the domain of morality. Contrasted with this basic moral quality of all human life, problems officially and popularly designated as moral frequently pale into insignificance and triviality. For example, the press frequently labels sexual issues as morals questions or charges. Although such issues do have moral significance, they are certainly less important than a moral appraisal of man's whole, wide, social life.

In all of this it is not hard to see the indefeasibly social character of Dewey's philosophy. He learned this first from the Hegelianism of his youth. For, let it be recalled, Hegel's system was a philosophy of culture and history. While the influence of the burgeoning American social sciences displaced that of German idealism in Dewey's mind, the social nature and significance of all philosophical thinking persisted. Early in his career, in *Reconstruction in Philosophy*, Dewey decried the philosopher's preoccupation with the technical problems of philosophy, and looked forward hopefully to a time when philosophy would consist of a consideration by philosophers of the problems of mankind.[16] This view stayed with him throughout his long life, finding expression in such later works as *Philosophy and Civilization*.[17] It also guided Dewey's own individual activities for social causes. He and his followers have found expression for their philosophic ideas along a wide front of liberal social causes, ranging through the decades from women's suffrage to civil liberties or to world peace and international order—to cite just a few illustrations among innumerable possibilities.

Supporting this activity is an underlying value judgment which might be stated as a moral commitment to science, education, and democracy as primary and fundamental human goods. Taken together they point to progress, or at least to the possibility of progress. To progress in this sense Dewey was as dedicated as his New England forbears had been to God.

For Dewey, democracy is not simply or primarily a form of political organization. Rather, it is something more basic and pervasive, informing and guiding not only politics or education but all aspects of social life. Against all authoritarian ways of social life stands the democratic way, in which social policies are formed by common and free discussion of the issues and by intelligent choices issuing from discussion. Such a free way of coming to judgments finds admirable illustration in science. Indeed, science may be said to practice precisely this way of making and testing judgments. Applied to human society, this way constitutes democracy. So it is that science and democracy converge, with a democratic way of education mediating between them.[18]

All these goods or goals converge on the possibility of progress or the improvement of the human situation. Dewey was far too sober a thinker to continue nineteenth century views of progress as a kind of cosmic escalator carrying man forever upward and onward. However, he did firmly believe that by taking thought man has the possibility of improving his lot in specific, concrete ways. This increment of human value in history, this improvement of the human situation, constitutes the still valid content of progress, and this in turn constitutes for Dewey and his followers a large part of the meaning of human existence.[19] This, or something like this, is the basic moral stance of the instrumental naturalist.

Philosophy of Religion

A word concerning the relation of this philosophy to religion is necessitated by the widespread impression of hostility. Is this not an atheist, godless philosophy? Critics have frequently leveled this charge, and exponents have lent credence to it. Yet, like so many half-truths in philosophy, this one is also a half-falsehood, and a misleading one, too. True, Dewey found little place for traditional institutional religion and traditional views of God. But this charge ignores the whole moral direction of his philosophy.

Naturalism's critical attack upon traditional ideas has been made with particular force upon traditional religion and theology which, it alleges, have functioned in wishful and compensatory ways to conjure up a whole world of make-believe or transcendental entities. Naturalism rejects the truth of these transcendent claims, and also points to the escapist motivation that calls them into being. Hence, most instrumental naturalists have responded to traditional theology and religion with views ranging from judicious agnosticism to blunt atheism. They have been more interested in criticism of religion than in construction or reconstruction.

Dewey himself, however, at least began the work of reconstruction. While he decried the noun or substantive, *religion*, in its traditional institutional forms, he envisaged more constructive forms for the adjective, *religious*, which he defined as a sense of the possibilities of existence, or of the possible union of fact and value in human existence. He even gave qualified assent to the use of the term, *God*, for this union in existence of fact and value.[20]

Dewey underscored the role of imagination in religious experience, or more precisely, in the religious quality which pervades all human experience. It is the function of imagination to envisage and project the goods or values of human life. Thus the free play of human imagination becomes itself a great and precious human value. Yet, in contrast to his contemporary, Santayana, who taught that imagination "supervenes" or hovers over the human world, Dewey insisted that it "intervenes," envisaging and then successively projecting the goals of human action, and providing us with the light and power to embody them in actual human existence.

In myth and ritual Dewey saw imaginative ways of celebrating the values that impart meaning to existence. At least this might take place in a truly healthy culture. In such a situation, religion would make no irrational and dogmatic claims on human credibility, and would impose no authoritarian standards on human behavior; rather, it would be a celebration of the values of the common life. To all this he added the emotion of natural piety by which a man might relate himself to the Nature whose child he inevitably and properly is.

SUGGESTIONS FOR FURTHER READING

As many of these works are classics that have appeared in numerous editions, only the most accessible publication is indicated.

Cohen, Morris. *Reason and Nature*. Glencoe: Free Press, 1953.

Cohen, Morris and Nagel, Ernest. *An Introduction to Logic and Scientific Method*. New York: Harcourt Brace, 1934.

Dewey, John. *The Influence of Darwin on Philosophy*. New York: Holt, 1910.

———. *Democracy and Education*. New York: Macmillan, 1916.

———. *Human Nature and Conduct*. New York: Modern Library, 1922.

———. *Art as Experience*. New York: Minton Balch, 1934.

———. *A Common Faith*. New Haven: Yale University Press, 1934.

———. *Reconstruction in Philosophy*. New York: New American Library, 1950.

———. *Experience and Nature*. Chicago: Open Court, 1958.

Frankel, Charles. *The Case for Modern Man*. New York: Harper, 1955.

Hook, Sidney. *Reason, Social Myths and Democracy*. New York: John Day, 1940.

———. *The Quest for Being*. New York: St. Martin's Press, 1961.

James, William. *Principles of Psychology*. New York: Holt, 1890.

———. *The Will to Believe*. New York: Longmans, 1927.

———. *Essays on Radical Empiricism*. New York: Longmans, 1938.

———. *Pragmatism*. New York: Longmans, 1946.

Krikorian, Y. V., ed. *Naturalism and the Human Spirit*. New York: Columbia University Press, 1944.

Lamont, C. *Humanism as a Philosophy*. New York: Philosophical Library, 1949.

Lovejoy, A. O. *The Thirteen Pragmatisms*. Baltimore: Johns Hopkins Press, 1963.

Nagel, Ernest. *Sovereign Reason*. Glencoe: Free Press, 1954.

———. *Logic without Metaphysics*. Glencoe: Free Press, 1957.

———. *The Structure of Science*. New York: Harcourt Brace, 1961.

Peirce, C. S. *Chance, Love and Logic*. New York: Harcourt Brace, 1923.

———. *Philosophical Writings*. New York: Dover Publications, 1940.

Ratner, Joseph. *Intelligence in the Modern World*. New York: Modern Library, 1929.

Schneider, H. *A History of American Philosophy*. New York: Columbia University Press, 1946.

White, Morton. *Social Thought in America*. Boston: Beacon Press, 1957.

IV
Linguistic
Analysis

ALONG WITH INSTRUMENTAL NATURALISM, existentialism, and phenomenology, linguistic analysis constitutes one of the major styles of contemporary Western philosophizing. Indeed, among academic philosophers of Great Britain and America at the present moment, it probably constitutes the most vigorous and numerous group of all. However, it claims our attention not only for this reason but for several others as well. By its own radical and sometimes revolutionary claims, it forcibly raises the question of philosophic method. As a movement it has claimed to be "the revolution in philosophy"—to quote the title of a volume expounding this way of doing philosophy.[1] For many students of philosophy, the appeal of linguistic analysis has been its combination of rigor and radicalism. Particularly in some of its earlier phases, it claimed to constitute a break with the history of traditional Western philosophy, and indeed with the idea of historical tradition in philosophy as expressed in our chapter 2. Yet, the history of linguistic analysis is itself significant, and is probably the most illuminating way to approach this philosophy.

Historical Background

Despite its somewhat sudden emergence on the American scene, this philosophic movement did not spring full grown and fully armed into the world, like Athene from the head of Zeus. Adherents of linguistic analysis have found traces of their way of philosophizing strewn through Western philosophy from Plato onward. However, it is to Hume that they look as father, or perhaps godfather, of their movement. Hume's single-minded empiricism, his clear distinction between empirical and logical statements, his deep hostility to all violations of these values, and above all his devotion to clarity and rationality, have been an inspiration to linguistic analysis. Kant's influence is less often acknowledged, doubtless because linguistic analysts also find much in Kant to quarrel with. Yet his distinction between analytic and synthetic judgments, his general concern with philosophic language and with the criterion of meaning are powerful influences on contemporary analysis.

Another stream of influence derives from the classical nineteenth century positivisim of Auguste Comte and his followers, with its emphasis upon natural sciences as the only reliable form of knowledge, and its correlative rejection of other, prescientific forms. Comte and his followers also inherited from Comte's early mentor, Saint-Simon, a strong sense of historic mission, which is still observable in some forms of linguistic analysis as a muted though still perceptible and operative messianism of science.

Still another historical source has been the development in the nineteenth and twentieth centuries of a new mathematical logic which has freed philosophical thinking from its age-long bondage to Aristotelean logic, and has provided both mathematics and philosophy with a bold new instrument or calculus by which to carry forward and to communicate its reasoning. With this new instrument has come also an impressive agenda of new problems and issues in the border territory between mathematics and philosophy. Mathematicians and philosophers have moved into this territory with vigor, diligence, and sometimes great originality, with the result that during the past half-century or so this borderland between mathematics and philosophy has been subjected to intense and fruitful cultivation.

All these lines of influence converged upon the Vienna Circle, which was a group of scientifically-minded philosophers and philosophically-minded scientists, who met for mutual discussion and cooperative work during the 1920s and 1930s. Moritz Schlick, who came to the University of Vienna in 1922 as a professor of philosophy, assumed a role of leadership in the Circle; but among the other participants were Herbert Feigl, Rudolph Carnap, Philipp Frank, Otto Neurath, Friedrich Waismann and Kurt Goedel. Karl Popper and Ludwig Wittgenstein, while not members of the Circle, were in close contact with it. The term, logical positivism, applied to the philosophic position of the group, pointed to its combination of philosophic positivism on the one hand and logical method on the other.[2] The philosophy of positivism, which was characterized by its founder, Auguste Comte, as the view that scientific or positive knowledge constitutes the only valid form of knowledge, was here formulated as a set of logical rules for the use of language. The effect was to rule off the playing field of meaningful cognitive activity, before the game began, any alternative or nonscientific forms of knowledge.

Contemporaneous with the Vienna Circle were important philosophic developments in England, especially at Cambridge. Between 1903 and 1913 Whitehead and Russell published their epoch-making *Principia Mathematica* as a statement of first principles of mathematics and logic.[3] Both men also participated in the movement of philosophic realism and naturalism, which attacked the reigning idealism of British philosophy. These developments in British philosophy were contemporaneous in turn with the coming of realism, pragmatism, and naturalism in American philosophy, as illustrated by the philosophies of James, Peirce, and Dewey of our last chapter. Among the leading figures of the English branch of the realistic movement was G. E. Moore of Cambridge, with his philosophy of common sense and common language. Moore's appeal to the experience and language of the common man was a weapon, honed to razor sharpness, for attack upon philosophers who appealed consciously or unconsciously to uncommon or esoteric forms of experience and language. Such philosophers illicitly shift the meaning of common words for their own philosophic purposes. Moore's method consisted of a very careful, painstaking scrutiny of philosophic ideas and words in the light of common sense and common language. The test of a philosophic idea or statement thus becomes its translatability into common language and common experience. Bertrand Russell (who once characterized Moore's commonsense philosophy as the metaphysics of the cave man) had his distinctive emphases and interpretations of the analytic way of philosophizing. In addition to his work in logic, Russell himself listed his definition of number (leading to an explanation of mathematics in terms of logic) and his theory of definite descriptions as his outstanding contributions to analytic philosophy.[4] To these achievements we shall return later in this chapter.

The consequence of these and other converging causes has been the emergence of the philosophic movement that we have labeled linguistic analysis. The label points to two or three continuing features amid the always changing and at times even conflicting forms of this philosophic movement. Speaking generally, the task of philosophy is either asserted or tacitly assumed to be (1) the analysis by (2) means of logic of the (3) language of other philosophers and of nonphilosophers, and sometimes of one's own language. There is, in other words, a threefold concern with analytic method implemented by highly sophisticated logical and semantical instruments, and applied to the varieties of human language, including especially philosophic language. Linguistic analysis continues, in other words, despite changing problems and emphases during its half-century of existence, still as analytic and as linguistic. So conceived, the task of philosophy becomes in effect to operate a clearinghouse for the words man uses. The reader is left to expand this fiscal metaphor to his own taste and satisfaction—dwelling, if he wishes, on the kinds of checks that clear and the various possibilities for bad checks, as well as standards of solvency. It is obvious that any such philosophy will necessarily emphasize the critical as against the constructive aspects of philosophic thinking, though as we shall point out presently, the latter is by no means absent from this philosophy.

The first form of linguistic analysis to exert infuence in England and America was the logical positivism of the Vienna Circle, especially as interpreted by A. J. Ayer's *Language, Truth and Logic.*[5] The coming of Hitler to Austria scattered the members and friends of the Vienna Circle to all parts of the free world, notably to England and America, with a consequent diffusion of their ideas. Waismann found his way to Cambridge, and Popper to the University of London, Frank to Harvard, Neurath and others to Chicago, Feigl to Iowa and then Minnesota, Carnap and Reichenbach to U.C.L.A. —to mention only a few leading figures in this dispersion of men and ideas.

The basic stance of logical positivism was that of a militantly critical philosophy on the attack against ideas that have allegedly served as a veil to cover unreason, and often injustice as well. Insofar as logical positivism was a constructive as well as a critical philosophy, it proclaimed a gospel of science in the service of humanity. While seldom an overt credo, this missionary enthusiasm for the gospel of science has been an observable and functioning element in logical positivism. At times it has also involved an intolerance for opposing ideas and a crusading zeal for its own program. Some philosophy departments have been known to reject and, as it were, to excommunicate adherents of other philosophies. At times, too, it has turned up decidedly odd combinations of attitudes, such for example, as a mingling of Marxist dogmatism and positivist skepticism in the same individual mind.

The chief weapon in the arsenal of logical positivism was the famous verifiability principle, which asserted that the meaning of a proposition consisted in the method of its verification. The similarity of this to pragmatism was pointed out in the last chapter. The critical impact of the principle was that if no such method of verification could be found, the supposed proposition was asserted to be meaningless or nonsensical. As interpreted by Ayer and others, this meant that most of traditional metaphysics, epistemology, and ethics, as well as traditional theology, failed this test and fell under this condemnation. The important new element in this critical attack was that these traditional bodies of supposed knowledge were not false—critics had been charging this for many years and centuries—but rather a meaningless babble of words. Since no clear method of verification was forthcoming, the putative propositions in which these bodies of traditional knowledge are uttered or written were labeled pseudopropositions, or meaningless concatenations of words. Hence, for example, the atheist as well as the theist is babbling; this whole area of discussion is ruled outside the field of meaningful language. Both the theist and atheist, the materialist and idealist, flunk the verifiability test and are condemned to the outer darkness of nonsense.

To be sure, verification is the appropriate method of testing only for the empirical or synthetic statements of common sense and of science. Logical positivism followed the distinction made by Hume and Kant between analytic and synthetic, or logical and empirical statements. The latter class comprises all statements about the world of things; and the former consists of the statements of mathematics and logic, all reducible to the form, $A = A$, and whose function according to the logical positivists is that of ordering or organizing the synthetic statements about the world. Beyond analytic and synthetic judgment so conceived and characterized, lies only the limbo of nonsense. Perceptive critics of logical positivism have noted here a double meaning of the term, *nonsense*, namely its common everyday meaning and the extended, hence metaphorical meaning employed by logical positivism.

An interesting application of this classification was Carnap's concept of the material mode of language. Logical statements Carnap termed the formal mode, and statements about matters of fact he termed the empirical mode. Statements in the material mode were those that seemed to be in the empirical mode, but turned out on examination not to be so, since there is no way to test them. For example, "this apple is red" is clearly in the empirical mode; and "this apple is real" sounds similar. However, upon examination there appears no way to test such predicates as "real" or "unreal." The whole gamut of metaphysical predicates and assertions turns out, according to Carnap, to be in the radically questionable material mode, which he then sought to eliminate by careful paraphrases that move such statements into either formal or empirical mode. So, for example, "the apple is real" is translated into the form, "The word 'apple' is a thing word," which is in the formal mode. Hence, by careful analysis of language, metaphysics is to be completely eliminated. What remains is commonsense experience (we dare not say "of the world," for this phrase is metaphysical and therefore meaningless) and the rules by which our reports of such commonsense experience may be ordered and reasoned about.

Carnap's analysis left a meager vestige of subjective meaning for metaphysical utterances. Such utterances are like lyric poetry, whose function is the expression of emotion. But these utterances tell us nothing about the nature of what philosophers used to call "reality" or "the world." Analogously, the logical positivists found only an emotive meaning in moral language. Thus the moral statement "killing is wrong" is to be paraphrased by the command "don't kill," based upon the strong negative emotion that is associated with the taking of human life.

As may be imagined, these positions were considerably elaborated and qualified in the course of argument. Nevertheless, logical positivism remained what it was in its first statement, a simple, forthright, critical philosophy, radical in its attack on traditional philosophy and in its proposals for reform. One counterargument had to do with the nature of the verifiability principle. Critical questions were raised concerning the nature of the principle, and how and to what it applied. As to the former question, some critics raised the issue of what sort of utterance the principle itself might be. If, as logical positivism asserted, all statements are either analytic or synthetic, what is *that* statement? If the meaning of a statement is the method of its verification, then what is the meaning of *that* statement? Various kinds of answers were attempted, none of them fully successful, ranging from the claim that the verification principle is itself an inductive generalization, to the suggestion that it functions as a proposal made pragmatically in order to achieve orderly or systematic knowledge. As to its application, there were puzzles relating to the fact that conclusive verification (or proof in the full logical sense) seems impossible in science; hence, science itself is threatened by the application of the principle—a result which no adherent of logical positivism could contemplate with equanimity. Proposals for a weaker form of validation, labeled not verification but confirmation (with its negative, infirmation) were offered.

One striking and fruitful suggestion was made by Karl Popper, in what he called the principle of falsifiability.[6] This proposal asserted that the meaning of any statement must include the grounds on which it might be falsified. Hence, statements that are true-no-matter-what, giving no clue to the grounds on which they might be judged false are, in effect, meaningless. The application of this principle to forms of utterance such as Freudian psychoanalysis or Marxist philosophy, as well as to the myth systems of many religions, show them to be meaningless verbiage. At least such was the intimation. This is an issue to which we shall return in chapters 6 and 7.

As logical positivists turned from criticism to construction, their devotion to science and humanity became clear. One project of this movement was the somewhat ambitiously entitled *Encyclopedia of the Unified Sciences*, which aimed at a philosophic foundation upon which scientific knowledge could be organized, purged of irrational elements, and presumably made available to serve the good of mankind.[7] While results fell considerably short of such large hopes, the project managed to produce a series of useful monographs on topics ranging from *Principles of the Theory of Probability* through *Foundations of Physics*, and *Foundations of Biology*, to the *Theory of Valuation*—the last by none other than John Dewey.

In a somewhat similar vein was the proposal termed "physicalism," whose program was to purge and reform the language of science so that its basic terms would be consonant with those of the physical sciences. In such a way science might rid its language of prescientific or irrational verbiage. Physicalism is similar to the naturalism of the last chapter in its devotion to science as the sole reliable form of knowledge. But to sensitive logical positivist ears, the terms nature and naturalism, sounded metaphysical. Hence, the claim of naturalism was recast into an assertion about language rather than about "reality."

Even as these proposals were made, changes were beginning to appear in the logical positivist position. True, some men such as Carnap, Hempel, Feigl, and Nagel, have maintained a lifelong allegiance to the principles outlined above, but others have moved onward to new and different positions. Bergmann was led to turn the charge of metaphysics on logical positivism itself in a volume entitled *The Metaphysics of Logical Positivism*, thus illustrating our first chapter's assertion of the undeniability of metaphysics.[8] Papers by Friedrich Waismann pointed toward a new multifunctional view of language. There are not just two, but rather there are many uses of language, argued Waismann in two papers entitled "Verification" and "Language Strata."[9] Each of these strata or levels has its own grammar, logic, and definition of verification, and most significant of all, its own distinctive use or function of words.

More than any other single man, the figure who embodied the changing forms of linguistic analysis, and also most influenced those changes, was Ludwig Wittgenstein. An Austrian who found his way to England in pursuit of such various interests as kite flying and higher mathematics, he also found his way into Bertrand Russell's lectures on philosophy at Cambridge in 1912. He spent World War I in the Austrian army, and jotted down in a notebook carried in his army pack what was to become the famous *Tractatus Logico-Philosophicus*.[10] This book was published in German in 1921, and in parallel English and German pages in 1922. In an allusive and aphoristic style, the author articulated a philosophy similar, but by no means identical, to logical positivism.

Despite the somewhat negative conclusion that most philosophical propositions are not false but senseless (*unsinning*), and a desire to dispense with philosophy as something to be surmounted or, in Wittgenstein's metaphor, as a ladder which, having been climbed, may be kicked away, nevertheless the *Tractatus* exhibits several significant metaphysical positions. For example, it expounds what is termed a picture theory of knowledge. "We make ourselves pictures of facts," declared Wittgenstein and then labored long to relate the picture to its referent.[11] He also characterized "the world" as constituted by the building blocks of atomic facts (*Tatsachverhalten*), a view clearly influenced by the logical work of Whitehead and Russell. Russell had posited atomic facts as entities in the world corresponding to the atomic propositions that were elements of his logical system. This hypothesis did not fare well in ensuing critical discussion, for atomic facts proved to be extremely elusive entities.[12] The *Tractatus* also asserted the world as "the totality of existent atomic facts"; and again that "the total reality is the world."[13] The world as the totality of facts is also declared to be value-neutral or *wertfrei*; or as Wittgenstein put it, "The sense of the world must be outside the world."[14] Stated theologically, "God does not reveal himself in the world." Apparently the world of which he spoke bore no relation to the value-oriented world in which humans live and act, and which Wittgenstein was to describe in his later works. The closing pages of the *Tractatus* wrestle with traditional issues of skepticism, mysticism, and the limits of intelligibility. The volume concludes with a well-known and characteristically oracular remark: "Whereof one cannot speak, thereof one must be silent."[15] Some have likened this to the religiously pregnant silence of the mystic, rather than the silence of the agnostic or skeptic.

The next several years Wittgenstein spent in Austria, first as a village schoolmaster, then in Vienna. He returned to Cambridge in 1928, offering his *Tractatus* as a doctoral dissertation the following year. He lectured at Cambridge from 1930 to 1936, and in 1937 succeeded to G. E. Moore's chair, continuing to lecture and teach intermittently until 1949. He died of cancer in 1951.

His posthumous publications included a successor to the *Tractatus*, entitled *Philosophical Investigations*, and also several books of lecture notes compiled by students, including those called, respectively, the *Brownbook* and the *Bluebook*.[16] In these works the reader sees taking shape a new postpositivist view of language and knowledge, strikingly different from that of the *Tractatus*. In the *Philosophical Investigations* the problem of language and its relation to the world is still central, but the idea of correspondence between scientific language and the world of atomic fact has been replaced by what may be termed a functional, indeed a multifunctional, view of language. In Wittgenstein's own words, men "play many language games" (*Sprachspielen*), each with its own rules and objectives.[17] The *Philosophical*

Investigations explore some of these games, specifying their rules and goals, distinguishing them from each other. The concept of language games was to prove an effective challenge to many inquirers to state and distinguish some of the many games which human experience and language show, and which presumably humans play.

Other thinkers, equally dissatisfied with the regnant logical positivism, were pushing on to similarly postpositivist views. We have already noted Waismann's paper on "Verifiability" with its emphasis on a contextual approach of verifiability, as well as that entitled "Language Strata," in which the idea of different languages, each with its own logical and semantical rules, and with "open texture" in the relation of language to reality was systematically urged. John Wisdom, who succeeded to Wittgenstein's chair at Cambridge, while immersed in the analytic way of philosophizing, had from the beginning of his career raised probing questions concerning the basic categories of analysis. As early as 1938 he was asking: "Is the verification principle true?" and "Shall we accept the verification principle?"[18] His somewhat cryptic response was that it is "the generalization of a very large class of metaphysical theories, namely all naturalistic, empirical, positivistic theories." Hence, while aiming at the elimination of metaphysics, the verification principle appeared in this view as metaphysical in character. In 1944 Wisdom's allusive and enigmatic essay entitled "Gods" projected new possibilities of meaning for artistic, religious, and even psychoanalytic forms of expression.[19] "The existence of God," he urged, "is not an experimental issue in the way it was." Not only the discovery of new scientific laws and facts, but the discernment of relations is humanly important. "Proust, Manet, Breughel, even Botticelli and Vermeer show us reality." So too, he intimated, do Freud and St. John. In his 1961 British Academy lecture entitled "The Metamorphosis of Metaphysics," he exclaimed, "How satisfactory to pass from a phase in which philosophical questions seemed to call on us to explore some country we could never reach, to see behind some veil we could never penetrate, to open some door we could never open to a phase in which . . . is made . . . only the demand that we should analyze a class of propositions we often assert, translate a class of sentences we often utter."[20]

Along with other shifts in the viewpoint of analytic philosophy came also vast changes in the goal or end of analysis. The logical positivists assumed that analysis could be complete or exhaustive, and also that it consisted in correcting verbal distortions or departures from either logical or empirical usage. Wittgenstein's *Tractatus* seemed to agree with both of these objectives.

During the postpositivist period of analytic philosophy, the metaphorical idea of diseases of language, along with the corresponding suggestion of therapy as the goal of analysis, have continued. However, the concept of any single standard and complete or exhaustive type of analysis seems to have disappeared. Rather, there are as many types of analysis as there are analysts, and what is more important, none of them is viewed as complete or exhaustive. Critics of analytic philosophy, while agreeing that analysis is an important part of philosophy's total task, have argued that it is by no means the whole of it. In the terms of our chapter 2, analysis embraces the critical aspect of philosophy, but largely ignores its constructive aspect.

By the nineteen fifties what had emerged was a wide variety of forms of linguistic analysis, some old, some new, some mixed old and new. Despite evident variety and even conflict within the movement, these forms continued to share a common approach to philosophy through the analysis of language. Language was and still is the filter through which philosophical concepts must pass. As to their own language, linguistic analysts share also a common style, careful, cautious, rigorous, clear and, more often than not, dry and dull. They also share a preference for small problems rather than large ones; the large ones must be broken down to small ones in order to be dealt with. Hence, the paper or brief essay rather than the book seems the normal form of philosophic expression.

As the student makes his way among the universities of the Anglo-American world, both the variety and continuity of linguistic analysis are apparent. Harvard's formulation differs from Princeton's or Columbia's, and all of these differ from Berkeley's or U.C.L.A.'s. Yet, of all the various formulations, the one that originated in and emanated from Oxford has been most influential through the fifties and sixties, as evidenced by such names as Ryle, Austin, Hampshire, Warnock, Pears, and Prior, to name only a few. More than any other single book, it was Ryle's *Concept of Mind*, published first in 1948, which opened the way to a new chapter in analytic philosophy.[21] Ryle had earlier declared what he termed his "reluctant conversion" to the view that philosophy's proper business is the analysis of language, in a paper entitled "Systematically Misleading Expressions."[22] Thus, for example, Platonic ideas might be termed systematically misleading since they are so readily confused with things. The same critical concern is manifested in *The Concept of Mind* in Ryle's attack upon the "official doctrine" that mind is a kind of private inner thing, object, or substance, within each individual body and accessible only to each individual by means of something pompously labeled "introspection." This doctrine of mind as an inner mental substance Ryle called "the fallacy of the ghost in the machine," and declared it to be a myth, which in turned he described as a "category mistake."[23] In a word, then, the official doctrine of mind is a single, vast, and agelong category mistake or cluster of category mistakes, which it is the business of analytic philosophy to lay bare and hence to correct once and for all.

In addition to Ryle's sustained attack upon this false and misleading view of mind, his book also gives constructive articulation to an alternative view that avoids the dualism of the Cartesian view and approaches mind publicly and functionally as an aspect of human behavior, always well-known to the common man and hence embedded in common language, and now to be given philosophical statement. Several features of Ryle's view of mind need underscoring. It is predominantly verbish, even adverbish, rather than nounish or substantive. Since the mind's various activities find expression in common language, the deliverances of language constitute a ready access to the processes and structures of mind. Ryle's view may also be characterized as consistently antireductionist. He is concerned to see mind as it *is* and *does*, rather than through the false mediation of a theory that reduces it to something else or explains it away.

Ryle states his purpose as "not to increase what we know about minds, but to rectify the logical geography of the knowledge we already possess." What is needed is "the continental geography of the subject." Both Ryle's criticism of the official Cartesian view of mind and his intimation of an alternative view have proven to be seminal suggestions for contemporary philosophy. He asserts that the exposition and criticism of "the powers, operations, and states of minds has always been a big part of the task of philosophers. Theories of knowledge, logic, ethics, political theory, and aesthetics are the products of their inquiries in this field."[24]

During the past two decades many new concerns have surfaced in analytic philosophy—many, though by no means all, traceable to sources or suggestions in Ryle and Wittgenstein. As Ryle indicates above, many of these concerns represent a renewal of interest in traditional philosophy. They are thus new perspectives on old, traditional issues of philosophy. In many cases they have led to renewed study of great figures in the history of philosophy, from Plato and Aristotle to Hume and Kant.

There is space here only for very brief comment on six of these contemporary concerns or themes, namely: (1) philosophy of mind, (2) theory of action, (3) ethics and value theory, (4) metaphysics, (5) logic and philosophy of mathematics, and (6) philosophy of religion.

Contemporary Themes

(1) What is currently labeled philosophy of mind may be described as a fresh approach and a new grouping of several old issues centering in the nature

and significance of mind. Central in the new approach are logical and linguistic methods and tools. For the human mind finds primary expression in language. Hence, many of the issues of philosophy of mind lie embedded in language, waiting to be lifted out, analyzed, and appraised.

Among the wide variety of issues that have interested philosophers of mind are the traditional regions of the mind's life, such as intellect, will, and emotion. For example, Ryle mounted a full-fledged attack on the concept of will, calling it as obsolete as the phlogiston theory of heat.[25] Others have arisen in defense, explication, and often redefinition, of will. Many writers have focused attention upon the traditional problems of perception and sensation. Other issues range from the nature of consciousness and self-knowledge to the relation of individual and social mind, and to the relation of thought to value and action. The relation of philosophical to psychological study of mind and philosophical criticisms of psychology have been the subject of several studies.

As to results, if philosophy of mind has not changed the world, it has yielded significant clarification of many traditionally muddled issues. It has shed new light on old problems. Also many of its questions have come to be seen as significantly overlapping action theory.

(2) Theory or philosophy of action owes its origin to several seminal suggestions made by Wittgenstein in his *Philosophical Investigations* and by Ryle in his *Concept of Mind*. Ryle argues for the primacy of "knowing how" over "knowing that." The latter, "knowing that," or intellectual knowledge, always occurs in the larger context of "knowing how," which in turn is clearly a species of activity, and as such is an aspect of the whole active life of the human self. Ryle, Wittgenstein, and others have also distinguished sharply between events which occur in the nonhuman regions of the world, and the actions of human beings, arguing that the latter cannot be reduced completely and without remainder to the former.

Once the issue of human action was posed, it led onward to other issues of many sorts. For example, Richard Taylor argued persuasively that deliberation concerning issues of choice or decision necessarily presupposes freedom of choice.[26] People will not continue to deliberate if they know that the aims or goals of choice are predetermined. A. I. Melden's *Free Action* argues, with the help of many suggestions from the later Wittgenstein, that the idea of free doing or action lies embedded in common language, and further, that other descriptions of human behavior necessarily presuppose these ideas.[27] So, for example, the simple act of raising one's arm is to be viewed as a directly perceived form of experience irreducible to other deterministic forms of explanation. Still other writers, such as Norman Malcolm, go on the offensive, arguing that mechanistic determinism as an explanation of the human self and its actions is radically self-contradictory.[28]

Stuart Hampshire treats human freedom as a kind of presupposition embedded in the words "I will . . . " in such expressions as "I will do act *a*," interpreted not as a prediction, but as a direct expression of intention.[29] Such intending or willing necessarily means free willing. Hampshire's *Thought and Action* uses action-theory as a new approach to many of the traditional problems of philosophy and of the humanities. A. R. Louch's *Explanation and Human Action* applies action-theory to a mordant critique of contemporary behavioral sciences.[30] These sciences, living in what might be termed a state of physics-envy, have slavishly imitated the successful methods of natural sciences, rather than developing methods appropriate to their own subject matter. The result is a word-game which is, more often than not, devoid of real meaning, and yields little or no genuine knowledge. Louch combines action-theory with a common language approach as a critical weapon to lay bare the tangled nonsense and half-sense of much of the verbiage of the social sciences.

A notable chapter in action-theory is John Austin's exploration of the performative function of language, in which language is approached as a highly distinctive form of action.[31] Austin contrasted performative with constative uses of language, the latter consisting of the reporting of facts. By contrast, in performative speech the words which we use actively *do* or *perform* something. For example, if I say "I promise . . . ," "I pledge allegiance . . . ," "I invite you . . . ," or "I apologize . . . ," my words are not reporting actions but are actually doing the acts therein embodied. These words, *invite, apologize, promise*, or *pledge allegiance*, and many more, all illustrate different kinds of performances that words do. Austin was led to classify the main types of performatives as (1) verdictives, which perform a verdict or act of appraisal, (2) exercitives, in which an action or decision is effected or carried out, (3) commissives, in which the self is committed to some action, (4) behavitives, in which an attitude is expressed, and (5) expositives, in which a thought or idea is set forth or expounded.[32] Austin was attracted to the view that there is also a performative component of "I know." Even the concept of truth has been analyzed for traces of performative meaning; to call a statement true consists at least in part of activities of certification or verification.

Austin's suggestion has called attention to aspects of language (and hence also to the thinking which language expresses or embodies) which other approaches to this subject matter have either neglected or have misstated. As Austin continued to analyze performative language, he was led to the conclusion that this was not so much a *kind* of language as a *function* of language. Thus, for example, such expressions as "I report . . . ," "I state . . . ," "I assert . . . ," may be classified as either performative or constative, according to use or context. Reporting fact or asserting the truth or falsity of statements are among the activities or performances of man. Hence, constatives may be classified as a subtype of performatives.

In passing, we may note in this connection the close parallel between what Austin termed a "speech-act" and what German existentialist theologians and philosophers of the hermeneutical movement have termed a *Sprachereignis*.[33] Clearly here is what may be termed a meeting of extremes in contemporary philosophy. We shall return to this issue in the next chapter.

(3) While there is a considerable overlap between action-theory and the traditional discipline of ethics, the latter by itself has received considerable attention from linguistic analysts. In the early logical positivist phases of the movement it was fashionable to reduce moral maxims like "killing is wrong" to commands like "don't kill," whose authority consists of the negative emotion engendered by society. This emotive meaning might even be reduced to the ejaculation, "ugh, killing!" A more sophisticated version of the same emotive meaning theory of ethics is to be found in Stevenson's *Ethics and Language*, with its emphasis on "persuasive definitions," that is, those definitions in which subsequent conclusions are covertly smuggled into the definitions which set moral argument on its way.[34]

The emotive meaning theory of ethics attracted a following, at least in part, because of the evident truth that our moral conclusions do seem to have an emotive as well as a rational or discursive component. Hence, the emotive meaning theory scored decisively against traditional rationalism which derived moral conclusions simply, indeed oversimply, as conclusions of rational arguments. Yet, the subsequent discussion has also shown defects in emotive meaning theories. How on the basis of this view alone can we explain the imperative aspect in moral discourse? It is not self-evident that the expression of emotion of itself generates moral imperatives. Again, how understand the general or universal reference involved in moral discourse?

As an illustration of the attempt to deal with these previously neglected aspects of moral experience, we may point to R. M. Hare's theory of prescriptive meaning.[35] Hare defines a prescription as a command that is universalizable. (Though Hare never says so explicitly, his writings suggest that a command seems to function as an act of approval or disapproval in the field of interpersonal relations.) He distinguishes between prescriptive and descriptive meaning in a manner similar to Austin's performative and constative distinction. While moral experience involves important incidental aspects of descriptive meaning, it is prescriptive meaning that, according to Hare, is central and definitive in ethics. Hare has carried on a lively polemic both against those who regard morality as comprehensible solely in terms of descriptive meaning on the one hand, and against the emotivists on the other.

What emerges is a set of categories that Hare regards as adequate for the consideration of what he terms "the logic of moral discourse." While this view of ethics has provided linguistic analysis with a way to cope with the traditional issues and problems of ethical theory, it still faces formidable problems if taken as a fully adequate view of the whole region of man's moral life. For example, Hare defines the good as the object of acts of approval; the good is that of which man approves.[36] Yet, this clearly calls for further analysis of such acts. What do we mean by "approve"? On what basis and in what contexts do such acts occur? To cite another kind of example, as mankind turns from philosophical ethics to social ethics, it is not clear how the linguistic approach will contribute, if at all, to specific and practical problems of moral guidance.

Concerning other forms of value, such as esthetic value, which is the subject of art and of the philosophy of art, and concerning value theory in general, linguistic analysis has had relatively less to say. Yet, there are intimations of concern as well as some suggestive leads for thought even in these regions. In the early days of logical positivism the gulf between fact and value seemed unbridgeable. The logical positivists had as firm a hold upon scientific fact as positivists can have on anything, but they banished all forms of valuation to the inner realm of the subjective and the emotional. (The equation between these last two terms, subjective and emotional, stands as an interesting monument to this philosophy, for a careful analysis of people's real emotions reveals many kinds of transactions with the objective world. In real life emotion is not cooped up in the subject but occurs as a way of relating man to his world.)

There are many recent and current attempts, not indeed, to bridge the gap, but to show how in fact it never really existed in the first place. One such attempt takes off from suggestions of Ryle and others that from the viewpoint of action (which has a primacy both for man and for philosophy) values are never found separated from fact. Only as we initially assume the primacy of scientific theory does the subjectivity of value emerge as a problem. From the viewpoint of active human existence, values and facts are always found mingled together as complementary aspects of reality. Hence the real question is: which values among those that compete for our allegiance are worthy of choice and pursuit? From this viewpoint, value-theory still remains agenda for linguistic philosophy.

(4) As we have seen, the early phases of linguistic analysis were militantly antimetaphysical. The stately nineteenth century mansions of metaphysics were rudely demolished by the logical positivists. But we have also noted the way in which Wittgenstein, Wisdom, and others found themselves inescapably dealing with metaphysical utterances or statements, as well as the metaphysical commitments forced by their own analytic methods.

Another significant figure in the resumption of metaphysics by linguistic analysis is W. V. Quine, Harvard logician and philosopher of logic. Among logicians Quine has been notable for the way in which he has worked his way through logical methods and activities to metaphysical or ontological conclusions. For example, his paper, "On What There Is," published in 1948, characterized existence pragmatically as "the value of a variable."[37] This was in effect to define existence in terms of logical or semantic function. Quine's critics commented that this definition yielded not what it means to *be*, but what is *said to be*.

More recent continuations of this line of thought have led Quine to what he has termed "ontological commitment."[38] A theory is said in logical terms to be committed to the sorts of entities over which its variables range. However, as Quine has pointed out, this range of entities will in turn depend upon the way in which the theory is formulated. Now, these ways are literally innumerable. Hence, what follows in Quine's view is a thorough relativizing of ontology and ontological commitment. Stated in plain English, what seems to emerge from all this is a combination of highly sophisticated logical theory and, in the application of logic to the world of reality, of old-fashioned pragmatism. Ontology seems in this perspective to be unavoidable, though the range and variety of ontological commitments seem literally limitless.

In some quarters the concern with metaphysics has increased to a point where it is fair to characterize analytic philosophy simply as a rigorous, analytic way of dealing with many of the traditional problems of metaphysical philosophy. Peter Strawson's *Individuals*, dealing with the existence of individual entities including individual persons, and his *Bounds of Sense*, a study of Kantian ontology, are cases in point.[39] Stuart Hampshire was led in 1950 to a notable study of Spinoza and, as we have already seen, in 1959 to a volume called *Thought and Action*, in which action theory functions as an entrance gate into many of the traditional problems of philosophy. Others have followed suit with studies of metaphysical problems and of important historical figures from Plato and Aristotle to Hegel.

This turn of events in analytic philosophy offers significant confirmation of the thesis advanced in chapter 2 that, since metaphysical philosophy deals with an undeniable aspect of the mind's life, namely, the idea of the unique, unlimited, all-inclusive totality of all things whatsoever, it cannot successfully be avoided. If we deny that we have a metaphysics we do not thereby successfully avoid metaphysical thinking, but rather find ourselves in the grip of unconscious metaphysics. It is an important part of the work of philosophical thinking to draw such unconscious assumptions into the full light of consciousness where they may be critically appraised. Happily, contemporary analytic philosophy has now developed to a point where this work is beginning to be done. Analytic philosophy recognizes that the question is not metaphysics or no metaphysics, but what kind of metaphysical thinking will we do. It is important in this connection to urge that there is still much ground to explore—or rather to reexplore—from this new perspective.

As we observe this aspect of the contemporary scene, we may imagine the shade of Wittgenstein smiling down upon his offspring, and asking what sort of language game *this* is. The question is a fair one and, seriously pursued, the answer may indeed be fruitful, not only for philosophy but for all the life of man's mind.

(5) Both the theory and practice of logic remain a central concern of analytic philosophers. As noted above, logic has continued to be fruitful for metaphysics and other branches of philosophy. Yet, the esthetic satisfaction of doing logic, so similar to the attraction of highly structured games like contract bridge and chess, remains an observably strong motivation for this whole area of study. Like these other games, logic also generates its own distinctive forms of virtuosity.

From the inception of this trend in the nineteenth and early twentieth century to the present, this has been a period of very great productivity in logic and related fields. As Bertrand Russell once remarked, whereas Aristotelean logic held thought in chains, the new logic has given it wings. The chains to which Russell referred were the subject-predicate form of analysis imposed by traditional Aristotelean logic upon all statements. The wings of the new logic provide the possibility of as many ways of analysis as the differing kinds of language demand.

Progress in both mathematics and logic has made it possible to formulate any part or area of either of these disciplines or, for that matter, any form of knowledge as a hypothetico-deductive system, which is to say, a system of statements in which one or more stand as postulates or assumptions and the others as theorems or conclusions. Both mathematicians and logicians have pressed toward the construction of ever more widely unified hypothetico-deductive systems, as well as studying the logical nature and behavior of these systems.

A giant step toward this end was taken by Whitehead and Russell's *Principia Mathematica* which, beginning with five postulates, involving any propositions, *p* and *q*, plus the symbols for alternation and negation, proceeded successively to the systems (or calculi), first of propositions, then of classes, and finally of relations. By means of his definition (following Frege) of number (to be discussed in the next paragraph), Russell was able to draw mathematics and logic together, deriving mathematics from the logical concepts above, or conversely reducing mathematics to logic. Previous mathematicians had been able to show all the entities of mathematics to be human constructions, with the notable exception of the natural numbers which, accordingly, were assumed to be part of the irreducible furniture of the world. The force of Russell's definition was to show that numbers too were logical constructions, whose elements were the classes or sets of logic.

The Frege-Russell definition of number is, in summary, that a number is a class of isomorphic classes. The number *two* will suffice as an illustration. The definition invites us to take any couple, say *a* and *b*, then go through the universe finding all other classes or sets that are isomorphic with this class consisting of couples. Isomorphism is the the relation of point-for-point identity of structure between the elements of two classes, as for example, the fingers on one's two hands. The class formed of all entities isomorphic with the original couple, *a* and *b*, is the number two.[40]

While Whitehead and Russell's achievement, as well as the work of other mathematicians and logicians seemed to bring even nearer the goal of a universal logical system embodying all knowledge whatsoever (a goal envisaged as long ago as Leibniz in his idea of a universal calculus), matters took a most unexpected turn with Goedel's incompleteness theorem in 1931. This theorem, which only belatedly received the attention it deserved, demonstrated that every formal or deductive system is necessarily incomplete.[41] While detailed study of the implications and consequences of Goedel's theorem is to date by no means either conclusive or exhaustive, it does appear to have delivered a fatal blow to the aspiration for a single, universal, all-inclusive, rational system. In the light of Goedel's theorem, any such logical systems must be judged impossible of fulfillment. If this is true, it is a conclusion of great significance for all of philosophy.

Meanwhile, still other philosophic issues arising from logic continue in liveliest discussion. One such issue stems from Kant's characterization of metaphysical statements as synthetic and a priori. As the new logic has developed, many if not all logicians have become convinced that no such statements are possible, that, in short, no true synthetic a priori statements exist. For example, one well-known philospher has asserted that no contemporary student who has had an elementary course in logic any longer takes this Kantian claim seriously.[42] However, on this important cluster of issues, there is a continuing dissenting minority who seem to believe that, in some sense, there are meaningful and true synthetic a priori statements, or more fundamentally, that the duality of analytic-synthetic is itself untenable.[43]

Another celebrated chapter in philosophical logic that has set in motion many further lines of thought is Russell's theory of definite descriptions. Philosophers ancient and modern had long puzzled over the status of apparently nonexistent entities like "the present King of France" and of statements which contain such terms, such as Russell's illustration, "The present King of France is bald." Using the conceptual categories of *Principia Mathematica*, Russell provided the following analysis of such expressions. There is an x such that for every y, if y exists and has the predicate a, then y equals x, and x has the predicates a and b. Stated in the less opaque language of ordinary prose, Russell's analysis may be said to consist of a conjunction of the following statements: "The King of France exists," "There is not more than one King of France," and "whatever is King of France is bald."[44] A notable element in Russell's use is his clear distinction between the existential and predicative interpretations of the verb, *to be*. By means of his analysis Russell believed that he had shown how such putative entities as "the present King of France" are logical constructions that might be analyzed or resolved into elements susceptible of empirical interpretation. Russell followed up with the metaphysical maxim that such logical constructions ought to be substituted wherever possible for fictional entities, thus reducing the metaphysical population of the world in conformity to Occam's razor. In passing however, we must also note that the theory of descriptions itself has in recent times come in for considerable critical discussion, notably in Strawson's paper, "On Referring."[45]

Work continues along many lines in logic. Within the fields of formal logic many workers toil at such projects as modal logic and tense logic. Study of probability and induction continues very much alive. Other workers continue in many important ways to reflect upon the philosophic implications and applications of logic.

(6) Still another front on which linguistic analysis has exerted observable influence is that of the philosophy of religion and theology. As we have seen, the logical positivists were either indifferent or scornful toward traditional religion and theology, even though, as we have seen, some of its adherents made an unconscious faith-substitute out of science. Theology, as

well as metaphysics, was banished to the limbo of nonsense. Yet, even at this early date, Willem Zuurdeeg combined logical positivist philosophy with Barthian theology in his *Analytical Philosophy of Religion*.[46] To many readers this view seemed to be a twentieth century version of the classical combination of philosophic skepticism and theological fideism.

In more recent phases of linguistic philosophy, many significant relations to religious thought and practice have emerged. Wittgenstein observed that men play many language games, thereby challenging those interested in the various different games to state their rules and goals, and to distinguish their language game from other games. To many students of religion this has constituted a standing challenge to characterize the religious use of language. What kind of language game is this, and how is it like and unlike other language games? This concern has tended to converge with other trends in theological study, such as an increasing concern with mythical language on the part of historians of religion, as well as the concern with words and meanings inspired by German existentialism in the so-called hermeneutical movement of Gerhard Ebeling and others.

Linguistic philosophers have concerned themselves with issues of religious thought, and theologians have reciprocated by excursions into linguistic philosophy. R. B. Braithwaite's Eddington lecture of 1953 entitled *An Empiricist's View of Religious Belief* viewed religious myths and doctrines as essentially consisting of morality plus emotion in a way that consciously recalled Matthew Arnold.[47] We have already alluded to John Wisdom's essay entitled "Gods." Following this came a volume of essays, edited by Flew and MacIntyre, entitled *New Essays in Philosophical Theology*, dealing with problems ranging from myth to miracle, and from the idea of God to the arguments for and against divine existence.[48] Paul van Buren's *Secular Meaning of the Gospel* sought to use linguistic analysis as the basis for a wholesale reinterpretation of Christian theology in secular humanist terms.[49]

What emerges from these and other similar works that might be added to the list is an increasing use of analytic methods in theological study. As noted above, this in turn converges with concerns with language derived from other sources. While no large-scale results are yet visible, undoubtedly this movement has contributed to clarity and rigor. This is a subject to which we shall return in chapter 12, on Christian theology as a philosophic option.

SUGGESTIONS FOR FURTHER READING

As many of these works are classics that have appeared in numerous editions, only the most accessible publication is indicated.

Austin, J. L. *How to Do Things with Words*. Cambridge: Harvard University Press, 1962.

———. *Philosophical Papers*. Oxford: Clarendon Press, 1962.

Ayer, A. J. *Language, Truth and Logic*. New York: Dover Publications, 1952.

———. *Philosophical Essays*. New York: St. Martin's Press, 1954.

Bergmann, G. *The Metaphysics of Logical Positivism*. Madison: University of Wisconsin Press, 1967.

Braithwaite, R. *Scientific Explanation*. Cambridge: Cambridge University Press, 1953.

———. *An Empiricist's View of the Nature of Religious Belief*. Cambridge: Cambridge University Press, 1953.

Carnap, Rudolph. *The Logical Structure of the World*. Berkeley: University of California Press, 1967.

Feigl, Herbert. *The Mental and the Physical*. Minneapolis: University of Minnesota Press, 1967.

Flew, A., ed. *Logic and Language* (I, II). Oxford: Blackwell, 1952, 1955.

Flew, A., and MacIntyre, A. *New Essays in Philosophical Theology*. New York: Macmillan, 1955.

Hampshire, S. *Thought and Action*. London: Chatto & Windus, 1959.

Hare, R. *The Language of Morals*. Oxford: Clarendon Press, 1952.

———. *Freedom and Reason*. Oxford: Clarendon Press, 1963.

Hempel, C. *Aspects of Scientific Explanation*. New York: Free Press, 1965.

Louch, A. *Explanation and Human Action*. Oxford: Blackwell, 1967.

Nagel, Ernest. *Goedel's Proof*. New York: New York University Press, 1958.

———. *The Structure of Science*. New York: Harcourt Brace, 1961.

Popper, K. *The Logic of Scientific Discovery*. New York: Basic Books, 1959.

Quine, W. V. *From a Logical Point of View*. Cambridge: Harvard University Press, 1953.

———. *The Ways of Paradox*. New York: Random House, 1966.

Russell, B. *Introduction to Mathematical Philosophy*. New York, 1919.

———. *An Inquiry into Meaning and Truth*. New York: Norton, 1940.

Ryle, G. *The Concept of Mind*. New York: Barnes & Noble, 1959.

Stevenson, C. *Ethics and Language*. New Haven: Yale University Press, 1944.

Strawson, P. *Introduction to Logical Theory*. London: Methuen, 1952.

———. *Individuals*. London: Methuen, 1959.

Van Buren, P. *The Secular Meaning of the Gospel*. New York: Macmillan, 1963.

Waismann, F. *Principles of Linguistic Philosophy*. New York: St. Martin's Press, 1965.

Whitehead, A., and Russell, B. *Principia Mathematica*. Cambridge: Cambridge University Press, 1903–1913.

Wisdom, J. *Philosophy and Psychoanalysis*. Oxford: Blackwell, 1957.

Wittgenstein, L. *Tractatus Logico-Philosophicus*. London: Routledge & Kegan Paul, 1922.

———. *Philosophical Investigations*. New York: Macmillan, 1953.

V
Existentialism

IT WOULD BE HARD TO IMAGINE two ways of philosophy more unlike each other than liguistic analysis and existentialism. They differ fundamentally in stance or attitude, as well as in the discursive content of philosophy. They differ also in style and method. While the linguistic analysts have written papers or articles on specific and carefully delimited topics, in a clear, dry style, the existentialists have written tomes, often far less than clear in style, devoted to the larger themes of philosophy, and frequently less than formally perfect in argument. While the linguistic analysts are almost entirely academic philosophers, the existentialists have frequently sought expression in literature and other arts, and even in theology. Methodologically, the linguistic analysts may perhaps be said to have used a microscope, while the existentialists have used a telescope.

One small bit of common ground is the term, *existence*, but even here difference outweighs similarity. For the analytic philosopher, existence is designated by the existential operator in modern logic (symbolized in *Principia Mathematica* by a backward and upside-down capital E).[1] As a primary or logically primitive symbol, this is undefined within the system; but existence is thus marked off as a category or concept to be accorded special and detailed philosophic analysis. The previous chapter noted Quine's view that existence is the value of a variable. In sharpest contrast, existence, as the term is used by existentialists, refers primarily to human existence, or the human situation. For the existentialists this is the region of existence that we know most closely and adequately; hence it becomes the primary source-region for the basic catagories of existentialist metaphysics or ontology.

While linguistic analysis is largely a movement of professional philosophers, existentialism has overlapped many fields, ranging from literature and other arts to theology. Existentialist writers have often been critical and suspicious of academic philosophy. Perhaps for these reasons, American and British academic philosophy has been slow to take existentialism seriously, to accord it full critical attention. Often, therefore, this philosophy has found its way into the academic curriculum through other disciplines and departments. Sometimes student interest has forced a consideration of existentialism as a protest against the apparent remoteness of linguistic analysis. Nevertheless it is a fact that in continental Europe existentialism, along with its close ally phenomenology, has virtually dominated the philosophic scene for the greater part of the present century.

The question often put by puzzled general readers in philosophy is: what is existentialism? This question points in several directions. As we have just seen, one is the meaning of the term, *existence*. Another closely related direction is the reference or extension of the label, *existentialism*. Just who are and who are not existentialists? Some expositions limit the label to a small group of French and German philosophers of the twentieth century (most of whom incidentally have at one time or another disavowed the term). Other expositions include a notable group of nineteenth century writers such as Kierkegaard, Dostoyevsky, and Nietzsche; and still others trace the origin of existentialism to medieval scholastics, or even find traces of existentialism in such figures as St. Augustine, or St. Paul, or the Greek tragedians. Still other classifications include as existentialists such poets as T. S. Eliot and W. H. Auden, as well as painters, and artists in other media, all under the category of existentialist art. Philosophic definition seems always to be plagued by the problem of borderline cases, but in this case the problem is particularly acute.

As in other ways of philosophy our approach to existentialism will be historical. Initially, at least, existentialism may be characterized as a movement embracing philosophy, theology, literature, and other arts, which began in the nineteenth century, came to maturity in the twentieth, and which centers in the question, what is man? Put more personally and poignantly, as existentialists often insist upon doing, the question becomes, who am I? Who am I really or actually, prior to all dogmas and theories about the nature of my being?

Sartre has said that in man "existence precedes essence."[2] This is to say, man *is* and knows *that* he is, before he knows *what* he is. His "that" refers to existence, and his "what" to his essence. (By *essence*, as here used, is meant no esoteric metaphysical entity, but simply and plainly *essential nature*.) Over wide areas of being or reality there is no shadow of separation or duality between these two aspects of being. My writing desk, my books, and typewriter show essence and existence in seamless unity. They exist; of this I have no real doubt. *What* they are, which is to say their essence or meaning, I may discover most readily by looking up the respective words in a dictionary. For an essence shorn of its superstitious connotations is simply the sum of the features necessary and sufficient for a thing to be what it is; and this is precisely what a dictionary seeks to embody in its definitions.

This unity of essence and existence holds good over much of organic as well as inorganic nature. The cow munching her cud in the pasture has apparently no questions about her essence, namely her bovinity, or cow-hood. Similarly the dog gives no evidence of conscious concern about his caninity. And so the matter goes for most living creatures.

With man, however, the case is radically different. Every serious human being of whatever creed or philosophy does ask himself, in one form or another, the question: what must I do and be to be genuinely human? Man's humanity, however we may define it, *is* a question. And this central human question in effect tears essence and existence apart in the human situation, and makes man's humanity a matter of conscious choice or decision. Man thus becomes the creature who must achieve or win his essence. As we shall see, how or indeed, whether, man can do this are matters on which existentialist writers disagree with each other. Caninity, bovinity are, as it were, gifts of nature to these respective creatures, but humanity is an aspiration and a dignity to be won—or lost.

This issue is beautifully expressed in an all too little known French novel entitled *You Shall Know Them* by Vercors.[3] It is the story of a young anthropologist, Douglas Templemore, who goes on a scientific field expedition to a remote region of New Guinea where he discovers what appears to be the "missing link" between man and his nearest animal relatives. Called the "tropis" (as short for *paranthropos*) by members of the expedition, these creatures exhibit many but by no means all the essential features of human beings. Their communication is on the borderline between animal cries and human words. In physical appearance also they appear to stand on the border between man and beast.

The central question is: are they man or animal? Are they or are they not human? The scientists resolve to do a crucial scientific experiment, namely to mate a tropi female with a human male. However the offspring turns out again to be borderline. Templemore decides to seek another kind of answer to the question. He deliberately kills the son he has fathered by a tropi female in order to force a legal definition of the human species. The climax of the book is Templemore's murder trial where the crucial question is the legal definition of man. The denouement or resolution comes in the form of a definition of the sort argued in the paragraphs above, namely, that man is the creature in whom the life impulse becomes self-conscious, thus forcing up to awareness the question: Who am I? What the author seeks to tell us by means of his story is that it is this radical and pervasive question that constitutes the defining feature of the human species.

From this view, two further distinctive features of the human situation follow as corollaries. The question, who am I?, is what William James called a forced option: namely, a situation where choice is inevitable, where in short I cannot *not* choose. This is so for the reason that my whole active life embodies and constitutes my answer to the human question: indeed it *is* my answer. Hence, second, my real answer to this question is not one that I make in an academic classroom, or write in an examination, or even in a book on philosophy: rather it is, again, the answer that I live out in action. Both of these peculiarities demand further analysis. However, this can better be undertaken after a glance at the history of existentialism.

Origin and Development

Like adherents of many other philosophies, existentialists find traces of their views scattered through the history of philosophy from the ancient Greeks to the present. To cite a particularly notable example, Pascal has been acclaimed as a forerunner of existentialism. His ideas concerning the grandeur and misery of man, his wager, his assertion that the heart has reasons that the head does not know, his rejection of Descartes' rational philosophy, his critical concern with religious faith—all of these anticipate important issues of existentialism.[4]

In this connection it will be useful to introduce the distinction between *existential* and *existentialist*, which translate into English Martin Heidegger's German terms, *Existenzial* and *Existenziell*.[5] The former refers to philosophical ideas or attitudes (wherever their occurrence) that emphasize or underscore existence in contrast to essence, while the latter refers to a philosophic movement of the twentieth century that has developed its own explicit philosophic categories for coping with the issues raised by the former. *Existenzial* may thus be rendered in English as *existential*, while *Existenziell* is *existentialist*.

The sources of existentialism lie within certain existential thinkers of the nineteenth century who have been aptly termed "the nineteenth century underground."[6] Beneath the nineteenth century's Crystal Palace of scientific progress and philosophic rationality lay an underground chamber containing intimations of deep trouble. Some of these intimations of troubles to come found expression in the early writings of Karl Marx, during the years when he was a young Rhineland editor troubled by the problems of the dehumanization and depersonalization of industrial workers. They found sharply divergent forms of expression in the intense religious reflections of Kierkegaard, in the somber novels of Dostoyevsky, and the violent aphorisms of Nietzsche.

It has been pointed out that many of the men whose writings were to constitute the sources of existentialism attended the lectures of Schelling in 1841–1842 at the University of Berlin on the subject *Die Philosophie der Mythologie und der Offenbarung*. The audience included many who would gain distinction in diverse ways. There was Karl Marx's friend and collaborator, Friedrich Engels, the historian Burckhardt, the anarchist Bakunin, as well as Sören Kierkegaard.[7]

Other names may also be added to the list of sources of existentialism. In Germany Feuerbach produced his *Essence of Christianity* in 1841, and in 1843 his *Grundsätze der Philosophie der Zukunft*. In the same year as the latter, Stirner brought out *Der Einzige und Sein Eigentum*.[8] In England, which incidentally has never been as deeply influenced by existentialism as has Germany, the writings of Darwin led men to focus attention on man as an actual organism. Yet of all the sources, undoubtedly the most influential were Kierkegaard (1813–1855) and Nietzsche (1844–1900).

Kierkegaard's philosophy must be viewed as an expression of his own pathetic, and indeed tragic, life. He protested passionately against Hegel's philosophy which he scornfully termed the "System," because it viewed existence, including personal human existence, as rationally derivable from Being, characterized by Hegel as the total system of rational essences. As Kierkegaard understood—or misunderstood—Hegel, all things flow forth in perfect rationality from this fountain of all Being. This meant to Kierkegaard that his own existence as an individual human being was reducible completely and without remainder to an item or element within this absolute rational System. With all the passion of his intense nature, SK, as he called himself, denied this, asserting his own existence as a primary fact of life from which all philosophizing must begin. In place of derivation within Hegel's system, SK posited as the basis of both actual thought and actual life a leap of faith. In place of Hegel's rationalism, he sought to find "a truth which is true for me, to find the ideas for which I can live and die." Taking his stand within existence, he alternately pilloried the System, and elaborated categories for the apprehension of existence as he found it in his own experience.[9]

Turning to his own existential categories, Kierkegaard first spelled out in *Either/Or* three different possibilities of existence, or ways of living, namely the aesthetic, the ethical, and the religious, among which every man must choose. Among the important categories for the last or religious way are freedom, anxiety, and paradox. We shall consider these basic ideas in turn. Freedom meant for Kierkegaard a human condition of infinite possibility.

Since in freedom man is like God, human freedom means that each man has a hand in making himself. Man's freedom can, however, destroy as well as create. Human freedom means that man has affinity alike with Nothingness and with God. His existence is in fact suspended between Nothingness and God.

Anxiety differs from animal fear in that the latter is a specific response to a specific threat.[10] In contrast, anxiety is a kind of free-floating fear that pervades one's whole personality. Far from being a response to a specific stimulus, it sometimes even pathologically creates its own objects. Anxiety rises out of man's double nature as free and finite. If he were only and simply finite or mortal, specific fears would not be transformed into anxiety. Contrariwise, if man were simply free spirit, anxiety would have no foothold in his nature. To repeat, anxiety is a product of man's combined freedom and finitude. Tillich and Rollo May are true to the spirit of Kierkegaard in making a distinction between normal and neurotic anxiety, the latter being pathological and hence yielding to adequate therapy, but the former being an essential and indefeasible condition of human finitude.[11]

Anxiety develops fully as despair or the "sickness unto death" which robs existence of hope and meaning. Anxiety in this sense is conquered by faith. While Kierkegaard never put the matter in these terms, faith, in his distinctive sense of this multivalued word, might be defined as that by which man successfully copes with the anxiety that is his human lot. Again, SK did not speak or write in these terms; his own formulation was more traditionally Christian and theological. Yet this implication was clearly present in his writings—waiting for others to draw it out and make it explicit.

Paradox was for Kierkegaard the logical or rational contradiction that reduced the System to nullity, as contradiction must always stultify any pattern of consistent argument. But it was SK's contention that if the facts are paradoxical, one must still cling to the facts and let the System go. For SK the Supreme Fact was the incarnation of God in Christ. Indeed, this supreme fact is forever paradoxical, for it means that the infinite has become finite. So at least argued SK.

Kierkegaard was a deeply devout man who sought to formulate his Christian faith as a way of understanding and living out his human existence. Yet he was as hostile to speculative theology and to the institutional church as to the Hegelian system. During his last years he lashed out in attack upon the state church of Denmark as a betrayal of Christian faith to middle-class respectability. Kierkegaard's agonized writings remained largely unnoticed until the twentieth century, when they were translated into German and English. Many twentieth century persons, both skeptics and believers, have felt that his descriptions of existence speak to their condition.

Superficially at least, Nietzsche is a polar opposite to Kierkegaard. A German pastor's son who turned against both Christianity and Christ, and a professor of classics who turned against philosophic rationalism as he found it embodied in the Western philosophic tradition from Socrates onward, Nietzsche turned for inspiration first to Greek tragedy with its Dionysian outlook, then to his own highly distinctive formulation of what the Germans call *Lebensphilosophie*.[12] His own life was a tragic protest against the illness and the limitations that held him prisoner and finally killed him.

In caustic aphorisms he pilloried middle-class respectability, which he believed lay like a pall over Europe. Like Kierkegaard's, his philosophy was in important measure a weapon of attack. Indeed, he spoke of "how to philosophize with a hammer!" The key concept of Nietzsche's philosophy, namely "the will to power," has been widely misunderstood as the will to dominate other people. Actually "the will to live" would be closer to Nietzsche's intended meaning, defining life as the free and creative activity of those rare individuals who dare really to live. The embodiment of this will to live is *Übermensch*, translated as "Superman," or better as "Overman." Nietzsche laid hold upon the then new scientific concept of evolution and used it—some would say misused it—for the purpose of saying that ordinary human nature is something to be transcended in the next stage of evolutionary development.

His attack upon both Jesus and Socrates as embodiments of traditional Western values was radical and thoroughgoing. Jesus and his ethic represent the resentment of the weak against the strong. Socrates and his rationalism, or rather his pseudorationalism, constitute a blanket of repression thrown over the strong and the vital. Hence Nietzsche pled for a "transvaluation of values" so that life, as he saw it, might win against all the forces that repress, inhibit, and kill.

If American and English academic philosophies have never taken Nietzsche in full seriousness, this is not the case in continental Europe, where his influence has continued strong from Spain to eastern Europe throughout the present century. In Germany the Nazis by a process of careful selection and distortion sought to make him their philosopher, but there is much in Nietzsche that is clearly anti-Nazi. He is widely read and studied in contemporary Germany, and has exerted strong influence, even on many readers whose own resultant philosophies differ fundamentally from his.

What was an underground movement of malaise and protest in the nineteenth century became a full-fledged philosophic movement in the twentieth century. In other words, existential became existentialist and existentialism or existentialist philosophy. This philosophy lists among its important contributors such names as Martin Heidegger (1889–1976), Karl Jaspers (b. 1883), Jean Paul Sartre (b. 1905), Albert Camus (1913–1960), Martin Buber (1878–1965), and Paul Tillich (1886–1965).

As a philosophic movement, existentialism has close affinity with a philosophy that in many important respects seems utterly dissimilar, namely, phenomenology. The founder and leader of phenomenology, Edmund Husserl (1859–1938), spent his philosophical career seeking a new method that would provide philosophy with a stable and scientific foundation. Husserl was a German contemporary of the realist movements in British and American philosophy; and these two respective types of philosophy have in common a protest in the name of science and the "real world" against nineteenth century idealism. Husserl began as a mathematician, and his early philosophic work sought to defend mathematics against psychologism, which is the tendency to interpret mathematical and logical thinking reductively in terms of psychological states. He continued all his life a vigorous opposition to this and other forms of reductionism.

Husserl's own phenomenological method began with a description of the given or presented contents of consciousness. In its ordinary occurrence, consciousness exhibits what Brentano before Husserl had called intentionality, that is, objective reference. In other words, consciousness is always consciousness of . . . , and as a preposition, "of" always occurs with some sort of object. However, in order to study consciousness we must "bracket" off the world or reality, and then focus our attention upon the direct, immediate data or given elements of consciousness. When this is done, what are thus directly presented to consciousness, according to Husserl, are essences. Phenomenological method consists, accordingly, of the direct and presuppositionless description of these essences, construed as the directly given contents of consciousness.[13]

In his lifelong exploration of these supposed deliverances of consciousness Husserl was led to dig ever deeper into the foundations of the human consciousness or mind. What is most important for his influence on existentialism and on other philosophies as well, was his view that consciousness is no passive white tablet on which experience writes its record, but rather is active in its encounter with the world. Therefore the real problem is not, as Descartes and Hume had wrongly supposed, how the mind can ever know the external world. The fact is that in intentionality the mind is forever going out to meet the world; and hence the real problem is how to bracket out the world long enough systematically to study the mind's relation to it.

Heidegger's *Sein und Zeit*, translated into English as *Being and Time*, was first published in Husserl's *Jahrbuch für Philosophie und*

Phänomologische Forschung.[14] Heidegger was Husserl's successor in philosophy at the University of Freiburg and, at first, he viewed his work as an application of phenomenology to the study of human existence. *Being and Time* may in this sense be characterised as an attempt at phenomenological study of human existence in history. However, it carried the additional and all-important implication of proceeding metaphysically through man to being. This was a radically new suggestion, for whereas traditional Western philosophy had approached metaphysics or ontology through cosmology, Heidegger sought to approach it through anthropology and history. So it was that his philosophy forked away from Husserl and phenomenology, as well as away from traditional Western metaphysics, and plotted its own new path to metaphysics or, as Heidegger preferred to say, to ontology.

Sartre also studied Husserl as well as Heidegger; and his work *Being and Nothingness* carried the subtitle *An Essay in Phenomenological Ontology.*[15] Similarly, Merleau-Ponty's *Phenomenology of Perception* shows the influence of both Husserl and Heidegger, but like Sartre's work, it moves away from both.[16] In a word, while phenomenology has continued to aspire to detached and scientific study of the nature of mind and self, existentialism has immersed itself in the issues and agonies of twentieth century culture and history. To some of these issues which recur in existentialist writing we must now turn our attention.

Existentialist Themes

A systematic presentation of existentialism would be a contradiction in terms. Kierkegaard and Nietzsche were antisystematists. Kierkegaard wrote contemptuously of the academic person who became a professor of somebody else's suffering. Yet the necessities of exposition compel us to compliance with at least the rules of grammar and coherence, which constitute the minimal elements of a system, if we are even to describe existentialism. The alternative is silence—or an incoherent cry. As a compromise between system and antisystem, which may yield us some understanding of existentialism, we shall state and briefly analyze six themes as they recur in the literature of twentieth century existentialism. While accents and emphases differ from writer to writer, and sometimes even clash, nonetheless taken together they will at least give us a beachhead of understanding. Let it be frankly conceded in advance that our choice of themes as well as the dramatis personae of existentialism, if not arbitrary, is at least a matter of choice in a field where others might well choose differently.

(1) The distinction between essence and existence, which may be termed

the defining feature of this philosophy, is by no means a discovery of existentialism. Etymologically *ex-istere* is a common Latin verb meaning to "stand out" or "step forth."[17] Accordingly, existence, or the existent, is that which stands out or steps forth from other aspects of being. The medieval scholastic philosophers distinguished between the *quod est* or the "that" of an entity, and the *quid est*, or the "what" of it. They also taught that while essence and existence, thus defined, are united in God, whose existence constitutes his essence and vice versa, they are sundered here below in all finite things. To this extent, Thomas Aquinas and his fellow scholastics were existentialists, as some recent writers have argued. However, they are so to this extent only and in this sense only.

More modern thinkers have formulated and elaborated this distinction in their own terms. In some philosophic systems it coincides with the distinction between possibility (essence) and actuality (existence). Modern empiricist philosophies have sought contact with existence at the point of direct sense experience. As we have previously noted, Hegel's system of idealism was notable for the bold way in which Hegel sought to derive existence from Pure Being, which he asserted to contain both essence and existence. In this respect existentialism resembles British and American realism in its protest against Hegelian idealism or essentialism. Seen against the background of the history of Western philosophy, what the existentialists have done is to hit upon a traditional distinction, developing and accenting it for their purposes.

(2) While the term, *existence*, applies to an aspect of all that is, or to all that has being, namely to that specific aspect which is distinguished from its essence, it is to that region of existence that each of us knows most immediately and best, namely his own self, that existentialism primarily directs our attention. Philosophically, this is a significant move, as we have noted, for traditionally Western philosophy has approached metaphysics through cosmology (which deals with the nature of the *kosmos*, or world). Existentialists propose to approach metaphysics through anthropology (which deals with the systematic study of *anthropos*, or man). This new approach is based upon the assumption that Being or Reality may be found in the human heart as well as in the structure of the world. Again, the premise of existentialism is that Being or Reality may be sought or seen in the human foreground of things as well or better than in the cosmic background.

What do existentialists find in their explorations of the human self and mind? While there are innumerable differences of emphasis, there is general agreement in a cluster of traits centering in man's freedom—that dreadful and unavoidable freedom which defines the human situation. Yet, while existentialism proclaims and urges freedom, it is often less than clear as to precisely what human freedom is and does.

Here we can attempt no more than a rough outline sketch of a subject worthy of vastly more detailed treatment. Let us begin with the suggestion that freedom may be approached as an aspect of developing human consciousness or awareness. Thus, a newborn human infant, while possessing awareness of objects, is in no real or actual sense free. His developing awareness of his own body and its various members is perhaps his first move in the direction of freedom. Gradually growing awareness of the difference between his own organism and other objects and organisms in his environment points in the same direction. A decisive step, or series of steps, is taken in the emergence of language, which enables him to fix objects and persons. In the emergence of language, it is interesting to observe that "I" is one of the last words to emerge in a growing child's vocabulary, following after "my," "us," "we," and "it."

In and through many of these developments, what begins to emerge is self-awareness, whose primary source lies in the capacity of language to make one's own being an object of awareness. It might perhaps be said that actual selfhood first emerges when the human organism acquires, principally though not exclusively by means of language, this capacity to be an object to and for itself. However, self-awareness means also self-transcendence, literally the power or capacity of the human self in imagination to stand free of itself, and indeed free of all fixed or given contexts, and to look at them. Self-awareness thus generates self-transcendence. Together they constitute the self as a self; and together they constitute the taproot of human freedom.

The concept of self-transcendence is often deprecated, especially by ordinary language philosophers as a murky Teutonic concept with no clear meaning. Yet if any reader wishes to perform a simple experiment to establish initial clarification, let him proceed as follows. Without any overt movement or activity let him in imagination stand free of himself and look at himself. Then let him stand free of the standpoint which he has just occupied and look at it. It will soon become apparent that such mental acts can continue indefinitely. This is functionally what the capacity for self-transcendence, or going beyond oneself, means.

Gilbert Ryle's *Concept of Mind* contains a notable analysis of this distinctive human capacity in terms of what he calls "the systematic elusiveness of 'I'."[18] Ryle discusses human acts, and successive orders or levels of acts. That is, whenever the object of one action is another of one's acts, the latter is constituted as a new "higher" order or level of action. It does not take much self-observation to see that this operation can go on indefinitely and that while "me" can be caught in such a net for orders or levels, "I" forever eludes such capture. Whether he intended this result or not, Ryle has provided in this analysis a good working conception of self-transcendence.

It is the distinctive capacity of the human self for self-awareness and self-transcendence that generates its capacity for freedom. Yet this capacity is itself never simply a fixed or given fact, but is rather a kind of indeterminate possibility, lifelong in its development and always partial and ambiguous in its realization. It is furthermore not located in a part or region of the self or mind such as the will (as faculty psychology claimed), but is rather a possibility of the whole human self as such. Indeed, we must also add that self and mind are not two things, but two functions of the same human being. The mind is simply and plainly the cognitive functioning of the self; the self, conversely, is the mind-in-action. In either case it is man who thinks or acts.

Human freedom so construed is never total or absolute, but always occurs and operates within fixed limits. For selfhood is first of all the capacity of a given, altogether particular human organism. This fact establishes immediately certain fixed limits in the needs of the organism for air, nourishment, excretion, and the like. The organism is a physical body, observing all the natural laws of such bodies. If I brake my car, I lurch forward according to the physical law of inertia; if I jump out a second story window, I am accelerated toward the ground according to the same law of acceleration as any inorganic body. My body is made of the same chemical elements as sticks, stones, and stars. I am in short not only free but finite and mortal—one creature among others in the world of animate and inanimate nature.

While my freedom always operates within limits, without which indeed freedom would not be a meaningful concept, it is not always possible to establish clear and sharp boundary lines for freedom's operation and its limits. For example, while some bodily or somatogenic diseases are clearly fatal, the psychogenic factors in many diseases are today being continually reappraised, thus pointing to a complex combination of psychic and physical causes of both illness and health. These psychic factors, be it noted, often involve the action of man's free self and mind. Again, while I cannot by taking thought add a cubit to my stature, I do nevertheless have the free option within broad limits of staying physically fit or of doing the opposite.

While the source of freedom is the human mind's capacity for self-awareness and self-transcendence, in any given situation the actual occurrence of freedom moves from inner attitudes or motives to overt action. In other words, I intend x, and then do x. Thus, free action becomes something that I do; and if as we asserted in the preceding chapter that part of contemporary analytic philosophy called action-theory is at all correct, statements of the form, "I do X" must be regarded as logically primitive assertions; they are logically primary or primitive in the sense of not being derivable from other statements about physical displacement or organic movement. To see the meaning or significance of one's actions, a person must first simply turn upon himself as he *does* something and observe what in fact takes place or goes on. Human actions are *done*, whereas physical events simply occur.

Furthermore, as we observed from action-theory in the preceding chapter, actions are freely done. To think otherwise, as for example in the hypothesis of mechanistic determinism, is to involve oneself in a tangle of self- contradiction. Looking at free human action, we can see alike its several aspects and the distinctive categories that are necessary to understand it. Its defining categories are (1) intention, or conscious purposiveness, (2) decision or choice and, (3) overt doing, either physical or mental. On this much, at least, existentialism and action theory might agree.

Freedom of action, moreover, has three aspects or facets, most readily characterized as freedom (1) *from*, (2) *of*, (3) *to* or *for*. It is freedom *from* external hindrances ranging from chains and prisons to psychological inhibitions or compulsions. In general, whenever any factor outside my volition determines my action, I am unfree, or in a state of bondage. But freedom is also *of* the self, and unless there be a self, existent and living within broad limits of normality, there can be no freedom. Abnormal behavior reduces the self to a "case," subject to medical care in the hope of restoring or regaining selfhood.

Freedom is also *to* or *for* aims or goals, namely to or for the goods or values toward which action is directed. Freedom that has been achieved or maintained at the first two levels, may still again be won or lost at this third level. For it is the case that some apparent values or goods are inherently self-destructive or self-contradictory in character; hence, action directed at them becomes involved in destructive contradictions. So it is that at the third level of freedom, *to* or *for*, man makes his bid for freedom in terms of the values or goods he serves. Some bids have a measure of success; others fail.

Our characterization of freedom as *from*, *of*, and *to* or *for* may be summarized in the definition of freedom as self-determination. This means that (always within finite limits) man makes or determines himself; he does so in terms of the values to which he is committed, and which he strives to realize. Indeed, even the conscious acknowledgment of finite limits can be an essential step toward freedom. The recognition of necessity, if not the whole of freedom, as Spinoza appears to have thought, is at least a necessary first step. Other essential steps are contained in the various features of freedom *from* and *of*, as discussed in previous paragraphs. They all constitute significant aspects of the total configuration that is self-determination, or more precisely, the human possibility of self determination. Taken as a whole, freedom of self-transcendence and self-determination, as we have sketched it here, may be understood as the freedom that stands at the center of the philosophy of existentialism.

Closely related to freedom is anxiety, which, as we learned from Kierkegaard, is a free-floating and pervasive fear characterizing man as such. Anxiety derives from the fact that man is free to envisage his finitude, his littleness, his mortality, in the midst of infinite or endless time and space. Seeing himself thus, he is anxious. As we saw in the previous section of this chapter, anxiety is of two kinds; normal anxiety, which is man's mortal portion, and on the other hand, pathological anxiety, namely, that which disorients man from the real world. While therapy can eliminate the latter, to abolish the former would in effect dehumanize man. Rather, with respect to normal anxiety, what is required is resources to enable each of us to cope with this aspect of the human situation.

Normal anxiety furthermore can issue in either creative or destructive patterns of action. Often it is the spur to creativity; but it can and sometimes does issue in egotism, arrogance, and violence, or in a defensive retreat from reality. Observation of one's self and of other human selves offers confirmation of all of these kinds of consequences.

(3) This last comment leads us on from freedom and anxiety to alienation or self-estrangement and evil, which are frequent and recurring existentialist themes. Man's freedom makes it at least an open possibility for him to miss the mark, to go astray from the destiny of becoming human. Paul Ricoeur has used the striking geological metaphor of "fault" for man, that is a "faulted" creature.[19] In these terms, freedom defines the fault-line in the human situation.

Since, in man, essence and existence are torn apart, it is possible for man to be involved in dehumanization or depersonalization, however these latter terms may be defined. From Hegel and Marx onward, the terms, *alienation* and *estrangement*, have been used for the many ways in which man's existence is separated and sundered from his human essence. For Marx and his followers this alienation and evil constitute a sociohistorical fact of worldwide and agelong significance.

In contrast to Marx, Kierkegaard spoke rather of the individual soul whose anxiety or "sickness unto death" leads inevitably to despair, unless a man has faith. With subtle perceptiveness he traced the ways in which the individual man apart from faith, seeks to avoid, evade, and masquerade the consequences of despair. For Kierkegaard the only cure for this mortal disease was faith, which again he depicted as an indefeasibly individual activity.

Among twentieth century existentialists Sartre and Camus are notable for their probing explorations of the nature of human evil. Sartre's concept of nausea stands for man's basic response to the godless, meaningless universe in which his life is cast.[20] In a word, human existence in a meaningless world is utterly disgusting, nauseating! Camus' novels, *The Stranger*, *The Plague*, and *The Fall*, may be characterized as a physician's successive attempts at diagnosing what Nietzsche termed "the disease which is man."

This existentialist concern with the nature of evil has frequently led to the charge of morbidity, pessimism, and decadence. Relatively few of the characters in an existentialist novel or play are normal or happy human beings. Why this preoccupation with evil? Many have asked whether this is not itself a phenomenon of putrescence? Does existentialism really present a fair or balanced picture of human reality?

Some critics have asserted that existentialists are compulsively preoccupied with evil. But to this charge the response might well be made that doctors have an analogous concern with illness. As to the charges of unrealism, morbidity, or pessimism, a similar reply may be offered. In an age of violence unparalleled in human history, of Buchenwald and Hiroshima, and the prospect of nuclear holocaust on a world scale, it is the part of honest realism to study the nature and causes of our human predicament. It may be truly asserted that twentieth century history has taken the category of the absurd out of the tomes of existentialist philosophy and written it into the history of our age. Verification of this assertion requires nothing more esoteric than reading the headlines of the daily newspaper. By contrast, those who simply turn away from these grim facts to a kind of chirpy, sentimental optimism are the truly unrealistic ones. The analogy between existentialist interpretations of evil with the orthodox Christian doctrine of sin has not escaped the attention of realists among the theologians from Kierkegaard to the Niebuhr brothers.

Another existentialist concept, closely related to alienation, and one which evoked much critical discussion, is that of Nothingness. It may be said that at the bottom of the pit of alienation and evil lies Nothingness. For Heidegger it is *Nichts* and for Sartre *Neant*, and analogous concepts recur through most of the existentialist writers.[21] Sometimes this concept has been the object of hostile philosophic attack, purporting to demonstrate the meaningless babble of existentialist thought. While the idea of Nothingness is by no means free of such semantic problems, the key to understanding seems to lie in the personal character of existentialist thinking. For *me* its primary reference is to *my* nothingness or *my* nonbeing, that is, my death. In this initial and preliminary sense at least, the idea becomes comprehensible and straightforward. But just as other concepts of existentialist thought can be generalized from their personal base, so this one undergoes a similar generalization. Conversely, the idea and the symbol, Nothingness, may be understood by tracing it back to its personal source and base, namely one's own nonbeing or death.

Along with existentialist diagnoses of the human disease, existentialist therapeutic suggestions must also be at least mentioned. True, some existentialist writers say in fact that there is no therapy; the human disease is fatal and has no cure. In fact, from the Greek tragedians to the present there has been a continuing tradition of persons who have held such a tragic view of the human situation. While others may not agree with this view, few would question its realism as well as its genuine human dignity. Such a tragic outlook seems to be the stance of men like Albert Camus.

One frequent existentialist proposal for therapy, or at least amelioration, is variously called authentic existence, good faith, or simply faith. The first term is from Heidegger's *Being and Time* in which the inauthentic existence of *Das Man*, the anonymous and faceless "one," is contrasted with life in its full human dimension of freedom and responsibility.[22] Authentic existence may be said to begin when a man is unwilling to continue as *Das Man*, and resolves, as it were, to take charge of himself and his destiny. Authentic existence means living in this full and distinctively human dimension of freedom and responsibility. Sartre's conceptions of bad faith and good faith are similar.[23] The former consists of an inner attitude of holding back from freedom and inner integrity, and then in turn, totally immersing oneself in or escaping into a social role. Such a course is a cowardly flight from the burden of free selfhood. Contrariwise, good faith means the inner integrity necessary to be and to live as a free self. Bad faith is dissimulation and hypocrisy; good faith is by contrast "truth in the inward parts."

Theistic existentialists have availed themselves of these categories for their definitions of faith. For Kierkegaard an attitude of genuine faith in God has many of the characteristics of Heidegger's authentic existence. It consists of a turning of the whole self in full freedom and integrity to God as the source of man's being. For Paul Tillich "the courage to be," that is, the courage to achieve and sustain a fully human life constitutes authentic existence.[24] As we shall soon see, Buber adds to this inner integrity and freedom a response of ethical love to one's fellow man. All of these as well as other similar proposals are to be regarded as proposals for healing or reconciliation of man's alienation or self-estrangement.

(4) From these considerations it will come as no great surprise that existentialists have been much concerned with ethics and human values generally. For Kierkegaard the ethical problem consisted of doing works of love which

are the spontaneous outcome of genuine faith. In sharpest contrast, Nietzsche pilloried Christian ethics as slave morality, and proclaimed a radical transvaluation of values so that man may move forward in Promethean freedom to *Übermensch*. The creative freedom of the superior individual was Nietzsche's primary value.

Sartre's form of existentialism has raised in radical fashion many of these traditional philosophic questions of ethics, and of values in general. As we have seen, freedom is for Sartre a radically individual possession; and in terms of his existentialist categories, Sartre has found interpersonal relations a virtually insoluble problem. He writes eloquently of the experience of being watched by another person, of the other's gaze as invading and violating *my* free selfhood. The other's freedom is thus my slavery. In depicting the love relationship between the sexes he seems to find only three possibilities, namely sadism, masochism, or indifference. The possibility of freely affirming the equally free life of another person seems not to occur to Sartre. Rather, as is said in *No Exit*, "Hell is other people."[25]

Sartre does derive a kind of moral norm from the individual's affirmation of his own freedom. He seems to assert that when I stand for my freedom I do so for all humankind. Yet, how this takes place, and the nature of this identification of my self and others goes unilluminated. Sartre also asserts that as I act, I literally create my own values. Hence, any thought of absolute value, or a norm above the individual, is both unfactual and undesirable. Yet, according to Sartre, man can be a kind of artist in the field of value creation. This is true both for moral, that is interpersonal, values and for other kinds as well.

Other existentialists have worked more fruitfully than Sartre at the problems of ethics. Jaspers, for example, speaks of "boundless communication" between human selves or, as others would put it, of communion.[26] This entails a genuine community of selves as both possible and desirable. From an independent perspective, similar sentiments are to be found throughout the pages of Gabriel Marcel.[27] For him too the community of persons is a prospect to be sought and cherished. However, it is Martin Buber whose writings provide most detailed depiction of what Buber himself has called I-Thou or person-person relations; and to Buber goes the credit for calling our attention eloquently and forcibly to this possibility of existence.[28] The words, "I-Thou," Buber took from Feuerbach, but the substance or content of this human relation he derived from his Hasidic Jewish heritage and eventually from the Bible. While his writings show remarkable lucidity of expression, Buber's thought is a complex synthesis of many influences, including Kierkegaard, Nietzsche, Hasidic mysticism, and the Bible.

According to Buber, human individuals achieve personhood not in isolation but in personal relation to other persons. Thus, the actual human situation is always persons-in-community. The full realization of personal relations is Buber's paraphrase for what the Bible calls *love*. Love in this ethical sense is not amiable sentimentality or erotic attraction, but precisely the intention to affirm personality equally in oneself and in others. For Buber the fulfillment of human selfhood occurs thus in the context of the correlative Biblical virtues of freedom and love. Hence, his thought has a moral and social quality that is lacking in other existentialists. Buber has held up the ideal of persons-in-community as the goal of human life. The good life, is as he put it, "the life of dialogue."[29]

Buber developed the religious as well as the moral implications of the I-Thou relation. Projected "horizontally," this relation defines human community and morality, but projected "vertically" as a way of relating man to ultimate reality, it provides a definition of the God-man relation. For Buber, this relation to God is direct and immediate. As he puts it, God, thus envisaged, can only be directly addressed, not talked about or rationally proven. Man can speak *to* God but not *about* him.[30] So conceived, the I-Thou relation constitutes a mysticism of communion deriving from Hasidism and the Bible. Much of Buber's later writing consisted of tracing the sources of this idea in the Bible and in Jewish history.

(5) Still another existentialist theme centers in the concepts of time and history. All the great existential thinkers of the nineteenth century were literally shocked into thinking and writing by what they believed to be the crisis of modern Western culture. This concern has continued in twentieth century existentialism, in which it has also given rise to reflection on the nature of history as such. This double concern with history is mirrored in the ambiguity of the word, *history*. For that term means both the human past, and the records and study of the human past; we speak both of studying history and of living or making history. Existentialist philosophy has been interested in both, yet lived history is clearly the primary meaning.

It is precisely the combination of freedom and finitude in the human situation that may be said to generate history as a basic form of human experience. Hence, to be human means to have a history, and vice versa. All of this seems to cohere with man's combination of finitude and freedom which was considered earlier in this chapter. So conceived, history might be characterized as the destiny of human selves writ large; conversely, a human self is a piece of history or historic destiny.

On this basis we can see why Heidegger, at the end of *Being and Time*, came to speak of history as the form of authentic existence.[31] As such, history is more than simply enduring or undergoing the experience of temporal sequence or the passage of time, though of course it does involve this. Rather, a man looks back to the past, and then moves with resolution into the open future. By a combination of resolution and understanding, man lays hold upon his past as a tradition and moves into the future. This is a movement aimed at realizing possibilities.

Among existentialist philosophers Jaspers has given specific attention to the academic study of history and to the categories necessary to carry it on, and incidentally to relate it to the kind of history mankind makes. Similarly, Paul Tillich and Reinhold Niebuhr have both addressed themselves to this problem, and have done so on the border territory between philosophy and theology. Here let it simply be said that the concepts of history and historical destiny are closely related to faith as well as to freedom. In a word, in his freedom, man acts by faith to respond to historic destiny. It is for this reason that the Biblically based faiths are sometimes called historical, in contrast to the cosmic and a-cosmic faiths of east Asia and south Asia. These are matters which we shall pursue in more detail in chapter 11.

Existential Thinking

An often overlooked feature of existentialism is its approach to, and interpretation of, cognitive activity or thinking. In his attack upon Hegelian rationalism, Kierkegaard made what seem to many readers extreme, and often downright irrational, comments in characterizing what he termed existential thinking.[32] In such existential thought, he asserted that passion is more important than consistency or logic, that the process of thinking is more important than its results, that there is no certainty but only continual striving, and indeed that continuing search is better than arrival or objective certainty. In a notable essay entitled "Existential Philosophy," Paul Tillich also addressed himself to "the existential thinker," distinguishing sharply between discursive and existential thinking.[33] Indeed, virtually all the existentialists have drawn a distinction in one set of terms or another between these two kinds of thinking. However, none so far as I know has yet undertaken the detailed or systematic characterization of existential thinking.

In the analytic tradition, Ryle has distinguished between "engaged" and "unengaged" thinking. Likewise, Austin's performative and constative utterance (discussed in the preceding chapter) might well be extended to performative and constative thinking. In the present study we have employed the metaphor of thinking in the grandstand and on the playing field, or from the respective viewpoints of the spectator or of the participant. In terms of modern Western philosophy, Kant distinguished between theoretical and practical reason, asserting the primacy of the latter.[34] At this point we can do no more than underscore this distinction, in whatever terms it may be made, and add that this is a subject urgently in need of vastly more detailed study than may be undertaken here.

Obviously, each of these ways of thinking has both its distinctive possibilities and its limits; and both must be considered in any full or adequate account of the mind's life. However, it is also fair to point out that the archtypal model for thinking in modern Western philosophy (perhaps indeed for the whole history of Western philosophy) has been the unengaged thinker sitting apart in his study, alone with his thoughts, and hopefully free of all commitments. That this is an egregious and misleading falsehood becomes clear as soon as we realize that most of human thinking takes place in the context of full participation in action, whether the action be that of a governmental official making foreign policy, a doctor making a diagnosis, or a traveler deciding which turn of the road he will take. Most people do most of their significant thinking on the playing field and not in the grandstand. It is, therefore, false and misleading to assume a grandstand model for what thought is like.

The thinking of the participants on the playing field shows fundamental differences from that of the spectators. For the thinking of the participants grows out of previous decisions and forms the context for subsequent decisions; and it is done in the context of man's active life. By contrast, the observer or spectator can continue to spin out his hypotheses indefinitely without involvement in action.

These observations lead to an important ontological question, namely: Is man most fundamentally a participant or an observer? Is man *really* (in whatever definition the reader may wish to give this word) on the playing field or is he in the grandstand? Is the human self in reality an action system or is it a form of contemplation or theory? It is not possible here to undertake an exposition, let alone an adequate answer, to this important question. Yet we can allude to the long tradition of voluntarism, extending back from Kant to Augustine and the Bible, which has defined both the human self and mind in voluntarist terms, namely, in terms of will and action. Of this continuing tradition the existentialists may be said to form the most recent chapter.

Existentialism's Impact

Some current writers speak of existentialism in the past tense, as something over and done with, noting for example that Sartre has moved from existentialism to Marxism. It is a fact that all the great existentialists are now either dead or very old men. Is existentialism still living or is it dead?

From our present perspective, it is possible to say that the existential thinkers of the "nineteenth century underground," as well as the existentialists of the twentieth century, called attention, often forcibly and even stridently, to aspects of the human situation that other men tended to ignore. As we have seen, among these neglected aspects are man's freedom, his alienation and evil, his paradoxical grandeur and misery.

What seems to be happening now as the great existentialists are passing or have passed from the scene is that many of these ideas about which they have written so intensely and often so persuasively are being incorporated into other men's thought. Some of these ideas, ironically enough, are even finding expression in academic philosophy, as witnessed by the present lively and widespread interest in the freedom of the will.[35]

One illustration which will concern us later in this study is the influence of existentialism on theology. A distinction has frequently been made between the religious and nonreligious existentialists. Actually this is less significant than the intense, deep, and critical interest of all the existentialists (whatever their own attitudes or conclusions) in man's religious experience. We shall return to this subject in chapter 11.

Psychotherapy and clinical psychology constitute another field that shows massive influence from existentialism. Indeed there is a movement, complete with organization and a journal, called "Existential Psychology."[36] Both in this group and outside it, students of psychology have learned much from existentialist probings of problems such as freedom, guilt, despair, suicide, and reconciliation. Not only psychologists, but social scientists of other disciplines have been influenced by Buber's conception of persons-in-community.

Beyond the academic disciplines, existentialist categories continue to provide many contemporary persons with a distinctive viewpoint from which to approach their world. To cite a single example, since the late 1960s and early 1970s, the youth of many nations have been deeply involved in bizarre and often violent forms of behavior ranging from the drugs, sex, and music of the hippies, through new and strange forms of revolution, onward to equally novel forms of religious experience. In this strange new context the existentialist categories of man's freedom and finitude, his quest for authentic existence, as well as his alienation and dehumanization, provide highly useful conceptual equipment for at least beginning the attempt to understand the age in which we live.

SUGGESTIONS FOR FURTHER READING

As many of these works are classics that have appeared in numerous editions, only the most accessible publication is indicated.

Barrett, W. *Irrational Man*. Garden City: Doubleday, 1958.

Buber, M. *Between Man and Man*. New York: Macmillan, 1948.

———. *I and Thou*. New York: Scribners, 1958.

Camus, A. *The Myth of Sisyphus*. New York: Knopf, 1955.

———. *The Rebel*. New York: Knopf, 1961.

Frank, E. *Philosophical Understanding and Religious Truth*. New York: Oxford University Press, 1945.

Fromm, E. *Escape From Freedom*. New York: Farrar & Rinehart, 1941.

———. *Man For Himself*. New York: Farrar & Rinehart, 1947.

Grene, M. *Dreadful Freedom*. Chicago: University of Chicago Press, 1948.

———. *Introduction to Existentialism*. Chicago: University of Chicago Press, 1959.

Heidegger, M. *Being and Time*. New York: Harper, 1952.

———. *An Introduction to Metaphysics*. New Haven: Yale University Press, 1959.

———. *What Is Called Thinking*. New York: Harper, 1968.

Husserl, E. *Ideas*. London: Allen & Unwin, 1931.

———. *Cartesian Meditations*. The Hague: Nijhoff, 1960.

Jaspers, K. *The Perennial Scope of Philosophy*. New York: Philosophical Library, 1948.

———. *Reason and Existenz*. New York: Noonday Press, 1955.

Kierkegaard, S. *A Kierkegaard Anthology*. Princeton: Princeton University Press, 1946.

Marcel, G. *The Mystery of Being*. Chicago: Regnery, 1966.

May, R. *The Meaning of Anxiety*. New York: Ronald Press, 1950.

———. *Existential Psychology*. New York: Random House, 1961.

Merleau-Ponty, M. *Phenomenology of Perception*. New York: Humanities Press, 1962.

Niebuhr, H. R. *The Meaning of Revelation*. New York: Macmillan, 1941.

Niebuhr, R. *The Nature and Destiny of Man*. New York: Scribners, 1941.

Nietzsche, F. *Basic Writings of Nietzsche*. New York: Modern Library, 1968.

Ricoeur, P. *Fallible Man*. Chicago: Regnery, 1965.

Roberts, D. *Existentialism and Religious Belief*. New York: Oxford University Press, 1957.

Sartre, J. P. *Existentialism*. New York: Philosophical Library, 1957.

———. *Being and Nothingness*. New York: Philosophical Library, 1957.

Spiegelberg, H. *The Phenomenological Movement*. The Hague: Nijhoff, 1960.

Tillich, P. *The Courage To Be*. New Haven: Yale University Press, 1954.

———. *Theology of Culture*. New York: Oxford University Press, 1959.

VI
Freud As
Philosopher

SIGMUND FREUD lived and died a physician and a scientist, and therefore doubtless turns uneasily in his grave at the thought of having his teachings construed as philosophy. Indeed, as I have worked on this chapter, an outlandish image has recurrently come to mind, namely that of meeting the great man at a meeting of the American Philosophical Association and asking, "But Dr. Freud, what is a nice man like you doing in a place like this?"

Nevertheless, this connection between Freud and philosophy persists, and in a variety of ways. While his own disclaimer of philosophy was clear enough, his teachings continue, notwithstanding, to function as a kind of philosophic vision for many people, or as a kind of functioning wisdom about the whole of life. These teachings have moved out in many directions in Western society, influencing the thought of social scientists, artists, journalists, and the common man, thus affording illustration once again that if any man deals comprehensively with the issues of the human mind, his work becomes philosophical in quality even in spite of himself. For professional philosophers, Freud's thought sets problems and challenges, and provides leads for thought in a wide variety of ways, as we shall soon see.

The Man and His Teachings

Sigmund Freud (1856–1939) moved to Vienna with his family at the age of four, and lived there until the year before his death, when he fled the Nazi invasion, finding asylum in England. He was in succession, student, graduate research assistant, doctor of medicine, university lecturer, professor extraordinarius, founder and leader of psychoanalysis. But from first to last he was physician and scientist—as a physician seeking effective means to heal the sick and, as a scientist, one of the great explorers and topographers of what has felicitously been called inner space.

In order to consider some of the philosophic issues and implications of Freud's teachings, we must first attempt briefly to summarize those teachings—despite the stark impossibility of giving an adequate account of Freud's thought in any few paragraphs. We shall list and sketch briefly five salient features.[1]

(1) Freud's method has both a logical and chronological priority in any summary of his teachings. His new clinical method for the exploration of the mind took shape slowly over several years. As a young neurologist, Freud cast about, seeking ways of gaining access to the problems of his patients. Following the lead of his colleague Breuer, he tried hypnosis as a way of penetrating the hidden depths of the mind. But he gradually dropped this in favor of what he called free association, namely the practice of asking the patient to say whatever came to mind, at first with Freud touching the prone patient's forehead. This method was gradually refined and sharpened, as for example, when he learned, at first to his dismay, that many of his patients' recollections were not to be relied upon. He supplemented free association, as the core of the psychoanalytic interview, with the study of dreams, the analysis of jokes, slips of the tongue, bodily gestures, and the like.

One matter of considerable significance was Freud's discovery of the phenomenon of transference.[2] At some point in the process of psychoanalysis the patient develops a strong and special interest in the analyst. At first this is strongly affirmative, but this stage may be followed by an equal and opposite negative interest. Freud was led to interpret this whole phenomenon as rooted in suppressed experiences of early childhood, which the patient now projected upon the analyst; and he regarded transference as an essential step on the road to healing.

Gradually Freud extended the scope of his inquiry. One such extension was from neurotic to normal personality, for he came to see that many of the problems which beset the former have a wide incidence among the latter. Another extension was from individual personality to the problems of culture or civilization. What emerged from all this is a Freudian vision, philosophic in character, of man and his place in the world.

During the crucial decade of 1895 to 1905 Freud's clinical method was provided with a structure of theory, consisting basically of three main ideas: namely, the unconscious mind, the splitting of the ego into levels or strata, and the pervasive character of sexuality. We shall consider these three crucial categories in turn, keeping in mind that together they constitute the heart of Freud's psychoanalytic theory.

(2) Freud was by no means the discoverer of the unconscious mind, or more precisely, the unconscious regions of the mind. References in Western literature date from Plato's *Republic*; and Indian and Chinese sages have been aware for many centuries of this region of the mind's life. Yet Freud may perhaps have been the first scientific explorer of this area of human experience. His method provided him with new access to these hidden regions. From the beginning he regarded the unconscious mind as characterized by desire or drives, or to use the traditional philosophic term, will, and also as having a dynamic power of its own. In the background of Freud's concepts lay such philosophic ideas as Schopenhauer's "world as will." The unconscious character of will means simply that here are aspects of experience of which the person is unaware, to which apparently he is denied conscious access.[3]

These characteristics of the unconscious in turn led Freud simultaneously to the concepts of repression and resistance. In many instances the unconscious contains images and ideas, or memories that have been ruled unacceptable, or antisocial, or dangerous, by and to the self. They are not for this reason exterminated, but rather are pushed down into a cellar or dungeon where they live a hidden subterranean existence. The door to this underground chamber is guarded by a censor who bars their return to everyday consciousness.

Often these subterranean dwellers exhibit the phenomenon of displacement. An image or idea moves into another region of the unconscious, forming new associations and then pushing up into consciousness in some new form or phenomenon which, accordingly, functions as a symptom or symbol. In this case the work of the analyst and his patient is to trace the symbol back to its original source, so that hopefully the patient may come to see it for what it is, and thus be able to begin coping with it.

The issues are similar in the case of dreams. Freud distinguished their manifest from their latent content; the first being what the dream seems to be about, and the second what it really means or signifies in the dreamer's experience. The task of analysis is then to make one's way slowly, painfully, and in the light of the individual's history, from the manifest to the latent content, in order to see what the dream is saying or trying to say. The case is similar with jokes, slips of the tongue (Freudian slips, as we have learned to call them), movements of the body, or even the clothes a person wears. Any or all of these phenomena may in fact be or become symbols, or symptoms, for the hidden, unconscious life of the self, if only we have eyes to see and ears to hear what is really being said.

Closely allied to repression is resistance. Not only are these elements of experience banished from consciousness, they actively resist apprehension and return. Freud early observed that his patients did not willingly or openly speak about the subconscious. Concerning these aspects of experience, he declared "they wear a heavy overcoat woven of a tissue of lies." It is the work of the analyst to remove this coat so that the patient may see for himself what are the real factors involved.

(3) Freud's discoveries concerning the unconscious led him to posit a splitting or fracturing of the self into layers. In his later writings he labeled three main strata as id, ego, and superego. The deepest level of experience, the id (in German *Es* meaning "it," as also the Latin *id*) has often been compared to a seething cauldron of primal drives or desires, each imperiously seeking its own fulfillment in pleasure. The id, in short, is dominated by the pleasure principle.[4] As has been suggested, it operates "as a transcendental unity of afference" for the whole of man's experience.

Opposed to the id in a state of declared or undeclared war is the superego, or the needs and demands of society, internalized in the self. Here lies the source of morality or of the categorical imperative which, in these terms, may be characterized simply as an imperative statement of society's requirements and demands. These demands are made to, or rather over against, the id whose whole direction and nature remain antisocial.

Caught between the opposing forces of id and superego is the ego, which may be described as the top layer of the id. Since it is conscious, the ego is ruled by the reality principle, in contrast to the pleasure principle, and its ideal role is to mediate between the opposing forces of id and superego. Freud's maxim, "Where id was there let ego be," expressed his hope that the forces of rationality and selfhood might win out, both in the individual and in the world. Yet, this was for Freud more a hope than an expectation. The forces of the id are too great and too powerful to be constrained easily or readily by the ego. Hence, it is to be expected that the agelong war of man's instinctual urges against civilization will continue, perhaps to the destruction of both.

(4) Simultaneously with his discovery of the unconscious mind and the splitting of the self, Freud came upon the pervasive character of human sexuality. His experience led him to believe that the basic energy of the human self or will is sexual or libidinal in nature. Conversely, sex is not simply one drive among others of adult or postpubertal life, but pervades the whole of experience and for the whole lifetime. Especially, Freud added, to the mingled scorn and consternation of his critics, it is an observable phenomenon in infancy and early childhood.[5]

The hypothesis of infantile sexuality yielded a no less important part of

Freud's theoretical structure than his account of the three stages in the development of personality. He argued that the aim or goal of all sexuality is pleasure, and that this pleasure is deployed upon one or another of the erogenous zones of the human body. Such pleasures, Freud asserted, moved through three phrases or stages during approximately the first six years of life. These stages are oral, anal, and genital. In the first or oral stage of development, erotic pleasure is concentrated in the region of the mouth in such activities as sucking and biting. In the second or anal period, pleasure is centered in the anus, first in the withholding and then in the passing of feces. In the third or genital period, the center of interest and pleasure moves to the genitals. After this follows a period of sexual latency lasting from the sixth or seventh year until sexual maturity is achieved in the thirteenth or fourteenth year.

In each of the three periods a cluster of personality traits comes to be organized around the respective erotic center. Also while maturity of development is achieved by moving from one stage to the next, there is always the possibility of fixation or arrested development, or of regression or perversion.

Coincident with the genital stage of development is the time of the Oedipus complex. The newborn infant's first love is for the mother as the source of nourishment and warmth. Yet, as Freud observed, the attachment of male children to the mother and of female children to the father soon becomes stronger. In the fantasy life of children of four to six years there is active rivalry with the parent of the same sex and a desire to take his (or her) place as sexual partner of the other parent. Frequently this arouses great hostility toward the parent of the same sex. Behind and beyond all the explicit and implicit mythology with which Freud invested his ideas concerning the Oedipus complex, this period of the child's development also features a challenge to parental authority (especially the parent of the same sex) with the concurrent development of the child's personality toward freedom and individuality.

Still another important possibility for neurotic development calls for comment here, namely, Freud's view of religion as an infantile neurosis, a kind of father fixation.[6] As Freud's biographer Ernest Jones summarized the matter, religion accepts as cosmic realities a small child's relation to his parents. As a philosophic naturalist Freud regarded any and all such transcendental knowledge claims as false and misleading. As psychoanalyst he believed he had traced them to their source and correctly diagnosed them as neurotic. Yet, he added, mankind is attached to illusions. While a few wise and courageous persons can free themselves from this infantile dependence and go on to live in the tragic freedom of adult life, there is no evidence that the majority of mankind will cease to live by illusion. For the universal neurosis that is religion, Freud saw virtually no cure.

(5) While Freud's primary aims were to heal the sick and to explore the hidden recesses of the mind, he was never oblivious to the wider social implications of his theories. These implications became more insistent with the years. Like Plato and Hobbes before him, he envisaged society as individual man writ large.

We have already alluded to the agelong warfare, as Freud saw it, between man's instinctual drives and the needs of civilization. Despite all our efforts at domestication, the id remains powerful and fundamentally antisocial. War and more particularly the First World War, was regarded by Freud as an eruption of aggressive instinctual energy, destructive or nihilistic in character. He was led in this connection to add to sex or libido another drive, namely, a death instinct. Hence, man is ruled by the twin deities of Eros and Thanatos, Love and Death.[7] Concerning the latter it may be said that there is an aggressive drive in much of human activity that is fulfilled in the relief of tension, or in a quieting of activity, which led Freud to suggest that the quiet of death is the end of life. He used the symbol of Nirvana for this peace of quietude or relief from tension.

Like the attending physician of a mortally ill patient, Freud was concerned to counsel a moderating of the demands of civilization upon the individual, so that the sufferings of the ego might be somewhat ameliorated. Yet he saw no cure for the human illness, no solution for the human problem—no real peace between man and society or within man himself. Freud's own aspirations were on the side of reason. He was indeed a great Jewish rationalist in the tradition of Maimonides and Spinoza. Yet his assessment of the human situation was tragic. His use of images and metaphors from Greek tragedy was more than coincidental. His appraisal of the human situation was clearly similar to that of Aeschylus, Sophocles, and Euripides before him. Such was the diagnosis of Dr. Freud, attending physician to Man.

Issues of Science and Rationality

The storms of controversy that have raged over Freud's ideas from earliest Vienna days to the present moment are an indication of their creative power. While we have no desire to be involved in these bitter polemics, which have ranged from civil wars among Freud's followers to angry denunciations of psychoanalysis and all its works, we must undertake some sort of critical evaluation. We shall deal briefly with two clusters of issues and criticisms, one centering in the problems of science and rationality, and the other in value and culture. In all we shall raise six questions, some of which incidentally might be classified with equal justification under either main topic.

(1) One charge leveled by many philosophic critics is that Freud's fundamental concepts and categories are so vague as to lack genuine and determinate rational meaning. In a word, Freud's teachings fall short of being reliable scientific knowledge. Karl Popper's "principle of falsifiability," which we discussed in chapter 4, is aimed directly at such systems as those of Freud and Marx.[8] It asserts that an essential ingredient of the rational meaning of any theory consists of the grounds on which it may be judged false. In effect, a theory or hypothesis that does not state or imply the grounds on which it might be judged false, that is in effect true-no-matter-what, is meaningless. There is, incidentally, strong irony in the allegation that Freud's teaching is irrational or unscientific, for no man has ever been more single-mindedly dedicated to the ideals of reason and science than Sigmund Freud.

Perhaps the most detailed of such critical analyses of Freud's thought is that of Ernest Nagel in *Psychoanalysis, Scientific Method and Philosophy*, edited by S. Hook.[9] Nagel opens his analysis with his own version of Popper's principle, namely, that any theory to be meaningful must yield specific, determinate consequences which may then be judged true or false by observation. Nagel also adds the requirement that at least some aspects of a theoretical structure must be rooted in observable reality. Such concepts as Freudian drives violate these canons of intelligibility, Nagel charges, since they have neither a clear basis in experience nor do they yield determinate, specifically testable consequences. Nagel is critical of the hypotheses involved in dream analysis, charging that they are not testable by publicly observable data, either in origin or in consequences. Nor is the psychoanalytic interview any help, for it is again neither publicly accessible nor repeatable. Furthermore, the analyst is far from being an objective observer. Quite the opposite, he directs the course of the narrative. Nor indeed are the therapeutic results of much use, for as a matter of objective statistical study they yield an impressive number of negative or neutral results. Hence, on the basis of the hard evidence, pro and con, in the case of the truth versus psychoanalysis, Nagel reaches the verdict "Not proven." What he seems to suggest might be summarized as follows: A modern mythology psychoanalysis may be, but science it is not. For the full weight of these arguments pro and con, including also several papers in defense of psychoanalysis, the reader is referred to the Hook volume cited above.

Few thoughtful persons will deny that this argument is a bewildering snarl of literally innumerable issues. To begin with, there are the difficulties of the field of study itself. It is enormously easier, at least in some important respects, to work with data perceived at the other end of a microscope or test tube than with the human self, which is not only an infinitely more complex system but also one in which the investigator is both, in some sense, observer and observed. Freudians have not helped in this issue when they have interpreted any and all opposition to their theories as examples of the Freudian concept of resistance—though such arguments ad hominem probably belong more clearly to the vulgarization of Freud than to Freud. One hastens to add that this vulgarization is a flourishing trend in itself.

Another basic question that impinges upon this and other issues is what will count as a fact. Many of the hostile critics of psychoanalysis wish to draw this circle narrowly (as we saw the philosophical positivists doing in chapter 4), limiting the area strictly to visual, auditory, and tactile data, a view which would effectively rule psychoanalysis off the playing field before the game begins. On this issue, our chapter 2's definition of a fact puts us clearly on the side of Freud. For in terms of our definition, there are "interior" as well as "exterior" facts, difficult though the former may be to get at, to test, and to check. Clearly, human reason must adapt itself to the job to be done rather than forcing the subject matter to conform to our presuppositions about ideal methods of inquiry. To cite a philosopher on Freud's side of this particular argument, John Wisdom has written: "A difference as to the facts, 'a discovery', 'a revelation', these phrases cover many things. Discoveries have been made not only by Columbus and Pasteur, but also by Tolstoy, Dostoyevsky, and Freud. Things are revealed to us not only by the scientists with microscopes, but also by the poets, the prophets and the painters."[10] However any of us individually appraises these issues, perhaps the most important thing to say is that the process of critical evaluation still goes on. In this case the jury is still out.

At this point a modest contribution to the philosophic clarification of psychoanalysis may be made by calling attention to two modes of knowing. Actually, this is a widespread distinction in contemporary philosophy, and is made in a wide variety of different terminologies and interpretations. Bertrand Russell distinguished between knowledge by acquaintance and inferential knowledge, James spoke of "knowledge about" and "knowledge by acquaintance," Bergson distinguished between intellect and intuition.[11] Dewey spoke of the difference between *knowing* and the direct *having* of experience. However characterized, here is a duality that runs throughout human experience; perhaps it may be labeled as the distinction between intuitive and discursive knowing. Yet, to limit the appellations, *knowledge* and *truth*, to either one form or the other, yields at most a verbal solution to what is a real problem. The other form continues to exist and to function, and to demand philosophic recognition of its existence as well as appraisal of its function.

In the case of psychoanalytic "insights," perhaps the least partisan solution is to call them knowledge of the first or intuitive sort which enter claims to knowledge of the discursive sort. These claims are then subject to further testing and checking by whatever means give promise of effectiveness. Surely the therapist and his patient would wish such a critical process to continue, for they have the most to lose from a false or misleading insight. In this respect, then, an insight may be said to function like the first formulation of a hypothesis which is then subject both to further delineation and development, and then to testing by whatever factual processes are available or may be devised.

This is a philosophic issue of widespread and recurring importance, for as we shall soon see, insights have their place not only in psychotherapy but in art, religion, morality—indeed throughout human personality and culture. To all of these fields the concept of insight is both pertinent and fruitful in the manner here suggested.

(2) Another closely related cluster of issues centers in the inclination of Freud and his followers to regard all reason as rationalization. This is to say, what we commonly call reasoning actually consists of the assignment of reasons belatedly or after the fact to conclusions that are really the product of subconscious causes. On this interpretation, reason is no longer the sovereign judge of interests and passions, but is covertly their paid advocate or lawyer, whose task is to make a case for ideas or attitudes, the true cause of which lies elsewhere. We shall meet an analogous concept in the next chapter, in the Marxist concept of ideology. In either the Freudian or Marxian form, we stand face to face with a philosophic issue which is both significant and pervasive in character, and which demands critical analysis. It will be worth our while to spend a few paragraphs on this issue, even though it may seem to divert attention momentarily from Freud.

The cruder forms of argument ad hominem to which this Freudian teaching sometimes leads, belong, let it be said again, to the popular vulgarization of Freudian teaching rather than to Freud himself. For example, who has not observed the ploy in argument, "You believe as you do because of wishful thinking," and then the counter move, "So do you!" At this point, significant or even interesting discussion becomes difficult for either party. Stated generally the argument runs: "Your thinking is the result of neurotic states, childhood fixations, wishful attitudes or other pathological circumstances, therefore what you say is invalid or untrue." However, when it is explicitly stated, this is so egregious and glaring an instance of the genetic fallacy (which is the mistaking of a *chronological*, or in this case a *psychological*, order for a *logical* order) that it is surprising so many people find it convincing.

Freud was by no means the first man to observe that reasoning is in fact sometimes powerfully and covertly influenced by passion or interest. That reason is the slave of passion is the explicit doctrine of philosophers as different as Spinoza and Hume. Yet, Freud was among the first scientific explorers of the unconscious region of the mind's life; and, clearly, the initial mapping of this relation between reason and interest is one of his great achievements.

Concerning the facts there can be no doubt. Our human minds *are* influenced by passion, and, doubtless, in more ways than any of us can become aware of. Human reason does, all too frequently, function as the hired lawyer or, indeed, the slave, of instinctual drives. Therefore, the hostile and defensive reaction of the traditional rationalist philosopher, namely, that this view subverts and destroys reason, may be ignored as both futile and foolish. Ironically enough, this rational defense against psychoanalysis seems itself to be strictly speaking a non sequitur. Suppose it does "subvert" or "destroy." Is it therefore untrue or invalid? Clearly, the conclusion does not logically follow from the premises.

As an example of such a simplistic, rationalist view, Brand Blanchard dismisses psychoanalysis with these words: ". . . there are psychoanalysts of the day who tell us that all thinking is at the mercy of just such factors as these, that it can never surrender itself to the control of the subject matter and follow the path of an objective logic, but is pulled about like a puppet by instincts, desires, and feelings. Such a position is, of course, self-destructive."[12] This is not the first time in human history that man, confronted with a strange new order of facts, has responded by denying their existence. Clearly, the only truly rational option is the opposite move of drawing the circle of reason widely enough to include the new facts, and then trying to understand them.

Yet, in the latter task Freud himself is less than helpful. For, while he introduced the term, *rationalization*, noted the incidence of the factual phenomenon, and sought scientific explanations of it, understanding of the philosophic significance of the issues involved was simply not Freud's central concern.

Let us begin a brief philosophic analysis of rationalization by the factual observation that, though he has much to say about other people's rationalizing that is illuminating, Freud himself also responded to problematic situations by thinking persistently, authentically, and searchingly—a fact that seems to have escaped his own notice. Freud reasoned and submitted his conclusions for the reader's rational appraisal. But suppose for a moment that he had applied psychoanalytic categories of explanation to his own cognitive activities? The effect would have been to reduce his own thinking to the rationalization of his own subconscious urges. How shall we solve this apparent dilemma? More generally, if it be assumed that reason functions *only* or *solely* as a paid advocate of interest, we may well ask why it is that interest seems to call for a lawyer? Why not the simple self-assertion of the interest? Is there not implied here a claim to rational justification or validity of some sort? Whence this strange claim? What is its significance?

We can do no more here than sketch in outline a solution that really deserves vastly more detailed argument.[13] What was said in chapter 2 concerning facts and truth will bear repeating in this connection. A fact was there defined as the referent of a true singular proposition, and truth was defined in terms of the adequacy of statement to referent, of thought to things. We also added the important idea of varying degrees of adequacy.

Our problem here, in the Freudian hypothesis concerning rationalization, is to account for the facts of this problem (namely, the problem of rationally posing and evaluating the human fact of rationalization) in ways consistent with our wider cognitive experience. An account that meets these tests may be characterized as an adequate, factual explanation or solution of this problem.

A rough sketch of a solution will consist of three assertions concerning the relation of our human minds to Reason and Truth. Taken together, I think they will yield a philosophic explanation of rationalization, as Freud's writings do not. Each of these following assertions cries out for more detailed philosophic analysis than present limits of space permit.

First, our human minds are finite, mortal, and relative; therefore, all our achievements of truth are likewise finite, mortal, and relative. Human truths are inherently partial, provisional, and tentative. They are partial, incidentally, in both issues of this word, namely incomplete and partisan. As St. Paul reminded the Corinthians, "we know in part . . . " He might further have added that we also know this is so.

Second, as a matter of fact observable alike in one's own experience and in that of other individuals and groups, our thinking is at times importantly influenced by interest or passion. Who of us has not had the experience of becoming aware of such influences, of seeing that his thinking has been conditioned or skewed by interest or prejudice or other conditioning factors? Incidentally, once a person becomes aware of such elements in his thinking, he is then at that moment able to begin coping with them. Until this moment of awareness his mind is at the mercy of these hidden forces. In this sense, at least, freedom is the recognition of necessity; the awareness of such "necessities" is, at least, the first step toward freedom.

Third, this awareness of our human finitude and relativity, and of the outside influences that press in upon our finite minds, presupposes in a very odd and unique way that which transcends these limits. In a word, our finite and skewed experience of rationality presupposes an awareness of Reason and Truth, pure and simple. Part of the oddness of this awareness is that Reason and Truth are never, apparently, direct objects of human apprehension, as particular objects and persons are, but are rather presupposed in all such actual awareness. We human beings are finite, and know that we are finite, thus presupposing awareness of norms or standards by which finitude is known as such. As we observed above, we not only know in part, but we know that this is so. As such we stand in the presence of Reason and Truth which are independent of our activities, and constitute both the standard and goal of our achievements in this field. By our awareness of these norms we are led to the knowledge of our finitude and partisanship.

In terms of this double awareness of Truth and of my truths, of Reason and of my reasoning, we are able adequately to understand Freud's concept of rationalization. Freud's view, as we have seen, does justice to the factual data involved. As a scientist Freud was satisfied simply to report the facts as he found them. Yet, if we attempt to construct a whole view of the situation solely out of such Freudian data, we shall be left in a hopeless and suicidal kind of relativism. How on the basis of this kind of evidence alone could we recognize rationalization as such? If all thought consists only of rationalization, then no process of thinking has any validity, including that involved in making the judgment that all thinking is rationalization.

But the observable fact is that we do at times recognize a rationalization as such, and this is sufficient to call into critical question the assertion that all thinking is rationalization. Once more, there is also the general fact about the life of our minds to which attention has been called, namely, that rationalized interests make claim to validity or justification. In this respect, the phenomenon of rationalization is similar to that of counterfeiting. In order to take place, it necessarily presupposes a standard of coinage. Analogously, our reasoning, imperfect as it always is, and corrupted as it often is, presupposes Reason as the standard and goal of its own activities.

However, these observations must not lead us to the opposite error, which we have previously identified with traditional philosophic rationalism. In terms of our present analysis, such a view would prematurely identify our thinking simply and completely with Truth and Reason, blithely overlooking the elements of finitude and interest that are such indefeasible aspects of human experience. Once again, what is needed is a double awareness of Truth and my truths, of Reason and my reasoning.

This view of the situation of human reason is confirmed by two widespread contemporary phenomena, namely, advertising and propaganda. In each of these cases there is both an element of interest and also a questionable claim to truth. In the case of both advertising and propaganda, there must be a standard of truth which is accepted by the recipients, and which is falsely simulated by the makers of the propaganda or advertising, if the advertising or propaganda is to be effective. A lie, to be effective, must clothe itself in the garments of truth. The interest involved in advertising and propaganda must be carefully concealed behind a façade of Rationality and Truth is these activities are to be practically effective.

These ambiguities of the human situation argue the existence of norms of Rationality and Truth, above the interplay of interests and the clash of finite claims. Yet no existent person or group is ever simply Rational—despite human pretensions to this effect. The power of Freud's instinctual drives is too great to be wholly subdued. Yet it is equally important not to let go our hold, mortal and finite though it remains, on the norms of Reason and Truth. For, once more, all our thinking is judged by these standards and directed toward these goals.

Issues of Value and Culture

Despite their focus upon healing the sick, Freud's writings deal comprehensively and basically with many issues of culture and personality. Indeed, no aspect of his teachings seems irrelevant to these wider issues, including those just considered under the heading of Reason and Science—which, after all, are fundamental features of both culture and personality. We shall consider briefly four more such issues: namely, Freud's doctrine of determinism, his view of religion, his impact upon imagination and the fine arts, and finally, his impact upon morality and ethics.

(3) Among Freud's most deeply held convictions was that of scientific determinism. He believed "hard determinism," as William James phrased it, to be a necessary postulate of science, and he was also convinced that this postulate was amply verified by the discovery of causes wherever he looked. Determinism is a view that has attracted the allegiance of many philosophers and scientists in every age, but was particularly popular in the nineteenth

century, due largely to scientific developments of this period. Yet, there is a fundamental problem here, both for Freud's therapist and the therapist's patient, and even more generally for man; for the experience of all three presupposes a freedom and responsibility which clash with the determinism that Freud expounded and adhered to.

The concept of determinism comes in many sizes, shapes, and qualifications. Its validity or invalidity may well depend upon the precise meaning given to it. In the case of Freud, he seems to have accepted a wholesale nineteenth century notion of scientific determinism, to wit, that all of reality consists of a single system of causal law and, therefore, that all things are comprehensible only in terms of efficient causes. This idea seems (a) to involve a self-contradiction and (b) not to be as Freud fervently believed, necessitated by science. Let us consider these charges in turn.

It is important to locate precisely the contradiction involved in this form of determinism. It is not to be found within the system of statements that elaborate this viewpoint (for such a system can surely be rendered internally consistent), but rather it is to be located in the active life of the person who, as one of his actions, asserts the truth of determinism. (This can in turn be put into propositions about his *act* of choice, which will then conflict with propositions asserting the truth of determinism.)

Let us see how this is so. Determinism in the sense in which we are dealing with it here, consists of the assertion that *all* events whatsoever are determined completely by prior efficient causes. Now, presumably, the determinist offers us this view because he believes it to be true, because, in short, he has considered the evidence pro and con, as well as the evidence for alternative nondeterminist theories and he concludes that determinism is true. Yet, if determinism is true, then it must include mental events as well as physical events, and among the mental events is his action of elaborating and accepting determinism. This too must, on the basis of his own theory, be rigidly determined by some order of efficient causation. In other words, he is irresistibly compelled to this conclusion because of prior biological, sociological, and other determining conditions. Now, if this line of thought be true, then the agent's experience of choosing on the basis of evidence, which is essential to the attribution of truth, becomes a cheat and an illusion. Here, then, are two lines of determination that clash head-on with each other.

It is, of course, easy enough to "solve" this problem by arguing, as some do, for different levels of determination or causation (including self-determinism or self-determination as discussed in our chapter 5); but the hard fact is that Freud did not make this distinction. His statement of determinism contains the above self-contradiction in stark form. Consistently carried through, we would have to conclude that Freudian psychoanalysis is susceptible of explanation solely and wholly in terms of the psychological constitution of its founder and followers. Tempting as it is, such a proposal must be rejected as one more illustration of the genetic fallacy.

The self-contradiction of determinism applies not only to the thinker, that is to Freud and the Freudian therapist, but also to the patient, trying to understand the disorders that afflict him and, practically, seeking to liberate himself from bondage. If determinism is true, then he too is caught between two conflicting lines of determination. For, first, if determinism is true, then it is true not only of his pathological behavior but equally of his attempts to seek a cure, and of his cured and normal behavior. It is true not only of him, but of the therapist as well. All yield to the absolute and sovereign sway of efficient determinism. Yet, as this patient acts, with the therapist's guidance, to seek and to find health, he must assume that he is acting freely and responsibly. More precisely he must assume that he is struggling painfully, sometimes fitfully, toward the goal of free or self-determined action. In order that this struggle may occur, one must assume that at the beginning of the therapeutic process the patient has at least an initial hold on freedom, and on the possibility of achieving it. At this point, Freud's determinism is breached.

The contradiction of the thinking determinist gives way to that of the acting determinist. It is ironical to observe that enough of Freud's teachings have seeped into the folklore to enable either ingenuous or ingenious people to use its deterministic explanations as excuses. For example, consider the student who, in attempting to exculpate a tardy paper, explained to his teacher, "As a result of early childhood training I have an irresistible compulsion to procrastinate." The teacher is said to have replied, "But I have an irresistible compulsion to punctuality." This kind of justification for actions raises insoluble problems for judges, deans, and others who must deal with persons-in-action, and who consequently must deal with them as free and responsible agents. Concerning the nature of freedom and responsibility, it must suffice here simply to recall to the reader's mind the preceding chapter's discussion of these issues.

The cul-de-sac in which Freudian determinism ends is needless, and yields readily to solution. First of all, it cannot be shown to be either a necessary postulate of reason in general or of science in particular. For the law of sufficient reason postulates that for everything there is a *reason*. Reality is, in other words, assumed to be a rational order in which for every entity there is some sort of Reason Why. However, efficient causes are only one variety of the species, reasons why. Indeed, it is an important part of reason's task to look and see what sort of reasons hold sway in the various regions of reality, as well as what sort of sway they hold.

In the case of science it seems plainly impossible to show that *all* science demands or presupposes the universal rule of efficient causal order. Rather, the functioning postulate of science must be interpreted in a looser, more open-textured way. It may be formulated as the assumption that there exist regions of order or determination in the universe. Precisely where they are located, what the nature of the order or determination is, and what its relation is to other patterns of determinate order are matters for specific factual inquiry. In this view, sciences may be characterized as so many hunting expeditions for whatever forms of determination may in fact turn out to exist. The experience of the natural sciences to date shows a wide variety of causes, reasons, or kinds of order in different regions of reality.

If nineteenth century science believed that it found efficient causation universally operative, this is by no means the case for twentieth century science. For example, in some areas of contemporary physics, there is a clear tendency to replace the concept of cause by that of law. More generally, to twentieth century science, the notion of cause shows a wide range of different meanings in different contexts. There is, in other words, an indefeasible contextual component in the meaning of the scientific concept, cause. Freud was convinced that his clinical practice verified his postulate of universal causation. A mind less convinced in advance might have formulated different interpretations of the patterns of reason and order that he actually turned up. In a word, Freud was frightened by what Gilbert Ryle has termed the "bogy of mechanism."[14] Twentieth century science and philosophy have done much to allay this false fear.

Of crucial importance for the sciences of man is the notion of self-determination. If this be admitted as a species of determination, the issue then becomes one of the kind of determination in terms of which explanation takes place, rather than the issue of determinism versus indeterminism. By self-determinism is meant the kind of occurrence in which, for example, my behavior of walking down the street is explained by the fact that I am going to the library for a book, or to the newsstand for the daily paper. This has sometimes been called teleological determination, purposive behavior, or final causation, and is at least prima facie a datum of human experience, not to be explained away by dogmas of determinism.

Common sense and common language testify, as we found reason to conclude in the preceding chapter, to a widespread identification of self-determination with freedom. At least several central aspects of what is usually meant by being free are included in the idea of self-determination. In free or self-determined action the causes of my action lie inside my volition rather than outside, and also they often lie in important measure in the future rather than in the past. It is to be observed that the experience of self-determination can be admitted as a real fact of human experience only if the sway of efficient determination over human action is assumed to be less than total.

As we have already noted, some writers who call themselves determinists treat self-determination as a new level of determination rather than as free action. In our view, this interpretation raises more issues than it solves. However, for the present discussion two comments are pertinent. (a) This is not Freud's view. He held firmly to the universal dominion of efficient causation. (b) These interpretations of self-determination as an emergent kind of level of determinism, if accepted, set limits on Freud's kind of determinism as components of the explanation of any particular event.

There is still a further distinction necessary to an understanding of Freud's thought on the issue of freedom. Let us call it a distinction between the concepts of determinism and bondage. The former we have already defined and discussed. Bondage is an idea here borrowed from Spinoza. It may be said to occur when the source of determination of one's actions moves from *inside* the volition to *outside* or *external* factors. Hence, bondage can happen only to a self originally or essentially free. Bondage occurs when a free self becomes enslaved or enchained. The chains may be of several sorts; they may be any set of factors external to a person's volition which become the real or effective determinants of his action. In Spinoza's view, they are all reducible to bondage to passion, from which the intellectual love of God provides emancipation—a profound but somewhat oversimplified view of the human situation. However, we bring this matter up here only in order to suggest that what Freud called "determination" or "overdetermination" may in many instances be more adequately viewed as forms of human bondage, from which both patient and therapist seek the patient's emancipation.

(4) We turn next to Freud's attack upon religion, and to some of the wider implications of his teachings for religious thought and practice. As we have noted, he attacked religion root and branch as an infantile father-fixation. Its neurotic character is apparent in the attitude of dependence upon an illusory celestial parent. At least three distinguishable assertions seem to be merged in Freud's charges: (a) the content of religious experience consists wholly of neurotic attitudes; (b) since the putative object of this form of experience is

nonexistent, the experience is therefore delusory; and (c) since the experience is wishful, it is therefore invalid or untrue.

Is the first assertion true or false? Is it factually true or false to assert that religious experience consists wholly and inherently of neurotic attitudes? Surely no candid student of religion would deny an extensive measure of factual truth to this charge, yet it is open to considerable question whether this is the whole truth. While admittedly there is much neurotic, defensive religion, there is at least the possibility of religious experience that is free and creative in character. This latter possibility Freud's view denies. Even more, it is open to question whether Freud's assertion is a truth about religion or about man. For, people who are wishful or neurotic in their religious attitudes seem to evince similar attitudes in other areas of experience, from family life to politics or to fine arts.

Yet, in the measure that there is factual truth in his charge, Freud is to be thanked for exposing these attitudes to public view. The more one looks at the kind of religious attitude that Freud denounced as wishful and illusory, the more similarity one sees to the kinds of religion denounced so unsparingly by the biblical prophets of ancient Israel. Indeed, the very idea of being necessarily "for religion" is in psychological terms a "defensive" attitude. In earlier and healthier ages, the free and radical criticism of religion was itself a religious task. At least it is such for all persons who stand in the tradition of prophetic religion.

The second assertion above, namely, that the object of religious experience is nonexistent (which Freud everywhere assumes and nowhere argues) is properly a philosophical statement, easily identifiable from chapter 2 as a form of philosophic naturalism or positivism. Freud or anyone is entitled to this view, but it ought to be philosophically argued rather than assumed as a self-evident postulate of science—which it is not.

The third statement above, namely, that since religion is wishful it is therefore untrue, explicitly asserted, is clearly a non sequitur. It does not follow that because a belief is wishfully conditioned, it is therefore invalid. At most, such conditioning may and ought to put us on guard to see whether or not the conclusion follows from the premises. As a matter of fact, it may be questioned whether wishful conditioning is invariably on the side of religious belief. There may well be actual situations where it will stand against the religious option, and incline a person toward the opposite. While Freud is saved from this example of the genetic fallacy by his ascetic renunciation of all or most extrascientific reflections, his followers have often fallen headlong into it.

While Freud's rejection of traditional religion, as he saw it, claimed to be total, many religious thinkers have found in his writings, both seminal suggestions as well as significant confirmation of important tenets of religion. Freud's descent into the depths of the self resembles that of many of the great religious explorers from St. Augustine to Buddha. His view of the self is one which recognizes and emphasizes the depth and inwardness of the self, in contrast to many contemporary forms of social science, which shallowly reduce the self to tendencies of behavior or clusters of social roles.

Freud's explorations of these hidden depths reveal, in his own terms, the same traditional problems of anxiety and guilt that have been the themes of traditional religion. Like Kierkegaard, Freud saw man as a creature torn by anxiety. Like Paul and Augustine, Freud saw human existence indefeasibly involved in guilt. While his prescription was fundamentally different from theirs, his diagnosis was strikingly similar.

David Bakan, among others, has also pointed to Freud's unacknowledged but unmistakable relation to the tradition of Jewish mysticism and of Biblical religion.[15] In both places we find images that Freud used to define and characterize human existence. In this specific respect, Freud was more religious than he knew or admitted. His basic categories are powerfully influenced by these traditions. Freud's general use of mythical language, whatever its motivation and significance for him, has done much to bring this language alive in the experience of contemporary men.

(5) The influence of Freud on imagination and the arts is less overt, but surely as powerful and as pervasive as his influence on religion. Imagination is the place of images in the human mind, and images are the terms alike of the psychoanalytic interview and the artistic experience. The positive impact of Freud on the arts has been to call attention freshly and forcefully to the role of images and imagination in both the creation and apprehension of the arts.

It is, of course, as easy as it is dangerous to push these similarities too far. For, in other respects, psychoanalytic experience and artistic experience seem utterly dissimilar. In the neurotic forms of experience with which Freud primarily dealt, images occur and recur with compulsive force in the life of a self that is literally the slave of their arbitrary and capricious power. Painfully, slowly, and with the help of his therapist, the neurotic makes his way to a few insights into their meaning, and thence to some degree of freedom.

In sharpest contrast, the images of artistic experience occur at what has been happily called "aesthetic distance." This is to assert that art takes the images of common daily occurrence, holds them off at a distance, consciously objectifying them, making them the content of an experience that is had and enjoyed as an end in itself. Whereas neurotic experience is an exercise in bondage, artistic experience is an exercise in creative freedom for both the artist and the beholder.

Again, as we have previously noted, both psychoanalytic experience and artistic experience employ the concept of insight as their characteristic way of knowing. However, psychoanalytic insight is achieved painfully and fitfully like a gleam of light at the end of a long dark tunnel, while artistic insight is the bright center of a whole nexus of relations that the work of art lights up.

(6) Freud's teachings impinge in numerous ways upon both moral practice and ethical theory. Ethical theory as such was not a primary concern of Freud, but other people who seek to cultivate this field are forced to wrestle with such Freudian concepts as his determinism, his hedonism, and his notion of the unending conflict between id and superego. Freud has at times been classified by popular thought as an ethical nihilist. This charge is wide of the mark. As Abraham Kaplan has well pointed out, Freud's strictures are upon the "law" but not the "prophets," which is to say, Freud's teachings are inimical to a fixed and closed morality, but not to an open and free morality.[16]

In this respect, Freud's own moral practice and example are as powerful as his theories. In moral practice Freud has sometimes been pictured as an immoralist. Nothing could be further from the truth. If he attacked some conventional morality, it was because he believed it was riddled with hypocrisy or heavy with needless repression. In respect to his own code, he was an austere moralist, serving the primary values of honesty, freedom, and reason with single-minded devotion; and he wrote these values into the structure of the psychoanalysis he founded and led. As Philip Rieff has clearly shown, Freud's was "the mind of a moralist."[17]

While it is still too early to predict how future generations and centuries will evaluate Freud and his teachings, at least the beginnings of a critical estimate are taking shape. We have pointed to the way in which he drew upon images and values carried for centuries in Jewish and Greek traditions. But perhaps above all Freud stands as a humanist. He sought to make man human, to restore somewhat the deep distortions wrought by constitutional flaws in man's nature; and the system of psychoanalysis he constructed is an instrument to this end. He is a humanist in the additional sense of defending the worth and dignity of man from attacks from either above or below, that is, from the tyranny of supernaturalism or the chaos of nature. Freud also belongs, as previously noted, to the long tradition of thinkers, dating from ancient Greece, who have envisaged human life as tragic. It may well be that he will go down in history as a tragic humanist.

SUGGESTIONS FOR FURTHER READING

As many of these works are classics that have appeared in numerous editions, only the most accessible publication is indicated.

Adler, A. *Understanding Human Nature*. New York: Greenberg, 1927.
Bakan, D. *Sigmund Freud and the Jewish Mystical Tradition*. New York: Van Nostrand, 1958.
Brown, N. O. *Life Against Death*. New York: Vintage Books, 1961.
———. *Love's Body*. New York: Random House, 1966.
Erikson, E. *Identity and the Life Cycle*. New York: International Universities, 1959.
Feigl, H., and Scriven, M., eds. *The Foundations of Science and the Concept of Psychology and Psychoanalysis*. Minneapolis: University of Minnesota Press, 1956.
Freud, S. *The Basic Writings of Freud*. New York: Modern Library, 1938.
———. *The Future of An Illusion*. Garden City: Doubleday, 1957.
Fromm, E. *Man for Himself*. New York: Rinehart, 1957.
———. *Escape From Freedom*. New York: Avon, 1965.
Hook, S., ed. *Psychoanalysis, Scientific Method and Philosophy*. New York: New York University Press, 1959.
Horney, K. *The Neurotic Personality of Our Time*. New York: Norton, 1937.
———. *Our Inner Conflicts*. New York: Norton, 1945.
Jones, E. *The Life and Work of Sigmund Freud*. New York: Basic Books, 1961.
Jung, C. *Basic Writings*. New York: Modern Library, 1959.
May, R. *Man's Search for Himself*. New York: Norton, 1953.
———. *Love and Will*. New York: Norton, 1970.
Outler, A. *Psychotherapy and the Christian Message*. New York: Harper, 1954.
Popper, K. *The Logic of Scientific Discovery*. New York: Basic Books, 1959.
Roberts, D. *Psychotherapy and a Christian View of Man*. New York: Scribners, 1950.
Sullivan, H. S. *Conceptions of Modern Psychiatry*. New York: Norton, 1965.
Tillich, P. *The Courage To Be*. New Haven: Yale University Press, 1952.
Trilling, L. *Freud and the Crisis of Our Culture*. Boston: Beacon Press, 1955.

VII
Marxism As
Philosophy

THE QUESTION raised in the preceding chapter concerning Freud now forces itself to our attention concerning Marx and Marxism, namely: Is this a philosophy and if so of what sort? For the orthodox and professional Marxist, philosophy has the restricted and technical meaning of "dialectics." To this we shall allude, but we shall not be limited to this narrow and partisan view of philosophy's nature and task. However, if one takes the whole body of Marx' teachings to be in some sense a philosophy, as we shall do in this chapter, one still faces important questions of definition and characterization. Shall we interpret Marx in his relation to Hegel as an Hegelian or post-Hegelian systematist? Or is he to be understood as one of the radical critics of Hegel? Still again, is Marxism to be understood as a nineteenth century scientific philosophy? Is Marxism, like Herbert Spencer's system, a nineteenth century philosophy of evolution? Is it, as its orthodox defenders claim it to be, a scientific theory of revolution and of the new society to come after revolution? Was Marx a Marxist—despite his celebrated denial that this was so? Fortunately, we do not have to choose exclusively any one of these or other options. For there are important elements of truth (and falsehood) in all or many of them. However we may choose to classify and characterize it, Marxism is still one of the systems of thought that has made world history in the first century of its existence. Whatever the reader may think of it, Marxism is the functioning philosophy and faith of many millions of human beings in all parts of the world. Hence, no philosopher of the twentieth century, professional or amateur, dare ignore it.

While professional philosophers in America and Great Britain have not taken Marxism seriously as a philosophy, this is not true of continental Europe (on both sides of the Iron Curtain) or of Asia. Not only is it the established philosophy of Communist countries; a looser, freer, and less authoritarian brand of Marxism, sometimes called Marxist humanism, occurs widely as a very lively philosophic option throughout continental Europe and Asia.[1]

Back of the philosophy stands the man, Karl Heinrich Marx (1818–1883). In the city of Treves, his father was a lawyer who in 1829 converted, with his family, from Judaism to Christianity, in order to avoid the discrimination that was then being forced once more upon the Jews of Germany. Marx' father seems to have been intellectually and spiritually a child of eighteenth century rationalism. It is also by no means irrelevant to note that Marx was the grandson of rabbis on both his father's and mother's sides of the family.

Marx was educated at the Universities of Bonn and Berlin where he came into contact first with Hegel's philosophy and then with the radical or "left" Hegelians. In 1841 he received the doctorate for a dissertation entitled "The Difference Between the Philosophies of Nature of Democritus and Epicurus." His radical views made an academic career impossible, so he turned in 1842 to journalism, first as a writer for and then as editor of Cologne's *Rheinische Zeitung*. However, this paper was suppressed for radical views only a few months after Marx joined it.

In 1843 he went to Paris in order to study socialism, taking with him his bride, Jenny von Westphalen. There he met his lifelong friend, supporter, and collaborator, Friedrich Engels. Expelled from Paris in 1845 he made his way to Brussels where in late 1847 he wrote the *Communist Manifesto*. It was issued early 1848.

He participated ineffectively in the revolution of 1848 in both France and Germany, and was actually tried for treason in the latter country. Though acquitted, he was expelled, and found asylum in England. Except for a few brief intervals, he lived the rest of his life in London where he continued to study, write, organize, and agitate until his death in 1883. He was for the decade from 1851 to 1861 correspondent for the *New York Tribune*. His life was scarred by bitter poverty, resulting in the death of three of his six children, and by continual ill health. He was sustained by his wife, and by an indomitable sense of mission. As a boy he had written in his juvenile diary in bad German poetry but in accurate prophecy concerning his own life:

Never can I pursue in quiet that which holds my soul in thrall, never rest at peace contented, and I storm without cease.[2]

As his life and thought unfolded, the content of his mission or vocation became the confident hope of impending social revolution, which he steadfastly believed would transform mankind from slavery to freedom. In the climate of opinion in which he lived, his sense of mission also generated an arrogant polemical quality of mind which, never doubting his own absolute truth, was intolerant and often grossly unfair to opponents. Marx seems to have bequeathed this quality to many of his followers.

From Hegel to Marx

Marx remarked that in Hegel he found the dialectic standing on its head, and that his achievement was to turn it rightside up. What then was the Hegelian dialectic which he righted and which served him at least as a point of departure?[3] The philosophy of Georg Friedrich Wilhelm Hegel (1770–1831) defies summary statement. Indeed, many observers would say that it defies rational statement of any sort, long or short.

Hegel's philosophic system was a complex synthesis of many elements, including (1) the concepts of reason and progress of eighteenth century France, wedded to (2) German romanticism and historicism. In the background were two other elements, (3) the sense of historic destiny derived from Christianity and, (4) an equally strong influence from mystical thinkers such as Eckhart and Boehme. In the struggle to understand Hegel it must never be forgotten that as a young man he turned from Christian theology to philosophy. Hence, it will not be misleading to approach Hegel's thought as a secularized, post-Christian version of the traditional Judeo-Christian drama of history. The key term in Hegel is the untranslatable German word, *Geist*, which functions in a way similar to *God* in Judeo-Christian discourse. Neither "Mind" nor "Spirit" is an adequate rendering; perhaps the two taken together come as close as possible. Here we shall leave it untranslated.

Geist begins as *subjectiver Geist*, that is, the mind or spirit of Man, revealed in human subjecthood, and notably in logic, which is said by Hegel to exhibit the skeletal structure of Geist.[4] However, once it achieves subjective statement, for reasons of its own, Geist alienates itself (the German word is *entfremden* and, once used by Hegel, was destined for a long and eventful history in subsequent philosophy) in Nature, which is accordingly *objectiver Geist*. This alienation is overcome in *absoluter Geist*, which is Geist deployed in human history and society. Society or culture (Hegel characteristically said "State") is for this reason viewed as embodied or incarnated Geist.

The reader will not be mistaken to observe in this last tenet concerning society both a seminal suggestion and a blatant prejudice. The seminal suggestion is the assumption that has provided agenda for a century of social scientists, namely, that human society or culture bears a significant relation to mind. Mind or Geist finds incarnation or embodiment in culture; hence conversely, culture is the fundamental expression of mind. The prejudice is, in Hegel's own words, the assumption that "the rational is the real, and the real is the rational."[5] These ambiguous words will bear several interpretations. Conservative interpreters hastened to read them as an assertion that existing society is the embodiment of Divine Reason. From this it follows that the all-important feature of any inquiry into the existing state of the world is to exhibit the rational pattern which, a priori, the inquirer knows to be there. Truly the status quo has never had a more confident exponent than Hegel.

Another aspect of Hegel's philosophy that proved equally important for Marx is its historical character. Geist moves through history in the characteristically Hegelian manner of thesis, antithesis, and synthesis, finding embodiment successively in Oriental society (of which Hegel was blissfully ignorant of everything beyond its supposed existence), the Greeks and Romans, and finally and climactically the Germans.[6] Hegel further boldly asserted this sequential order as the progressive history of freedom. In the first phase, one man, namely the emperor or headman was free; in the second some men were free; but now, in the case of the Germans, all are free.

One hastens to interject that Hegel's view of freedom was derived from the Kantian view of autonomy, which means that in freedom the self gives norms or rules to itself, which in turn is a Germanic way of saying self-determination. As we saw in the last chapter and will have occasion to observe throughout our study, self-determination is the central aspect of human freedom. However, in Hegel it is not empirical persons who "give norms to themselves" but absoluter Geist who does so—a view that enabled Hegel to draw the conclusion that this spirit of freedom resided in the Prussian state of his day.[7] Once again, Hegel combines seminal suggestions with egregious error. In this case, Hegel had valuable insights concerning the nature of freedom, but in the concrete application and practice of freedom he failed miserably.

For European history Hegel availed himself of the radical medieval idea of three historical ages, namely, of the Father, of the Son, and of the Holy Spirit. In Hegel's formulation the first age extended through Charlemagne, the second from Charlemagne to the Reformation, and the third from the Reformation to Hegel. The plausibility of this grandiose vision of history was dependent upon ignorance of many historical details and an equal willingness to blur well-known facts. Yet for all this, it did present the picture of history as linear and dramatic rather than cyclic in nature; and it did underscore the sociopolitical character of history—features of the greatest importance for Karl Marx.

Following Hegel's death his followers split into two camps, right and left Hegelians, the former dedicated to the pedestrian exposition of conservative aspects of the master's philosophy, and the latter pushing toward new, radical (and sometimes most un-Hegelian) interpretations. It is a fact of some interest that from the latter sprang some of the most creative and influential lines of thought in nineteenth century Europe.

Among the left Hegelians was Ludwig Feuerbach (1804–1872) who took the decisive step of naturalizing Hegel's Geist, that is, of asserting Nature rather than the Spirit to be the ultimate reality, or, conversely, of asserting a naturalistic universe. Feuerbach was a philosopher of religion who sought to fit religion into his naturalistic view of reality. He did so by means of the Hegelian category of alienation, arguing that the putative entities of religion, namely gods, demons and the like, are in reality aspects of man's own nature that have been alienated and then asserted to have objective reality. In Feuerbach's view, they are all *Wunschwesen* or "wish-entities." Feuerbach's *Essence of Christianity* argued for a humanist, naturalist view of religion.[8] Marx took his stand with Feuerbach, punning that everyone must be baptized in the "fire-spring" (which *feuerbach* means in German). As we shall soon see, in other matters, he pushed beyond Feuerbach.

What Marx meant by his remark about turning the dialectic rightside up was that in Hegel he found the dialectic of history as a movement of Geist, whereas he came to believe that the determining factors in human history are not ideal or spiritual but material in character. Mind is an emergent from matter and not vice versa. Consciousness presupposes existence, and not existence, consciousness; and existence is built squarely upon a material foundation. This became the first premise of Marx' philosophy.

Marx and His System

It is of the greatest importance to see Marx' philosophy as an expression of his life. What the world has come to know as the Marxist system did not spring immediately and full-grown into existence. Rather, it came late in Marx' life as a systematic working out and elaboration in political and economic terms of his earlier philosophical ideas. Marx left the university as a radical Hegelian. His intellectual life from this time onward can be divided into two periods. First was the decade of brilliant discovery, of venturesome new philosophical formulation, approximately 1840 to 1850; second was the period from 1850 to the end of his life, which was concerned with the application and elaboration of his philosophy to the realities of politics and economics. Intellectually the second period was also a time of system building and of system defending as well as counterattack on enemies, defectors, and renegades. During this second period Marx was also concerned practically with organization, agitation, and revolution, through which he sought to apply his philosophy to the political order and history. The philosophical ideas of the first found detailed sociopolitical elaboration and application in the second.

Marxian scholarship in recent decades has shed new light on Marx' philosophic origins, as revealed by his early and, until recently, unpublished works. These range from his doctoral dissertation, to journalistic articles written for the *Rheinische Zeitung*, to philosophic and economic manuscripts written during 1843–1845, and to the *Critique of Hegel's Philosophy of Law*, *The German Ideology*, and several manuscripts unpublished and unfinished during his lifetime.[9] In these writings Marx is revealed as a philosophical radical, measuring existing society against his own austere and pristine humanistic ideal. In the ideal human society, man is, or rather will be, free, creative, cooperative, rational, and in harmony with nature. He will in short be truly human, and Marx regarded his philosophy as an instrumentality to this end.

It is important to spell out the main features of Marx' humanistic ideal. Man in his truly human selfhood will have first of all a creative and fully cooperative relation to his work and to his fellowman. His work will be a creative expression of his humanity. His consciousness will no longer be skewed and corrupted by ideology; he will in short be genuinely rational, and reason will guide the course of both individual and social life. Moreover, he will live in harmonious order with nature, which in present capitalist society he exploits and violates.

Yet, as Marx looked around himself at nineteenth century Europe, what he saw was an utter negation or antithesis to this genuine humanity. Man was at his neighbor's throat or on his back, his mind was stained and skewed by the false consciousness of ideology, at odds with himself and with nature. To the question why this should be so, Marx replied with his own interpretation of the Hegelian category of alienation. Man is dehumanized or alienated from his true humanity. His existence is torn apart from his true essence. The heart of this alienation moreover lies according to Marx in the capitalist economic system that separates man from his work, making both himself and his work commodities to be bought and sold in the market place. The taproot of alienation is, in a word, capitalism and all its works.

Marx' humanism was moreover eschatological, in the precise sense that he confidently believed that in the next age of history, alienation would be overcome, and man's essence and existence would be once again harmoniously united. Once the capitalist system has been replaced by Communism, the sun will rise on a new age of humanity. It would be false to Marx to speak of this next age as the Kingdom of God, for the idea of God is a product of man's present alienated consciousness; but surely and clearly it will be the Kingdom of Man. And Marx continued all his life to believe that this Kingdom was immediately at hand.

If in later life Marx talked less about this philosophic vision of the new age and more about the details of economics and politics, it was not because he had abandoned the vision. Rather as a philosopher of concrete experience he was giving detailed application and embodiment to his earlier vision in the life of human society. Early in his career Marx wrote the following prophetic words, fulfilled in his own individual life if not in the life of human society: "Just as philosophy finds its material weapons in the proletariat, so the proletariat finds its intellectual weapons in philosophy. And once the lightning of thought has penetrated deeply into the virgin soul of the people, the Germans will emancipate themselves and become men."[10]

Marx continued to study, to write, and to publish, even as he sought to participate in the events that his writings interpreted. After the failure of the revolution of 1848 he settled down in London to produce the great political and economic works which together comprise the system called Marxism: in 1852, *The Eighteenth Brumaire of Louis Napoleon*; in 1859, *A Contribution to the Critique of Political Economy*; in 1871, *The Civil War in France*; and in 1875, *A Critique of the Gotha Programme*. The first volume of *Das Kapital* was published in 1867; volumes II and III were edited by Engels after Marx' death, appearing from 1885 to 1894, while the notes for the fourth volume on surplus value were edited by Kautsky and published from 1905 to 1910.

What emerges from this vast quantity of writing is a philosophic system in the grand style of the nineteenth century, that is, a single system of categories in terms of which a total comprehensive explanation of all reality is attempted. His system remains specifically Hegelian in at least one respect, namely, that history moves dialectically from thesis through antithesis to synthesis. Once he had embarked upon the venture, Marx seems to have had no doubts about the legitimacy of system building, and in particular the final truth of his own system.

A prominent feature of the system is the author's abhorrence of the term, *romanticism*, and his extremely high valuation of scientific ways of thinking. Romanticism constituted for him emotion unrelated to reason or to the world of reality, whereas science was a way of reasoning concretely and critically about the real world. Marx did not hesitate to claim scientific status for his methods and his results; he sought to dedicate *Das Kapital* to Charles Darwin, and was dissuaded only by the latter's demurrer. Marx believed that he had discovered the "law of motion" of capitalist society; and Engels asserted that his work concerning human society might be compared to that of Darwin in the biological sciences. In evaluations of this sort concerning Marx and Marxism the twentieth century student will correctly and ironically see a curious kind of romanticism of science.

But what is the Marxian system? What kind of intellectual mansion did Marx erect? While an adequate answer to that question is far beyond present limits of space, we can at least sketch the pillars of this imposing philosophical edifice.

(1) The first pillar is what traditional Marxist literature has called *historical materialism*. The term, *materialism* stands for the metaphysical assertion that reality is material in nature, rather than spiritual, organic, or of some other sort. But of course the important question is what in specific detail this assertion is taken to mean or imply.

There is one egregious popular misconception that can be cleared up immediately. It turns upon two widely different and logically independent uses of the words, *materialistic* and *materialism*. In current American discussion, a widely popular journalistic and homiletic usage equates materialism with action in terms of self-centered, or acquisitive, or narrowly hedonistic motives and goals. This view seems to locate human good very largely in the stomach. For this usage the label, *moral materialism*, has been suggested; and it will function satisfactorily provided we see that moral materialism is altogether independent of metaphysical materialism, which we have defined as the view that reality or being is material in character. Hence, to observe that Marx held to the second but not the first comes as no surprise to anyone except the professional anti-Communists of popular platform and press. Indeed, the confusion between the two kinds of materialism constitutes a very dangerous ambiguity, for the good reason that in fact in recent history the appeal of Communism has been in terms not of cynical moral materialism, but rather in precisely opposite terms of lofty, even heroic or fanatical idealism.

There is another issue of considerably greater philosophic importance that Marxists have formulated as the difference between mechanistic and dialectical materialism. In this connection, a recent study of Marx' teachings points out that Marx himself never used the terms, *historical materialism* or *dialectical materialism*, though they are of frequent incidence in Engels, Lenin, and other Marxist writers.[11] Nevertheless, this distinction seems clearly implicit in Marx' writings and is given explicit and detailed articulation in later

Marxist philosophical writing. Mechanistic materialism may be said to be defined by the assertion that reality is "nothing but" matter in motion—all else is appearance. Thus it commits the "nothing but" fallacy, that is, the fallacy of reductionism. In explanation and in reality, all of being is held to be reducible to matter in motion.

Dialectical materialism does not deny the existence of the human spirit and of spiritual relations, but it argues that material factors and relations are underneath all reality as its foundation. Hence, mind or spirit "emerges" from matter, though in the end it is asserted to be explicable in terms of matter. Clearly, the reality and significance of finite or human spirit are more plainly acknowledged and have larger scope in dialectical than in mechanistic materialism. However, despite their many disagreements, these two forms of materialism agree in a common denial of infinite spirit or God.

To mechanistic materialists, particularly during the nineteenth century, the basic images and concepts of their philosophy were derived from physical science. Not so for Marx. His matter is not that of the physicist, but of the economist. For him the fundamental reality is the economic system of production by which every society turns out the material goods of food, clothes, and shelter necessary for human survival. Upon this economic foundation, the superstructure of law, politics, education, science, religion, and all the rest of culture, is erected. Marx put the matter in these words:

> The first premise of all human history is of course the existence of living human individuals. The first fact to be established, therefore, is the physical constitution of these individuals and their consequent relation to the rest of Nature. . . .
> . . . the totality of these relations of production, constitute the economic structure of society—the real foundation on which legal and political superstructures arise and to which definite forms of social consciousness correspond. . . . It is not the consciousness of men that determines their being but on the contrary their social being determines their consciousness. . . .
> From this starting point, it (i.e., Marxist philosophy) explains all the different theoretical productions and forms of consciousness, religion, philosophy, ethics, etc., and traces their origins and growth by means of which the matter can of course be displayed as a whole . . . at each stage of history there is found a material result, a sum of productive forces capital and circumstance . . . which also prescribes for its conditions of life and gives it a definite development, a special character. . . .[12]

We shall return later in this chapter to critical appraisal of these philosophical views of Marx. Meanwhile, here it is enough to observe that the real problem involved in Marx' materialism is the precise nature of this relation of determination which is asserted to hold between the material foundation and the structure or superstructure that is erected on it.

(2) The second pillar of Marxian philosophy is the doctrine of economic determinism. Closely allied to historical materialism, it asserts that the determining factors in all human events are economic in nature. This is to say, the way in which men produce the material goods necessary to support their life determines all else about their common life. The preceding quotations from Marx might be said to illustrate not only historical materialism but also economic determinism as well. Marx was fond of speaking of the economic foundation of society, and the superstructure of culture (ranging from politics to religion) erected on this economic base. Again, the crucial issue for this philosophy is the nature of the relation between foundation and superstructure, and on this issue Marx is far from clear or unequivocal.

One all-important application of the idea of economic determinism is to law and the state. In Marx' view these structures will reflect the economic organization of a society. As Lenin was later succinctly to put the matter, the state is simply the executive committee of the ruling class to maintain its dominance and accomplish its ends of repressing the masses. Hence too, coercion and violence are essential attributes to the state. Marx asserted this view in these words:

> Since the State is the form in which the individuals of a ruling class assert their common interests, and in which the whole civil society of an epoch is epitomized, it follows that the State acts as intermediary for all community institutions, and that these institutions receive a political form. . . . Civil law develops concurrently with private property.[13]

An aspect of economic determinism of particular interest to our study is the concept of ideology. Marx took the word from an obscure philosopher of the French revolution named Destutt de Tracy, and for both men the term embraced education, science, art, religion, philosophy, and related aspects of a society. For Marx all of these idea systems are part of the superstructure erected upon an economic base, and are thus subject to the rule of economic determinism. Far from being above the battle lines, they exist within the limits set by, and subject to the purposes of, the ruling economic class. Marx' various uses of the term, *ideology*, range from the objective recognition that an idea system is a part of a culture to the negative value judgment of a corrupted, distorted consciousness resulting from causal factors in capitalist society. In the former sense Marxist thought is one ideology among others, but in the latter sense it constitutes that supreme truth which is above and beyond the false consciousness that is ideology.

One particular aspect of ideology, namely religion, elicited unconcealed hostility from Marx. Everyone, including those who have never read a line of Marx' writings, seems to know that Marx denounced religion as the opiate of the people—incidentally, first in his analysis of Hegel's philosophy of law in 1844. But seldom do these nonreaders take the trouble to understand the terms of this denunciation. Marx derived from Feuerbach the view of religion as natural and human in origin. That is to say, he received from Feuerbach the view of the gods and demons as alienated human wish-entities. To this he added his own social thunder, charging that the socioeconomic explanation for this escape mechanism is that by dreams of another world the masses are kept acquiescent to their masters in this world. There is also genuine pathos in such remarks of Marx as that religion is "the heart of a heartless world."[14]

(3) The third pillar of the Marxist mansion is the doctrine of the class struggle. Social classes are real entities for Marx—as real for him as the state for Hegel, or as cultures to a cultural anthropologist. Classes are defined in terms of their source of income, namely, wages, land, or profit derived from capital; and almost from the beginning of history classes have been pitted against each other in inexorable and agelong conflict. Engels depicted the beginning of human history as a primitive communism. But mankind departed from this Marxist Garden of Eden when the landlord and the soldier combined forces to subjugate and enslave the worker. Ever since, they have lived off his toil. Hence, the relation of exploiter and exploited, of robber and robbed, has prevailed throughout history. The toiling masses work to produce the necessities of life, only to be robbed of a large part of their output by those who hold power over them. *The Communist Manifesto* states the matter in these words:

> The history of all hitherto existing society is the history of class struggles. Freeman and slave, patrician and plebeian, lord and serf, guild-master and journeyman, in a word oppressor and oppressed, stood in constant oppostion to one another, carried on an uninterrupted, now hidden, now open fight, a fight that each time ended either with revolutionary reconstitution of society at large, or in the common ruin of the contending classes.[15]

Modern industrial society continues the historic struggle of the classes, but with one all-important difference. The inner dynamism and contradictions of capitalism drive it inexorably toward revolution, and beyond revolution to a new revolutionary socialist society. The capitalist, as he piles up capital, is forever in search of new markets, first at home and then overseas. For his own impoverished workers are unable to buy back the fruits of their own labor. Meanwhile, with a similar inexorability, the industrial working class increases its size, its misery, and its militancy. All aspects of this situation conspire together in approved dialectical Hegelian manner to create a revolutionary situation. As the *Communist Manifesto* observes, "What the bourgeoisie therefore produces above all is its own grave diggers. Its fall and the victory of the proletariat are equally inevitable."[16]

(4) The fourth pillar of Marxism is revolution; and as the historic events of nineteenth century Europe unfolded, Marx studied the dynamics of revolution. He concluded that in this decisive and climactic phase of human history every instrumentality of human society and culture must be devoted to defeating the bourgeoisie; first gaining and then guarding the victory of the proletariat. Marx continued to believe that the revolution was imminent. He was also sure the struggle would be violent, bloody, and cruel. No ruling class in history has ever peacefully relinquished power, and the modern bourgeoisie is no exception. Therefore, the proletarians must forcibly wrest power from their enemy and then by means of a dictatorship of the proletariat must defend their hard-won victory. All of these conclusions were confirmed in his mind by the bloody experience of the Paris Commune of 1871.

In the further future as the threat of counterrevolution recedes, the state will diminish and eventually cease to be an instrument of repression, leaving only its administrative functions. It is interesting to note that it was Engels and not Marx who used the metaphorical phrase, "the withering away of the state."[17] Nevertheless, during the revolutionary period the struggle is total. This means that the absolute allegiance not only of soldiers and political leaders but of ideologists as well must be maintained. Scientists, artists, teachers, and philosophers are soldiers in this war, and there is no place above the battle lines. As we have noted, Marx regarded religion as inherently reactionary and hostile to the revolution. However, for philosophy he found a continuing place in the rational guidance of revolutionary social action.

(5) Marx was reluctant to give details concerning the society of the future except to note that, as the new humanity fights its way free of the chains and habits of the past, there will be progressive liberation for all, a final healing and overcoming of man's agelong historic alienation from his true humanity. Labor will no longer be a badge of servitude, but will become an expression of humanity. Except for the administration of things, the state will have ceased to exist. As Engels put it, mankind will have stepped from prehistory to history, from necessity to freedom. Then in that happy future mankind

will be able to inscribe on its banners: "From each according to his abilities, to each according to his needs."[18]

Such then in briefest, barest outline are the main themes of Marxist philosophy. It has undergone many changes and transformations and appears in many conflicting versions. There are marked differences among Marx, Engels, and Lenin, not to speak of their differences from those whom they despised as revisionists or social democrats. Between the differing versions there have often been acrimonious polemics and even bloodshed. Yet in one form or another, Marxism is the functioning philosophy—and we may add, the faith—of many millions of living men.

Critical Issues and Questions

From its beginning to the present, Marxism has been the target of critical analysis, and often too of hostile attack of many kinds. Here we shall note five areas in which critical discussion of Marxism continues very much alive.

(1) Let us begin the task of critical evaluation with the terms, *materialism* (which Marx used) and *historical* or *dialectical materialism* (which has been the traditional label from Engels to the present day). As we have seen, the word *materialism* carries a heavy negative charge in current popular usage (at least in the West, and particularly in America). This is doubly so if it is joined with the adjective, *Marxist*. Yet if we can get past this popular disaffection with words, what we find here in this philosophy is many issues strikingly similar to the realist and pragmatist philosophies widely prevalent in America and England in the first half of the present century. For example, the reader will recall the naturalism of John Dewey discussed in chapter 3 and the realism of British and American philosophers considered in chapter 4. Marxism resembles these Western philosophies in their common critical protest against Hegelian idealism. There is more similarity than difference over wide areas of metaphysical and epistemological doctrine between what Marx called materialism and the philosophies of Dewey, Lovejoy, and others of their generation in America, and such British figures as Whitehead, Russell, Moore, and Broad. If we accept the recent suggestion of Avineri's book, *The Social and Political Thought of Karl Marx*, to the effect that Marx is more clearly dialectical than Engels and Lenin (concerning whom Avineri suggest that they were in their own Marxist terms mechanistic materialists) then this similarity is clearer than ever.[19] This similarity, be it underscored, lies in the regions of metaphysics and epistemology; in ethics and social philosophy the differences remain deep and fundamental.

There is a further difference that is rooted in the character of Marx' philosophy as a system in the grand tradition of metaphysical systems. This feature of Marxism prompts us to recall chapter 4's reference to Karl Popper's principle of falsifiability. Does Marx' materialism explain no-matter-what or, on the other hand, is it a system from which determinate consequences may be deduced? In a word, does Marx' philosophy pass or fail the falsifiability test? A reasoned answer to this question is by no means easy, simple or short. It will have to suffice here to say summarily that different answers seem to emerge from different parts or sections of Marx' writings. Some passages fail this test, others pass it, sometimes with distinction.

If we take as our illustration of Marxist philosophy the so-called three laws of dialectics as formulated by orthodox, traditional Marxist philosophy, a negative result seems clearly forthcoming. These three laws are (1) the interpenetration of opposites, (2) the transmutation of quantity into quality and, (3) the negation of negation. Their crucial deficiency is that they provide no unequivocal way of deriving specific and determinate consequences in terms of which they may be tested. Thus, for example, Lysenko made one application to biological science, and his opponents another. Marxist philosophy, officially so-called, provides no clear way of deciding which is the right and which is the wrong application.

(2) The Marxist doctrine of economic determinism is likewise a complex snarl of several issues. It is possible to formulate from Marx and from his successors two versions of this doctrine, which may be called, respectively, the stronger and the weaker. The first or stronger form asserts plainly and boldly that all social causation is or may be reduced to economic causation. The second or weaker form asserts with convenient ambiguity that economic causes set outer limits within which many other forms of social causation operate. Within these outer limits, innumerable economic and other noneconomic conditioning factors operate as part-causes of historical events. However, Marxists have an exasperating way of moving back and forth between these two formulations of their thesis. Pursued in one, they flee to the other. Both the weaker and the stronger interpretations are fully grounded in the writings of Marx and Engels, who also exhibit this same disconcerting ambiguity. While tactically there is a certain unconscious astuteness in this move, it can hardly be regarded as a contribution to human understanding.

Obviously, the influence of economic conditions upon all human affairs is pervasive and in some cases decisive; and as we have already observed, Marx may claim credit for having turned the spotlight of attention upon this fact. Yet Marx and Marxism do not receive high grades for the precise or accurate delineation of the nature and limits of this influence and its relation to other determinants. Distinctions betwen necessary and sufficient conditions, and between full-cause and part-cause, would be useful in correcting and clarifying Marxist philosophy at this crucial point.

The decisive criticism of economic determinism is the blunt fact that, useful as this hypothesis is in some circumstances, there are simply and plainly many human situations where other than economic factors are decisive. To cite a simple illustration, Marxists are fond of explaining nationalism in economic terms as a political façade for the economic interests of the ruling class. As this is being written, the suicidal and homicidal nationalism of Israelis and Arabs in the Near East makes daily news. It is clearly impossible to explain these phenomena wholly in economic terms. Indeed, in this as other cases, people are led to actions that are actually against their economic interests. Other illustrations will come readily to mind.

Another controversial aspect of economic determinism centers in the world, *determinism*. As a good nineteenth century scientific metaphysician, Marx insisted upon determinism as essential to scientific explanation. He believed that only a world in which all events are netted together in a web of causal sequences can be rational or scientifically explicable. Determinism was therefore for Marx as for Freud a kind of presupposition of scientific reason. Again, for Marx as for Freud, it was a presupposition that he believed to be borne out by factual investigation of the world. As we have seen, Marx found economic causes wherever he looked.

In passing, there is in Marx' philosophy a significant complication of this issue that recent scholarship has turned up. If we distinguish between the writings of Marx and Engels, as Avineri among others insists we must, the latter appears as more clearly and simply determinist in outlook than the former. Hence, the problems that plague determinism are much more clearly present for Engels than for Marx. In Marx' writings the issues of freedom and determinism are handled more carefully and more critically.

Nonetheless, we must assert against Avineri that there are still many passages in Marx' writings in which determinism appears to ride roughshod over freedom. Marx frequently declaims eloquently on the inevitablity or inexorability of historical events. With a stark Hegelian necessity, capitalism is said to move to its self-destruction and onward to its antithesis in socialism. But then Marx' language shifts to that of praise and blame, he chides the evil capitalists as oppressors and robbers, and praises the proletarians as history's heroes.[20] Clearly there is a contradiction here. If history moves with the kind of inexorable necessity so grandiloquently stated by Marx, the villains are not to be blamed for their villainy, and the heroes are not to be lauded for their virtue. Both are completely the creatures of their socioeconomic circumstances. If human events are adequately comprehended in this Marxian deterministic explanation, then freedom of choice of decision is an illusion. Similarly, with freedom goes responsibility; and with responsibility goes also the language of praise and blame, which is such a significant part of Marx' rhetoric and thought. Contrariwise, if freedom of choice and responsibility are real facts, then the kind of necessity asserted by Marx is to this extent mistaken.

To say this is by no means to deny the existence of other kinds and combinations of necessity and freedom. Quite the contrary, this is to call for a formulation of freedom and necessity in mutually compatible terms, for both freedom and necessity are real facts of human experience, calling for adequate analysis and understanding. Negatively stated, what we here assert is simply that Marx and his followers express a form of determinism that is incompatible with the freedom which they also presuppose, and that they seem blissfully unaware of this contradiction. Hence, they are firmly impaled on the horns of the dilemma of freedom and determinism.

(3) What shall we say in critical evaluation of the Marxian concept of ideology, especially as it applies to philosophy? There are close parallels here at many points to the Freudian concept of rationalization as discussed in the preceding chapter. In both cases there is the claim to have discovered a decisive element of interest or passion which influences or even completely determines the mind's distinctive activity of thinking. In the case of Freud, this interest is the compulsive, wishful force of the id, while in Marx the determining force is class interest. In both cases human reason is asserted to be the slave of subrational forces. In both cases, incidentally, the charge is pressed with greater vigor in the case of other people's thinking than in the case of one's own thinking. In the case of Marx, the concept of ideology as alienated consciousness, distorted and corrupted by economic interest, claims to be the conclusion of an extensive and detailed historical analysis of human society.

In assessing the Marxian concept of ideology, we recall the three assertions by which in the preceding chapter we sought to appraise Freudian rationalization. First, our human minds are finite or mortal, and therefore all our truths are relative or provisional in nature. It is because we "know in part" that all our achievements of knowledge are partial, and hence are forever subject to further study. Second, it is a matter of observable fact that our thinking is influenced by extrarational factors, instinctual drives as Freud insisted, and economic interests as Marx argued. Yet, third, this very apprehension of our finitude and of the interests that press upon us presupposes an awareness of a Truth that stands above the clash of interests and finite claims. Indeed, our awareness that we "know in part" necessarily presupposes a norm of Truth and Rationality above or beyond all our finitude and partiality.

In terms of this double awareness of Truth and truths, of Reason and reasons, we are able to do justice to the elements of important truth in the Marxist concept of ideology, without falling victim to its fallacious aspects. For example, in these terms I can at least begin to perceive that my thinking is influenced by the fact that I am a middle-class American, a university professor, and the like. Becoming aware of these factors, I can at least begin to cope with them, and press onward toward greater adequacy of thought.

From the viewpoint of this double awareness, as we argued in the preceding chapter, we are able to avoid two equal and opposite errors. One is the traditional rationalism that blissfully denies the existence of the powerful, nonrational forces that press upon our minds and pervasively influence our thinking. The observable fact is that no man, no party, no people is ever as simply rational as philosophic rationalism often supposes. Claims that this is so, even when made by Marxist groups, serve simply as a rational façade for interest. Whether a man looks within his own heart, or abroad at the strife of parties and systems, he cannot avoid the conclusion that there is an ideological taint in all thinking—including his own.

Yet the equal and opposite assertion that human thinking consists of "nothing but" rationalization is a curiously incoherent and illogical assertion. If this were so, we would not be able to recognize ideology as such. But the fact is that at least sometimes we do recognize it; and this seems necessarily to presuppose a kind of Archimedean point, above the clash of interests, which enables us to recognize ideological claims as such. As we argued in the preceding chapter, these ideological claims function in our mind's life much as conterfeiting does in the monetary system. It presupposes a standard of coinage.

The ambiguous human situation is then that we stand under a norm of Reason and Truth that we acknowledge, but which is not ours to possess or control. There is a kind of negative acknowledgement of this norm in the very concepts of rationalization and ideology as such. Our thinking is sustained and judged by this norm, all our achievements are directed toward this goal and measured by this standard. Otherwise, we would fall headlong into a self-stultifying relativism. By this double vision we perceive our limits and distortions as well as our achievements of rationality.

Attention must be called at least in passing to an all-important difference between Freud and Marx. Marx pointed eschatologically to the society of the future in which all the alienation and distortion of the present age will be overcome. No analogous fulfillment is discernible in the thought of Freud.

(4) What evaluation may reasonably be made of Marx' attack upon religion, and the continuing hostility of Marxism to all forms of traditional religion? It is hardly necessary to point out that along with charges of "materialism" and "atheism," this is a feature of Marxism that fuels the fires of professional anti-Communism in contemporary Western society, especially in America.

Yet, more thoughtful religious people have long been wary of being maneuvered into a stance in which they are always "for religion" and "against irreligion." From the days of the Hebrew prophets onward there has been a built-in principle of criticisim in the Judeo-Christian tradition, in terms of which the religious criticism of culture begins with the criticism of religion. The prophets' strictures upon the religion of their time, in the name of the Lord, were the first in a long prophetic tradition. While Marx would certainly have rejected this interpretation of his thought, there seems good ground for placing him in this prophetic tradition. In the name of justice and righteousness, Marx, like Amos and Isaiah and many others before him, denounced an immoral and unworthy religion. Let it be plainly and factually asserted that a very great deal of extant religion is precisely what Marx said it was, namely, the opiate of the people.

Granting this, the further question is whether this is all there is, whether in short Marx' description covers the whole of religion. Or is there rather a religion of justice and mercy and faith that eludes Marx' attack? If there is, and there clearly seems to be, then Marx' description is to that extent wrong and inadequate. Indeed, Marx' view of religion seems unable to explain the passionate sense of justice exhibited in his own writings.

His charges were also informed and guided by his philosophic naturalism which held that transcendent claims of every sort are false and misleading. However, if we find, as many philosophies of the past and present have found, some reasonable basis for such transcendent claims, then this part of Marx' argument also falls to the ground. For the moment it must suffice to call attention to this issue as one with which subsequent chapters will deal.

Finally, there is a powerful though unconscious strain of religious conviction that moves through Marx' philosophy and the Communist movement which stems from him. We shall turn in a moment to the characterization of this religious element in Marxism. Here let it be said that if this be granted, then Marxism's hostility toward traditional religion must be judged as the intolerance of a new and somewhat strident faith toward other older religions—a phenomenon for which there are many parallels in mankind's religious history.

Marxist Myth and Religion

Looking now at the Marxist system of thought as an integral whole, how shall we understand it? As its protagonists often claim, is it a scientific philosophy or even a science? It appears to commonsense observation to be a complex synthesis of many elements, of which we have been able to hint at only a few. It is sociology, economics, political theory, philosophy, and many more things. But underneath this complex structure lies a conviction very similar to that which in more traditional systems has found expression in myth and religion.

The word, *myth*, is used in so many variant ways that we must specify our present meaning. Sometimes *myth* is taken as synonymous with *fiction* or *untruth*. However, in our present usage we have in mind the great myth systems of the world, whether of the Greeks, the Hebrews, or the peoples of south or east Asia. These myths are systems of imaginative or poetic forms, usually narrative in character, by which man has sought to come to terms with his world. The terms of such myths are powerful images of a sort similar to the basic terms of poetry.

In the case of the Judeo-Christian or Biblical myth, one of its functions is a statement of the drama of history. In this respect the Biblical myth is the background of such books as St. Augustine's *City of God*. It is in this sense also that Judeo-Christian myth forms the background and the presupposition of Marxism.

In a word, Marxism is implicitly myth and religion, which is to say, myth and religion that do not recognize themselves as such. More specifically, it is a secularized version of the Biblical-Augustinian myth of history. Looked at in the wide perspective of the faiths and philosophies with which this book is concerned, Marxism may be accurately characterized as a Judeo-Christian heresy—or in other words a skewed, distorted version of the myth of history that underlies and informs Judaism and Christianity. Both the positive relation and the distortion may be seen by comparing the two renderings of the myth of history.

The Biblical-Augustinian version of the myth begins with the Garden of Eden and the Fall of Man, while the Marxist version begins with primitive communism as its Eden. The Marxist Fall may be said to have occured when the landlord and the soldier joined forces to subjugate and enslave the worker, thereafter living off his toil.

The plot of the drama of history in the traditional Judeo-Christian version of the myth of history is the interaction of the Lord God and his people, the latter interpreted first as Israel and then as mankind. In the Christian, as contrasted with the Jewish version, it rises to climax with the coming of Christ, and proceeds onward through church and world history to Judgment Day.

According to the contrasting Marxist version, the plot of this narrative is the historic struggle of the toiling masses of history against their successive oppressors and spoilers. The Marxist drama approaches its climax with the coming of industrial society, with its industrial proletariat (the messianic class), and with the coming of the Messiah (Marx). The proletarian revolution, which is the "final conflict," ushers in the New Age, which is at once the Marxist Kingdom of God and New Jerusalem.

The Marxist eschatology is clearly similar to that of millennialists throughout Jewish and Christian history. While it speaks a modern secular language, the emotions and attitudes of Marxism are similar to those of Jehovah's Witnesses and other such groups, ranging from the Biblical book of Revelation to the present day.

Several specific features of the Marxist myth may be briefly noted. In the wide perspective of the philosophies and faiths of the world as we seek to survey them in the course of this book, the historical character of the Marxist myth as well as its parent Biblical-Augustinian myth contrasts with the cosmic and a-cosmic myth systems of south and east Asia. As a consequence, Marxism burst upon these Asian cultures as something radically new. However, to the West it is only the most recent variation of the West's own mythical foundation.

We have called Marxism a Judeo-Christian heresy.[21] A heresy may be defined as a skewed or distorted version of the truth. The common truth here involved is the historical character of existence. From the orthodox viewpoint, one distortion of Marxism lies in its view of the nature of human evil (or sin) and its cure. The orthodox view of sin asserts that it is the arrogant pride of man by which he overreaches his creaturely status, seeking to be, as the Bible puts the matter, "as God." For Marxism, evil is rather to be understood as acquisitiveness or the lust for property, which presumably will be completely overcome in socialist society.

The radical difference between these two views of evil or sin may be seen by contrasting the ways in which human evil is dealt or coped with. The traditional Judeo-Christian view is that all men are sinners, and that therefore sin will infect every society. As a consequence, the orthodox Judeo-Christian traditions may be characterized as anti-Utopian. In sharpest contrast, the Marxist prediction of a perfect society must be placed in the tradition of Utopian thought and aspiration that has been such an important feature of the modern West. True, as Reinhold Niebuhr argued, the Marxists have been "hard" Utopians rather than "soft" Utopians.[22] They are hard alike in their cynically realistic appraisal of prerevolutionary society and in their fanatical devotion to revolution. Nevertheless, their dream of a perfect human society must be accounted soft or sentimental romanticism. Along with other forms of Utopianism, this illusory goal of a perfect society located somewhere in the human future functions to misguide action in the present.

In the preceding chapter we suggested that Freud's view of human existence might be compared to Greek tragedy. How shall we characterize Marx? What model or paradigm is appropriate for this view of the human situation? Is it not melodrama? In Marxism the Biblical and Augustinian drama of history becomes melodrama, with all the customary features, such as the division between good guys and bad guys, the overdramatic crisis in which the heroine in direst peril is rescued at the last moment by the hero, and they live happily ever after.

Yet, melodrama is always unconvincing as a depiction of the human situation. The audience goes wistfully away from the theatre reflecting that life is never quite like that. Why then is Marxism so convincing to so many people around the world? Why is it such a likely or plausible tale to so many people? Certainly it is not because of the overdrawn major plot of the drama, but rather because in a very great many detailed and down-to-earth ways, it seems the answer to the facts of human existence. And, in history, that seems sufficient justification for most persons for any faith or philosophy.

The religious quality of Marxist myth leads to one final observation. Professional anti-Communists, as well as many traditionally religious people, often join in diagnosing the evil of Communism as its "godless atheism." This diagnosis seems wide of the mark. In the first place, a closer look at human history shows that atheists are really not very dangerous people. In the rough and tumble of human history the skeptical attitude implied in this atheistic view is ineffective rather than dangerous. The danger of Communism is in reality quite the opposite of atheism; it is idolatry, which is not the absence of belief in God, but is rather the passionate attachment to a false god.[23] In another connection we have quoted Reinhold Niebuhr's aphorism that when man plays God, he becomes the devil to his fellowman. The Communist role in "playing God" has been eloquently depicted in Koestler's *Darkness at Noon*.[24] It is characteristic of a fanatical religion to produce the intolerance and savage cruelty to opponents that are the observable traits of "believing" Marxism in action. Communism, then, is not nonreligious, but is rather a new and fanatical religion. Far from being atheist, it is idolatrous in the precise sense of devotion to a false absolute. Its secular vesture does not successfully conceal its religious content.

SUGGESTIONS FOR FURTHER READING

As many of these works are classics that have appeared in numerous editions, only the most accessible publication is indicated.

Althusser, L. *For Marx*. London: Penguin Books, 1969.
Avineri, S. *Social and Political Thought of Marx*. New York: Cambridge University Press, 1962.
Bennett, J. *Christianity and Communism*. New York: Association Press, 1962.
Berlin, I. *Karl Marx His Life and Environment*. New York: Oxford University Press, 1963.
———. *Four Essays on Liberty*. New York: Oxford University Press, 1969.
Bloch, E. *A Philosophy of the Future*. New York: Herder & Herder, 1970.
Bottomore, T. *Karl Marx Early Writings*. London: Watts, 1965.
Bottomore, T., and Rubel, M. *Karl Marx*. Harmondsworth: Penguin Books, 1961.
Burns, E., ed. *A Handbook of Marxism*. New York: International Publishers, 1935.
Calvez, J. Y. *La Pensée de Karl Marx*. Paris: Seuil, 1956.
Easton, L., and Guddat, C. *Writings of Young Marx*. Garden City: Doubleday, 1967.
Feuer, L. *Marx and Engels*. Garden City: Doubleday, 1959.
Garaudy, R. *From Anathema to Dialogue*. New York: Herder & Herder, 1966.
———. *The Turning Point of Socialism*. London: Collins, 1970.
Hook, S. *From Hegel to Marx*. New York: Humanities Press, 1950.
Kellner, E., ed. *Christentum und Marxismus Heute*. Frankfurt: Europa, 1966.
Lichtheim, G. *Lukacs*. London: Collins, 1970.
Lukacs, G. *Existentialisme ou Marxisme*. Paris: Nagel, 1948.
Marcuse, H. *Reason and Revolution*. Boston: Beacon Press, 1960.
———. *One Dimensional Man*. Boston: Beacon Press, 1964.
Mehring, F. *Karl Marx*. New York: Covici Friede, 1935.
Mills, C. W. *The Marxists*. Harmondsworth: Penguin Books, 1963.
Sartre, J. P. *The Philosophy of Jean-Paul Sartre*. New York: Modern Library, 1966.

VIII
The Central
Tradition
of Indian
Philosophy

OUR STUDY so far has focused on philosophies originating in the modern and contemporary West. For the next four chapters we shall be dealing with non-Western philosophies, Indian, Chinese, and Japanese. Western people exhibit a curious ambivalence toward the Orient or "the mysterious East," as they sometimes label the great Asian civilizations. On the one hand there is uncritical adulation that expects to find the lost secret of life somewhere in this mysterious region. But, on the other hand, the arrogant parochialism of the West continues, despite protestations to the contrary, and more significantly, despite significant contemporary beginnings of good study. Consider such a fact as that among the innumerable books on the history of philosophy, only a very few (for example, those by Bertrand Russell and Will Jones) have the modesty and accuracy to insert the adjective "Western" before "philosophy."[1] Perhaps it is not wide of the mark to suggest that these two opposite attitudes toward Asia are two sides of the same coin. In both cases, what they lack is decent respect for the peoples of Asia combined with a genuine curiosity really to know them and their civilizations. This book is dedicated to the proposition that these are worthy and timely ideals.

As we embark on our Asian journey we must prepare to leave behind many of the familiar scenes and landscapes of Western thought and to prepare ourselves for new and unfamiliar sights. Of Indian, as of other non-Western traditions of philosophy, the question is often raised: But is this philosophy? For one thing, as we have previously noted, India never had an eighteenth century enlightenment with its massive secularization of Western thought and life. As a consequence, Indian philosophy and religion are still closely entwined in ways that puzzle and repel many contemporary Western philosophers. Moreover, Indian religion, in its endless variety and its stark unlikeness to the familiar forms of Western religion, is even more baffling to Western observers than is Indian philosophy.

Whether Indian philosophy is really philosophy or not will likely turn out to be either a merely verbal question on the one hand, or on the other hand, a further exercise in Occidental ethnocentrism that, in effect, denies the label philosophy to unfamilar—and to us, new—forms. In any event, we shall be content here to introduce the reader to these Asian forms of thought, and then let him decide the issue for himself.

Even the commonest terminology in this field is open to serious dispute. For example, the now familiar label of "East-West philosophy" is seriously defective in that it brings together under the rubric, "East," cultures as dissimilar as India and Japan, or India and China. For, as we shall see in the chapters that follow here, the central philosophic tradition of China is cosmic, while that of India is a-cosmic. In the former case, the world of nature and society constitutes the whole of reality, beyond which literally nothing real or significant exists. By contrast, the seers and philosophers of India's central tradition have looked continually beyond the world of nature and society to a transcendent realm or goal, in terms of which the everyday world is devalued.[2] This contrast between India and China has many significant observable implications. For example, asceticism is a very widespread Indian practice, while in China its absence is almost total. Another implication is the radical transformation of Buddhism, originally an a-cosmic Indian system of thought and devotion, when it interacted with the cosmic culture of China.

Further delimitation of our topic is necessary. This chapter is devoted to what we have labeled the central tradition of Indian philosophy, with only occasional glances at the many other diverging forms and traditions. However, it is important immediately to recognize that these many other forms did and do exist, even though we shall not be able here to deal with them. Even as delimited, our present task is difficult enough, involving as it does almost three thousand years of philosophic activity, as well as many concepts both unfamiliar and difficult to the Western student.

Beginnings

In the opinion of modern scholars, a people who called themselves Aryans (the word means "noble") pushed into northwest India from the plains of central Asia about the middle of the second millennium B.C. During the next five hundred to a thousand years they moved south and eastward, both conquering and in turn being conquered by India. Their first literature, the

Rig Veda, was probably complete by 1000 B.C., making it the world's oldest extant literature.[3] The 1,028 hymns of the *Rig Veda* are devoted to gods as many and various as the deities of the Olympian Greeks. In this populous Vedic pantheon, Varuna was a sky god, Agni was fire, Rudra was a capricious and sometimes malevolent Dionysian figure, Rita was cosmic order, and Indra was the hard-fighting, hard-drinking divine champion of these Aryan tribesmen. Many patterns of myth have been traced among these poems. Sacrificial ritual was the central and pervading theme. The tenth and last book of the *Rig Veda* is also characterized by the same sort of mythical approaches to philosophy that characterize Hesiod's writings in Greece. One of these ancient and anonymous poems, namely *Rig Veda* X, 129 is remarkable for its anticipation of the later course of Indian philosophy and hence is worth quotation in full:[4]

> Non-being then existed not nor being:
> There was no air, nor sky that is beyond it.
> What was concealed? Wherein? In whose protection?
> And was there deep unfathomable water?
> Death then existed not nor life immortal;
> Of neither night nor day was a token.
> By its own inherent force the One breathed windless:
> No other thing than that beyond existed.
> Darkness was at first by darkness hidden;
> Without distinctive marks this all was water.
> That which, becoming by the void was covered,
> That One Thing by force of heat that came into being.
> Desire entered the One in the beginning:
> It was the earliest seed of thought the product.
> The sages searching in their hearts with wisdom,
> Found out the bond of being in non-being.
> Their ray extended light across the darkness:
> But was the One above or was it under?
> Creative force was there, and fertile power:
> Below energy, above was impulse.
> Who knows for certain? Who shall declare it?
> Whence was it born, and whence came this creation?
> The gods were born after this world's creation:
> Then who can know from whence it has arisen?
> None knoweth whence creation has arisen;
> And whence he has or has not produced it:
> He who surveys it in the highest heaven,
> He only knows, or haply he may not know.

Many notable concepts lie hidden in the tightly packed lines of this ancient religious and philosophic poem. For example, the gods are asserted to be parts of the cosmos, in sharp contrast to the Biblical Creator of heaven and earth. Again, the closing lines express a bold skepticism. However, most notable of all is the concept of That One Thing (in the Vedic language, *tadekam*) which is asserted as the source or origin of all else. This is the first intimation of the Reality (later to be called *Brahman*) destined to dominate India's central philosophic tradition.

Also at least implicit here is *moksha* or man's salvation by emancipation from all finite, mortal bondage. It is impossible to say when this idea first found explicit articulation. Yet, as we shall presently see, it found varying expression in most of the philosophies of ancient India. We shall find different interpretations in the philosophies of Buddha and Mahavira, and later in this chapter in Hinduism.

Following these hints and suggestions of the *Rig Veda*, Indian philosophy came to its first full flowering in the seventh and sixth centuries B.C., during the historic period of the Eurasian continent that our chapter 1 called the Axis Age. By this time there had been civilized societies in Eurasia from Greece and Egypt in the West to China in the East for at least a millennium, and in some cases for two or three millennia. But, during the centuries of the Axis Age (roughly 700 to 400 B.C.) there were new stirrings of life in many of these civilizations, marked as we have seen, by the first clear emergence of individual selves upon the stage of human history. Strong men broke the tight hold of archaic civilizations upon the individual, and individual selfhood came to be. From the first philosophers of Greece and the prophets of Israel to Zoroaster, Buddha, Confucius, and Lao-tze, outstanding men asserted and lived out their individual destinies. It is by no means coincidence that most or many of these men were philosophers.

The new development was fostered by various sociopolitical causes and conditions, as, for example, in China the decay of the Chou dynasty, and in Greece and elsewhere the rise of the commercial classes. In India, older, smaller, and more democratic city-states were giving way to larger state systems.[5] Also in India the age was marked by a kind of world-weariness that led many men to the wilderness, there to practice asceticism and to meditate.[6]

The rise of philosophy in India, be it noted, was roughly contemporaneous with its first flowering in Greece; and in both cases it was marked by the vigorous growth of many diverse schools of thought. For example, when Siddhartha Gautama (later to be called the Buddha) set out on his celebrated seven years of philosophic search, he went successively to six philosophic teachers, namely an antinomian, a rigid determinist (whose sect, the Ajivakas, lasted on in India until the sixteenth century A.D.), a materialist, an atomist, an extreme ascetic who founded the Jain system, and a skeptic. To this list of schools of philosophy must be added, most importantly of all, the seers and metaphysicians of India's nascent central tradition who were also the authors of the *Upanishads*, as well as the Buddha's own subsequent and boldy original philosophy.[7] As we shall argue in the next chapter, Buddha was not only a religious founder but the author of a genuinely original and creative philosophy. It is too bad that this ancient flowering of philosophy is hidden from us in the mist that obscures so much else in ancient India. Adequate sources are simply not available for detailed historical study.

As just noted, prominent among these ancient Indian philosophers were the anonymous authors who composed the *Upanishads*. The word, *upanishad*, means "to sit apart"; and the image is that of a group of students gathered around a teacher or guru in the forest for discussion of the great themes of human existence. Their similarity to the dialogues of Plato has often been noted. There are well over a hundred *Upanishads*, but of this number some ten to fifteen are really important. The names of some of these are *Chandogya, Brhad-Aranyaka, Isha, Katha, Kena, Prashna, Mundaka,* and *Mandukya*. The earlier are in verse, and the later in prose. All seem to date from between 1000 and 500 B.C. For orthodox Hindus, they constitute together with the Vedic hymns and other documents called *Brahmanas* ("priestlies") and *Aranyakas* ("forest books"), the whole body of Vedic literature, and hence they are sacred scripture. The Hindu categories are *shruti* (namely that which is "heard" by the seers, and hence is holy scripture), and *smriti* (that which is "remembered," that is, a religious classic).

It is important to point out that the contents of the *Upanishads* express no single unified system of philosophic or religious doctrine. Rather, they contain a wide variety of teachings on every topic discussed. Yet, while there is no single system, there is nevertheless a major cluster of ideas, attitudes, and images that taken together does form a single viewpoint and, accordingly, constitutes the primary source of India's central philosophic tradition. At least six philosophic and religious themes are joined together in this single cluster; we shall discuss them briefly in turn.

(1) Brahman (etymologically, *bhr* means "to grow," or "spring forth") is the single absolute and self-subsistent reality underlying all things. We have already met it under the name of "That One Thing" (*tadekam*) of *Rig Veda* X, 129. Several metaphors are used to point to this reality. It is said to be one, it is said to be imperishable, it is the person or spirit (*purusha*) revealed in sun, moon, and all things, it is world-soul, it is word, wisdom, the root of

the tree, the salt which pervades the water, and many, many other things. It is also pertinent to note its similarity to Plato's Idea of the Good, and Absolute Beauty, or to Aristotle's Being-as-Such, Plotinus' One, or Hegel's Absolute Spirit. Still other interpretations of this One Supreme Reality await us in subsequent chapters of the present study.

In any of its innumerable guises, Brahman may be approached in either of two ways, negative or affirmative. To begin with the negative way, if we take any commonplace object and strip away successively all the predicates that make it this particular thing, when we have completed this task, only Being or Brahman remains. This, briefly stated, is the *via negativa*, the negative path, to the Absolute. However, we may take an opposite route to the same goal, beginning with the same commonplace object and adding one by one every other object that "is," "exists," or "has being." When we have amassed all such objects together, the defining feature of this unique logical class or set turns out, paradoxically enough, to be this same Being or Brahman.

(2) Still more significantly, this absolute reality can also be sought inwardly as well as outwardly. One may descend into the self, stripping away, one by one, all the particularizing attributes of oneself until, at the bottom of this deep well, one finds the *Universal Self* or *Atman*. Many of the Upanishadic seers regarded the Atman as a kind of inner absolute. The Atman is, to repeat, not the individual human self but rather the Universal Self, or universal form of selfhood, of which individual selves are mere passing illustrations.

(3) The climactic statement of the *Upanishads* is the identity of Brahman and Atman, or in the Sanskrit, *Tat tvam asi*, "that art thou." It means, briefly, that each individual self is a broken fragment of the Universal Self, which is then in turn asserted to be identical to the external Absolute or Brahman. We are all then parts of a single great Whole. Our highest destiny is to realize this and thus to be absorbed in Brahman, and hence from this supreme viewpoint also to see the unreality and evil of all that falls short of this One Absolute Reality. This recurring philosophical idea (which our chapter 2 termed the philosophy of unitive mysticism) has never been more clearly or eloquently expressed than by the seers of the *Upanishads*. From this ancient spring flows India's central philosophic tradition, which is the subject of this chapter.

Around this central cluster of ideas, several others group themselves. (4) To many men in the archaic world from Greece to China occurred the moral insight, "as you sow so shall you reap." The Indians called this insight *Karma*, the "law of the deed," and they made it an inflexible, inexorable and universal law. They also joined it to *Samsara*, which is "rebirth" or "transmigration." Thus *Karma-Samsara* came to mean that through endless cycles of existence man reaps the fruits of good and evil deeds. Small wonder the Indians envisaged bliss as escape from this never-ceasing wheel of existence.

(5) Man's destiny after death is the theme of several *Upanishads*, but is explored most fully in the *Katha Upanishad*. This document is a conversation between a young man named Nachiketas (about to be sacrificially killed by his father) with Yama, the god of the underworld. The latter is properly reticent concerning what lies beyond, but is led at length to say in effect that man's highest destiny after death is, once more, absorption in Brahman.

(6) The ethical implications of this outlook are strewn throughout the dialogues of the *Upanishads*, but they are admirably summarized at the end of the *Brhad Aranyaka Upanishad* in "What the thunder said" (which incidentally is the source of a famous passage in T. S. Eliot's *Wasteland*). Like much else in this and other *Upanishads*, it is in Sanskrit a wordplay, "*da da da*," pointing in pun to three verbs meaning "control or discipline yourselves," "give," and "be compassionate." From these three virtues have stemmed both the ethical theory and the moral practice of India's central philosophic tradition.

Several recent historians have emphasized that this monistic idealism of the *Upanishads*, as it is often characterized, has never completely dominated the field of Indian philosophy. Heinrich Zimmer, Ninian Smart, and others point to the fact that while the philosophy of the *Upanishads* is monist and idealist, there are other continuing strands of thought that are both realist and pluralist in outlook.[8] Of these differing views, Zimmer emphasized Jain philosophy (of which more in the next chapter). Indeed, among the six orthodox Hindu philosophies four are, as we shall soon see, realist and pluralist in outlook, hence in varying degrees of disagreement with the central tradition.[9] There is thus a great deal of continuing diversity in Indian philosophy, superficial appearances to the contrary notwithstanding.

Growth continued during the centuries that immediately followed the completion of the *Upanishads*, roughly 500 B.C. to A.D. 1. About the beginning of the second century B.C. a sage named Badarayana summarized in his *Brahma Sutras* (also called the *Vedanta Sutras*) the cluster of ideas from the *Upanishads* to which we have just called attention. *Sutra* means literally "a thread," and the Indian texts or documents called by this name consist of aphoristic written summaries of statements intended to be elaborated in oral discussion and reflection. Badarayana's *Brahma Sutras* was an essential historical link in the development of India's central philosophic tradition.

From approximately the same period of ancient Indian history came two other highly significant documents, the *Manu Shastra* (which means "the law code of Manu," who was the Adam as well as the Moses and Noah of the Indian tradition) and the *Bhagavad Gita*. The former is still the authoritative law code of orthodox Hindu life and worship. While caste is mentioned in earlier sources, it is here fully acknowledged and considerably elaborated. In the code of Manu, the reader sees Hinduism taking shape or assuming its recognizable historical forms. In the Manu code is the characteristically Hindu idea of the four *ashramas* or stages on life's way: that of the student, the householder, the holy seeker, and the emancipated one. A man begins as a student of religion under a guru, then graduates to the role of householder. Having performed the duties of these first two stages, he is then free to become a wandering ascetic seeking the final stage of salvation or emancipation. If he succeeds in his quest, he becomes a *sanyasin* or one emancipated from all mortal bondage. Hinduism, as it developed, prescribed duties and fulfillments for each stage. Characteristically there is in Hinduism something for everybody and for every stage of life.

From this same period came also the idea of the four ends of man (*caturvarga*), which are respectively, *dharma, kama, artha,* and *moksha*. The first, dharma, is righteousness or good moral conduct, according to the best standards of Indian society. Dharma stands in contrast though not in conflict to the second, kama. *Kama* means "desire" or "love," and like the Greek *Eros* is both a common noun and the proper name of a god. In both cases the gods preside over the wide ranges of human experience ranging from wide varieties of sexual experience to highly idealized or sublimated forms of desire and aspiration. In India the *Kama Sutra* is a gentleman's guide to the varieties of sexual experience. But kama also extends to the highest reaches of idealized aesthetic experience in the arts, thus in effect both legitimizing and integrating this whole domain.

Artha, by contrast, means "material advantage" and includes both political and economic power. Americans might plausibly translate it as "success." Its ethos was of course traditional Indian society. Artha, so conceived, is the subject of the *Artha Shastra*, a document often attributed to Kautilya, chief minister of Chandragupta Maurya of the fourth century B.C. In a manner strikingly similar to Machiavelli, it deals in cynically realistic fashion with the methods and issues of wielding political and economic power. Zimmer classifies it as a philosophy of "time" rather than of "eternity," of the city of this world rather than of the heavenly city. Hence it provides clear demonstration that India's social thought is not as world-denying as some Western students have supposed.

The fourth and highest end of man is moksha, or emancipation from all mortal bondage. As we have seen, this goal is intimated in *Rig Veda* X, 129, and more clearly in the *Upanishads*, and is spelled out in detail in subsequent Indian thought. For many Western readers it is a baffling and unworldly ideal, for as Zimmer has remarked, virtually all the traits and values of individual personality (which the modern West cherishes as supreme goods) are here treated as fetters or chains of mortal bondage.[10] In varying ways this traditional Indian ideal tells mankind that finitude or mortality constitutes enslavement. If one wishes to be truly free, he must by intellectual vision and practical discipline of life, emancipate himself from the prison house that is the world. With varying interpretations and emphases this conception of human emancipation has dominated traditional Indian thought from its inception to the present.

Perhaps one way to make this difficult and strange idea clear to the twentieth century West is to contrast it with the dominant Western view of freedom as self-determination in action. I am free, says Western man, when I am rid of external fetters and also have met the inward prerequisites for an active life in which I am autonomous or self-determining, in which, in a word, I make my own choices and live my own life. No, says the ancient Indian, this is not yet full and true emancipation. The full ideal of freedom will not be achieved until I have literally transcended all mortal limitations, attaining oneness with Absolute Reality.

The difference can also be seen in the traditional religious ideals of final fulfillment in India and the West. Judaism and Christianity speak of a life in heaven where good men still as individual persons live in blessed communion with their Maker. Hindus and Buddhists look forward to an exalted state where all individual existence is completely transcended. What is empirically involved in this difference may perhaps be expressed as contrasting and conflicting valuations placed upon human individuality. Indians conceive of individual existence as something to be transcended, while Jews and Christians value it highly enough to think of the next world in individual terms. Truly, what men profess about the hereafter often provides important clues for their values concerning the here-in.

Undoubtedly the most important document of the later centuries B.C. in India is the *Bhagavad Gita*.[11] Originally a part of the great epic called the *Mahabharata* (the Indian *Iliad*), it has had for many centuries its own independent existence, and is clearly the most widely read and influential of India's religious writings. It is primarily a religious or devotional classic; but in India in contrast to the West this does not preclude philosophical implications of the highest importance as well. In a word, the genius of the *Gita* is a synoptic unity of outlook, such that everything previous to it seems to flow into it, and most that is subsequent flows out of it. In this feature of the *Gita* we also correctly observe an important trait of the Indian mind, namely an unwillingness to exclude anything, and a corresponding desire to include literally everything in a single synoptic and comprehensive outlook. It is as though the Indians had deliberately repealed Aristotle's three laws of thought, namely, identity, noncontradiction, and excluded middle. Hence, each thing is not only what it is, but shades imperceptibly into what it is not. Likewise, there are no complete and final exclusions or contradictions, but rather continuity extending unbroken over all that is or appears to be. Anyone who has gazed at the façade of a south Indian temple, crammed as it is with sculpture over its entire surface, and then compared this to the simple rational outlines of the Athenian Parthenon, will at least begin to understand this quality of Indian thought.

The *Gita* is a Sanskrit poem of eighteen chapters, having the form of a conversation between the warrior, Arjuna, and his charioteer, who turns out to be the god, Krishna. Arjuna, summoned to fight in the impending battle (which is the climax of the *Mahabharata*), suddenly feels pacifist scruples, or compunctions about the carnage and evil consequences of war. Krishna persuades him in the end to do his warrior's caste duty; but in the course of the argument he also manages to touch upon most of the themes of God, man, and man's well being. Drawn into the fabric of the *Gita* are at least five important threads of Indian philosophic and religious thought: (1) Upanishadic monism, (2) Vedic ritual, (3) Sankhya-yoga, (4) Buddhism and, (5) most important and characteristic of the *Gita*, namely *bhakti*, which is the devotional and theistic relation of lord and devotee. All are woven together into a remarkable unity of outlook.

(1) The first thread, namely, what we have called Upanishadic monism, is simply but plainly present in the background as a kind of widely acknowledged assumption concerning man's chief end as emancipation or moksha. (2) The second, namely Vedic sacrificial ritual, finds expression as a kind of abstract allegorization of the Vedic ritual relation of gods to man. This is interesting for its contrast to Greek religio-philosophic development. For in Greece the philosophers mounted a critical attack upon Greek religion, often radical in its aim and spirit. This attack, which came to its climax in the Sophists and in such documents as Plato's *Republic*, contributed to the markedly secular atmosphere of Greek society. For such trends there are virtually no parallels in India. Instead of attacking popular polytheism, Indian philosophy allegorized it under the Vedic maxim, "Reality is one but the sages speak of it in many ways." This has enabled monistic Indian

philosophy to live in apparent harmony with a still luxuriant popular polytheism, as indeed it does in the *Bhagavad Gita*.

(3) The philosophy of the *Gita* is by no means limited to monistic Vedantism, as the main philosophy of the *Upanishads* came traditionally to be labeled. As we shall see in the next section of this chapter, the Sankhya and Yoga systems, at first separated and then joined together, enjoyed a long and independent career in ancient Indian philosophical history. Here it must suffice to note that the many passages in the *Gita* alluding to yogic practice, to matter-spirit dualism alike in man and the universe or to the repeating cycles of history, all probably originated with Sankhya-Yoga philosophy.

(4) Buddhist influence is more controversial, but several references in the *Gita* to ascetic practices and meditation in order to achieve the enlightenment of nirvana sound too much like Buddha's philosophy to deny a high probability to this source.[12] If this is so, it means that the *Gita* provides illustration of the recurring Hindu strategy of meeting competition by incorporating large elements of the opposition in one's own thought. The Lord Buddha contended for many centuries with Krishna, Shiva, and many others for the allegiance of Indian minds and hearts. The eventual reabsorption of Indian Buddhism by Hinduism seems clearly foreshadowed by the treatment of Buddhist teaching in the *Gita*.

(5) Clearly, on any reading the dominant theme of the *Gita* is the personal and devotional relation of Lord Krishna to his devotee, Arjuna. Such devotional thought or bhakti is present in documents that are many centuries older than the *Gita*, but in Indian history the *Gita* is its major source and greatest inspiration. The climax of the *Gita* occurs in Books XI and XII in which Arjuna asks for a convincing manifestation of Krishna; the response comes in an awe-inspiring theophany which in turn elicits from Arjuna an attitude of complete faith, love and devotion. As we shall see, this type of religious thought and devotion constitutes in Indian history a kind of foil for Advaita Vedantism; it has had important illustrations and consequences from that day to this.

Taken as a whole, the *Gita* teaches the three *margas* or "alternative paths to salvation," that of works, of knowledge, and of devotion. The first or karma marga had been traditionally the path of ritual works, but the *Gita* transforms it into a combination of ritual and moral works, and adds the significant and creative ethical notion of disinterested action, or, stated in the *Gita*'s own metaphor, of action without regard for the fruits of action.[13] The path of knowledge, or *jnana marga*, consists not of ordinary secular knowledge, but rather of that intuitive philosophic vision of Reality which, experienced existentially, is sufficient to achieve emancipation. Yet in the view of the *Gita* this is a hard path, to be trodden by only a chosen few who have strength, competence, and time to endure and to practice its rigors.[14]

For the *Gita*, clearly the best path is that of devotion, or bhakti marga, which consists of the passionate love of the human heart given in response to the grace of a personal Lord or *Ishvara*. This preference is woven into the structure of the poem. In chapter VII, 4–7 Krishna tells Arjuna that he, Krishna, has a lower and a higher nature, a distinction that in course of explanation turns out to be similar to the relation of God and nature in Western thought. The "higher nature" is Krishna's personal lordship, and the "lower nature" becomes the universe over which this lord holds sway. Krishna's personal nature grows from this point onward, reaching its climax in the magnificent theophany of chapter XI, which is also the climax of the poem.[15] Here Krishna reveals himself to be the lord of all creation, and Arjuna responds appropriately with an attitude of loving devotion or personal faith. So it is that bhakti or personal devotion to a deity established itself in Indian thought as a way of salvation.

For Arjuna, as for countless Indians before and since, the personal Lord is Krishna; yet Hinduism has always offered its adherents the widest possible choice in deities. Any such choice, sincerely and wholeheartedly followed, suffices for salvation both here and hereafter. Among the many paths to the One Reality, the devotional path of the *Gita* has had wide and long influence in Indian history. Contrasted with the paths of work and of knowledge, devotion is a popular way. The shopkeeper or tradesman who has neither time nor aptitude for the other two ways, can carry within his heart as he goes about his daily work the love of a personal Lord.

Hindu Philosophies

As we have seen, the last centuries B.C. and the first centuries A.D. marked the emergence of what is popularly termed Hinduism. The English term is modern (first used in 1834), and is largely Western in use as well as in origin. This means that most Hindus in human history have not known or called themselves by this name. Furthermore, the word itself is apparently a Persian mispronunciation of the name, Sind, for the region and river now known as Indus. Such is the checkered history of the word that is widely used to stand for the central tradition of Indian religious thought and practice. Hinduism is a way of both philosophic thought and religious practice. While our interest centers in the former, we must not forget that this has always existed in close and vital relation to the latter.

Crucial to the emergence of Hinduism was the concomitant rise and spread of Buddhism. Buddha's movement was at first simply one more ancient Indian brotherhood of monks, like so many others of that time and place. There was, at first, much in Buddha's way that all Indians might and subsequently did affirm. But there was controversy as well. Hindus came at length to label Buddhism along with Jainism and Carvaka or Indian materialism as "heterodox" or "heretical." All three denied the authority of the Vedas. For Buddha this involved (as we shall see in the next chapter) his opposition to caste. His brotherhood of monks was open to all castes. Increasingly, Lord Buddha was a strain on the catholicity and tolerance of the ancient Indian spirit. Religiously he seemed à rival to Shiva and Vishnu for the allegiance of man's heart. Philosophically such Buddhist systems as that of Nagarjuna were attacked by orthodox Hindu thinkers as both negative and escapist.

Out of this centuries-long process of argument and discussion emerged the six orthodox Hindu philosophies or *darshanas*. The criterion for "orthodoxy" was, again, the acceptance of the authority of the *Vedas*, including caste. The word *darshana*, often used as a Sanskrit and Hindi translation of the Greek term, "philosophy," is from the Sanskrit verb, *drsh*, meaning "to see." Hence it is literally and etymologically a perspective or viewpoint. These six orthodox viewpoints all had independent origins, and in varying degrees also independent existences. However, in the course of Indian history they have all tended to be drawn into a single tradition under the domination of the sixth way, Vedantism. Hence, in modern times, they appear as elements of a single tradition, or more precisely, as different strands of a single rope.

The six orthodox darshanas are (1) *Nyaya* (Logic), (2) *Vaisheshika* (Atomism), (3) *Sankhya* (Distinctionism), (4) *Yoga*, (5) *Mimamsa* (Exegesis) and, (6) *Vedanta*.[16] Tradition has also tended to group the first two and the second two in pairs. As we have previously noted, these two pairs, or all of the first four philosophies, are realist and pluralist in outlook, and thus, according to the hypothesis of Heinrich Zimmer, are related to the ancient pre-Aryan past of India rather than to the Aryans and their Vedic literature. As we have already noted, Zimmer, and after him Ninian Smart, assert two source regions of Indian philosophical thought, one going back to the remote pre-Aryan past and the other originating with the Vedic Aryans. The former is realist and pluralist in outlook, and the latter is idealist and monist. The fifth and sixth darshanas are clearly Vedic in origin, though different from each other in their interpretation and use of Vedic thought. The fifth has maintained a kind of solitary and separate identity, and the sixth has established itself as India's central philosophic tradition. It represents the culmination of the monist and idealist thought of the *Upanishads*.

(1) The first, *Nyaya*, is traditional Indian logic. The word *Nyaya* means literally "justice," but here the meaning is justice in inference or in reasoning processes. Originating in the *Nyaya Sutras* of Gautama of the third century B.C., Nyaya consists of an analysis of reasoning processes, which parallels Greek logic in some respects, though it contrasts in others. Significantly the *Nyaya Sutra* offers its logical knowledge as a means to "supreme felicity," that is, to salvation or emancipation. It specifies four ways to knowledge, namely, perception, inference, comparison or analogy, and word or verbal testimony. These four ways have been accepted by all Indian philosophers except the Carvakas or materialists who characteristically accept only sense perception as a valid basis for knowledge. Buddhist and Jain philosophies also developed their own distinctive and contrasting types of logical analysis. Nyaya also features a five-part syllogism, in contrast to Aristotle's three-part formulation. First is the proposition to be established, as, Socrates is mortal. Second is the reason, namely, because he is a man. Third is the universal connection plus illustration, namely, whatever is man is mortal, for example, John, George. Fourth is the application, so also Socrates. Fifth is the conclusion, Socrates is mortal. Compared with Western logic, the reader will note the verbosity of this Indian formulation. Nyaya also lists many different kinds of fallacies and debater's devices, both valid and invalid, for the student's consideration and use.

(2) Tradition has paired the Logic School with Vaisheshika or Atomism. The term *Vaisheshika* means "particularity," hence, Atomism. This school propounded an atomic theory of matter at a historical period roughly contemporaneous with the first Greek atomic theory. It also displayed a penchant for analyzing everything into lists of irreducible and particular elements. Thus, for example, there are four different kinds of atoms, namely, earth, water, fire, and air. There are initially seven categories of existence, namely, substance, quality, activity, generality, particularity, inherence, and nonexistence; but these are in turn reducible to three, namely substance, quality, and activity, corresponding to the nouns, adjectives, and verbs of the Sanskrit language. There is likewise an irreducible plurality of human souls, each of which is asserted to possess a substantive and eternal reality. Otherwise, asks this school, how could karma be meted out to each individual? In passing, all traditional Indian philosophies except Buddhism and materialism agree in asserting the eternity of selfhood or spirit, in either pluralistic or monistic terms.

In Indian history the atomist school has provided a realist and pluralist metaphysics to accompany Nyaya logic. Some scholars have argued that originally Atomism was atheistic or nontheistic; but however this may have been, in their traditional formulation, both Logic and Atomism argue for God as the Prime Mover of the world. They use this argument for God, incidentally, alone among Indian philosophies—and virtually alone outside the monotheistic religious traditions of Judaism, Christianity, and Islam.

(3) *Sankhya* and *Yoga*, while originally separate, have also long been paired together by tradition, Sankhya supplying the metaphysics, and Yoga the practice. The word *Sankhya* means "discrimination," that is, between matter and spirit; and the system turns upon the primary distinction between matter (*Prakrti*) and Spirit (*Purusha*), both in the universe at large and in the individual human soul. The individual person in turn achieves his emancipation by distinguishing existentially, or in his own life, between matter and spirit. Indeed, the real or true self is by definition eternally free. Hence, the task of actual selfhood is to achieve a realization of this fact, thus liberating oneself from the delusory appearances of matter. These appearances, however, are extremely persistent, and Sankhya offers a subtle analysis of them. Within the individual self or soul, Spirit (Purusha) forgets its true nature and becomes involved with matter (Prakrti); and this combination results in the three gunas or constituents of selfhood. These are, respectively, *sattva, rajas,* and *tamas.* The first is the element of light and truth, the second is the passionate or spirited element, and the third is the heavy dark element of spiritual inertia. Readers familiar with Plato's philosophy will note a similarity to his analysis of the self in the allegory of two steeds and charioteer. In the Sankhya philosophy the aim is to rise by knowledge and discipline, through the three gunas to a point transcending them all, thence to emancipation or moksha.

The interplay of spirit and matter in the universe at large leads, indeed, to the step-by-step emergence or development of the empirical universe. We dare not call this process evolution, though it has sometimes been likened to Western philosophies of evolution. For, in the first place, in terms of its own value system, it is not evolution or progress, but rather devolution or regress. In the second place, it happens not just once, but in endlessly repeating cycles or pulses. These repeating cycles constitute what, from a human viewpoint, seem exceedingly vast eons or ages of time.

Nature, matter, or Prakrti is by itself inert, according to Sankhya; but the attractive power or Purusha stirs it to action. Once this action begins, it moves through a cycle of differentiation and development that yields the universe as this appears or presents itself to human minds. It also yields individual selves or egos. However, in many of the turgid pages of this philosophy it is utterly impossible to see clearly whether it is the universe or the individual ego whose development is being described. But this is perhaps inevitable in a philosophy that correlates the development of microcosm and macrocosm. In the concept of Prakrti, Sankhya speaks for all traditional Indian philosophy; it says that the beginningless and endless world is simply and plainly *there*. We will also find an analogous idea in Chinese philosophy. Aristotle's world is similarly eternal.

(4) The avowed aim of this combined cosmology and psychology is, once more, emancipation. While *Sankhya* provides the philosophical basis, *yoga* contributes the practical discipline. The word *yoga* means "yoke," though in Sanskrit this term has a perplexing variety of meanings and connotations ranging from "that which joins together" to "that which is to be endured." Yoga came also to mean any path to emancipation whether trodden by philosophic and religious insight, by rigorous disciplining of the body or a combination of both. The *Yoga Sutras* of Patanjali, of the second century B.C. are the classical source for Yoga philosophy and practice. The *Hatha yoga* tradition has emphasized physical exercise and discipline. While their sources and early existence were apparently independent, Yoga was subsequently joined to Sankhya philosophy, and then in the course of later centuries both were largely absorbed by Vedanta. With many variations and emphases it provides an eightfold path to salvation—or should one say an eight-rung ladder to emancipation? The eight steps as outlined by Patanjali are as follows: (1) *yama* or general moral discipline, (2) *niyama*, advanced or ascetic discipline, (3) *asana*, bodily exercises and postures, (4) *pranayama* or breath control, (5) *pratyahara*, withdrawal of senses to within the self, (6) *dharana* or concentration, (7) *dhyana*, meditation and, (8) *samadhi* or emancipation.

In a general way these steps provide a practical way or path to the liberation or moksha described philosophically by Sankhya. We shall also see in the next chapter how similar this way is to Buddhist meditation. Even more generally, we observe here in *Sankhya-yoga* one more distinctive formulation of what chapter 2 called mystical experience and philosophy. We have also noted Sankhya-yoga as a major philosophic influence upon the *Bhagavad Gita*.

(5) *Mimamsa* or exegesis stands alone among orthodox Indian philosophies; the word means "explication" or "exegesis of a text"; in this case, of the Vedic literature, which Jaimini, the fifth century B.C. founder of the school, held to be absolutely inspired and inerrant. It is interesting to find

this example of religious literalism (called in Protestant Christianity "fundamentalism") in the Indian tradition. So absolute, indeed, is the authority of the Vedas for this school that it denies the existence of God who wrote them or is above them, for such a divine being would derogate from these sacred scriptures. Therefore, there must accordingly be no God. Mimamsa is, in other words, atheistic fundamentalism.

It does contain an interesting and sophisticated theory of words, which a Western reader might label as Platonic realism. These meanings subsist independently of human perception and use. Furthermore, Mimamsa teaches that man's apprehension of meaning and truth is necessarily and inherently valid, the model being a faithful reading of Vedic literature, which, a priori, is absolutely true. From all of this it is concluded that, since true cognition as such is ipso facto valid or true, only falsity need be explained or established by argument. Other Indian schools have drawn upon Mimamsa's analysis of meaning and truth.

As we shall see in a later section of this chapter, Mimamsa has had a significant revival in nineteenth and twentieth century India due largely to the work of Swami Dayananda Sarasvati and the Arya Samaj which he founded. Dayananda led a "back to the Vedas" movement in Hinduism, which also combined militantly anti-Western and anti-Christian elements. Jaimini's Exegesis school of philosophy continues to find ready acceptance in the cultural-nationalism of Dayananda's many followers in twentieth century India.

Vedantism

(6) The sixth orthodox system is called *Vedanta*, which means "end," "fulfillment," or "realization" of the Vedas. It is thus the fulfillment of the line of thought that began in the *Upanishads* and led through Badarayana onward to such classical expositors as Shankara and Ramanuja. It is also called *Uttara Mimamsa*, which may be freely translated as "higher criticism," that is, of the Vedic literature. This is in contrast to Jaimini's *Purva Mimamsa* which in Western textual terms is "lower criticism" of the same Vedic literature.

The form of this philosophy has consisted largely in commentaries on Badarayana's *Brahma Sutras*, which by this time had become virtually a sacred text. The phenomenon of doing philosophy as a commentary on a sacred text is by no means limited to the Indian tradition. Students in the history of Western philosophy know that Thomas Aquinas and his fellow scholastics of the Middle Ages of Europe elaborated their comprehensive systems as commentaries on the texts of the Bible and the church fathers. This way of philosophizing by commenting on a sacred text has also had other notable exemplifications, as we shall presently see, in Judaism, in Islam, and in the Confucian tradition of China.

Among the twelve classical or traditional commentaries on the *Vedanta Sutras*, that of Shankara has long held first place. While the lore surrounding this great man is extensive, few facts concerning his life can be indisputably pinned down. Even his dates are debated, though A.D. 788–820 seem most probable. He was a south Indian, who managed to crowd into his brief thirty-two years of life several careers, as ascetic, monastic reformer, scholar, devotional poet, and greatest of all, philosopher. His *Advaita Vedanta* system stands not only as the definitive formulation of India's central philosophical tradition but as one of the great metaphysical systems of the world's history.

A great many texts, some of them undoubtedly spurious, have been attribued to Shankara. He was, however, in all probability the author of devotional poems to Shiva which combined his own devotion to Lord Shiva with his underlying austerely monistic metaphysics. His *Crest Jewel of Discrimination* (in Sanskrit *Vivekachudamani*) is an admirable summary of his philosophical and mystical vision.[17] So also in his *Atmabodha*, translated as "Self Knowledge" (though the Western reader soon discovers that it is intuitive or mystical knowledge of the single transcendental, or absolute self, which is referred to—not one's own individual human self).[18] Shankara also wrote scholarly commentaries on the sacred documents of Indian thought including many principal *Upanishads* and the *Bhagavad Gita*. His rendition of the latter is still accepted by scholars as the standard text. However, Shankara's most important philosophical writing was his commentary on the *Brahma Sutras* or *Vedanta Sutras* of Badaranya.

Shankara's method turns upon the two terms, namely, "superimposition" (*adhyasa*) and "discrimination" (*viveka*). The former means both literally and logically the attribution of a predicate to a subject. But for a philosophical monist like Shankara, it carried the additional meaning of predicating something unreal of something real, that is, of Brahman. Hence superimposition means the attribution of finite and false mortal predicates to Brahman. The Sanskrit words *adhyasa* and *adhyaropa* derive from terms for the flattering language of eulogy addressed by poets to kings or by lovers to their mistresses. From the viewpoint of Absolute Reality (which Shankara was convinced he held), such attribution is ultimately false and must be stripped away. The process of stripping away successively these false predicates is the philosophical task of discrimination (viveka), at the end of which lies the crest jewel of wisdom, or as Shankara's title puts it, of discrimination. As to this crest or crown jewel, the source of the metaphor is the widely recurring story of the jewel that a man seeks all over the world only to find it has been around his own neck the whole time. The Great Identity of Brahman and Atman is this crest jewel, declared Shankara.

For Shankara, Reality is Brahman and Brahman is Reality. Beside this there is only *maya* or the illusion of finitude. Brahman is simply and plainly self-subsistent reality. Of the apparently real things in our empirical world, it is invariably true that they are caused by something else. If, then, we strip away these false causes, what is left is self-caused Being. Similarly, Shankara strips away time and change, and hence derives timeless eternity as a further trait of Brahman. That this Brahman is the origin or cause of the world of appearances appears less immediately obvious. As he develops this line of thought, Shankara appears to rely upon the metaphor of a self and its manifestations in action; and we add that in Shankara's valuation, action is lower and less real than contemplative vision. Of Brahman we can say simply that it absolutely and supremely *is*. From this *is*ness or being flow all its other characteristics, its unity, its truth, its supremacy. As such, it is the good and goal of all human striving. Human philosophy has seldom in all of mankind's history contructed as uncompromising a monism as Shankara's.

To the devotional religion that Shankara himself cherished, he conceded philosophically only a qualified reality and virtue. His formulation was *saguna Brahman* and *nirguna Brahman*, or Brahman with qualities or Brahman without qualities.[19] Among the qualities of Brahman are those that constitute an *Ishvara* or personal Lord (in Shankara's case, Lord Shiva, to whom he wrote excellent devotional poetry with all the fervor of the *Bhagavad Gita*). But Shankara, the philosopher, grasped this nettle firmly and asserted that above, beyond, and more real than saguna Brahman is nirguna Brahman, or the Absolute Reality in which we truly live and move and have our being. From this highest viewpoint of all, a personal God and personal religion are to be understood simply as concessions to human frailty and finitude.

Beyond Brahman is only maya, the illusion of finite existence. The word *maya* is from the verb *ma* meaning both "make" and "measure." In Indian thought before Shankara it had meant such various things as a god's power to act and to get things done, or the divine making of the world or of special objects in the world. But successive generations of unworldly philosophical reflection had devalued the everyday world and all things within it as a whole. A key thinker in this long process had been the Buddhist philosopher Nagarjuna who, during the second century A.D., taught that all things are *shunya* or "emptiness." We shall consider him in the next chapter. Shankara criticized Nagarjuna in particular and Buddhism generally as escapist, but his writings show that he was more influenced by them than he either admitted or knew.

Shankara uses several metaphors to depict the highly qualified and deficient reality he accords to maya. It is, he says, the sport or play of Brahman, thus denying it the serious reality of work. Or, it is like the mistaken perception which imagines that the rope is a snake. Again, it is like the conjurer's trick. Shankara is explicit in his assertion that the empirical everyday world has its proper measure of empirical, everyday reality. As long as we live and act on this level we properly regard it as real. There are, in short, two kinds of truth, everyday truth and transcendental truth. Only as we come to see this world *subspecie* Brahman do we perceive its "unreality," or delusory appearance.

An issue of some importance to twentieth century Western philosophy concerns the precise meaning or interpretation to be given such assertions of the "unreality" of the world. It is an interesting fact that some forms of nineteenth century Western philosophic idealism made assertions strikingly similar to that of Shankara, labeling the world as "mere appearance." Many twentieth century philosophers arose in protest and in defense of the everyday world. For example, G. E. Moore wrote celebrated papers "in defense of common sense," in "refutation of idealism," and specifically, in "proof of the external world."[20]

A careful reading of Shankara can help in appraising or reappraising this issue. For one thing, as we have seen, Shankara does not deny the existence of the world of appearance if we take our stand on the level of everyday experience. Hence, Moore's strictures lose their force if aimed at Shankara. It is only when a man takes the viewpoint of transcendent truth that he comes to see the "unreality" of the world. Furthermore, stated in twentieth century terms, what seems involved here is not the flat, factual nonexistence, but rather the *devaluation* of the everyday world. Shankara's Vedantism, like classical Western Platonism, holds to a union of fact and value, or of being and goodness with the corollary concept of degrees of being or fullness of being. According to this philosophy, whether in its Indian or Western form, Being is one, good and true. *Ens est unum, bonum, verum*. From such a viewpoint, devaluation entails relative nonexistence, and vice versa.

For Shankara and his tradition of Advaita Vedanta, the vision of Brahman produces emancipation, for the good reason that it destroys the illusion of separate, finite existence. Once avidya or ignorance is destroyed, the mind's gaze turns to its proper object and it is absorbed first figuratively then literally in this supreme object. This and this alone is man's chief end and supreme good. This is all and enough.

This may have been all and enough for Shankara, but it was neither for some of his readers and critics. Chief among these was Ramanuja (b. 1038) who wrote into his commentary on the *Vedanta Sutra* drastic criticisms of Shankara's monism. There is, he argued, no adequate proof of Shankara's Great Unity. In the manner of a modern analytic philosopher, he argued that speech and perception are sufficient evidence to show the reality of concrete and differentiated entities. Otherwise, how would ordinary nouns and verbs have arisen? Consciousness furthermore is not a single universal system, but rather is an attribute of limited conscious selves.[21] What is more important, such limited conscious subjects persist into the hereafter, where the state of released souls is one of participation in Brahman rather than of total absorption. Ramanuja's view was notably closer to Judeo-Christian theism than was Shankara's monism. Ramanuja himself was a devotee of Vishnu; and the continuing tradition of his followers has emphasized active and devotional elements against the stark monistic vision of Shankara. As we have seen, this tradition originates in the *Bhagavad Gita*, extends through Ramanuja who wrote a notable commentary on the *Gita*, down to contemporary Indian philosophers.

Other critics, such as Madhva (1197–1276), were even more radical than Ramanuja in their attacks upon Shankara's monism. Yet none of his traditional critics has equaled the influence of Shankara, nor the architectonic and comprehensive unity of his philosophical system.

Modern Revival

Modernity came late to India and largely in the form of Westernization. This has meant that many Indians have clung to premodern ways of thought and life in the guise of defending their tradition against aggression from the West. Actually, India's responses to the West have ranged across a wide spectrum. But among those who responded, we shall find a very remarkable succession of nineteenth and early twentieth century thinkers whose thought and lives have breathed new vitality into Hindu philosophy and devotion, and who have thus exerted a powerful impact upon Indian life as well. For Hinduism the nineteenth was indeed a great century, marked by renewal of many sorts.

First among these great nineteenth century figures chronologically, and other ways too, was Ram Mohan Roy (1777–1833). Born a Bengali Brahman he rose as high as then possible for an Indian in the Indian civil service. Resigning while still a young man, he devoted his life to a combination of scholarship and reform. He was among the first modern Sanskrit scholars and translators. Assisting a Scottish Presbyterian missionary in translating the Bible into Bengali, he is said to have converted his colleague from Calvinism to Unitarianism. He sought to defend Hinduism against Christian missions by purging it of evils such as polytheism and *sati* or widow burning. To achieve his reforms he organized the *Brahma Samaj* an organization that sought to graft onto Hindiusm such features as congregational worship and a humanitarian social ethic. Roy died in the arms of Unitarian friends in Bristol, England in 1833; but a notable succession of followers carried on the work which he began. Among these were three generations of Tagores. Following Roy's death, Dwarkanath Tagore, one of India's first capitalists, gave his support and leadership to the Brahma Samaj. He was followed in this role by his son, Debendranath Tagore, who was the father of Rabindranath Tagore (1861–1941) whose book of poetry, *Gitanjali*, won India's first Nobel prize for literature in 1913.[22]

Rabindranath Tagore's poetry stands in the great devotional tradition of the *Bhagavad Gita* and Ramanuja's writings. In the background as a kind of pervasive influence is a modernized version of Vedantist philosophy. But in the foreground is the way of personal devotion expressed in poetry of high quality. Like others of his generation, Tagore also sought to unite religious philosophy with public affairs. With Gandhi, Tagore was active in the movement for India's independence and nationhood. He was also the founder of one of India's best universities *Shantiniketan* (the name means "abode of peace"), named for its location at his family's summer home, and devoted to humanistic studies.

A radically different stance was taken by Swami Dayananda Sarasvati (1824–1883), a staunch Indian nationalist and enemy of all things Western or Christian. He sought to reform Hinduism by going back to the *Vedas* which he envisaged as the source of all human good, including even such modern achievements as natural science and democratic government. As previously noted, he made extensive use of Jaimini's Mimamsa or Exegesis School of Indian philosophy. Dayananda founded the Arya Samaj to serve as the vehicle of his program. In the strong nationalism of present-day India, this organization continues in vigorous life.

A still different posture was taken by Ramakrishna (1836–1886) and his chief follower, Vivekananda (1863–1902). Ramakrishna, far from being a philosopher, was an illiterate religious genius, who possessed the kind of charisma that has great power in India. He attracted a large following to his temple at Daksineshwar outside Calcutta. His oral teachings, written down by followers, were saturated with Vedantist thought, partly the result of his own intuitive genius and partly the result of an old Vedantist philosopher who had been one among his several teachers.

Among the large number of Indians who came to consult Ramakrishna was a young lawyer named Narendranath Datta who, as he thought, was en route to study in Great Britain. Changing his name to Vivekananda he stayed for life as Ramakrishna's devoted disciple, as founder of the Ramakrishna Order, and as Hindu missionary to the West. Philosophically, Vivekananda proclaimed a liberal version of Vedantism, which has had wide appeal to Western as well as Indian minds. For example, at the Parliament of Religions at the Chicago World's Fair in 1893, Vivekananda's philosophy and personality dominated the whole event. He continued as a missionary to the West for Vedantist thought and devotion until his untimely death in 1902. His influence was strong on a whole generation of Indian leaders who as young men came under his spell.

Mohandas Gandhi (1869–1948), while not a philosopher in any literal sense or in any academic sense, is notable for his sensitivity to philosophic and religious issues, and for the way in which he gave them powerful expression in sociopolitical action. The range of these influences on Gandhi extends from the Jain concept of noninjury (ahimsa) to Vivekananda's Vedantist philosophy of Indian culture. Asked by Radhakrishnan to contribute an essay for a volume entitled *Contemporary Indian Philosophy*, Gandhi responded with a single page which said in effect: my life is my philosophy and my religion.[23]

Among twentieth century Indian philosophers the names of Aurobindo (1872–1950) and Radhakrishnan (1888–1975) are preeminent. Both men produced philosophies that brought Indian and Western thought together; both were Vedantists in the tradition of Shankara, though both undertook critical revisions of Shankara's idea of maya. For both men philosophy and life fuse into a unity; in India's traditional way, philosophy becomes a whole way of life.

Aurobindo was the son of a skeptical Bengali medical man who sent him to England for education. He returned home with a Cambridge degree with honors in Greek and Latin classics to take up an Indian academic career. At home in India he was led more and more to the study of India's own classical heritage. In the early years of this century he was also drawn increasingly into the Indian Congress party's agitation for Indian independence. As a member of the extremist wing of the Congress, he was jailed, falsely it now seems, for alleged participation in a bombing plot, and, while in jail, had a vision of Vivekananda coming to him and telling him to empty his mind and prepare for God. On release he withdrew from politics, made his way to the south Indian French enclave of Pondicherry, there to establish an ashram for meditation, study, and writing.

During the following four decades of his life, in a vast output of writings on many subjects, but especially in his multivolume work, *The Life Divine*, Aurobindo managed to construct his own metaphysical system of philosophy.[24] He called himself a Vedantist, and his mind was steeped in Shankara's writings. Sometimes he labeled his views "integral yoga." However, he was also profoundly influenced by nineteenth century European philosophies of evolution. The universe, he declared, is a process of cosmic evolution, and we are all individual parts of this vast process. This universal evolutionary process progresses successively, in Aurobindo's words, from matter to life, to mind, to supermind, then on to its climax in the life divine. For the Western reader the greatest obstacle to understanding Aurobindo is the lack of precise or clear definition of these somewhat grandiose concepts. However, the reader will not be far wrong to think of successive levels of emergent evolution—a concept of considerable popularity in the West during Aurobindo's lifetime. Thus, the highest stage may be interpreted as an evolved, perfected state of mankind and the world.

All of this vast system Aurobindo believed susceptible of expression in terms of Shankara's Advaita Vedantist thought—with one exception, namely, maya. Shankara's unworldliness had produced the concept of maya, and in the modern, twentieth century world this tenet stands in drastic need of revision. The everyday empirical world is indeed not unreal but real, declared Aurobindo. It is the base—one is tempted to say the launching pad—from which we take off. Yet, if matter is real, we nevertheless proceed (as in English syntax) from real to more real and thence to most real. The contrast is accordingly not one of real versus unreal, but of degrees of being or reality culminating in a Supreme Reality that transcends our highest superlative terms—an idea with which Western philosophy has been familiar since Plato and Plotinus.

Aurobindo's metaphysical system has been compared with that of Teilhard de Chardin. Both men are professedly philosophers of evolution. Both philosophies seek to be metaphysical systems in the grand style. Both make a large place in their systems for mystical vision. Both men, be it added, have been less than fortunate in the group of less than critical followers who have gathered as disciples around their teachings. Both men have drawn hostile fire from philosophers for whom a grand system of the universe is less important than clear and reasonable thinking on matters of specific experiential detail.

Sarvapelli Radhakrishnan has been modern India's philosopher-statesman. First student, then professor of philosophy in several Indian universities and at Oxford University, he has been a pioneer in making Indian philosophy available to the West.[25] When India achieved independence in 1948, he became the first Indian ambassador to Russia, then successively vice-president and president of India.

Like that of Aurobindo, Radhakrishnan's philosophical orientation was Vedantism, though like Aurobindo he found it necessary drastically to revise the traditional concept of maya. Like Aurobindo, he gave a central place to the relation of philosophy to religion. That which the philosopher says in his conceptual language, the religious person says in his language of powerful images, and also practices in his life.[26]

Radhakrishnan was a vigorous and lifelong opponent of all forms of particularism in both philosophy and religion. Laying hold upon the tradition of tolerance in the Hindu idea of Universal Spirit, Radhakrishnan found all the great philosophies and faiths of the world saying the same thing—each in its own way, and in terms of its own symbols. His was a *philosophia perennis*, or at least it aspired to be such. It is also a contemporary statement of the view which our chapter 2 termed *monistic mysticism*. It is, in chapter 2's terms, both mysticism as experience and as philosophy. The former is the direct experience of the religious devotee, which for Radhakrishnan is only a direct, intuitive way of knowing what the philosopher is able to characterize in detail in his philosophical system. Radhakrishnan made much of the resemblances of his philosophy to Western forms of philosophic idealism, seeing in both of them different formulations of the same "philosophy of the spirit."[27]

Critics of Radhakrishnan have not been slow to point out the vagueness of his basic concepts and his somewhat cavalier way with specific factual details. Even more, they have found in his mixing of East and West an eclecticism that misses the concrete virtues of each. Indian critics have at times also severely criticized his historical interpretation of the Indian tradition.

Meanwhile, at the present moment, in the nineteen seventies, the great nineteenth and early twentieth century revival of Hindu thought seems to have spent its force. As these words are written, Aurobindo has been dead for twenty years, and Radhakrishnan has just died. No figures of comparable magnitude appear on the present horizon. In philosophy as well as politics India seems to have run out of great men. What the future holds for Indian philosophy is today as uncertain and problematic as it is for Indian politics.

SUGGESTIONS FOR FURTHER READING

As many of these works are classics that have appeared in numerous editions, only the most accessible publication is indicated.

Basham, A. N. *Hinduism*. London: Weidenfield Nicolson, 1960.

———. *The Wonder That Was India*. London: Sidgwick Jankson, 1970.

Bernard, T. *Hathayoga*. London: Arrow, 1960.

Brown, W. N. *Man in the Universe*. Berkeley: University of California Press, 1966.

Danielou, A. *Hindu Polytheism*. Princeton: Pantheon Books, 1964.

Dasgupta, S. *Indian Idealism*. Cambridge: Cambridge University Press, 1962.

———. *A History of Indian Philosophy*. Cambridge: Cambridge University Press, 1963.

de Bary, W. T., ed. *Sources of the Indian Tradition*. New York: Columbia University Press, 1958.

Deutsch, E. *Advaita Vedanta*. Honolulu: East-West Center Press, 1969.

Deutsch, E., and Van Buitenen, J. A., eds. *A Source Book of Advaita Vedanta*. Honolulu: The University Press of Hawaii, 1971.

Edgerton, F. *The Bhagavad Gita*. New York: Harper & Row, 1944.

Griffith, R. T. *Hymns of the Rig Veda*. Benares: Lazarus, 1896.

Hiriyanna, M. *Outlines of Indian Philosophy*. London: Allen & Unwin, 1964.

Hume, R. E. *Thirteen Principal Upanishads*. London: Oxford University Press, 1931.

Moore, C. A., ed. *The Indian Mind*. Honolulu: East-West Center Press, 1967.

Morgan, K., ed. *Religion of the Hindus*. New York: Ronald Press, 1953.

Mueller, F. M. *Hymns of Rig Veda*. London: Trubner, 1877.

———. *Upanishads*. Oxford: Clarendon Press, 1900.

———. *Six Systems of Indian Philosophy*. New York: Longmans, 1928.

Nakamura, H. *Ways of Thinking of Eastern Peoples*. Honolulu: East-West Center Press, 1964.

Naravane, V. *Modern Indian Thought*. New York: Asia Publications, 1964.

Potter, K. *Presuppositions of India's Philosophies*. Englewood: Prentice Hall, 1963.

Prabhavananda, S. *The Spiritual Heritage of India*. Garden City: Doubleday, 1964.

Radhakrishnan, S. *Indian Philosophy*. London: Allen & Unwin, 1962.

———. *The Principal Upanishads*. London: Allen & Unwin, 1968.

Radhakrishnan, S., and Moore, C. *Source Book of Indian Philosophy*. Princeton: Princeton University Press, 1957.

Zaehner, R. C. *Hinduism*. New York: Oxford University Press, 1966.

———. *The Bhagavad Gita*. Oxford: Clarendon Press, 1969.

———. *Concordant Discord*. Oxford: Clarendon Press, 1970.

Zimmer. *Philosophies of India*. New York: Meridian Press, 1957.

IX
Buddhist
Philosophy

IN THE PRECEDING CHAPTER we characterized Siddhartha Gautama, called by his followers the Buddha, as the boldest and most original philosophic mind of ancient India's Axis Age. Now we must explain this assertion, and give some account of Buddha's philosophy and of the main philosophies of his followers. Like Hinduism, Buddhism is both a way of philosophical thought and of religious devotion. As in Hinduism, our attention will be focused on the former, but we will fail to understand Buddhist philosophy if we forget that it has been conjoined throughout its history with a highly distinctive way of devotion and faith. In this chapter we shall be concerned with Buddha as philosopher and with some of the philosophies that grew and flourished in India and southeast Asia within the Buddhist tradition, leaving for the following chapters the story of Buddhism's interaction with the culture of China, and also the emergence of that distinctively Japanese form of Buddhism called Zen.

Attention has already been called to the flowering of philosophy in ancient India's Axis Age, and to the wide variety of philosophies which then flourished. As the reader will recall, Buddha explored and rejected no less than six widely different teachings and teachers before undertaking and achieving his own original philosophic formulation.[1] Among those teachers was one who, despite Buddha's rejection of his way, demands a word of comment, both for his contrast with Buddha and for his general significance in Indian philosophy. This was Mahavira, as his followers called him (an honorific title meaning "Great Man"; his name was Nataputta Vardhamana), the founder of the Jain sect and philosophy.

Mahavira was a contemporary of Buddha. His dates are uncertain, though 588–527 B.C. seem most probable. Like Buddha he grew up as a ruler's son in a small northeast Indian kingdom, in an age when small states were being superseded by larger political units. Also like Buddha he renounced the life of a noble for the ascetic's quest for enlightenment and salvation. Both men founded monastic brotherhoods that cut across caste lines in a time when those lines were hardening, hence suggesting the conclusion that they were rebels against caste.

Mahavira as well as Buddha left behind a system of philosophy and a community dedicated to using that philosophy as a kind of road map to blessedness, or salvation, conceived as emancipation or *moksha*. Along with Carvaka or Indian materialism, Jainism and Buddhism have been judged by Hinduism to be heterodox (*nastika* in contrast to the six *astika*, or orthodox systems). The common feature of their heterodoxy is that all three deny the authority of the *Vedas*.

There are, however, equally important differences between the ways of Mahavira and of Buddha. While Buddhism has interacted creatively with many Asian civilizations, and claims over three hundred million adherents, Mahavira's followers number only a million and a half people, all in India. Mahavira's way of devotion has emphasized extreme asceticism, against which it is probable that Buddha consciously formulated his "middle way." While, as we shall presently see, Buddha's philosophy has continued to grow and develop in many forms throughout south and east Asia, Jain philosophy has suffered from a rigid and ossified traditionalism.

In terms of the preceding chapter's distinction between Indian philosophies that are monist and idealist, and those that are realist and pluralist, Jain thought is clearly of the latter type. Hence, its traditions have been traced back to the very ancient pre-Aryan past of India. Heinrich Zimmer regards it as the archtypal model for this ancient type of thought, in his view antedating the origin of both the Nyaya-Vaisheshika and Sankhya-Yoga systems, which are the orthodox Hindu examples of the realist-pluralist type.[2]

Along with everyone else of his time and place, Mahavira accepted the concepts of *karma*, *samsara* and *moksha*, though he placed his own highly distinctive philosophic interpretation on each of them. In accordance with his realism and pluralism, Mahavira taught the real substantive existence and the eternity of individual souls. Indeed, such souls exist as indestructible spiritual monads in all living things, thus leading to the ethic of noninjury (*ahimsa*) to all. Since all living things contain souls, all must be respected. He also taught a matter-spirit dualism, alike in the individual person and in the universe. Hence, emancipation or moksha consists of cleansing the matter off one's soul in much the same way that barnacles might be scraped off a ship. This cleansing process includes the ethic of ahimsa, a rigorous ascetic practice or observance, and meditative study of Jain philosophy. The process includes also removing the stains of karmic matter, of which there exist some thirty-odd kinds, the effect of which is to stain the soul a variety of colors ranging from black and blue to yellow and white. Mahavira's ingenious and highly elaborated theory of karmic matter seems to have incorporated a threefold scheme of the types of personality, similar to the theory of the three gunas of Sankhya-yoga discussed in the preceding chapter.[3] According to this Jain teaching, one should aim at a transparent soul, unstained by any karma. However, of the various kinds of karma, milky white is least evil and black is worst. These images and ideas may also be observed in the iconography of Jain sculpture, with its milky white and glassy transparent images of Jain heroes.

In contrast to Hindu notions of absorption, or of Buddhist nirvana, Jain realism postulates a heaven where men still exist as individuals in a place called *Isatpragbhara*, at the top of the universe. Far from being absorption, this state of blessedness is called *kaivalya* or isolation. The path to salvation is long and hard and, furthermore, must be walked in one's own strength. There are no saviors who extend a helping hand to travelers on this road.[4]

Theologically, Jain thought is not agnostic but strictly atheistic, arguing rigorously against belief in a creator or savior deity with many of the same skeptical arguments used by David Hume in eighteenth century Europe. Not only is belief in a lord or savior rationally unfounded, it also fosters attitudes of neurotic dependence.

Jain teaching also tells of not just one founder, Mahavira, but of a long tradition of twenty-four such men, of whom he was the last. It calls them *tirthankaras* or "ford-finders."[5] The metaphor refers to fording the river that separates the present world from blessedness yonder. While Mahavira and his twenty-three predecessors discovered this ford, each man must make his crossing in his own strength to the further shore.

Jain philosophy includes an extreme and severe pessimism about the world and all its wretched inhabitants. For most suffering creatures the world is hell, from which there is no possible escape. However, Jain philosophy teaches that the human condition constitutes a kind of escape hatch from the universe of suffering.[6] Along with other Indian philosophies Jainism teaches a cyclic view of history, but it outdoes the others in the vastness of its endlessly repeating pulses or cycles of historical time. From this grim and ceaseless wheel of time, man's only hope is to escape to blessedness yonder. Along with these teachings has gone a morality of extreme asceticism featuring the strictest vegetarianism, as well as ahimsa or noninjury to all living creatures. The latter teaching still leads Jain monks and nuns to wear a gauze mask lest they unwittingly swallow an insect, and to carry a small broom with which to sweep insects from their path. This same compunction early in Jain history led its people to abandon agriculture (lest they injure earthworms and other similar creatures) for the marts of trade. Most Jains are still merchants or shopkeepers.

Among the significant philosophic features of Jainism have been its logic and epistemology. These include a doctrine of sevenfold predication (*saptabhangi*) and of intellectual relativism (*syadyada*, which literally means "the way of perhaps").[7] The world is assumed to be too complex for any single predicate or statement to grasp fully or adequately; hence, truth lies in holding to the relativity of all viewpoints and statements. All assertions may have some measure of truth, but none by itself is simply true or false.

Buddha's Philosophy

Turning from Jain philosophy to that of the Buddha and his followers is a move from a system of the ancient past to a living philosophy of this world today—one of the living options of our title. Yet, the source of this living twentieth century philosophy was first a young Indian noble, then a mendicant seeker after truth, of the sixth century B.C.

It is difficult to strip away the encrusted traditions of centuries, and to get at the life and thought of the historical Buddha, particularly when this is not a project of compelling interest to the Buddhists themselves. The best we can do is to extrapolate backwards in time from the earliest source documents, which may be said to express what Buddha meant to his followers of early centuries.[8] What emerges is a portrait somewhat more human and lifelike, less stiff with stylized tradition than that of Mahavira. Clearly, Siddhartha Gautama was a man great in thought and life, and as is often the case with great men, his thought and life were not separated, but thoroughly interfused with each other.

In typical Indian fashion, Buddhist tradition has woven stories of many preexistences, and also of Buddha's supernatural birth. Warned of events to come, Buddha's father sought to shield his young son from the latter's appointed destiny. However, his efforts were to no avail, for, seeing "the four passing sights," namely, an old man, a sick man, a dead man, and an ascetic, the young prince was shaken loose from his attachment to the world. At the age of twenty-nine he renounced his royal life and set out on seven years of search for enlightenment and emancipation. As we have noted, his search took him in vain to many of the teachers and philosophies of the time.

Much of any man's philosophy can be seen in his rejections. In the Buddha's case he rejected first of all the aristocratic social world into which he was born, and which, following his enlightenment, he diagnosed as a scene of wretchedness born of compulsive desires. However, he also rejected several of the prevailing philosophic and religious isms of his day. Brahman metaphysics seemed to him a meaningless and useless word game. Jain asceticism seemed to him an error equal and opposite to worldly indulgence. In agreement with Mahavira and in opposition to bhakti, he also rejected what modern psychologists might call the neurotic dependency involved in popular devotional religion. Rather, asserted both of these ancient Indian thinkers, man must save himself. All of these ways were, in Buddha's words, teachings that "do not edify," which is to say, in relation to man's real problem and its solution, they are meaningless and useless. The similarity of these strictures to the analytic philosophy described in chapter 4 is striking and will appear even more so as our exposition proceeds. Buddha, as well as contemporary analytic philosophers, was concerned to expose the futility of meaningless philosophic and religious questions. Hence, his search continued.

Buddhist tradition asserts that the climactic experience that made Prince Siddhartha the Buddha (popularly "the enlightened one," but more accurately "the awakened one") took place under a pipal tree (henceforth a "bo tree") at Bodhgaya in northeast India. If we seek to explicate the metaphor of awakening, the question arises: from what state to what other state of consciousness did he then wake up? If we focus attention upon the metaphor of illumination, we ask: from what darkness to what light did this experience lead him? Adequate answers to these questions would consist of nothing less than the whole content of his thought from this experience to the end of his life. For Buddha had sought an answer for seven years; and the next forty-five years of his life he spent teaching others by precept and practice what he found as the answer to his life's question.

Once more we must rely upon Buddhist tradition that has formulated the content of Buddha's experience and thought in summary fashion as the Fourfold Noble Truth and the Noble Eightfold Path. A. L. Basham has pointed out that the Fourfold Truth is significantly cast in the terse language of ancient Indian medicine, the first two statements constituting diagnosis, and the third and fourth statements constituting therapy.⁹ Buddha would presumably accept Nietzsche's remark that man *is* a disease, since his therapy entailed a complete transcending of the human or mortal condition. In passing, it is interesting also to note the recurrence of metaphors of disease and therapy in twentieth century thought about the human situation from Freud to Existentialism and, even further, to Wittgenstein's "therapeutic" analysis in linguistic philosophy. Buddha, too, thought in these terms. Let us note his diagnosis and therapy for man.

The first of the Four Truths is that existence is misery or wretchedness (*du:kha*), the second is that this misery or wretchedness is rooted in compulsive craving (*trishna*), the third is that misery can be overcome by eliminating craving, and the fourth is that this can be accomplished by walking the Noble Eightfold Path. This path seems also to have been formulated deliberately as a middle way in discipline and ascetic practice, between the extremes of worldly indulgence and of Jain asceticism. To change the metaphor, the Noble Eightfold Path may be seen as a kind of eight-rung ladder to nirvana. The rungs or steps of this ladder are: (1) right understanding, (2) right thought, (3) right speech, (4) right action, (5) right livelihood, (6) right effort, (7) right meditation, and (8) right emancipation or rapture. Such was the content of Buddha's awakening; such was his terse diagnosis and prescription for the human condition.

To many Western readers it seems morbidly pessimistic to say that existence *is* misery. They would argue that existence *has* its wretched and tragic aspects, but it *is* nevertheless something positive. To put the issue in different terms, Buddha seems to have regarded all human affections or motives as compulsive cravings; hence, emancipation comes radically by breaking their hold upon us, and transcending them completely. Yet, granting the existence of some such compulsive attachments, is this a fair or factual characterization of the *whole* of man's emotional or affective life? Are there not other more amiable, more humane forms of feeling? Whatever our twentieth century Western answer to this question may be, Buddha's answer seems to have been negative.

Like the nineteenth century German philosopher Schopenhauer, Buddha seems to have regarded all life, indeed all existence, as an expression of a vast blind will to live, a kind of universal urge to grasp, to have, to be. Hence, all creation writhes in agony. Man especially is the slave of passion, and in such slavery there is no peace. The only possible peace lies rather in rising above mortal passion, in breaking the fetters that bind us to the human and creaturely condition.

As we have seen, the root of this mortal misery lies in compulsive desire, or ignorant craving and attachment. Again Buddha's diagnosis finds parallels in the West. Spinoza found the source of human bondage in passion, and analogously found the source of salvation in the liberating force of knowledge or truth. Freud, too, proposed a similar diagnosis and therapy. Like Buddha, Freud found the cause of mortal misery or neurosis in the compulsive, enslaving libidinous urges of the id. Both Buddha and Freud found in knowledge the existential power to break these chains that hold men in bondage, though Freud was less hopeful than Buddha of man's full emancipation.

Along with most Indians of his age, Buddha accepted the ideas of karma, samsara, and moksha, though he offered his own distinctive interpretation of all three. Karma-samsara is the law of the deed whose consequences extend from one incarnation to the next, and so on endlessly. But where Hindu teachers taught that man must strive obediently through many successive incarnations to achieve emancipation, Buddha taught radically that his philosophy as formulated by the Four Truths and the Eightfold Path constitutes a power strong enough to break the chains and liberate man immediately in a single moment of insight—and, one adds, regardless of caste.

Man's goal of emancipation Buddha called nirvana, and again, for the Western reader, explanation is necessary. First of all, this term must be regarded as Buddha's distinctive interpretation of the common Indian ideal of emancipation or moksha. Etymologically, *nir* is the negative prefix, and *vana* means "breath" or "spirit." Ananda Coomaraswamy has suggested that precise etymological parallels from Sanskrit to Latin would yield us the term *despirated*, (as an opposite to *aspirated*).[10] Others have translated nirvana as "blown out," meaning the blowing out of the flame of passion, which is the source of misery. This distinctive interpretation of moksha or emancipation is linked in Buddha's life and also in Buddhist tradition with the experience of meditation or meditative thinking. By meditation Buddha and others after him have achieved awakening or nirvana.

In traditional Buddhist interpretation, nirvana is a state of being beyond all mortal craving, and like other Indian versions of emancipation it is also literally beyond all finite existence. To Western minds such a state has seemed as negative as death itself; the aspiration for nirvana has often been characterized as the longing for a quiet death. Yet this interpretation collides head-on with the Buddha's explicit statement to his first followers that nirvana was not to be equated with extinction. Buddhists argue at length that nirvana is not negative, but actually superaffirmative. It only seems negative to us mortals because we are still the slaves of misery and passion, and our poor human imaginations cannot yet even picture the bliss of nirvana. Certainly, in any case, nirvana has functioned throughout Buddhist history as a supremely affirmative symbol.

The conjunction of Buddha's thought and life yields another essential tenet of his teaching. Having achieved awakening, he was faced with the choice of opting immediately for nirvana, or of remaining in mortal surroundings long enough to tell other mortals the good news of deliverance. Buddha chose the latter course, and thus he provided the Buddhist tradition with its archtypal model for compassion (*karuna*), which is the principal and primary Buddhist moral virtue. Tradition represents the Buddha as torn by the temptation to opt immediately for complete detachment and emancipation. But, faithful to his destiny, he chose the way of compassion for his fellowmen.

Buddhist ethics have always shown a tension between the ideals of detachment and of compassion.[11] The logic of compassion is that while man is still enslaved, his passions are egotistical, and self-centered. Enlightenment breaks the chains of this slavery to self, enabling one freely and spontaneously to affirm the lives of his fellow humans and, even more widely, of his fellow creatures of all sorts. This aspect of Buddha's faith and thought may be described as a vision of universal salvation or blessedness.

Against this process of salvation or the achievement of blessedness, it is the negative power of *avidya* or ignorance, which is to say of an ultimately false view of the reality of the world and of the self, that holds us in bondage. Affirmatively stated, it is the liberating knowledge, imparted by the Buddha to the effect that the self and the world are unreal, which breaks the chains and sets us free. Again we observe the striking similarity between Buddha's views and twentieth century interpretations of therapy, ranging from Freud to Wittgenstein. For both, man begins in a state of bondage to false and misleading ideas; and for both, therapy consists not of solving problems, but, in Wittgenstein's words, of dis-solving false problems.

To these central tenets about man and his emancipation, Buddha added very little else. His disciples came to him asking questions about the existence of gods, of substantial souls, of life after death, and of a substantial world. To all of these questions Buddha gave the tight-lipped answer that they were questions which "did not edify"; from the viewpoint of man's disease and its cure, they were meaningless and irrelevant.[12]

He did add a few further ideas as guards against distortion of his central teachings. One such was the doctrine of *anatta* and another that of *anicca*. The former means no-soul (*an-atman*), and it asserts that what we regard as a substantial soul or ego is really only the temporary juxtaposition of five passing *skandhas* or elements that come together at birth, giving the appearance of substantive reality, but which will separate at death. One of Buddha's early followers likened the skandhas to the spokes of a wheel.[13] Together they form a wheel, but when they fall apart the wheel ceases to exist. Western readers have frequently likened Buddha's view of the self to that of David Hume, who looked within himself and saw no unified and substantial self but only a rapid succession of impressions.

This no-soul doctrine posed a problem for Buddhist karma, for if there is no substantial soul to transmigrate, what is the carrier of karma? Buddhist thinkers wrestled desperately with this problem, and one of them was led to suggest that karma is like a flame passed from torch to torch, even though individual torches are consumed and fall back into nonexistence.[14]

Corresponding in the external world to anatta is anicca, which is the doctrine of no enduring substances. What to common sense seem to be permanent substances are really only slow-motion processes. Even the supposedly everlasting hills are worn away by erosion. Nothing in the universe is exempt from the gnawing tooth of time and change. Wherever he looked, Buddha found change and decay, and hence he concluded that universal flux is the law of the universe. Along with Heraclitus (and more recently Whitehead) Buddha adhered to a metaphysics of process. Different as they are in other ways, all three of these philosophers find as the last word for the universe, not being, but becoming.

In Buddha's case it is particularly important to note the religious motivation for these philosophical teachings. For Buddha, as we have seen, man's problem is his compulsive attachments. Yet, man clings to these objects of desire because they seem real. However, this seeming is delusory and ignorant. In ultimate truth these objects are not real, but are as unreal as a dream. Hence, it follows that the issues of perdition and salvation lie in discerning the difference between ignorance and knowledge. The former condition consists of the ontological mistake, as it were, of taking the world of appearance as real. Contrariwise, salvation conceived as emancipation consists of passing from ignorance to knowledge, or as it happened to the Buddha, of waking up from the dream of appearances to the truth and reality of nirvana. As Buddha's followers have put the matter, it consists of passing existentially from the samsara world to the nirvana world.

In their efforts at understanding, Western students have applied many modern Western predicates to the Buddha's philosophy. It has been variously characterized as naturalistic, humanist, agnostic, and positivist. However, other writers, in critical reaction, have denied some or all of these adjectives, arguing that such predicates applied to Buddha's philosophy are flatly and plainly anachronistic. For one thing, do they not suggest a break with sacred tradition, and assert a modern secularization of holy things that was altogether foreign to Buddha and his age? Clearly, we shall have to sift the claims implicit in these adjectives in order to get at the truth and avoid error.

As to naturalism, Buddha did seriously question supernatural powers and man's religious dependence on them; but it must immediately be added that he did so in a context radically different from the modern West, in which this word and idea have come into being. A similar remark may be made of Buddha's humanism. Man is the center of his concern, but in a sense radically different from that of the American Humanist Association.

Thomas Huxley invented the term, *agnostic*, in nineteenth century England, where a whole cluster of meanings gathered around it. Buddha likewise questioned the existence of gods, future life, and much else, but in the very different historical and philosophical context that they were not relevant to man's central and crucial problem. Still again, positivism was Auguste Comte's nineteenth century word for the claim that only modern natural scientific knowledge is truly reliable or valid. Buddha made a somewhat similar claim, but for knowledge of an utterly different sort, namely, that which correctly diagnoses and prescribes for the human disease or condition.

In the manner of his age in ancient India, Buddha gathered a group of followers about himself in a monastic brotherhood like many another such brotherhood before and since. To the brotherhood he entrusted the task of spreading his teachings. Each year during the rainy season Buddha took his company of followers to a private retreat for discussion and renewal. When the rains abated, the monks went out to teach in the cities and villages and countrysides of India. His last words to his followers as he lay dying, may be said to epitomize his philosophy: "All mortal things decay, work out your own salvation diligently."

In the centuries immediately following Buddha's life, the brotherhood or *Sangha* continued and prospered. There was a succession of ecumenical Buddhist councils which did such things as codifying the sacred scriptures and regulating the life of the community. Three centuries after the Buddha, the great Indian emperor, Ashoka, third of the Mauryan dynasty, was converted to Buddhism. Known to us through the pillars and inscriptions he spread over wide regions of India, Ashoka became a zealous Buddhist layman.[15] While he followed a notable policy of toleration for all religions, he also used his position to advance the cause of Buddhism, sending missionaries to Sri Lanka and probably also as far as the Middle East, and establishing shrines, chapels, and resthouses along the routes to pilgrimage sites. As a result of Ashoka's influence, what had been a monastic brotherhood became a universal religion, with many of the appurtenances of institutional religion. Ashoka has been called the Constantine of Buddhism.

From Ashoka's time for the next several centuries, Indian Buddhist philosophy also underwent notable development. First of all, several different schools of philosophical interpretation arose to argue for their respective understandings of Buddhist doctrine. There was lively debate of such issues as the metaphysical nature and status of the external world, of the human self, of dharma, nirvana, and much else. Considerable disagreement exists among contemporary historical scholars concerning the number and nature of the different schools of Buddhist philosophy as well as their tenets. Some documents claim as many as eighteen differing schools and philosophies. At least four or five were historically significant. Early in Buddhist history one group called itself *Theravada*, meaning the "tradition of elders," and hence claiming to stand in apostolic succession from the Buddha and his first followers.[16] Another called itself *Mahasanghika*, meaning "the great assembly." Still another group called itself *Sarvastavada*, literally "the way of the reality of everything." Precisely what this last group stood *for* or *against* is not clear, particularly in view of Buddha's denial of the reality of both substantive souls and substantive objects.[17]

As these discussions continued, one group of schools coined the term *Mahayana* for themselves and *Hinayana* for several of the others. The word *yana* means "vehicle," or even more concretely, "ferryboat"; *maha* means "great," and *hina* means "little." The image involved is that of a ferryboat which carries people across the river that separates this world from bliss and blessedness yonder, or as Buddhists put it, from "the further shore" where the miseries of this world are left behind for the joy of nirvana.[18]

The image and concept of the large ferryboat meant that in effect there was room on board for all sorts and conditions of men. Mahayana Buddhism, in other words, adapted itself flexibly to both the religious and the philosophic needs of mankind. Particularly, it gave greater scope and freedom to laymen as against monks. Hence, on the one hand, it became more and more a religion in the conventional and institutional sense of a system of holy forms; and on the other hand, it also developed significant new philosophies. We shall want to look at Mahayana philosophies, but first let us glance at the Theravada philosophies which formed the main opposition to Mahayana.

Theravada Philosophy

That form of Buddhism which the Great Vehicle labeled as the Little or Lesser Vehicle understandably preferred its own designation of Theravada. The claim to be in the tradition of the elders set limits on its development in both philosophic speculation and ecclesiastical organization. In both respects the claim to apostolic succession pledged Theravada not to go beyond the Buddha and his first followers.

Historically, in Sri Lanka and Southeast Asia, Theravada Buddhism won out, becoming the established form, while Mahayana won out in India, Tibet, China, and Japan. In the Theravada world, Buddhism has continued as primarily a monastic community surrounded by the world, and wherever possible radiating its influence into the wider society. It has remained a community of monks (and also of nuns), who affirm a distinctive philosophy, and practice a distinctive way of devotion. It is thus a way for individual people to walk the path to nirvana, while cultivating along the way a quiet Buddhist compassion for fellowmen. This is the path first discovered and explored by the Buddha; and because he was the way-finder his memory is revered and his statues are garlanded. However, according to Theravada theology, the Buddha is now in nirvana and is thus beyond the reach of prayer or petition. Hence, Theravada's characteristic attitude is that of meditation, in contrast for example, to Judeo-Christian prayer or worship.

Theravada thought has added only a few features to the Buddha's own austere depiction of the path to blessedness, and it has prided itself on this fact against the speculative philosophies of Mahayana. One addition has been the doctrine of *Bodhisattvas*, or Buddhas-in-the-making (*Bodhisattva* means "body of light"). The claim is that there is not one unique Buddha, but rather that there is a multiplicity of such figures, though far fewer in Theravada than in Mahayana.[19] In Theravada there are said to be some eighteen to twenty-four Bodhisattvas conceived as Buddha figures ready to enter nirvana, but who have remained in the samsara world in order to help suffering fellow creatures on the upward path to nirvana. By far the most popular such figure in Theravada is Maitreya (or Metteya, in the Pali language), who is the Buddha of the age to come.

The Buddhist view of history, Theravada and Mahayana alike, is cyclic.[20] The wheel of history revolves continuously, without beginning or end. This is an image and a concept which Buddhism shares with Jainism, Hinduism, and other ancient Indian philosophies. As the wheel turns endlessly and over incredibly vast periods of time, human fortunes in history ebb and flow. According to the Buddhist version of this idea, each *kalpa* or revolution of the wheel is divided into four quarters, the first of which is decline, the second, quiescence, the third, advance, and the fourth, realization. Then the cycle begins again; the wheel commences another revolution. The Western conception of the progress of mankind with its implication of the unique, once-for-all course of history encounters no sharper contrast than with this traditional Indian cyclic view. These two contrasting views of history also carry with them profoundly different feelings toward that piece of history which is an individual human life.

One philosophic idea greatly emphasized by Theravada, and having to do with the working out of karma, is called the chain of dependent origination (*Pratityasamutpada*).[21] It may perhaps be characterized as a description in terms of Buddhist philosophy of the way in which one damned thing follows another. For it specifies the way in which, as a result of ignorance, the phenomenal world comes step by step into being. The twelve links in this chain of dependent causation are (1) ignorance or avidya from which arise (2) volitional activities, which in turn produce (3) consciousness relinked to existence, (4) mind and matter and, hence, physical existence, (5) the six senses, (6) impressions, (7) feeling, (8) craving, (9) attachment, (10) the process of becoming, (11) rebirth, and (12) old age and death. The religious motivation is clear if we note that to break the first link, namely, ignorance or avidya, has the consequence of snapping the whole chain. To Western readers this idea appears remarkable, alike for its subjectivity and for the curious ordering of its elements.

In summary then, Theravada Buddhism instructs its followers, as Buddha taught his first converts, that we mortals come out of past karma. We are here in the world because the past gives birth to the present, and because the wheel of life continues ceaselessly to revolve to every recurring present. For the foolish man the wheel simply continues its endless revolutions. But to the wise man the human condition is the opportunity to rid himself of the burden of past misdeeds, and to place himself on the Middle Path to reach the blessed state in which sorrow and misery give way to joy and reality. To be emancipated from worldly life and absorbed in what is true and timeless, this is man's chief end.

Mahayana Philosophies

As we have seen, during the centuries of its vigorous life in India, Mahayana or the Great Vehicle was characterized by religious developments that made its truths more readily available to the common man. But there were also philosophic developments that kept pace with the religion. While these new speculations claimed to be simply an extension of the Buddha's philosophic intention, to the modern reader as to the Theravada Buddhist, they seem to go far beyond anything recorded of the historical Buddha. In short, there was room on board the Great Ferryboat for all sorts and conditions of humans, even for speculative philosophers.[22]

Particularly important among the religious developments of Mahayana were those centered in the doctrine of the Buddha. While Theravada multiplied Buddha figures, Mahayana multiplied them much more, and also significantly changed their function. Bodhisattvas were transformed from Buddhas-to-be into sacrificial saviors holding out helping hands, dispensing grace, to the whole suffering creation; and vowing not to enter nirvana until the whole universe is saved. Many of these suffering saviors bear striking similarity to the figure of Christ in Christianity. Among these virtually innumerable Bodhisattvas, the most important were Lord Avalokita, who descends to earth age after age to help miserable mortals; Manjusri, Bodhisattva of wisdom; Vajrapani, stern foe of evil; and Maitreya, Buddha of the future age.[23]

In addition to Bodhisattvas, Buddhist theology distinguished other types of Buddha figures. As we have seen, Bodhisattvas begin their ascent to nirvana from a human base, but defer their final assumption to nirvana in order to save others. By contrast, *Manushi Buddhas* are now in nirvana, beyond the reach of human petitions and of mortal woe. Gautama Buddha is one such. But there are also *Dhyani Buddhas* (literally "meditation Buddhas") who begin their ascent not from a human base, but from some other region of the universe. Important among this last type is Amitabha who began as a solar spirit.

In Buddhism as in other religious traditions, some persons took the way of personal devotion to Buddha, or to some particular Buddha figure, notably Amitabha. Historically, this is ironical in view of Buddha's own apparent rejection of the devotional way; but it was destined to become a significant feature of Chinese and Japanese Buddhism centering in Amida or Omito, as Amitabha came to be called in East Asia.

Buddhist theology also produced the doctrine of the *trikaya*, or three bodies of the Buddha. These three bodies are (1) *Dharmakaya*, body of essence, (2) *Sambhogakaya*, body of bliss, and (3) *Nirmanakaya*, body of manifestation.[24] The root metaphor underlying this doctrine seems to be that of emanation of light from a central source or sun. From the Dharmakaya as the source, light and truth emanate in successive circles to all the world. The Nirmanakaya is such an emanation or manifestation in the human world. Between source and manifestation later Buddhist theology added Sambhogakaya. To the primal reality of Dharmakaya all things will in the end return.

Trikaya doctrine has often been compared to the trinity of Christianity. However, the similarity seems to lie principally in the number *three*. Beyond this, the contrast with Christian trinitarian doctrine is more significant than the likeness. For the ancient church fathers of Christianity taught both the absolute uniqueness and the full incarnation of Christ. In other words, they asserted that there is one and only one Christ, and that he actually took on human flesh. From this position, they rejected such proposals as repeated existences for Christ, and a multiplicity of Christ figures. Most emphatically of all, they rejected the ancient gnostic proposal of an apparent but not real or truly human incarnation.

On all of these points of doctrine the Buddhists held opposite views. They taught that the Buddha has lived through innumerably many incarnations, and that there are in fact a very great many Buddha figures. Nor were they concerned to urge a real incarnation for Buddha; an appearance seems to be quite sufficient. Thus, from a Christian viewpoint Buddhism is an avowedly gnostic or docetic religion, while from a Buddhist viewpoint, Christianity is still bogged down in the illusion of material existence.

To the twentieth century student of religions it is perhaps not the somewhat esoteric speculative details of these two theologies, Buddhist and Christian, that are important, but rather their respective visions of human existence. For what men say about transcendent realms frequently provides important clues as to their present life values. In this case, Christianity, and
Judaism as well, place a high value on what the contemporary West would
call the "real world," including especially its material aspects. Buddhist
values, by contrast, appear transcendental and spiritual in character, with a
consequent devaluation of the world of daily experience.

An important philosophic development in Mahayana was the emergence
of two new and great Buddhist schools. *Madhyamika*, the Central School,
and *Yogacara* also called *Vijnanavada*. Nagarjuna, the founder of Madhyamika, stands as one of the great figures in Indian philosophy and indeed of
the world's philosophies.[25] A biography written in fifth century A.D. China
says that he was a south Indian, converted successively to Hinayana and then
to Mahayana Buddhism. A luxuriant folklore has grown up around his life,
though few details are truly certain. He seems to have been the court philosopher for an Indian Buddhist king, possibly Kanishka, who ruled in northwest India (A.D. 78–123). Writings attributed to him show awareness not
only of the prevailing varieties of Buddhist philosophy, but also of Hindu
philosophy. It has been suggested that the title *Madhya* or "central" meant
that his philosophy stood midway between the extremes of nihilism (which
putatively taught the absolute unreality of everything) on the one side, and
the realism of Sarvastavada of the other. Another, better-founded suggestion
is that his school was "central" between the earlier realist schools and the
later idealist schools of Buddhist philosophy. In this respect Nagarjuna has
been likened to Kant in modern European philosophy. Like Kant, he undertook a transcendental criticism of all preceding realisms; and also like Kant,
from his philosophy stemmed later idealist systems.[26]

Even through the aphoristic sutra style of his writings, we can still discern
in Nagarjuna the power of an original philosophic mind. Religiously his intention was clear, that is, by means of his own distinctive philosophical
method to fulfill the religious intention of the Buddha, namely, to emancipate men from ignorance and bondage to the bliss and peace of nirvana. His
method consisted of a dialectical attack upon all other philosophies, with a
view to showing that they were riddled with internal contradictions, and
hence that their supposed referents were unreal. Students of Western philosophy will correctly observe here a striking parallel to the dialectical method
of F. H. Bradley in late nineteenth century England.

When Nagarjuna's dialectic had done its work, what was left? The translation by Stcherbatsky of Nagarjuna's *Madhyamika Sutra* renders the result

as "universal relativity," which is to say, a kind of universal contingent existence of all things.[27] Of all things that claim existence, none truly or really *is* or *exists*; all simply and only *appear* to be. They come into apparent existence, and then they pass away. All things whatsoever are relative, and the relativities are fraught with internal contradictions. Nothing, absolutely nothing, really and truly *is*.

Nagarjuna displayed the rigorous consistency of his dialectic by applying it not only to all things in the world but to Buddha and nirvana as well. Not even Buddha or nirvana truly *is* or *exists*.[28] They too are entities to be included in the universal flux and relativity. The religious motivation of this reduction may perhaps become clear to Western readers if they will consider a parallel case from the Judeo-Christian tradition. It is possible for pious people to become, in the popular phrase, "hung up" on God, on Christ, or on heaven. Indeed, such attitudes appear to be of rather widespread occurrence in current Western popular religion. From a Buddhist viewpoint, any such hang-up in any tradition whatsoever may fairly be characterized as the sort of craving or compulsive attachment that produces bondage. Nagarjuna's method was to show that all the objects of such attitudes lack real being, thereby freeing mankind from attachment to them.

By his uncompromising and unqualified dialectic, Nagarjuna arrived at what he called *shunya*.[29] All, absolutely all, is shunya. But what is shunya? The word is the Sanskrit term for zero in the number series. Hence, it is analogous etymologically to the Latin *nihil*, whose primary and literal meaning is the same. Yet, as philosophic and religious symbols, nihil and shunya have developed in very different ways. The terms, *nihilism* and *nihilist*, as commonly used, carry a very negative charge. By contrast, shunya is a nothingness that is happy, joyous. This affirmative quality may be seen from the significance of shunya in Nagarjuna's thought. As we have argued, the religious motive in Nagarjuna's dialectic is to lay bare the illusion of existence and so to free man from bondage to finite things. Once this basis is seen to be ignorance and illusion, then man will be freed for, or to, the bliss of nirvana or shunya. Thus, from Nagarjuna's time onward, shunya functions in Buddhist philosophic thought as a synonym for supreme felicity. Paradoxical as it may at first seem to Western students, here is Happy Nothingness.

As we saw in the last chapter, later Hindu philosophers, notably Shankara, attacked Nagarjuna, charging him with escapism and egotism. In other words, his nihilism was alleged to deny any reality to the everyday world, and his quest for salvation was alleged to be self-centered and egotistical. Apparently Shankara was not well acquainted with the actual teaching of Nagarjuna, for there is an element of joyous and generous affirmation in the latter's writings; and philosophically, he was clearly not the kind of nihilist that Shankara charged. In fact, Nagarjuna asserted the reality of the everyday world in precisely the same fashion that we noted in the preceding chapter for Shankara.[30] Like the later Hindu philosopher, Nagarjuna asserts that only if one assumes a different, transcendent viewpoint, can he discern the empty or unreal character of the everyday world. Apparently Shankara was more influenced by Nagarjuna than he knew or cared to admit.

In discussing Shankara in the preceding chapter, we raised the question of precisely what takes place or goes on in such philosophic moves as assertions of the illusory character of the everyday world. We noted the fact that twentieth century philosophers of common sense and common language have often taken this assertion literally and so have had little difficulty in reducing it to nonsense. Yet, as we argued, this is to miss the real point of such utterances. Whether in Shankara, Nagarjuna, or elsewhere in numerous occurrences in the history of the world's philosophies, such assertions seem to claim a quite different meaning. This is shown in the present instance by Nagarjuna's clear assertion that if approached and viewed on an everyday level, the everyday world is real. What he is asserting from a transcendent viewpoint is rather a comparative *devaluation* of the world of appearance. Indeed, Nagarjuna taught that the samsara world and the nirvana world are not different realms or regions, as other Buddhists have argued. Rather, they are the same world seen from different perspectives or viewpoints.

Like Shankara, Nagarjuna wrote from a philosophic viewpoint which, in contrast to modern Western philosophical separation of fact and value, asserted (or more precisely, presupposed) fact and value to be indissolubly united. What, then, he was claiming in the doctrine of shunya was that from the transcendent philosophic viewpoint which he asserted, the world of appearance received a negative valuation. We shall meet this view again in other traditions and in other symbolic forms elsewhere in the world. Whether one accepts or rejects it, it is important to see what it means—and does not mean.

Like Kant in the history of modern Western philosophy, Nagarjuna and his central philosophy proved to be only a temporary stopping place on the road to idealist philosophies of Buddhism. The most important systems of Indian Buddhist idealism was the Vijnanavada or Yogacara associated with Asanga and Vasubandhu who probably lived in the fourth or fifth century A.D. Like many modern Western forms of idealism, this system posits, as its basis or foundation, an absolute or cosmic consciousness. This they called *Alaya Vijnana* (literally, "receptacle consciousness") meaning that this absolute and all-inclusive consciousness *contains* or *includes* all other more individual forms.[31] From this pure source are successively derived all the various kinds of things that constitute the world. One Buddhist document lists eight successive forms of consciousness. From the source in receptacle consciousness is derived secondly, "mind consciousness" in general, and from this in turn individual "mental functions," and thence the five forms of sensory awareness. Correlated with these forms of consciousness are respective realms of the world.

In different terms and different metaphorical symbols, students of philosophy meet similar philosophers in many different parts of the world. For example, Plato and Plotinus in the ancient Greco-Roman world used the metaphor of light emanating from the sun for the relation of Absolute Being to the successive realms or regions of becoming or appearance. Western mystics have also used the metaphor of a fountain from which pour forth successively all forms of reality.

Our sketch of Indian Buddhist philosophies has been necessarily brief and selective, tracing only a few main lines of development and describing only a very few salient ideas. During the centuries of Buddhism's ascendancy in India, roughly from the time of King Ashoka to the fifth or sixth centuries A.D., Buddhism occupied a central place in Indian thought and life. And from its Indian base it also began its long journey from India along the central Asian routes to China, Korea, and Japan. The next chapter will pick up the story of Buddhist thought at this point.

Meanwhile, Buddhism began its period of slow decline in India, the land of its birth. The reasons for this decline are by no means well understood. As noted in the preceding chapter, one partial reason was the resurgence of Hinduism, which led in turn to an absorption or reabsorption of Buddhism into India's central tradition. Thus, Buddha came to be regarded as one of the nine main avatars or incarnations of Vishnu. In the competition for the loyalty of Indian hearts, the Lord Buddha lost out to Shiva, Vishnu, Krishna, and others. Numbers of Buddhist followers greatly declined.

Yet, as a heretical system of philosophy, Buddha's teachings endured as an important influence on the Indian mind and culture. In contemporary times there has been a considerable revival and recognition of this influence. Current Indian historians and philosophers have sought to reclaim the Buddha as one of India's greatest sons, speaking of classical India as "Hindu-Buddhist civilization." Indians place the Buddhist King Ashoka's lions on their postage stamps and the Buddhist wheel of dharma on their nation's flag. In addition to this recognition of historic influence there are also notable revivals in contemporary India of Buddhist forms of both thought and faith.

SUGGESTIONS FOR FURTHER READING

As many of these works are classics that have appeared in numerous editions, only the most accessible publication is indicated.

Bahm, A. *Philosophy of the Buddha*. New York: Harper, 1959.

Benz, E. *Buddhism or Communism*. Garden City: Doubleday, 1965.

Brown, W. N. *Man in the Universe*. Berkeley: University of California Press, 1966.

Burtt, E. H., ed. *Teachings of the Compassionate Buddha*. New York: Mentor Books, 1955.

Carus, P. *The Gospel of Buddha*. Chicago: Open Court, 1898.

Conze, E. *Buddhism, Its Essence and Development*. New York: Philosophical Library, 1951.

Coomaraswamy, A. *Buddha and the Gospel of Buddhism*. Bombay: Asia, 1956.

Davids, T. W. R. *Buddhism: Its History and Literature*. New York: Putnam, 1896.

de Bary, W. T., ed. *The Buddhist Tradition*. New York: Modern Library, 1969.

Eliot, Sir Charles. *Hinduism and Buddhism*. London: Routledge & Kegan Paul, 1957.

Getty, Alice. *The Gods of Northern Buddhism*. Oxford: Clarendon Press, 1928.

Hamilton, C., ed. *Buddhism: A Religion of Infinite Compassion*. New York: Liberal Arts, 1952.

Keith, A. B. *Buddhist Philosophy in India and Ceylon*. Oxford: Clarendon Press, 1923.

Morgan, K., ed. *The Path of the Buddha*. New York: Ronald Press, 1956.

Murti, T. R. V. *The Central Philosophy of Buddhism*. London: Allen & Unwin, 1954.

Nakamura, H. *The Ways of Thinking of Eastern Peoples*. Honolulu: East-West Center Press, 1964.

Robinson, R. *The Buddhist Religion*. Belmont: Dickenson, 1970.

Stcherbatsky, T. *The Conception of Buddhist Nirvana*. New York: Humanities Press, 1965.

Streng, F. *Emptiness: A Study in Religious Meaning*. New York: Abingdon, 1967.

Suzuki, B. L. *Mahayana Buddhism*. New York: Macmillan, 1969.

Takakusu, J. *Essentials of Buddhist Philosophy*. Honolulu: University of Hawaii Press, 1947.

Warren, H. C., ed. *Buddhism in Translations*. Cambridge: Harvard University Press, 1953.

Zimmer, H. *Philosophies of India*. New York: Meridian Press, 1957.

X
Chinese
Philosophy

CHINA VIES WITH INDIA for distinction of being the oldest continuous living civilization on earth. Yet the dissimilarity between these two civilizations is also as sharp and as total as any on earth. In contrast to the heavily sacral tradition of India, Chinese society is distinctly secular. Much Indian thought is marked by a reaching out for a transworldly absolute with a consequent alienation of man from the everyday world of nature and culture, whereas in China nature and society are the massive continuities, constituting together the existing universe or cosmos, beyond which nothing exists. India's religious tradition is marked by ascetic practices, many of them extreme and bizarre; China is characterized by a general abhorrence of asceticism as a violation of the human body, which is an integral part of the good cosmos. Furthermore, our bodies are given us by our parents, hence to violate one's body by asceticism is an offence against filial piety. Again, India tends in language and thought to abstraction; by contrast China is indefeasibly concrete.

Most of these differences may by summarized by saying that India's central tradition is a-cosmic, while China's is cosmic. *Kosmos* is the Greek word for the world of the city-state set within its natural environment; hence *cosmos*, as we shall use the term, may be characterized as the realms of nature and society taken together as comprising the real world. What is even more important is that the terms, *cosmos* and *cosmic*, stand for a distinctive type of life orientation that emerges among the archaic civilizations of Eurasia, extending from Greece and Egypt in the west to China in the east. In his *Cosmos and History*, Eliade has contrasted this cosmic orientation with the peculiarly historical understanding of human existence that is characteristic of the Judeo-Christian West.[1] At this latter view we shall look in chapters 12 and 13. Here we may note that in the modern period Chinese philosophers tend to regard the Judeo-Christian Bible with mingled scorn, bewilderment, and amusement. Viewing the world of nature and society as the sum total of reality beyond which literally nothing exists, the Genesis creation story becomes absurdly false. For, beyond or above the world or cosmos there is no divine creator, but rather only nothing. Furthermore, all men of reason know that the universe or world, far from being called into being by a deity is simply in itself everlasting. To such a Chinese cosmic view, the mythical stories of the Bible seem childish fables, unworthy of serious study.

A cosmic orientation has further implications. It means a harmonious and coherent system of nature and society, of which gods, man, and objects of nature are members together. In a word, the universe is a great city-state, of which all are citizens, and in which there are no breaks or radical discontinuities. To the contrary, the cosmos is informed and pervaded by what may be termed a principle of continuity. John Wilson has even used the term, *consubstantiality*, for this relation, meaning partaking of a common, continuous substance extending over the entire universe.[2] Moreover, this coherent and continuous order of the cosmos is essentially timeless. At least, historical change is conceived to be minimal and derivative, and time is usually understood in cyclic terms by analogy with the yearly cycle of nature. The relation of man to the universe, as microcosm to macrocosm, is a frequent theme of cosmic cultures. With varying emphases this cosmic orientation, with its accompanying interpretation of all human things, characterizes ancient civilizations from Greece to China. In passing, the similarities between these two great civilizations, Greece and China, at opposite extremities of Eurasia are striking indeed. Both are aristocratic, humanistic, and aesthetic, as well as cosmic in outlook. The great dissimilarity lies in their languages.

China's cosmically conceived civilization was already old when philosophy first flowered in the declining or feudal period of the Chou dynasty (ca. 600–300 B.C.). Even then, China looked back to at least two millennia of civilized life, and already the Chinese mind had assumed the conservative stance that was to characterize it until the coming of Communism in the twentieth century A.D. By 600 B.C. China had already gathered her culture into a series of classical books which functioned as reservoirs of traditional values maintained under the custodianship of scholar-sages. Several canonical lists of classics, ranging from four to thirteen in number were current.[3]

All included the *Shu Ching* or *Classic of History*, the *Shih Ching* or the *Classic of Poetry*, the *I Ching* (which was at once a diviner's handbook and a compilation of folk philosophy), and the *Li Chi* or *Book of Rites*. The canonical list that prevailed consisted of five classics, namely, the four just mentioned, plus the *Ch'un Ch'iu* or *Spring Autumn Annals*. To the five classics, the Confucians later added the four books, namely, Confucius' *Sayings*, the *Mencius Book*, *The Great Learning*, and the *Doctrine of the Mean*. The existence of such volumes and lists, let it be said again, underscores the nature of China as that civilization in which guidance for life was sought from classical books interpreted by elderly scholar-philosophers. Confucius is often said to have edited one or more of the classics.

Some of the values and themes of the Chinese classics are worth noting. First is the idea of a classic itself, which is that of a book which, while falling short of being sacred scripture, nonetheless constitutes an authoritative norm, allegiance to which is affirmed by calling it a classic. The values and themes of the classics find expression in a series of powerful and recurring images. Prominent among these images are Heaven, Earth, Man, and the Central Kingdom. The first refers not to a celestial abode for postmortem existence, but rather to the vault of the sky (*T'ien*, the Chinese character for Heaven means "sky" and also, significantly, "day"), conceived as the source of the authoritative norms and values that give meaning to human life. The Mandate of Heaven (*T'ien Ming*) is a corollary concept, which imparted to individuals and to society a sense of vocation and mission. The end of life for the individual and for society is to discover and to perform the Mandate of Heaven. For the emperor this mandate conferred upon him a divine sanction somewhat similar to the Western divine right of kings.

In China, as in other cosmic cultures, the complement to Heaven is Earth. It is interesting to note in this connection that, unlike many other lands from Greece to Japan, China's central tradition did not personify these forces as personal deities, Father Heaven and Mother Earth. Earth is the source, through agriculture, of material goods essential to human survival, hence sacrifices to Earth marked the seasons of the agricultural year. From an early time the Chinese emperor, acting as a representative of his people, performed elaborate and prescribed sacrifices to Heaven at summer and winter solstice, and to Earth at spring and autumn equinox.

In the center of the flat disk of earth lay the Central Kingdom of China. The Chinese have never called themselves "Chinese," a word designating the far-western province of Ch'in, whose duke became the first emperor, Shih Huang-ti (221–207 B.C.). Rather, they have called themselves *Chung Kuo*, the Central Kingdom, and from their most ancient times to the present moment they have fervently believed that this is so. The Chinese have always regarded it as the proper relation of the Central Kingdom to the rest of the world, that the leaders of the latter should bring gifts to the former.

Under Heaven, on Earth, and in the midst of the Central Kingdom stands Man; and as W. T. Chan remarks, if there is a single feature that characterizes Chinese philosophy throughout its long history it is humanism.[4] The Chinese never doubted that the fulfillment or realization of the distinctively human possibilities of existence constitutes man's chief reason for living. Like Greece, the philosophy and the whole culture of China has been humanist in outlook.

The Chinese classics show other recurring images and themes as well. Several of these will be described in the next section in our exposition of Confucius' teachings, for Confucius declared himself to be an editor rather than an author, "no originator, but a lover of the ancient teachings." Three of these themes were already old when Confucius laid hold of them. One was *yin* and *yang*, or the dual energy-modes of the universe, which combine in various ways to constitute everything in nature and society. Yang was the active, light, male principle, and yin the passive, dark, female principle. While yin and yang pervaded all ancient Chinese thought, they received distinctive emphasis from the Taoists, and we shall return to them in this connection. A second recurring image was *hsiao* or filial piety, and a third was *li*, or propriety. While filial piety began with respect amounting to reverence for one's own parents, it expanded to embrace a similar attitude toward one's whole family past and present, toward the Chinese kingdom as a large family, and indeed toward all that is old or ancient. Hence, filial piety came to mean (in the words of Santayana's definition of piety) a "reverent attachment to the sources of one's being." Hsiao was celebrated in China's elaborate funeral rituals. As a complement to filial piety, li asserted the principle of good form, initially in matters of etiquette and daily human dealings, but then extending out continuously to the world itself as a sphere of well-ordered, harmonious relations. Presupposed in all of this was the nicely ordered feudal pyramid of Chinese society, in which everyone found his station in life and lived under Heaven's Mandate.

Presupposed also is a sharp social distinction between the aristocratic philosophy of the gentlefolk and the popular superstitions of the masses. The latter outlook is characterized by a great number of good spirits (*shen*) and evil or capricious spirits *(kwei);* and popular religion consisted, in altogether practical fashion, in maintaining the good will of the former and averting the ill will of the latter.

However, in China as in other aristocratic cultures, the gentleman-scholar stood aloof from these popular superstitions, and sought his guidance and fulfillment in philosophy. It was in this sense that Y. L. Fung, writing as a Neo-Confucian of the twentieth century, observed somewhat condescendingly that, while Western nations are religious, the Chinese tradition is philosophical.[5]

Chou Philosophies

The Han dynasty historians spoke of the "hundred schools of philosophy" which flourished in the preceding Chou dynasty. The Chinese word here translated as "philosophy" is *hsüeh* or "learning." The compound character, which is often used to translate *philosophy*, *che hsüeh*, is modern in derivation and is probably influenced by the West. It means literally, "wisdom-study." However, the two elements of which it is composed are both ancient, going back to pre-Han times. *Che*, meaning "wisdom," is similar to the Greek, *sophia*, in its reference to knowledge as a whole, though the Chinese term has a distinctly more active and practical meaning.[6] Confucius, incidentally, used the term *hsüeh* (without *che*) for the philosophical knowledge that was the goal of his studies. Some critical writers have seriously questioned whether che hsüeh constitutes "philosophy" in any proper sense of the Western word and idea. The answer here, deliberately assumed and offered for the reader's consideration, is that in China as in India there is a body of writing and thinking substantially similar to what in the West is termed philosophy. The reader is invited to consider the issue as this chapter proceeds, and then to decide for himself. The Chinese character, *chia*, is translated as "school" and means literally "house" or "household." Hence, these are traditions and communities of philosophy.

When the hyperbole of a "hundred Chou schools" is reduced to historical fact, they turn out to be six. These six main Chou schools of philosophy are (1) the *Ju Chia* of Confucius, (2) the *Tao Chia* of Lao tze and Chuang tze, (3) the *Mo Chia* of Motze, (4) the *Yin Yang Chia* of the magicians and practitioners of occult arts, (5) the *Ming Chia* of Hui Shih and Kung-sun Lung, and (6) the *Fa Chia* of Lord Shang, Han Fei and Li Ssu.[7]

Y. L. Fung, twentieth century historian of Chinese philosophy, has proposed a sociological hypothesis for the origin of these schools.[8] The *Ju* or Confucian school began with the court scribes and chroniclers. Indeed, this is what the term *Ju* means. The great twentieth century scholar, Hu Shih, once wrote a notable essay arguing that the Ju were the court sages of a previous dynasty, and were already obsolete in Confucius' time. Hence, it was characteristically Confucius' achievement to revive a bygone class and custom.

Fung attributes the Tao school to hermits or recluses from society. Others would amend this slightly to read disillusioned intellectuals who failed of acceptance in high official circles. The Mohists seem to have sprung from the lower levels of the feudal nobility. The Yin-Yang school is attributed to practitioners of the occult arts, always a large and busy group throughout Chinese history. The Ming school, devoted as it was to logic and semantics, is attributed to lawyers, debaters, and other professional users of words. Finally, the Fa school (often translated as the "legalist" school, since *Fa* means "law" in Chinese) is attributed by Fung to the "men of methods," that is, to the practicing politicians.

(1) Most important of the Chou philosophers and indeed the most important individual in Chinese history is the man known to the West as Confucius. The Chinese know him as *Kung fu tzu* (Master of the Kung family) or familiarly as *Chung-ni*. Along with many other Chinese names and terms, the name "Confucius" is a latinized or westernized version which originates with the sixteenth and seventeenth century Jesuit mission in China.

Confucius' life may be pieced together from a Han dynasty biography, eked out by references in the writings of his disciples, including their records of his own spoken words. He was born in 551 B.C. in the province of Lu, which lies at the base of the Shantung peninsula in northeast China, and died there at the age of seventy-two in 479 B.C. He was reared by his widowed mother, to whom he was greatly devoted and who, at great sacrifice, saw that he had a traditional aristocratic, liberal education. While still a young man he opened a school which was destined to become the ideal model for all schools of Chinese history, just as Confucius became the paradigm of the Teacher and Scholar.

His school taught the six traditional Chinese academic disciplines, namely, ritual, music, archery, chariot driving, writing, and mathematics. While many of the students were sons of nobles, Confucius was proud that no student was ever turned away for lack of money. By education in social ethics he sought to prepare young men for careers in governmental service.

In his middle fifties Confucius undertook an assignment in government, only to be framed, with consequent loss of face, by other less righteous officials. Then followed a period of thirteen years of wandering, with a small band of loyal students or disciples, in search of a ruler who would be wise enough to accept Confucius as his advisor. The search proved futile. During these years Confucius was sustained by his strong sense of vocation and mission, which he understood in terms of the Mandate of Heaven. Heaven had given him a job to do, he believed, and the meaning of his life was to carry out this divinely given assignment. The content of this assignment was the reestablishment of the good order of the early Chou dynasty, which in Confucius' time had fallen into disorder and disintegration. The ideal age for Confucius, as for other Chinese sages, lay in the past rather than the future. Hence, renewal was asserted to consist of a return to this idealized past.

Failing in this mission, Confucius came home to Lu in old age to spend his last years as a scholar and editor. One of the five classical books, *The Spring Autumn Annals*, is said to have been compiled by him, and he may well also have done editorial work on others. In any event, Confucius pored over classical books until his death.

To the Western student Confucius' teachings often seem bland and solemn, sometimes even pompous, platitudes. But to the differently attuned minds of the Chinese, they have been the words of life. Perhaps this has been so because the teachings of Confucius do such an excellent job of collecting and expressing the traditional Chinese values discussed in our previous section.

Indeed, as we have seen, the main themes of Confucius' teachings were his interpretations of traditional ideas and images. As already noted, one such was li, translated as "etiquette," "decorum," or more broadly, "harmonious order." In Confucius' mind there was no gap between etiquette and ethics. On the one hand, etiquette is infused with moral significance, and on the other hand, ethics is not conceived as a heavy-handed moralism, but as an aesthetically conceived harmonious order of society.

Confucius spoke also of hsiao or filial piety, and lent the weight of his authority to the view that family has a higher priority than government in man's allegiances. Thus, if one's father steals a sheep, the son sides with the father and not the government—a priority that the Chinese Communist party has lately labored to reverse.⁹ In Confucius' mind, respect for parents is broadened to include a general reverence for seniority. This attitude is deployed socially in what Confucius termed the five great relations, namely, of (1) father for son, (2) husband for wife, (3) older brother for younger brother, (4) emperor for subjects, and (5) seniors in general, relative to youth. The reader will note that none of these relations is between equals; rather all are asymmetric. For Confucius this asymmetry becomes a generalized respect for the old and the past.

In the three virtues of *jen*, *shu* and *yi* we come to the heart of Confucian humanism. *Jen* (pronounced "wren") combines the Chinese characters for "man" and "two"; and has been variously translated as "benevolence," "love," "human-heartedness," and by W. T. Chan, as "humanity."¹⁰ It seems to mean "humanity," with the accent on human fulfillment or realization in social context. *Shu* means "reciprocity" or "mutuality," and is summarized in the Confucian maxim: "Do not do to others what you do not want them to do to you."[11] The negative formulation of this well-known aphorism is more a matter of Chinese grammar and Oriental reserve than of moral substance. For the attitude expressed is the mutuality of self and other, which is strikingly similar to the Golden Rule of Jesus. *Jen* and *shu* are given social application in *yi* or righteousness. Here then is a conservative, aristocratic, but actively social ethic.

Confucius' ethical philosophy is summed up in the figure of *chün tze*, or Magnanimous Man who, like the same figure in Aristotle's Nichomachian ethics, is an aristocratic scholar-statesman whose social conscience impels him to a position of leadership in the community. Like his Greek parallel, Confucius' Magnanimous Man follows an ethic of the middle way or golden mean. No aspect of classical Chinese culture shows the similarity of Greece and China more clearly than this striking parallel between the ethics of Aristotle and of Confucius.

One notes throughout Confucius' teaching the absence of any detailed metaphysical speculation. Confucius was a moralist and social philosopher rather than a metaphysician. A closely related question may also be raised whether Confucius' teachings are in any sense religious, or whether on the other hand they constitute simply a system of ethics without religious support or context. Much depends here on what is meant by *religion*. If we mean Western monotheism, then obviously the teachings of Confucius have no relation whatever. Indeed, in Western terms Confucius might be termed an agnostic humanist. More specifically, when his disciples asked him about life after death, he replied in effect "one life at a time." When they asked about gods he replied, "reverence the gods or spirits, but stay aloof from them."[12] Asked about prayer, he replied cryptically, that his praying had been going on for a long time. Certainly this credo does not add up to burning religious zeal.

Yet, at other points, religious elements are clearly detectable in Confucius' teachings. The definition offered in our chapter 2 for religion was "a system of holy forms." In Confucius' teachings, these holy symbols are Heaven, Earth, and Man, though it must immediately be added they carry a notable low voltage charge of holiness. Furthermore, these holy symbols also found ritual expression in the system of sacrifices to which Confucius was devoutly attached. When a follower questioned this interest, Confucius replied, "You love the sheep but I love the sacrifice."[13] Lin Yutang has wryly remarked that if Confucius were a Christian, he would surely be a high church Anglican.

In addition to his ritual concern, Confucius also had, as we have noted, a strong sense of vocation and mission.[14] Heaven had appointed him to restore the good order of the early Chou dynasty, and this vocation or calling gave meaning to his life. If either or both of these elements count as religious, then Confucius was religious. Perhaps it might be said that, in the terms of chapter 2's definition of religion, this is in historic fact what being religious has meant in Chinese history.

(2) The second Chou philosophy, Taoism, has been a foil for Confucianism throughout Chinese history. It is said to have begun with Lao tze (this name is actually a title meaning the "Old Master" or the "Old One"), an older contemporary of Confucius and the traditional author of the *Tao teh ching*, the Classic of the Way and its Power. While many modern scholars have questioned Lao tze's authorship, the balance of scholarly opinion seems at the present moment to be that he at least began the process of authorship, to which other later hands made additions. In any case, the *Tao teh ching* is what it is, regardless of authorship.

It stands as the primary source of China's indigenous mystical tradition. The major theme is the nature of *Tao*, which is a common Chinese character meaning "way," "path," or "street." The verb "to know" in Chinese is *chih tao*, literally, "to know the way." However, Taoist thought has taken this common word and given it highly distinctive meaning. In this new and unique usage, Tao means the "great way of the universe, the cosmic Tao." As such, it constitutes the way of life for man. To find it is to live, and to miss it is to fall short of life.

Yet the Tao is hard to find, and even harder to describe or characterize, for "the Tao that can be named is not the true Tao," says the *Tao teh ching*.[15] Like the object of the mystic's quest in many other traditions, the Tao is ineffable or inexpressible. That is to say, it transcends the ordinary secular world to which language refers. In China as in other traditions, this poses the question of how to express the inexpressible.

A study of the *Tao teh ching* yields a consistent answer to this question, which is not only of fundamental significance to the comprehension of the Tao, but constitutes also a clue for the understanding of mysticism generally. The *Tao teh ching* recommends silence first of all as the appropriate response to the inexpressible; as it were, to punctuate the difference between the ordinary secular world and the Tao. This silence functions as a kind of preface for what is to follow. Thereafter, the task of expressing the Tao, of saying the unsayable in human speech, consists of a combination of negation, paradox, and metaphor.

The *Tao teh ching* is marked by a cluster of metaphors by which man's mind and tongue seek to lay hold of the Tao as an object transcending everyday experience. Parenthetically, we note here the explicit absence of the traditional metaphor of height. The Tao is never said to be *above*; quite the opposite, it is said to *pervade* the cosmos. In the Tao we live and move and have our being; however, our human problem is that we do not know it as such.

Among the recurring metaphors for the Tao are: the spirit of the eternal feminine, the valley, the uncarved block (before the sculptor lays violent hands upon it), water (which is low and useful and conforms to the shape of any container), and One.[16] Such is the Tao! As the *Tao teh ching* puts the matter, "not knowing what to call it, we call it One."[17] From this "One begets two, and from two spring the myriad things of the phenomenal world." The "two" of the preceding statement are the yin and yang of the traditional Chinese world view; and the *Tao teh ching* gives its own distinctive statement to these principles. In contrast to the active or yang quality of Confucian thought, the authors of this book were devoted to the passivity of yin.

A closely related theme in the *Tao teh ching* is the anti-Confucian polemics that may now be found strewn through the text. Abandon righteousness and humanism, said Lao tze, meaning, abandon the artificiality of Confucius' activist social ethic.[18] In place of Confucian "do-goodism" Lao tze recommended a natural, spontaneous and often passive way of blending oneself into Nature's Way.

All of this found expression in the principle of *wu wei*, sometimes translated as "inactivity," but better rendered as "acting only in accordance with Tao."[19] Don't fight the universe, said Lao tze, suggesting that the Confucians were doing just that. Rather, let Nature or Tao flow through your spontaneous impulses to a free and natural expression. While not total inaction, this did lead to a social ethic of minimum action. In place of the active pursuit of social welfare, Taoism prescribed what might literally be termed laissez-faire. "Rule a great state as you would cook a small fish," said Lao tze, that is, with minimum handling.[20] This ethic envisaged a society of small villages far away from the artificialities of Chinese court life, provincial or imperial. It also pled for peace, charging that war was a gross violation of the Tao. Such was the message of the tight-lipped, often cryptic and paradoxical, aphorisms of Lao tze, destined to have an influence over Chinese minds second only to Confucius.

What Lao tze left unsaid, his follower Chuang tze (388–295 B.C.) carried through to witty and paradoxical conclusions in both word and deed. For Chuang tze, as for Lao tze, the one great reality is the Tao, beside which all else, if not unreal, is a vast mass of contradictory opposites, to be alternatively pilloried and ridiculed. Never elsewhere in world history has mysticism achieved such an alliance with sophisticated wit. Chuang tze spoke of the interplay of opposites within the great whole of Nature. Thus, for example, if a man sleeps in a damp place, rheumatism is the result; however, the eel thrives on such conditions. Monkeys live in trees, but humans would be uncomfortable in such a habitat. What emerges from all this is a kind of universal relativity.[21] This attitude is pushed to an extreme epistemological conclusion in Chuang tze's question about his dream: "Once I dreamed I was a butterfly, then I awoke. But now I do not know whether I am a man who dreamed he was a butterfly, or a butterfly now dreaming he is a man."[22]

Chuang tze embodied his message in actions. For example, he was fishing when the ambassador of the king came, bidding him come to the royal court as councilor and bureaucrat. Wryly he asked the emissaries if they recalled the fossil turtle at the court. Then pointing to a live turtle, he asked which they would rather be. They replied, of course the latter. Chuang tze responded, "I too will stay here and wag my tail in the mud."[23] Chinese history records no more complete rejection of the Confucian ideal of public service.

When Chuang tze's wife died, his friend Hui Shih (a philosopher of the School of Names) visited him and found him sitting on the floor beating on a pot and singing. Hui Shih exclaimed in shocked surprise, "This is too much." "No," explained Chuang tze, "at first I was grieved, but then I realized that she had come out of the universe by the universal processes of Nature and now she has returned and is at peace in the great house of the universe. So why should I grieve?"[24] Again the reader sees here a deliberate rejection and deliberate affront to Chinese funerary customs, so dear to Confucius and his followers. Often mingled with other later systems of thought such as Ch'an Buddhism, the wit and the imaginative vision of Lao tze and Chuang tze were destined to live on in Chinese philosophy.

(3) One system of thought with which Taoism formed a natural blend was the so-called Yin Yang school. As we have noted, in Chinese thought, yin and yang are dual energy modes which, in a variety of combinations and permutations, inform and indwell all things natural and human. This means that if we have the key to these indwelling modes we may understand the processes of the universe. The concrete, contextual character of the Chinese language lent itself fully to this task. In such terms, diviners foretold the future of individual people and of the empire, as well as reading the ways of Nature. They interpreted signs and prodigies in terms of yin and yang, and they pushed a kind of natural speculation almost to the threshold of chemical science. The Yin Yang school also produced such various protophilosophical products as a kind of process-metaphysics (in what was called the doctrine of the ceaseless "self-transformation of things").[25] It also produced

a hedonist ethic in such documents as Yang Chu's *Garden of Pleasure*, with its teaching that if by pulling out one hair from my head I might save the world, I would not do so.

(4) Among Confucius' first critics in ancient China, along with Lao tze and Chuang tze, was Mo tze (479–438 B.C.). Founder of a school of social and religious philosophy widely influential in ancient China, Mo tze criticized the sophisticated feudal class-structure of society that is implied throughout Confucius' teachings. In contrast, he argued for a simple equalitarian society of farmers, villagers, and king. He was even more critical of the extensive and expensive Confucian funerary rituals. Again, where Confucius sought his ideal model for society in the early Chou dynasty, Mo tze went further back; his ideal was located in the early days of the previous Shang dynasty. Still again, in contrast to Confucius, who had given the strong impression of Heaven as impersonal, Mo tze taught that Heaven is personal. It is accessible to our petitions, and speaks its (or rather *his*) will through oracles.[26] This has led some Western students to see in Mo tze the beginning of a personal view of God, in contrast to the dominantly impersonal view of Heaven throughout Chinese history.

Mo tze was also what the modern West would call a utilitarian in ethics. He confidently believed that the consequences of righteous dealing would be social well-being, and that conversely the wages of evildoing would be paid off regularly by Heaven in social ill-being. Hence, he argued, all that a people needed for a good society was a beneficent and democratically minded ruler.

Mo tze's teachings were notable in still another respect. Neither in Confucius nor in any other ancient Chinese teacher is there any strong sense of human sin or evil. Rather, the general consensus of ancient China was that human nature is basically good. Yet, Mo tze outdid the others in teaching the basic goodness of human nature, thus beginning a centuries-long discussion of this topic. We shall return to this theme as it unfolds in different teachers and philosophies.

(5) The *Ming Chia* or school of names, represented by Hui Shih (380–305 B.C.) and Kung-sun Lung (b. 380? B.C.), constituted an ancient Chinese school of semantic analysis of surprising sophistication in selection and treatment of themes.[27] The documents that we have from this school contain lists of paradoxes and problems emerging from the use of language. Hui Shih laid it down that "the greatest thing has nothing beyond itself . . . the smallest thing has nothing within itself," thus setting limits for man's thought about himself and the universe. He declared in paradox that the sun at noon is declining, and the creature born is the creature dying. Kung-sun Lung argued that a white horse is not a horse, for how could the same entity

have at the same time two such conflicting predicates as "white" and "horse"? These ancient Chinese logicians even went so far as to raise the basic epistemological question of reference, namely, of how human predicates can "reach" or extend to the world. While their school did not survive the ancient world, its influence continued strong in other traditions, such as Taoism.

(6) The sixth school, *Fa Chia*, is usually translated misleadingly as "legalism." *Fa* means "law" in China, but the Chinese concept of law has more the meaning of power of enforcement than of equal justice. This school, originating in the practice of politicians, found expression in the writings of Lord Shang (d. 388 B.C.) and Han Fei (d. 233 B.C.).[28] Significantly, it became the established philosophy of the short-lived but very important Ch'in dynasty. The duke of Ch'in became by conquest Shih Huang-ti, the First Emperor. He proceeded by ruthless suppression of opposition to the unification of China, to the building of the great wall, the grand canal, and much else. Finding opposition to his severe rule centering in traditional scholars, he ordered, on pain of being buried alive, the confiscation of all their books. As might be guessed, this tyrannical act was less than fully successful; the scholars and their classical books outlived the emperor.

The Fa school taught a doctrine of hard, cynical, Machiavellian realism. Man, they said, is not generous but basically selfish and hedonist in outlook. Since this is the case, any ruler who wishes to continue to rule must establish a system of harsh punishment and equal and opposite rewards. Only so can the refractory material of human nature be shaped into an orderly and peaceful society. Such a society would ideally consist of farmers, soldiers, and an absolute monarch. The Fa philosophers were particularly hostile to scholars and merchants, with their decadent tastes and restive ways. As already noted, the Fa school bears striking similarity to the teachings of Machiavelli in the modern West. In both theory and practice, the Fa school and the Ch'in dynasty overplayed their hand. Following the death of Shih Huang-ti and, in a few years, of his weak son, the dynasty fell, and was succeeded by the Han, which became the great classical dynasty of ancient China, contemporaneous with and similar to Rome in the West. When the Ch'in dynasty fell, the Fa philosophy fell with it.

Han Philosophies

During the last centuries of the Chou dynasty, Confucian philosophy underwent significant development, particularly at the hands of Hsün tze (298–238 B.C.) and Mencius (371–289 B.C.) who centuries later were to be designated respectively as the heterodox and orthodox champions. In their own time, they were viewed merely as two scholar-philosophers working out their own teachings by means of commenting on Confucius. Hsün tze is particularly interesting for his skeptical, realistic, and somewhat cynical turn of mind.[29] He pushed beyond Confucius in his blunt assertion that Heaven is impersonal and is therefore unaffected by human rites and petitions. He did not for that reason recommend abolition of the sacrifices and other ceremonies. Rather, they should be retained for their aesthetic qualities. Even more, Hsün tze taught that human nature is natively evil or self-centered. Man is by nature both egotist and egoist. He is also a hedonist. Therefore, any goodness that occurs will be because the refractory material of human nature has been successfully molded by effective teaching and by government. Hsün tze was incidentally the teacher of the legalist, Han Fei.

Opposed to Hsün tze was Meng ko or Mencius who accepted Confucius' teaching of the goodness of man, and pushed it even further. Against Mo tze, who had taught the equal or indiscriminate love of all men, Mencius taught discriminating love, that is, love precisely fitted to the social status of its recipient. Thus, I do not love a serf in the same way as I love my father or the emperor.[30] Mencius also taught that the ruler is responsible to and for his people, and that under some rare circumstances rebellion against an evil ruler is justified. These tenets constitute the basis for the somewhat anachronistic assertion by some Western writers that Mencius taught "democracy."

The Han dynasty (200 B.C.–A.D. 220) was the high point of ancient Chinese civilization, and Confucianism became its established philosophy, a position which it continued to hold until the fall of the Manchu dynasty in 1912. Like most establishments, this one was a complex affair combining in its Confucian synthesis much continuing political practice in the manner of the legalists, or Fa philosophers, as well as a novel element of metaphysical speculation in the style of the Yin Yang and Taoist schools.

The leading actor in this political-philosophical drama was a court astrologer, advisor, and philosopher, named Tung Chung-shu (179?–104 B.C.). It was he who in 136 B.C. composed the imperial decree making the teachings of Confucius the official philosophy of the empire.[31] Having himself risen through the examination system he developed and extended its influence. He also successfully recommended to the emperor an official public university, in which the presribed curriculum was Confucius' teachings, and whose graduates would supply the government's civil service. By the first century B.C. there were three thousand students, and in the later Han period there were no less than thirty thousand in this university.[32]

Tung Chung-shu was a philosopher in his own right, and his teachings sought to draw together in a single, synthetic metaphysical system most of the previous and current lines of thought. Under the dominant symbols of

Heaven, Earth, Man, and the Mandate of Heaven he also undertook a successful rational justification of the Han imperial system. Tung Chung-shu's metaphysics, worked out as scholarly commentaries on the classics, began with the notion of the cosmos or universe as a never-ceasing process of self-transformation. The dual energy-modes of yin and yang define alternating movements in this universal flux. Out of the different combinations and permutations come the five elements or agents, namely, earth, air, fire, metal, and water. These in turn combine to produce both the different kinds of natural objects and of human events. By his knowledge of these processes, Tung professed to predict future events in both nature and society for the imperial court.[33]

Tung also had his own distinctive view of human nature, sufficiently like that of his master, Confucius, to make him orthodox, and sufficiently new to make him an original thinker. He said, in a word, that the original material of human nature was neither good nor evil but neutral. Hence, the crucial importance of a good education and a good political system to mold the human clay into rational and civilized patterns.

Tung Chung-shu was what present-day young people might scornfully call an establishment figure, that is, an advisor to emperors and a philosopher of the status quo. But there were others who were neither of these things. Notably, Wang Ch'ung (A.D. 27–100) was a skeptic and a mordant social critic. All that Hsün tze had already said about the impersonality of Heaven, Wang repeated with new emphasis.[34] Heaven, he declared scornfully, is not a farmer or a mulberry girl for man. In short, no anthropomorphic models apply. Rather is it the case that natural phenomena like thunder and lightning, and sun and rain take place in complete indifference to man. Wang was also particularly disdainful of the view that a man's soul or ghost lives on after his body decays. This is groundless superstition. Rather, the truth of the matter is that out of the ceaseless processes of the universe an individual life emerges, has its day, and then ceases. Only the endlessly self-transforming universe endures.

Wang Ch'ung was also a trenchant critic of court scholars and others who simply mouth the tradition that they have received, never reflecting critically upon it. Hence, what they pass on is not wisdom but custom and superstition. Wang was thus a founding member of the long and distinguished tradition of Chinese skeptics and critics. The Indian tradition has a few parallels for this type of mind. In the West, from Lucretius in ancient Rome to Bertrand Russell in twentieth century England, there is a similar tradition of critical minds who have written and reflected in biting attack upon human follies and vices.

Chinese Buddhism

Like Rome in the West, the Han dynasty of China fell. In both cases the fall was more like a gradual subsidence. The date of A.D. 200 is given for the end of the Han empire. It was followed by three centuries of disintegration and turmoil during which China came as close to real discontinuity as at any time in her five millennia of history. What is important for us to notice is that when the Han dynasty fell, it almost pulled down the Confucian philosophy that was so closely identified with it. True, during the next three centuries scholars continued to read and to comment on Confucius and the Confucian classics, but they did so with new accents and emphases. Hence, Confucius, while not abolished, was pushed to one side while attention was once more given to the Tao and also to a new teaching, namely Buddhism.

As during the Dark Ages of Europe men sought refuge in monasteries from the darkness and the storms of their time, so in China also they sought to escape from the general disorder of the age. Some sought refuge in a Taoist Garden of Pleasure, and others in a Buddhist monastery. We must look briefly at both options.

As to the first, there was between A.D. 200 and 500 a revival of the school of Lao tze and Chuang tze, called by Western scholars Neo-Taoism, and by the Chinese the Dark Learning, *hsuan hsüeh*.[35] Notable in the Dark Learning was a group Taoist aesthetes called the Seven Sages of the Bamboo Grove, celebrated throughout subsequent Chinese history for their combination of mysticism with sophisticated and worldly wit.[36] One of them, Juan Chi, is said to have had himself followed by a servant carrying a jug of wine and a spade, the former to refresh him when thirsty and the latter to bury him if he fell dead. Another of the sages, Lio Ling, was accustomed to walk nude about his house. Accosted by his friends, he replied, "I take the whole universe as my house and my house as my clothing. Why then do you enter my trousers?" These sages deliberately cultivated spontaneity to the point of living by one capricious impulse after another. Thus, one of them opened the window of his house on a night snowfall, which reminded him of a distant friend. Moved by this impulse he traveled all night to see the friend. But then as he was about to knock on the door he obeyed a new impulse to return home. Still another of these sages was given two cranes, and in order to prevent them from flying away he clipped their wings. This made the cranes appear despondent. So when the cranes' feathers grew again, their human owner let them fly away.

Another tale recounted of Juan Chi's family that they were great drinkers. They did not bother with cups, but sat on the floor and drank from a large jar. When the pigs came into the house they joined in drinking from the same source. The reader will correctly observe in these stories a deliberate affront to Confucian social decorum. He will also note what modern Western historians might label a "back to nature" movement.

However, the Dark Learning also had implications and formulations that were more specifically philosophical. Hsiang Hsiu and Kuo Hsiang appear to have been the authors of a book called the *Kuo-Hsiang*, which drew out consistently and in explicit detail the conclusions of Chuang tze's logic and metaphysics.[37] Chuang tze had remained agnostic regarding the existence of a creator; the *Kuo-Hsiang* book boldly concluded that since evidence was lacking, there was no Creator. Rather, there exists only the universe itself in endless process of self-transformation. Moreover the Tao is no-thing, in the strictest sense of these words, namely, it is not any one thing or determinate combination of things. Hence, the Tao is plainly and simply the way of the scheme-of-things-entire. Moreover, concluded the *Kuo-Hsiang*, Heaven (or *T'ien*) denotes no one thing or determinate combination of things, but just the universe or the scheme-of-things-entire, to which the wise man will naturally and spontaneously attune his life.

This Taoist revival, while interesting in itself, is also important for its relation to Buddhism's coming to China. First of all it helped to provide a vocabulary for the incredibly difficult task of translating Buddhist documents from Sanskrit to Chinese. Even more, it helped to create a climate of feeling and thought in which Buddhism could be heard and heeded. For example, the Taoists, in contrast to the Confucians, possessed a Chinese word and idea translatable as "emptiness," which could be put at the service of Buddhists. Also, as we shall presently see, the Tao became virtually a synonym for the Buddha-nature.

Buddhism made its first appearance in China during the later Han dynasty, but it was during the third through the fifth centuries, following the Han, that it gained at first a secure foothold, then widespread acceptance. During the T'ang dynasty (A.D. 618–906) China was known as "Buddha land." However, in the Sung dynasty (A.D. 960–1279) which followed, Confucianism counterattacked, regaining for Confucius his central place in China's tradition, pushing Chinese Buddhism to a secondary place from which it has never recovered.

The interaction of Buddhist faith and Chinese culture must surely stand as one of the most intrinsically interesting encounters in man's cultural history. For Buddhism came to China as an a-cosmic Indian system of thought and devotion. China approached this interaction as the Central Kingdom, cosmic in its outlook and scornful of all claims to wisdom or truth from outside its own bounds. As we shall see, the interaction wrought basic changes both in Buddhism and in China.

As to the actual process of transmission, small groups of Buddhists gathered in China around some particular Indian text or philosophy that had been brought from India, thus imparting from the outset a sectarian quality to Chinese Buddhism.[38] The difficult process of translating Buddhist texts into Chinese took place over a long time and involved the labors of many men, but no name is better known or more significant in this respect than that of Kumarajiva. The son of an Indian father and a Kuchan mother, he was converted first to Hinayana, then to Mahayana Buddhism. Carried as a war captive to the Chinese capital of Anyang, he was given the task of heading a team of translators. He was awarded the title of Preceptor to the Nation from 401 to his death in A.D. 413.

The records of this time show considerable resistance and hostility to Buddhism as a foreign and most un-Chinese philosophy. In contrast to Confucian public service, Buddhist nirvana appeared to many loyal Chinese minds an empty and selfish goal. Buddhist ascetic practices seemed a violation of the body given to each person by his parents, hence a violation of filial piety. The Chinese, to whom family was the basic loyalty, pronounced a similar condemnation against the celibacy of Buddhist monks. As a crowning objection, Buddhism was asserted to be an outlandish foreign idea never once mentioned in the Chinese classics.[39]

But Buddhism not only journeyed to China, Chinese students made the reverse journey to India either by land over the Asian trade routes and through the mountain passes, or by the even longer sea voyage. They came to learn and to meditate at Nalanda, world center of Buddhist studies in northeast India and at other places as well; and they returned home laden with manuscripts, ikons, and even more important, with Buddhist ideas and attitudes. There is record of more than two hundred Chinese student-pilgrims who made this dangerous but illuminating journey during this period.

In China several clusters of Buddhist sects took shape. Three such clusters had lasting existence, (1) *Ching tu* or Pure Land, (2) *T'ien t'ai*, and (3) *Ch'an*.[40] The first was a reassertion in Chinese terms of devotional Buddhism, whose existence we noted in India. Philosophically its importance is that of one more instance of a significantly recurring religious attitude, namely, that of personal devotion to a savior. As we noted in chapter 1, this type is similar to the bhakti tradition of Hinduism. In the preceding chapter we also noted its beginnings in Indian Buddhism. Other illustrations will be found in Hasidic Judaism, in Muslim Sufism, and in Christian mysticism. Here then is a recurring type which interprets religious experience by the metaphor of human love or devotion for another person.

T'ien t'ai, which in English means "Heavenly Terrace," was named for the mountain in east-central China where its principal monastery was located. Among its founders is one of the great philosophers and religious figures of Chinese history, the monk Chih K'ai (A.D. 538–597). A war orphan, he became a student of philosophy, and gained distinction for his ability at metaphysical speculation. Then, however, he fell under the influence of a teacher, Hui-ssu, who convinced him that philosophical speculation and religious practice must be held together, like the two wings of a bird. Chih K'ai concentrated his study on the celebrated *Lotus Sutra*, finding in its pages the double emphasis he sought; his followers in this tradition have continued this concern. He established a monastery where philosophy and religious practice might be joined together. From Chih K'ai has stemmed the *T'ien t'ai* tradition of China and the similar *Tendai* of Japan. The philosophy of Chih K'ai and his followers, which provides a metaphysical foundation for religious devotion, is a system of Buddhist idealism in which all the many realms of the world emanate from and return to One Absolute Reality. It stemmed from the philosophic idealism of Indian Buddhism noted in the preceding chapter.

By far the most intensely Chinese as well as the most boldly original among the forms of Chinese Buddhism is *Ch'an*. The word is the Chinese translation of the Sanskrit *dhyana*, meaning "meditation."[41] Ch'an is said to have been brought from India to China by Bodhidharma (A.D. 460–534), about whom a luxuriant folklore has grown up, but little reliable information is to be had. He is known as the first patriarch of the Ch'an sect. However, the effective beginning for what Ch'an was to become occurred at the time of the fifth and sixth patriarchs, Hung-jen (601–679) and Hui-neng (638–713). The latter appears as one of the outstanding figures of Chinese religious and philosophic history.

Hung-jen is said to have announced a competition in verses to determine his successor. A favorite candidate, Shen hsiu (605–706?), who subsequently became leader of the Northern School of Ch'an, submitted the following aphoristic summary of Buddhist truth as he understood it:

Our body is the tree of Perfect Wisdom
And our mind is a bright mirror
At all times diligently wipe them
So that they will be free from dust.[42]

Hui-neng, at this time a supposedly illiterate kitchen worker at the monastery, and a southerner from the region of Canton, submitted the following
verse, notable for its play of paradox:

> The tree of Perfect Wisdom is originally no tree
> Nor has the bright mirror any frame
> Buddha-nature is forever clean and pure
> Where is there any dust?[43]

He followed with another verse which pushed paradox even a step further,
and also specifically opposed Shen hsiu's verse:

> The mind is a tree of Perfect Wisdom
> The body is the clear mirror
> The clear mirror is originally clear and pure
> Where has it been affected by any dust?[44]

Tradition says that Hung-jen called Hui-neng secretly to his room, invested
him with the robe of office, but told him to flee for his life. However this
may have been, the Southern School of Ch'an, famous for its doctrine of
sudden enlightenment, was set on its way by Hui-neng. In contrast to this
teaching, the Northern School taught the validity of gradual enlightenment.

We shall pursue the Ch'an path of meditation more fully in the next
chapter, which deals with its Japanese offspring, Zen. However, at this point
we note in Ch'an what may appropriately be termed the thorough Sinifica-
tion of Buddhism—that is, its assimilation to the main stream of Chinese
culture. In Ch'an teaching, action is affirmed as more important than speculative thinking. The avowedly practical aim and goal of action is enlightenment, similar to the Buddha's experience under the Bo tree. Yet in Ch'an,
enlightenment is freshly construed as insight into the meaning of the universe and the individual's part in it. Unworldly Indian ascetic practice becomes in Ch'an simply the strict regimen and discipline of the Ch'an monastery and the Ch'an way. Traditional Buddhist metaphor is transmuted into
Chinese paradox and wit, much of it drawn from the Taoist tradition. In the
kung-an (Japanese *koan*) exercise, paradox often moves from words to deeds,
a kung-an or koan being a paradox pondered and even sometimes enacted
by the novice as part of his training. We shall return to this matter in the
next chapter.

But conversely, China was also significantly changed by Buddhism. For
the populace the vivid stories of the regions of Buddhist hells and heavens
added a supraworldly dimension hitherto lacking in Chinese thought. For
the Chinese intellectual, Buddhist metaphysics had the same effect, surroun-

ding nature and society with a wider and more colorful universe. Buddhist compassion brought to Chinese ethics a wider and more spontaneous charity toward fellow creatures.[45] Buddhist mediation gave to the Chinese mind a new viewpoint from which to look at the world. It has been well said that if it were not for Buddhism, Chu Hsi, the great Neo-Confucian philosopher, would have been impossible. To Neo-Confucianism, as this philosophy is known to Western scholars, and to its counterattack upon Buddhism we must now turn our attention.

Neo-Confucianism

Even in the days of Buddhism's supremacy, a few staunch Confucians held the line against the invasion of foreign ideas, and for China's traditional ways. One such was Han Yü (768–824), essayist, Confucian scholar, and enemy of Buddhism. He wrote an essay upbraiding the emperor on the latter's public acclamation of a Buddhist relic. Instead, wrote this angry sage, this "stinking bone" ought to have been cast upon the rubbish dump, and the priests of Buddha thrust back into secular life. Han Yü also wrote on the perennial Confucian theme of the goodness of human nature. He sought to call his fellow scholars back from their dalliance with Buddhism to the ancient way of their people as contained in the Chinese classics.

In the T'ang dynasty, Han Yü' s was a lonely voice, but during the next dynasty, the Sung, Neo-Confucianism became a major movement, mounting a successful campaign against Buddhism, culminating in the great philosophic synthesis of Chu Hsi. The foundation was laid by the philosopher, Chou Tun-i (1017–1073), in his two treatises, *An Explanation of the Diagram of the Great Ultimate*, and *Penetrating the Book of Changes*. Tradition asserts that a Taoist priest gave Chou a diagram of the universe, for which he then sought philosophic explanation. However this may be, his philosophy provides the foundation for Neo-Confucian metaphysics and ethics. His first book begins with the exclamation, "The Ultimate of Non-being and also the Great Ultimate!"[46] The Great Ultimate (*T'ai chi*) had been known to Chinese thinkers from at least as far back as the Han dynasty appendix to the *Book of Changes*. By the time of Chou Tun-i, it had become both a powerful symbol and a widely recognized concept. *T'ai* means "great" or more precisely, "supreme," and the Chinese character, *chi*, contains two radicals, one of which Y. L. Fung has identified as originally the ridgepole of a tent, and the other of which suggests pervasiveness or comprehensiveness. It will perhaps not be far wrong to suggest that here is the ridgepole for the great tent of the universe.

In relation to our whole project in this book, it may be urged that here is the term in Chinese philosophy for *Ultimate Reality*, comparable to *Brahman* in Vedantist thought, to Aristotle's *Being-as-such*, Plotinus' *One*, or Eckhart's *Gottheit*. It is therefore significant to observe its exposition and development by successive members of the Sung Neo-Confucian tradition following Chou. It is also interesting to note Chou's equation of the Great Ultimate and the Non-ultimate or Ultimate-of-Non-being, as a Chinese, Taoist-influenced formulation of both the negative and affirmative Absolute. To his metaphysical reflections, Chou added a note of tranquility which showed Taoist and Buddhist influence, declaring, "the state of absolute quiet and inactivity is sincerity." Despite Taoist influence, Chou was even more concerned with the themes and spirit of Confucianism.

Shao Yung (1011–1077), the Pythagoras of this remarkable group of philosophers, found an ontological reality in numbers, or conversely, he found numbers embedded in reality.[47] The Great Ultimate had the number One, and embedded in Heaven were the other odd numbers, 3, 5, 7, 9, while the numbers of Earth are 2, 4, 6, 8, 10. By means of the interaction of Yin (Earth) and Yang (Heaven) Shao managed to derive the numbers of many things in Heaven and Earth. He also quoted the admonition of the *Book of Changes* to "investigate principle" or *li*. (It is important to note that this *li* is a different Chinese character from its near-homonym, *li*, which we rendered as "harmony" or "good order" earlier in this chapter. Indeed, the number of near-homonyms for *li* are said to run into the hundreds, all being the same in sound except for tone, but being quite different written Chinese characters. As we shall soon see, the present *li* soon developed in Neo-Confucian philosophy into something very similar to Plato's ideas.)

Where Shao Yung found reality to consist of such things as numbers and ideas, Chang Tsai (1020–1077) was a philosophic naturalist who asserted all reality to be composed of *ch'i* or material force.[48] Chinese material force differs from its Western relative, matter, by having its own built-in force or dynamism. In terms of Newton's equation, $F = ma$, it is not just "m" but "ma." So conceived, ch'i is for Chang Tsai the basic stuff of the universe. Hence, Chang may be termed a naturalist and materialist and, as might have been guessed, he has been acclaimed by Marxist thinkers as a Chinese forerunner of Marx and Mao.

Chang identified ch'i with the Great Ultimate itself. It pervades the universe and constitutes the underlying material of which, reality, in its ceaseless processes of transformations of evolution and devolution, consists. In these terms, Chang sharply attacked Taoist nonbeing and Buddhist emptiness. Nothing is empty or vacuous. Ch'i is everywhere and always; it constitutes the basic stuff of the whole vast relational system of the universe.

In addition to his metaphysical concerns, Chang is also celebrated as a moral philosopher for his "Western Inscription" (so-called because he hung it on the west wall of his study). This remarkable summary of Neo-Confucian thought begins with the declaration:

> Heaven is my father and Earth is my mother, and even such a small creature as I finds an intimate place in their midst.
> Therefore that which fills the universe I regard as my body and that which directs the universe I consider as my nature.
> All people are my brothers and sisters, and all things are my companions.[49]

The inscription moves through a long list of traditional ideas and persons that supply the ingredients of *jen* or human fulfillment and then onward to the conclusion:

> Wealth, honor, blessing and benefits are meant for the enrichment of my life, while poverty, humble station and sorrow are meant to help me to fulfillment.
> In life I follow and serve Heaven and Earth. In death I will be at peace.

Like the other Neo-Confucian philosophers, the two Ch'eng brothers, Ch'eng Hao (1032–1085) and Ch'eng I (1033–1107), were statesmen and governmental officials. These brothers also marked a division between what were to become the two historic versions of Neo-Confucian philosophy. One version or school, called by Y. L. Fung "the school of mind," that is, subjective or intuitive mind, began with the older brother, Ch'eng Hao, and led on through Lu Hsiang-shan (1139–1193) who was a contemporary of Chu Hsi, to Wang Yang-ming (1472–1529). The other school, called by Fung "the school of Platonic reason" (though "Aristotelean reason" might be more appropriate) began with Ch'eng I and led on to the great Chu Hsi.[50]

On a first reading, the Ch'eng brothers show great similarity to each other; it requires careful scrutiny to see that Ch'eng Hao's views are more intuitive and subjective than his younger brother's. Even then their agreements may well seem more important than their differences. Both brothers taught that all things are composed of li and ch'i, form and matter, though they differed with each other slightly but significantly on the details of this analysis. Ch'eng Hao emphasized the identity of one's own mind with universal mind, with the implication that by exploring the former one comes to know the latter, and eventually to be united with it. Ch'eng I's somewhat more objectively-oriented philosophy led on to Chu Hsi. Together these two, Ch'eng I and Chu Hsi, are called by the Chinese the "Ch'eng-Chu school."

Chu Hsi (1130–1200) brought Neo-Confucianism to its highest point of development. His philosophy is an architectonic synthesis, which incorporates all or most of the preceding elements of Chinese thought. Even Buddhism constituted an important, though negative, influence in Chu Hsi's system. Chu stands along with Shankara, Aristotle, and Thomas Aquinas as one of the great metaphysicians of world history. In active life he was a strong patriot and a devoted public official. However his opinions were too vigorous and too free for his contemporaries, so that he was repeatedly dismissed from public office. Chu was also a great scholar, who, among many other achievements, established official texts of the Chinese Classics. It was Chu who labeled Mencius orthodox and Hsün tze heterodox. To the five classics he added the four books, namely, *The Teachings of Confucius, The Teachings of Mencius, The Doctrine of the Mean,* and *The Great Learning*, as the syllabus for civil service examinations, an official arrangement which lasted until 1912. To his White Deer Grotto in Kiangsi province students gathered from all parts of China for study, lectures, and philosophic discussion.[51]

For Chu Hsi Reality is T'ai Chi ("the Great Ultimate") which combines in itself form and matter, li and ch'i, though li or principle seems to have a priority. For, he asserted, the Great Ultimate is simply the li or principle of all things, and of the highest good. It is not spatially conditioned, so as to be *here* or *there*, but rather pervades and indwells all things whatsoever. Lao tze had said that the Tao is in all things, and Buddhist philosophers had said that the Buddha nature is in all things. Continuing this tradition, Chu argued that the T'ai Chi is in all things, and not in part, but in whole. In other words, the Great Ultimate in its totality is to be seen in every least thing in the universe. For this somewhat puzzling relation he used the metaphor of the moon (in contrast to Plato's metaphor of the sun for the idea of the good) whose light is reflected on all the objects on which it shines.[52] The Great Ultimate, he adds, is also similar to the top of a house or the zenith of the sky.

Chu insisted upon the interdependent character of li and ch'i, form and matter, in all things. In words strikingly similar to Aristotle criticizing Plato's supposed doctrine of discarnate ideas, Chu Hsi says that there is no li apart from ch'i, and no ch'i apart from li. Together they are said to be components of all determinate things, in a way amazingly analogous to the form and matter of Aristotelean substances. The reader can only conclude that similar minds widely separated from each other in time and space sometimes find similar solutions to similar intellectual problems. In terms of li and ch'i, Chu was able to move onward to a highly unified conception of that comprehensive process of processes which is the universe. His was a dynamic and relational view of reality.

Chu was also a good Confucian humanist for whom jen or humanity is the highest good and the sum of all virtues. For man fits into the universe as one in whom all relations and all principles (li) find expression. He is related to the world as microcosm to macrocosm. As an intellectual and sage, Chu Hsi also gave a high place to what the Chinese classics call "the investigation of things" and "the extension of knowledge." In Chu's interpretation, they combined aspects which to the Western reader may well seem widely diverse. On the one hand, the investigation of things looks to Western eyes like a kind of protoscientific natural history or observation of nature. The sage observed the world in order to understand the li or principles of things. But this same practice shows striking analogies to Buddhist meditation; the sage investigated things as a kind of quasi-religious ritual.

As a philosopher and sage, Chu stood aloof from the spirits, the *shen* and *kwei*, of popular religion. As we have previously noted, intellectuals in many religious traditions take a similarly critical view of popular anthropomorphism. In Chu Hsi's philosophic system, the shen and kwei are transformed from good and bad spirits into impersonal principles in the universe.

Along with his Neo-Confucian predecessors and contemporaries, Chu was an avowed enemy of Buddhism, which he regarded as "empty," that is, devoid of material and social content, as well as "selfish" in its search for individual salvation. Some of his strictures show no very close acquaintance with actual Buddhist texts and ideas. However, at other points, such as his metaphysical system he betrays a strong influence, unconscious though it was, from Buddhism. Such are the ways of philosophic controversy. Philosophers frequently oppose most effectively by assimilating large elements of the opposition.

The other branch of Neo-Confucianism, the so-called school of mind, achieved its definitive expression several centuries later in the Ming dynasty figure, Wang Yang-ming (1472–1529). Like Chu Hsi before him, he was a general and governmental official, and like Chu, the force and candor of his ideas led to frequent dismissals and official disfavor.[53]

Wang's thought has a more strongly intuitive quality than Chu's. He emphasized the traditional teaching of the sage's being "of one body with all things in the universe." In all men there is some of this lofty principle of unity, Wang taught. Hence, in order to achieve goodness, a detailed knowledge of the objective world is not so important as to turn within oneself to the innate principle of unity and goodness. And when a man intuitively *knows* this good, he normally and naturally *does* it. Hence, in its full reality, knowing is the same as doing. Negatively stated, if I do not *do* the good, this is evidence that I do not really *know* it.[54] Thus Wang taught the unity of thought and action, a principle which has elicited the approval of Mao Tse-tung, the twentieth century Chinese communist leader who, despite this agreement, undoubtedly finds much else in Wang with which he can only disagree.

Modern and Contemporary Tendencies

Modernity came late to the Central Kingdom, and in the form of Western gunboats and soldiers who, during the nineteenth century, assaulted the decadent Ch'ing or Manchu dynasty, though paradoxically in the Tai Ping rebellion of 1840–1855, foreign military power actually supported the Manchu rulers against the rebels. Confucian advisors counseled either resistance or slight concessions to the West. Both proved futile, and in the revolution that followed in 1911–1912, both the Manchu dynasty and their Confucian advisors fell. In the social and political storms that have enveloped China during the twentieth century it is impossible at the present moment to see what elements of China's great tradition have perished and what elements, if any, survive.

On the political scene, the democratic regime of Sun Yat-sen replaced the Manchus in 1912. With Sun's death in 1925, he was followed by the more conservative and traditional Chiang Kai-shek. The Chinese communist movement, surviving international war and repression by Chiang, seized power as the People's Republic of China under Mao Tse-tung in 1949. Chiang fled with his army to Taiwan. During these decades of whirlwind, Chinese philosophy has continued very much alive, both at home on the Chinese mainland, on Taiwan, and even overseas as well. Some of the main issues and problems are dramatically illustrated in the thought and life of three leading figures, Hu Shih (1891–1962), Fung Yu-lan (b. 1895), and Mao Tse-tung (1893–1976).

Hu came to America on a Boxer indemnity scholarship at first to study agriculture at Cornell, but transferred to Columbia to study philosophy under John Dewey. Writing a dissertation on logical method in ancient Chinese philosophy, he received the doctorate degree, and returned home to participate in the tumultous life of the times. As befitted a disciple of Dewey, Hu's philosophy was that of a modern Western liberal. He sought to win China from her traditional teacher, Confucius, to a new teacher, John Dewey.

In China he rose rapidly to leadership in what has been called "the new culture movement." With the founder of the Chinese Communist party, Ch'en Tu-hsiu (1879–1942), Hu edited a student periodical entitled *The*

New Youth. Both editors mounted a full-scale attack on Confucianism as out of date and irrelevant for life in the modern world. Hu sought literary and linguistic reform, but above all he sought to replace Confucius' teachings with the liberal scientific and democratic way of life and thought as expressed in Dewey's philosophy. His own scholarly interests continued on a wide front, extending from literary criticism to political theory and practice, and during his long life he contributed learned papers to many discussions as well as energy and leadership to many liberal social causes. As a liberal devoted to the ideal of individual freedom, he found himself in an ever-increasing opposition to Communism. When the Communists came to power he fled to Taiwan, where he died in 1962.

Like Hu, Fung was educated in philosophy at Columbia University, but unlike Hu, he was led first to a restatement of philosophy in traditional Confucian terms. Until 1950 Fung called himself a Neo-Confucian of the Ch'eng-Chu school, and in books and lectures in China, Europe, and America he expounded this viewpoint. If Chu Hsi's viewpoint had been Neo-Confucian we shall have to call Fung's formulation Neo-neo-Confucian, for he expressed in the *Spirit of Chinese Philosophy* a twentieth century cosmopolitan philosophy fabricated out of Neo-Confucian materials. The four ideas of *Li, Ch'i, Tao* and the *Great Whole* or *T'ien*, provided him with traditional concepts which, by liberal reinterpretation, became the materials for a contemporary philosophy in the tradition of his Confucian forbears.

However, the march of political events harshly intruded upon Fung's Confucian philosophizing. The Communists came to power in 1949. In 1950, one of his sons, on joining the Communist party, denounced his father as reactionary. Within a year Fung recanted his Neo-Confucian philosophy and espoused Marxism. Since his conversion from Confucius to Marx and Mao, he has continued at the University of Peking, seeking to adapt his philosophizing to the new China and its masters. Full information is lacking, at least to Western students, as to these new forms of philosophy. However, we do know that he has reread Chinese philosophical history, reinterpreting such figures as Hsün tze, Wang Ch'ung and Chang Tsai as forerunners of Marxism, while condemning Confucius, Mencius, and the orthodox Confucian and Neo-Confucian tradition as "feudal, idealist and reactionary."

Vastly more important than the liberal democratic Hu or the late convert Fung, at least for the present and the forseeable future, is the Marxist philosophy of Mao Tse-tung. Unlike the first two, Mao's education and indeed his whole life have occurred within the boundaries of China. Mao emerged significantly as an organizer of peasant revolt in Hunan during the 1920s, leading an unsuccessful rising in 1927. He continued to work in the rural hinterland, and in 1931 was elected chairman of the Soviet Republic of China. In 1934–1935 he was one of the organizers and leaders of the famous Long March of the Chinese Communists some 6,000 miles from Kiangsi province to the far northern province of Yenan. From this base the struggle against both Chiang Kai-shek and the Japanese invaders of China continued. After World War II Mao led the civil war against Chiang, culminating in victory in 1949.

Mao's Marxist thought appears to constitute a break, a radical discontinuity in the long historical continuity of Chinese culture. After more than twenty centuries of loyalty to Confucius as teacher, China appears now to have a new teacher in Karl Marx. In some important respects this appearance is true, though in others—and who can yet say which is more important—the Chinese tradition continues.

Over extensive areas of social and philosophical thought and practice, Mao's writings dutifully expound the philosophy of Marx and Lenin as set forth in our chapter 7. He denounces Confucius as the ideologist of a feudal conservatism and, what is a radical shift for China, points to an ideal age not in the past but in the revolutionary future.

Yet the careful reader notes some telltale changes in Mao's Marxism. For one thing, certain features of style persist. In the style of Chinese gentlemen for several millennia, Mao writes poetry and does calligraphy. Indeed, Mao's *Little Red Book*, while differing utterly in content, follows the style of Confucius' *Lun Yü* as a book of aphoristic teachings for the guidance of social life.

Turning from style to content, Mao's brand of Marxist philosophy shows at least one radical and highly significant difference from the versions of Marx and Lenin. For the latter two the industrial working class constitutes the messianic class that will lead the revolution and usher in the New Age. For Mao, it is not the industrial working class but the Chinese peasantry. For Mao as a practical leader totally immersed in political action, this may be regarded as a pragmatic adjustment to reality. Yet, it constitutes a fundamental change in Marxist philosophy. It also establishes significant links with Chinese history, pointing back to the Tai Ping rebellion of the nineteenth century, to other earlier peasant risings, and to China's archaic and perennial village communities.

Whether the elements of continuity or discontinuity will prove more important in Mao's thought yet remains to be seen. Indeed, what the future holds for Chinese philosophy, as for Chinese civilization, is at the moment clouded with uncertainty. Whether traditional Confucian civilization is now over and done with, with China moving into the future with Marx and Mao as teachers; or whether on the other hand China will assimilate these new teachers as she has done so often in the past and then continue on her traditional Chinese way—all this at present writing hangs in the balance.

Yet, whatever the future may hold, China's long past with its great and central tradition of philosophy stands as one of history's great achievements of the human mind. No perceptive reader, whatever his own background and viewpoint can fail to learn from it the jen or humanism that is its central theme.

SUGGESTIONS FOR FURTHER READING

As many of these works are classics that have appeared in numerous editions, only the most accessible publication is indicated.

Benz, E. *Buddhism or Communism*. Garden City: Doubleday, 1965.

Chan, W. T. *Religious Trends in Modern China*. New York: Columbia University Press, 1953.

———. *Sourcebook of Chinese Philosophy*. Princeton: Princeton University Press, 1963.

———. *The Way of Lao tzu*. New York: Liberal Arts, 1963.

Chen, K. *Buddhism in China*. Princeton: University Press 1964.

Creel, H. G. *Chinese Thought from Confucius to Mao Tze-tung*. New York: Mentor Books, 1960.

———. *Confucius and the Chinese Way*. New York: Harper, 1960.

Day, C. B. *The Philosophers of China*. New York: Citadel, 1960.

de Bary, W. T., ed. *Sources of the Chinese Tradition*. New York: Columbia University Press, 1960.

———, ed. *The Buddhist Tradition*. New York: Modern Library, 1969.

Fung, Y. L. *The Spirit of Chinese Philosophy*. London: Paul Trench, Trubner, 1947.

———. *A Short History of Chinese Philosophy*. New York: Macmillan, 1960.

Hughes, E. R. *Chinese Philosophy in Classical Times*. New York: Dutton, 1960.

Moore, C. A., ed. *The Chinese Mind*. Honolulu: East-West Center Press, 1967.

Morgan, K., ed. *The Path of the Buddha*. New York: Ronald Press, 1956.

Reischauer, E., and Fairbank, J. *East Asia: The Great Tradition*. New York: Houghton Mifflin, 1960.

Takakusu, J. *Essentials of Buddhist Philosophy*. Honolulu: University of Hawaii Press, 1947.

Thompson, L. *Chinese Religion*. Belmont: Dickenson, 1969.

Waley, A. *Three Ways of Thought in Ancient China*. Garden City: Doubleday, 1956.

Wilhelm, H. *Change*. London: Routledge & Kegan Paul, 1961.

Wilhelm, R., ed. *I Ching*. London: Routledge & Kegan Paul, 1970.

Wright, A., ed. *Confucianism and Chinese Civilization*. New York: Atheneum, 1965.

XI
Zen as
Philosophy

ZEN, argued the late D. T. Suzuki, is neither religion nor philosophy but simply and uniquely Zen.[1] We shall hope presently to understand the unique aspects of Zen to which Suzuki bore witness. However, we propose initially to approach Zen with the hypothesis that it is a form of religious experience and a form of philosophy, both of which are highly distinctive formulations of what our chapter 2 called *unitive mysticism*. Such at least is the hypothesis that we shall seek here to test on the relevant factual data.

Yet before we can begin any of the various interpretations of what Zen is or is not, we need to get straight a few fundamental historical facts. First of all, Zen is Japanese and as we shall soon see, its relation to Japanese culture is a highly significant aspect of its total nature. Second, it is a species of Buddhism, different in important ways from other forms and incorporating elements from other traditions such as Taoism, but nonetheless thoroughly and distinctively Buddhist in its central features.

Historically, Zen is the inheritor of a threefold legacy from India, China, and Japan, and cannot be understood if any of the three is ignored. Chapters 8 and 9 looked at ancient India in which Buddha lived, thought, and taught, and in which his followers continued for several centuries. The preceding chapter noted the way in which Buddhism interacted with Chinese culture and practice to form Ch'an. It will now be necessary to look at the Japanese background and context of Zen.

Japanese Tradition

Compared to China, Japan's history is short and recent. Civilization came to Japan during the T'ang dynasty of China (A.D. 618–906). Extending back of this period was an age of many centuries of barbarism, and then of indigenous culture that laid the foundation for civilization, and that has persisted throughout Japanese history in the form of Shinto. Shinto is most readily characterized as Japan's indigenous religious tradition. It is the civic religion of Japanese values or the Japanese way of life, though ironically the name, *Shinto*, is Chinese, meaning "the way of the gods." The analogous Japanese term is *Kami no michi*, and the gods or *kami* are the innumerable and primeval gods, spirits, or holy powers, of Japanese nature and society. The records of their lives, of their fights and loves, their alliances and misalliances are preserved in the pages of the Shinto scriptures, the *Kojiki* and the *Nihongi*; and these kami may be said to live on today as they have from the beginning of Japanese history in the Shinto shrines that still dot the Japanese landscape.[2]

The kami did not disappear when Buddhism came to Japan, but rather made alliances in typically Japanese fashion with Buddha figures to form something called *Ryobu Shinto*, the twofold way of the gods. The most important kami is *Amaterasu Omikami*, the sun goddess.[3] (It is noteworthy that here the sun is a goddess rather than a god as in so many other traditions.) Amaterasu's symbol is still on the flag of the Japanese people, who look to her as children to a divine parent. She is still said to be the divine ancestor of Japan's ruling house (though the present emperor renounced his divinity in 1946 after the disaster of World War II); and her symbol, a mirror, signifies her presence at the great Shinto shrine at Isé.[4]

Of all the world's living religions, Shinto is probably the clearest or purest illustration of the cosmic or nature-culture type. Hence, for readers who have noted previous references in these pages to religions of this type, Shinto will present few surprises. However, what is surprising is the tenacious vitality of Shinto in Japanese history. It is even more surprising to see the way in which Shinto has sought to adapt itself to the twentieth century world and especially to the highly secular postwar Japan in which the emperor is no longer divine.[5]

Yet, one thing which Shinto is not, and makes no pretensions to be, is philosophical. There is no Shinto theology or philosophy. Indeed, this may be taken as a first indication of the wider fact that there is no Japanese philosophical tradition comparable to the philosophic traditions of both India and China. There have been philosophers and philosophies in Japan; in earlier days imported from the Chinese mainland, and in modern times, from the West. We shall also presently argue that in some minds Zen has functioned as a highly distinctive kind of philosophic vision. But none of this adds up to a continuing philosophic tradition, comparable to those we have encountered in India and China.

Historically, Japanese culture as a whole has been marked by successive borrowings or importations, first from the Asian mainland and more recently from the West. Yet to this it is necessary to add immediately that the Japanese have put their unique stamp on what they have taken from others. Of the innumerable illustrations of this dual process of appropriation and adaptation, the example closest to our study is Buddhism. Buddhism came to Japan from the Asian mainland of China, but once in Japan it put down roots into Japanese soil and grew into distinctively Japanese forms. The result is that Japanese Buddhism is at least as Japanese as it is Buddhist.

All this testifies to the pragmatism of the Japanese mind, which is to say, a willingness to accept reality as now constituted, and, beginning with present reality, to mold and remold it, step by gradual step, to one's purposes.[6] One consequence of this trait is that the Japanese alone among the great Asian civilizations have succeeded in building an advanced industrial and technological society. Furthermore, Japan's achievement of modernity has not, as in the case of other peoples resulted in the ruthless destruction of her traditional culture. Rather, in Japan the old and new dwell together in apparent harmony. Jet aeroplanes fly over an ancient and traditional landscape. The traveler on the world's fastest train from Tokyo to Kyoto looks out the window at sacred and timeless Mt. Fuji. Japan's ancient monarch continues to reign over a thoroughly modern nation.

Buddhism first found lodgment in Japan in the sixth century. In A.D. 522 a mission from southern Korea brought Buddhist ikons, sutras, and ideas to the royal court. However, an epidemic of disease, occurring soon thereafter, was interpreted as the anger of the traditional gods at the newcomers, with the consequence that Buddhism was wiped out. A second mission, some thirty-five years later in A.D. 587, made a permanent beginning.[7]

It is significant to see what Buddhism first meant—and did not mean—to the Japanese. At first the subtle philosophies of Chinese Buddhism fell as seed on stony ground. Prince Shotoku, one of the first important individuals in Japanese history, was an ardent Buddhist layman, concerned not with theory or philosophy but with the practical consequences of the new faith. He preached or lectured on Buddhist sutras in the royal court, seeking converts to the new faith. What is even more important, he included devotion to the Three Treasures, that is, the Buddha, the Dharma, and the Sangha, in his Sixteen Point Constitution of A.D. 604.

In the years that followed, the Japanese characteristically were more concerned over issues of correct performance of ritual and of discipline for the monastic community than with an adequate understanding of Buddhist philosophy. More than once they sent to China for instructions in matters of ritual and organization. During the Nara period (A.D. 710–784) Buddhism became the established religion of the imperial court, its monks exercising great influence on the government. The six Nara sects, as they are labeled, represent successive importations of elements of Buddhist thought and devotion from China. It was during this period that Emperor Shomu built and dedicated the *Daibutsu* (the "Great Buddha") at Nara.[8] Yet, as in the case of so many other establishments, this one overreached itself, with the consequence that in 794 the emperor moved his capital from Nara to Kyoto in order to escape these ecclesiastical influences, and to give himself greater freedom of movement.[9]

Main Forms of Japanese Buddhism

The Nara period of Japanese history was followed by the Heian (794–1192) and the Kamakura (1192–1368) periods, during which Buddhism in Japan at last put down roots in the soil of Japanese culture, becoming in effect, Japanese Buddhism. Like its parent, Chinese Buddhism, it divided into many diverse sects. Some of these paralleled the Chinese sects discussed in the previous chapter. However, all of those that endured did so because they incorporated valuable elements of Japanese culture.

In A.D. 804 two young Japanese Buddhist monks set sail for China on the same embassy. They were Saicho (767–822) and Kukai (774–835) known to Japanese history, respectively, as Dengyo Daishi and Kobo Daishi, and the founders, respectively, of the *Tendai* and *Shingon* sects. Both men have left their mark not only on Buddhism but also on Japanese history, as the title, *Daishi* ("Great Teacher"), indicates. Saicho returned home the following year with the essential features of Tendai, and Kukai the following year with the main features of Shingon or esoteric Buddhism. Recent Japanese census figures list twenty Tendai sects numbering 2,261,272 family units, and forty-nine Shingon sects with a membership of 11,567,243 family units.[10] Kukai particularly has been a very great culture hero of Japan, having apparently excelled in everything from calligraphy to road and bridge building.

During the disorders and disintegration of the later part of the Heian period, a new popular religious movement arose in Japanese Buddhism. Wandering saints and poets went through the streets of Japanese cities singing the praises of Amida Buddha, as a loving savior, willing to help all who called upon him, and to those who were saved, promising fellowship with Amida in the next world, or as they put it, in the Pure Land. The greatest among these devotional saints and founders were Honen (1132–1212) and his follower Shinran (1173–1262) founders, respectively, of the *Jodo* and *Shin* sects. The most recent official statistics list 16,899,289 family units as members of Pure Land sects.[11] In origin and nature they have been popular religious movements. They constitute an expression in Japanese Buddhism of what we have termed *devotional religion*, or the mysticism of communion. Like this attitude in other traditions, Pure Land has emphasized a loving relation to the Savior, celebrated in the Nembutsu ("Hail Amida Buddha"). Repeated in genuine faith this confession is said to guarantee bliss yonder in the Pure Land of Amida. Along with this has gone a characteristic emphasis on conversion of the heart and on personal faith in Amida Buddha, with accompanying vivid pictures of both Heaven and Hell. In a somewhat untypically Buddhist fashion, these sects have also emphasized a doctrine of human sin or man's evil heart. They have also spoken of two ways to salvation, one of *jiriki* (or "self-power") and the second of *tariki* (or "other power"). The first was said to be extemely hard, and the latter, as exemplified by Pure Land, was said to be an easy path to salvation. This is important also for Zen whose Japanese founders proclaimed their way as jiriki. Clearly, the Pure Land sects constitute a religious, and not primarily or principally a philosophic phenomenon.

As has happened in other times and places, devotional religion in medieval Japan elicted sharp and hostile criticism as an otherworldly distraction of energies needed for life in this world. In the case of Japanese Buddhism, the most important and most hostile critic was Nichiren (1222–1282), prophet, God's angry man, and founder of the Nichiren sects. His self-adopted name, *Nichiren*, meaning in Japanese "sun-lotus," expressed the combination of Buddhist and Japanese values that has ever since characterized the group of sects stemming from him. Nichiren denounced Jodo and Shin in unsparing terms as otherworldly distractions of energies needed for the service of Japan. He also warned his fellow countrymen of the then impending Mongol invasions, and freely interpreted the failure of these expeditions as divine deliverance. He was a kind of Japanese Buddhist Elijah, or in American terms, a John Brown. Nichiren Buddhist sects today number over 25,917,097 families, including notably the most rapidly growing religious movement in Japan, formerly known as *Soka Gakkai*, but currently (at least in the United States) preferring to be called *Nichiren Shoshu*.[12] This ardently missionary group is making a considerable number of converts not only in Japan but also overseas, particularly in western United States.

From the later Heian and Kamakura period came also the two principal founders of Zen Buddhism, Eisai (1141–1215) and Dogen (1200–1253). Both of these men visited China to study and meditate in Ch'an monasteries. Both returned home to Japan well schooled and strongly persuaded in the Ch'an way. Through them the Ch'an legacy, as summarized in the preceding chapter, was bequeathed to Japan, where it came alive as Zen.[13] The words for meditation, Sanskrit *Dhyana*, Chinese *Ch'an*, and Japanese *Zazen* testify to this threefold process of transmission and transformation from India to China to Japan.

Eisai made two trips to China, first in 1168 and again in 1187. On his second trip he wished also to push on from China to India. Prevented from this, he returned home as a full-fledged master of the Chinese *Lin chi* or Southern School, which in Japanese became *Rinzai*. Eisai was also the father of Japanese tea-culture. Tea drinking had apparently begun in Ch'an monasteries as a mild stimulant to meditation and enlightenment, and before Eisai had found his way to Japan. Yet to Eisai goes the credit for sponsoring tea drinking in his native land. His tract "Drink Tea and Prolong Life" was addressed to a Kamakura shogun whom Eisai sought to divert from alcohol to tea. Eisai's preaching had a strongly nationalistic tone as is seen in the title of his book *Zen for the Preservation of the Nation*. Finding opposition to his teaching at the imperial court in Kyoto, he moved to Kamakura where the young nobles of the new Kamakura shogunate gave him a ready hearing. Eisai and his followers of the Rinzai Zen sect became schoolmasters for the children of these nobles, who approved the strong inner-directed kind of character which Zen developed.

Dogen, founder of the Soto Zen sect, stands as one of the greatest religious personalities and also one of the greatest philosophic minds of Japan's history. The son of noble parents, he was orphaned at the age of seven and, following his mother's dying request, he turned from politics to Buddhist meditation. Ordained a Tendai monk, he continued to seek for what he could regard as a fully adequate way. He sought Eisai's guidance, and at his suggestion went to China in 1223. In China he was on the verge of despair when enlightenment came to him under the tutelage of the great monk Juching in 1225. Dogen's enlightenment occurred in what must be regarded as a highly philosophic context for this climactic religious experience. It is said that the experience came to him as he pondered the phrase, "the dropping off of body and mind," which might be freely translated into English as the transcending of the duality of body and mind.[14] Apparently it was the recurring problem of body and mind together with the unitive vision which solved the problem, that brought enlightenment to Dogen.

Returning home, he proclaimed his teachings not as a new sect but as simply good basic Buddhism. Central to Buddhism for Dogen was the practice of meditation or zazen, and he gave explicit and strict instructions for its practice. In contrast to Eisai's advocacy of the koan exercise, Dogen advised against it as a distraction from the central business of meditation aimed at enlightenment or satori.

His attitudes toward traditional Buddhist devotional forms ranged all the way from respect to scorn. In general, he regarded the traditional symbols as aids to meditation, yet, once when a hungry man begged at his monastery door, he handed him the money that had been collected for a halo for the Buddha image, telling him to use it to buy bread. The true goal of Buddhism was not veneration of ikons but meditation and enlightenment.

Dogen accompanied the practice of meditation by a philosophy that Heinrich Dumoulin, historian of Zen, calls "religious metaphysics," and which he likens to the neoplatonic philosophy of Plotinus in the West.[15] For this philosophy, the unitive idea or the One of Plotinus' system constitutes the supreme reality from which all things proceed and to which they return. For Dogen, this return is called satori or enlightenment. Dogen also emphasized the relation between what he called primal and acquired enlightenment.[16] The former is a native endowment possessed by all human minds, similar to the Fourth Gospel's "light which enlightens every man." By contrast, acquired enlightenment is that which takes place in the experience of satori. Dogen further argued that acquired enlightenment consists of a restoration and fulfillment of primal enlightenment.

In a sense, Dogen's philosophy of Zen may be characterized as a standing, lifelong protest against all dualities and dualisms, together with the desire to push beyond them to the unitive vision and its distinctive wisdom. So conceived, even practice and enlightenment are seen not as two things but, in essence, one. Likewise, the nirvana world and the samsara world are one, seen under different aspects. In all beings the Buddha-nature is in some way present, hence all are really and truly one. So, indeed, all is summed up in One; and One is directly experienced in satori.

The impetus of life and thought emanating from Eisai and Dogen set Zen on its historic way. We shall return to other aspects of this subject in the next section of this chapter. Meanwhile, we may summarize this sketch of Zen beginnings with the observation that Zen had the good fortune to be on hand at a crucial time in Japanese history. Hence, the Zen way has been closely interwoven with the central concerns of Japanese culture, ranging from government and swordsmanship to landscape gardening and flower arrangement.

Aspects of Zen

Turning our attention from history to analysis and evaluation, we ask what Zen is or consists of. To this question Philip Kapleau's book, *Three Pillars of Zen* gives the traditional threefold answer of meditation, practice, and en-

lightenment.[17] To these three pillars we shall venture to add a fourth and
fifth, namely, Zen's significance for Japanese culture and, despite Zen's own
protests and denials, its distinctive philosophy.

(1) As its name announces, Zen is a way of meditation, even though Kapleau refuses to translate *zazen* as "meditation," substituting contextual
description and exposition of what he holds to be the altogether unique way
of meditative practice labeled only as *zazen*.[18] However, it does seem possible to indicate at least some of the ways in which Zen is both similar to and
different from other ways of meditation that our study has encountered. Zazen is, of course, Buddhist meditation in the context of the extremely rigorous but highly flexible and pragmatic discipline to be described below. First
of all, it is meditation whose normal base of operations is the *zendo* or meditation hall of the Zen monastery. However, in most reliable expositions, the
comment is immediately added that meditation does not end in the meditation hall, but extends out into the world. For the true man of Zen, his meditation becomes independent of external circumstances, becoming a whole
way of life, and hence, a quality of everything he does and is.

The Zen way of meditation also seems typically Japanese in its combination of rigor and flexibility. For example, while the lotus or half-lotus posture for the human body is generally recommended, variations are suggested
according to the individual needs of people. One may even meditate while
seated in a chair.[19] Again, the normal procedure is meditation within the
context of Buddhist devotional symbols, visible and invisible, audible and
inaudible. Yet, there is also in this tradition a strong awareness of the way in
which these symbols can become fixations or hang-ups rather than "fingers
pointing." The great exemplar of Zen is the Buddha, yet Zen declines to be
hung up even on Buddha. Many Zen writers also point to Zen meditation as
the real substantive core of other traditions, Christian, Muslim, Hindu,
Jewish, or of no tradition.

Meditation aims at the climactic experience of enlightenment or satori. If
meditation is compared to the path up the mountain then enlightenment is
the view from the summit. Though satori is indescribable apart from direct,
firsthand experience, it is still this desirable and valuable goal which functions as the object of the seeker's quest as he toils his way up the mountain.

The inner mental content of the experience of meditation seems to consist
of two elements or aspects, one negative and the other positive. The first, or
negative element, consists of cutting one's mind free from enslavement to
the concerns of the intellect and the intellect's exclusive and sovereign sway
over all of life. By intellect is meant the discursive mind as it operates in all
the various phases of daily thought and life in the world, and in the view of

Zen the intellect must be—not destroyed—but dethroned. Affirmatively, meditation may be characterized as the practice of spontaneous openness or receptivity such that, when the climactic experience of enlightenment happens or comes, one will be ready to receive it. During meditation, the meditating person is encouraged to let his mind roam free in a way reminiscent of Freudian free association. Then, in the midst of such receptiveness, the supreme insight happens, often in ways and times least expected, and always in ways beyond human control and prediction, which is to say, beyond the control and prediction of man's discursive or calculative mind.

(2) The practice of Zen consists of all the activities that accompany and facilitate meditation, and thus stimulate and sustain enlightenment. It consists, first of all, of guidance by a master or *roshi* who has himself trodden the path and has thus gained his credentials as a guide for others. The wisdom and the disciplined lives of Zen roshis are matters of common testimony. So too is their unique combination of the two traits of humor and seriousness. Truly, these men have earned the right to the obedience they require of their students and seekers.

Zen practice includes also the rigorous common life of the Zen monastery where daily work symbolizes and expresses the life of the spirit. It is significant to observe that the otherworldly asceticism that is so common in India becomes in Japan a rigorous and disciplined way of life within the present world. So it is, also, that the man of Zen first comes out of the common, secular world, but after his enlightenment returns to it with the fruits of his experience.

A disciplined and moral way of life are basic prerequisites for Zen seekers. Once these are achieved, the path up the mountain consists of meditation and practice under the watchful eye of one's roshi. He will probably apply a combination of what Suzuki terms "verbal methods" and "direct methods."[20] The former include periodic interviews, in which the roshi and the student discuss the latter's problems, and the roshi offers whatever guidance he deems wise. Among the verbal methods may be such devices as paradox, for which Zen is well-known. The Zen uses and significance of paradox seem to be twofold: first, by the force of the apparent contradiction involved, to shake and shock a person free from enslavement to the discursive intellect, and second, to serve as a finger pointing toward enlightenment.

For example, the student is told "to understand is not to understand," or "empty handed I go yet the spade is in my hands."[21] A study of these and many other paradoxes involved in Zen teaching seems to yield two distinguishable types, first, those that by paradox call attention parabolically or allegorically to some aspect of Buddhist teaching, and second, the sheer paradoxes that appear (to this observer at least) simply to stand as such. The latter might perhaps be characterized as Zen "shaggy dog stories," whose function is simply and solely their shock effect. The paradox "not to understand is to understand" is clearly the former sort, for what is being said here is that not to understand (intellectually) is to understand (intuitively), and so to achieve enlightenment. Similar meanings, often parabolic or even allegorical in nature, may be discerned through many of the paradoxical words of Zen aphorisms.

To such verbal methods of teaching, Zen adds direct methods. To words it adds deeds, thus accentuating the unity of words and deeds. The deeds begin with the discipline of the meditation hall, including the "stick of mercy" as it is called, by which drowsy seekers are beaten out of their lethargy by blows across the shoulders.[22] By pointing, or beating, or sitting in silence, the Zen master may underscore or emphasize whatever lesson he feels his student needs to learn. All such methods serve to underscore the existential character of Zen.

We have already noted the fact that while Eisai made extensive use of the koan exercise, Dogen held it to be a distraction from the central business of meditating. The two traditions of Rinzai and Soto Zen have continued these respective attitudes. In Rinzai the koan is used as a kind of enacted paradox on which the student is required to fix his attention over extended periods of time.

Some koans have become famous, as for example Joshu's answer, "*mu*," to the question of whether the Buddha nature is in a dog.[23] Generations of Rinzai students have focused their mind on *mu*, which is, in effect, a qualified negation. But what precisely is the qualification? That is the question. Almost as famous is the teacher's question, "What is the meaning of the First Patriarch's visit to China?" and the answer, "The cypress in the front courtyard."[24] Here, behind the façade of unreason, is to be found Zen's insistence on the reality and significance of concrete objects of the everyday world, such as a particular cypress tree.

Some koans raise fundamental and perennial philosophic questions, as for example the roshi who held up a stick saying, "If you call this a stick you affirm, if you call it not a stick, you deny. What is beyond affirmation and negation?" His question raises, doubtless unwittingly, sophisticated questions of logical theory that still continue to perplex philosophers, as for example the logicians and analytic philosophers of our chapter 4.

The list of paradoxes and koans is literally and characteristically endless, but perhaps the koan exercise may best be illustrated by D. T. Suzuki's preface to one of his last expositions of Zen to a Western audience. He began with these words, "In the West to be or not to be is the question. But in the

East to be is not to be, so there is no question.'' Hopefully the reader has by now acquired enough insight into Zen for him to see that this is not a shaggy dog story. Hopefully too, he has by this point in our study become sufficiently concerned with East-West relations to take this koan as a subject for further reflection and study.

(3) As we have asserted repeatedly, the aim of meditation and practice is enlightenment, called by Zen, *satori* or *kensho*. Both of these Japanese terms have the etymology of "seeing into one's nature." In either case, here is Zen's formulation of what chapter 2 called the direct experience of unitive consciousness. Hence, satori may be described as the experience, in the context of Buddhist symbols, of oneness with all things whatsoever. In satori, man experiences a supreme and absolute unity surpassing all divisions.

Following William James' celebrated and controversial list of the important traits of mystical experience in *The Varieties of Religious Experience*, D. T. Suzuki listed eight traits or characteristics of satori. The following list of six main traits of satori is the present author's free and revised rendering of both James and Suzuki.[25]

Suzuki's first trait of satori is irrationality, yet it soon becomes clear that what he means is independence of control by man's discursive reason or intellect. No person ever finds enlightenment at the conclusion of an argument. Even more strongly, let it be said that satori is not so much something we may *do* as something that *happens* to us. In such ways as this are asserted the outer limits of man's intellect with respect to this whole region of experience. As was suggested above, Zen believes that the discursive intellect must be dethroned. To be sure, expositions of Zen have sometimes gone beyond these limits, and have flatly asserted unreason. Sometimes, indeed, Zen's irrationality has erupted in such behavior as book burning. To this issue we shall return in the section below on Zen's philosophic content.

Second, satori is asserted to be intuitive, or to partake of the nature of immediate insight. The testimony of those who have experienced it is that it happens with all the force of direct, immediate experience. In Whiteheadian terms, it occurs in the "mode of presentational immediacy." And, as we have argued, it happens to a person in ways independent of, or even against, his own wishing or willing. The concept of insight may perhaps provide a clue for the exposition of satori for people who disclaim any acquaintance with mystical experience. Let such readers recall the common experience of having an insight. As is sometimes said, the insight "occurs" to them. Then let them raise this experience of insight to the nth power, and let them extend it to cover all reality. This, or something like this, is satori, the Zen experience of enlightenment. It is supreme and total insight.

Third, closely allied to its intuitive quality is what Suzuki calls its momentary character. It comes and goes, and does not endure continuously or indefinitely. To be sure, this is a matter of conflicting emphases between the Rinzai and Soto sects. For the former have traditionally taught sudden enlightenment, while the latter have taught that enlightenment is gradual, more like a steady illumination than a sudden flash of light. Yet, it is at least possible that there is a valuable truth in both these emphases, the differences being those of relative emphasis and of different temperaments. In this connection it is notable that, even for a Rinzai follower, an enduring or steady illumination is desirable, while the advocates of gradual illumination by no means deny that some precise or abrupt moments may be more luminous than others.

Fourth, Suzuki speaks of the "affirmative quality" of the Zen experience and also of its "feeling of exaltation." Other witnesses speak also of the note of joy and peace. Perhaps we may interpret these affections as the emotive accompaniments of the achievement of a new unity of the self that occurs in all genuine mystical experience. Actual human selves always exhibit varying degrees of disunity or inner division, and of their opposites, namely unity or integration. Such selves ever seek greater integration. Obviously, any such new integration is an occasion of joy, harmony, and victory, even though it sometimes takes place in the midst of continuing turmoil in the self and the world.

Fifth, Suzuki speaks also of a "sense of the Beyond" (the capital letter is his), and he immediately adds that this sense carries an impersonal rather than a personal feeling tone. It is possible to understand both the Beyond and the impersonality within the context and meaning of enlightenment. For, as was said above, the content of the mystical experience is the direct experience of one's total unity with Reality or Being. Obviously, any such experience, genuinely and directly undergone, brings the sense of overcoming narrow boundaries and fixed limits, and of the inexhaustability of the Reality of which one's self is a small part or aspect. Indeed, genuine religious experience, in whatever tradition, involves some such perception as this infinitude of Being.

Sixth, in the wider context of his writings, Suzuki's use of the term, *impersonal*, may be seen as a way of distinguishing Zen experience from the strong and unequivocal personalism of the Judeo-Christian relation to God. He is concerned to make clear that Zen has no such personal deity or savior. As we have noted, it is, in Japanese terms, jiriki and not tariki. Yet, granting all this, it may be questioned whether the term, *impersonal*, is not misleading. For a person's relation to sticks and stones, to pens and pencils—in short, to things—is the usual meaning of *impersonal*. It would be truer to the experience to say *transpersonal*, meaning that, in this unique experience, both categories, personal and impersonal, have been left behind in an experience whose uniqueness can only be captured, if at all, first by direct experience, and only thereafter expressed by metaphorically extended images or symbols.

(4) Zen's symbols are undeniably Japanese, and to Zen's relation to Japanese culture we must briefly turn our attention. Zen is a part of Japan, being both influenced by and influencing the whole culture of which it is a part. The roshis in whom the Zen way is incarnated are indefeasibly Japanese persons and cannot be understood apart from this altogether basic fact. Their thought and lives are steeped in the culture of their nation. If we compare this Japanese branch of Buddhism with the Buddhism of India or of Southeast Asia, the ingredient of Japanese values becomes clear.

Japan shares with China what we have termed a cosmic outlook or orientation. To this the Japanese added their own intensity of nature, their peculiar brand of pragmatism, and their occasional eruptions of irrationality.[26] All of these distinctive values find expression in Zen. Again, the Japanese share with the Chinese a love of the concrete or the particular, in contrast to India's flights of abstraction. Zen is a form of Buddhism which, instead of fleeing from the concrete to the abstract, insists rather in seeing the abstract in and through the concrete particular things and persons of everyday life. Zen is an expression of this distinctive East Asian relation of the universal and the particular.

In this connection, both China and Japan have had a strong, clear, and sharp aesthetic sense, especially for the beauty of nature—an attitude that grows readily out of their cosmic orientation. Humans intuit the universe of which they are parts, and they do so by means of powerful and expressive symbolic forms. Zen is the inheritor of this cosmic legacy, seeing in nature symbols of the eternal spirit of which nature is the embodiment and expression.

Zen is not only influenced by Japan but also, in turn, has exercised pervasive influence on Japanese culture. Herein lies a major difference between Buddhism in China and Japan. In the former country the national tradition was fully developed long before the coming of Buddhism. However, in the case of Japan, Buddhism was on the scene during the formative period of the national tradition and, hence, was woven into its basic patterns. No branch of Buddhism has been more widely or deeply influential than Zen.

We have already noted that the Rinzai followers of Eisai became schoolmasters to the Japanese nobility who saw correctly in Zen an influence for strong, inner-directed character education. This trait in turn produced a brand of inward courage that made Zen effective in swordsmanship and other military practices. Yet one must immediately add that this military courage was also tempered by Buddhist humanitarian scruples concerning the limits of aggression against a fellow human being.

Muso Kokushi, Zen abbot and master, and the plainspoken counselor to emperors and shoguns, was also the first Japanese landscape architect. He designed a garden as a fitting environment for the teahouse and its ceremony. All of these had Buddhist symbolic meaning as well as characteristically Japanese beauty. Sesshu's landscape paintings and Basho's haiku poetry continued the same tradition. Indeed, it is difficult to find any major achievement of Japan's traditional culture that has escaped Zen's pervasive influence.

(5) Zen philosphy or influence on philosophy is harder to make a case for, despite what Father Dumoulin calls Dogen's "religious metaphysics." For how can one make a philosophy out of the rejection of philosophy? The question is a fair one, but Zen shows the way in which it has, in fact, been done.

First of all, let us note with Suzuki that the context of Zen is the whole Mahayana tradition of Indian and Chinese Buddhism. This includes the basic conclusions of Buddha's thought, but also and even more, it means the thought of Nagarjuna and other Mahayana philosophers as carrying Buddha's intention to its consistent philosophic conclusion. No conclusion of Nagarjuna was more important for Chinese and Japanese Buddhism than his view that the samsara world and the nirvana world are the same reality seen from different, or opposite, viewpoints. This statement enabled Chinese and Japanese Buddhist philosophers to interpret Buddhism as a truth about the cosmos. Zen inherits this line of thought.

But what of Zen's irrationalism, its doctrine of no-mind, and its occasional outbursts of book burning and sheer depreciation of reason? These elements in the Zen tradition are not to be denied. They point, however, to a fundamental truth, namely, that there is another kind of truth that is not under the sovereign sway of the discursive intellect. At its best, this insight is the discursive intellect's own insight into its own limits or boundaries; and, at its best, is precisely what Zen says. However, its worst is an overplaying and distortion of this fundamental truth, which manifests itself as antirationalism and obscurantism. Both the best and the worst are to be found in the Zen tradition.

At its best, Zen constitutes an incisive statement, in the distinctive symbol system of Japanese Buddhism, of what our chapter 2 called the philosophy of mysticism. Here, as elsewhere, there have emerged not only the practical disciplines necessary for the experience, but also the philosophic concepts necessary for the expression of the unitive vision of mysticism, with its fundamental theme of the One and the many and their interrelations. It is, indeed, this philosophic vision that Zen has nurtured and sustained in Japanese history. Zen presents itself to the twentieth century world not only as a form of mystical experience, but also as a highly distinctive formulation of what we have called the philosophy of mysticism.

The Significance of Zen Today

We return now to Suzuki's remark concerning the uniqueness of Zen, with which this chapter began. Suzuki's judgment is correct in the precise sense that Zen involves a highly distinctive symbol system; and, in terms of this system, Zen offers to the seeker an interpretation of the mystical vision that is unique in many of its emphases and accents. In these ways, then, Zen is unique, or at least highly distinctive. Some Zen roshis have refused to translate Zen terms and source documents from Japanese into other languages, arguing that only in the Japanese language can it be truly and accurately understood.

As in the case of any unique or highly distinctive entity, the student must here work his way, by a combination of sympathetic imagination and hard study, into the context in which Zen symbols have meaning. This problem may be likened to that of understanding the meaning of a subtle poem in a new and unfamiliar language. In a word, in the study of Zen, and even more in its practice, this kind of direct experiential dimension is necessary if Zen is to be meaningful.

Yet, having said this, and Suzuki to the contrary notwithstanding, let it also be said once again that Zen is an example of what throughout this volume we have called mystical experience and the philosophy of mysticism. It is, indeed, these more general aspects of Zen that render it approachable and intelligible to people of many different times and places. And let it be added, it is the personal experience and testimony of many people of our time of both East and West that Zen constitutes a timely and wise expression of this mystical view of man and the universe.

Despite Zen's contemporary significance, the most persuasive and widely comprehensible statement, even for twentieth century minds, will nevertheless be a traditional Zen symbolic form. Hence, we conclude this chapter with Hakuin's famous "Song of Zazen." Hakuin (1685–1768) was the Zen leader and reformer whose thought and life were most responsible for the modern revival of Zen. The translation is by Shibayama, roshi of Nanzenji monastery, Kyoto.[27]

All beings are primarily Buddha.
It is like water and ice:
There is no ice apart from water;
There are no Buddha apart from beings.

Not knowing how close the Truth is to them,
Beings seek for it afar—what a pity!
They are like those who, being in the midst of water,
Cry out for water, feeling thirst.
They are like the son of a rich man
Who wandered away among the poor.

The reason why beings transmigrate through the six worlds,
Is because they are lost in the darkness of ignorance;
When they wander from darkness,
How can they ever be free from birth-and-death?

As for Zazen taught in the Mahayana,
No amount of praise can exhaust its merits.
The Six paramitas—beginning with the Giving, Observing the Precepts,
And other good deeds, variously enumerated,
Such as Nemutsu, Repentence, Moral Training, and so on—
All are finally reducible to Zazen.

The merit of Zazen even during a single sitting,
Erases the countless sins accumulated in the past.
Where then are the Evil Paths to misguide us?
The Pure Land cannot be far away.

Those who, for once, listening to this Truth
In all humanity,
Praise it and faithfully follow it,
Will be endowed with innumerable merits.

But if you turn your eye within yourselves
And testify to the truth of Self-nature,
To the truth that Self-nature is no-nature,
You have really gone beyond the ken of sophistry.

For you, then, open the gate leading to the oneness of cause and effect;
Before you, then, lies a straight road of non-duality and non-trinity.
When you understand that form is the form of no-form,
Your coming-and-going takes place nowhere else but where you are,
When you understand that thought is the thought of no-thought,
Your singing-and-dancing is no other than the voice of Dharma.

How boundless is the sky of Samadhi!
How refreshingly bright is the moon of the Fourfold Wisdom!

At this moment what do you lack?
As Nirvana presents itself before you,
The place where you stand is the Land of Purity,
And your person the body of the Buddha.

SUGGESTIONS FOR FURTHER READING

As many of these works are classics that have appeared in numerous editions, only the most accessible publication is indicated.

Bellah, Robert. *Tokugawa Religion*. Glencoe: Free Press, 1957.

Burtt, E. *The Teachings of the Compassionate Buddha*. New York: Mentor Books, 1954.

de Bary, W. T., ed. *Sources of Japanese Tradition*. New York: Columbia University Press, 1958.

———, ed. *The Buddhist Tradition*. New York: Modern Library, 1969.

De Martina, R.; Suzuki, D.; and Fromn, E. *Zen Buddhism and Psychoanalysis*. New York: Grove Press, 1963.

Dumoulin, H. *A History of Zen Buddhism*. New York: Pantheon Books, 1963.

Earhart, B. *Japanese Religion*. Belmont: Dickenson, 1969.

Hamilton, C. *Buddhism: A Religion of Infinite Compassion*. New York: Liberal Arts, 1952.

Kapleau, P. *Three Pillars of Zen*. New York: Harper & Row, 1966.

Moore, C. E., ed. *The Japanese Mind*. Honolulu: East-West Center Press, 1967.

Morgan, K., ed. *The Path of the Buddha*. New York: Ronald Press, 1956.

Nakamura, H. *The Ways of Thinking of Eastern Peoples*. Honolulu: East-West Center Press, 1962.

Ono, S. *Shinto, The Kami Way*. Rutland: Tuttle, 1962.

Ross, F. *Shinto: The Way of Japan*. Boston: Beacon Press, 1965.

Reischauer, E., and Fairbank, J. *East Asia: The Great Tradition*. New York: Houghton Mifflin, 1960.

Stryk, L. *Zen Prayers, Sermons, Anecdotes*. Garden City: Doubleday, 1963.

Suzuki, B. L. *Mahayana Buddhism*. New York: Macmillan, 1969.

Suzuki, D. T. *Manual of Zen Buddhism*. New York: Grove Press, 1960.

———. *Essentials of Zen Buddhism*. New York: Dutton, 1962.

———. *Zen Buddhism*. Garden City: Doubleday, 1965.

Takakusu, J. *Essentials of Buddhist Philosophy*. Honolulu: University of Hawaii Press, 1947.

XII
Christian
Theology
As Philosophy

THIS CHAPTER TITLE will doubtless strike some readers as a contradiction in terms. Theology is theology and philosophy is philosophy, and like East and West in the old adage (although hopefully not contemporary fact) never the twain shall meet. Speaking historically and traditionally, theology may be defined and construed as the internal self-understanding of the Christian faith, practiced by professing Christians—and so this line of thought continues—also addressed to Christians. Sometimes, as for example in the *Church Dogmatics* of Karl Barth, it has been explicitly limited to those within the Christian church.[1] This view of theology has often elicited the charge, from those outside this closed circle, that the whole enterprise is one gigantic rationalization after the fact. Philosophy, on the other hand, claims to have no prior commitments—at least none that are exempt from critical scrutiny. Hence, philosophy in contrast and opposition to theology is free to follow where the factual evidence leads. Philosophy also professes a universality of outlook that makes it impatient with all particularisms. Thus, when theology has claimed final or absolute truth, philosophy has stood up to oppose such claims. Such at least have been some of the relations between theology and philosophy, and we shall do well to acknowledge them at the beginning of a chapter that is devoted to a different view of their relations, actual and possible.

There are some obvious difficulties in this traditional view of the relation of theology and philosophy. Some of the great figures of the past have surmounted the barriers and have been at once theologians and philosophers. Augustine is legitimately studied both as theologian and philosopher. So too are Thomas Aquinas and his fellow scholastics, past and present. To take a very different historical example, if we classify David Hume and his writings on religion as philosophy, and the orthodox responses to Hume as theology, in effect what we have done is to build a Berlin wall through the middle of an argument when in fact no such barrier exists.[2]

Yet it is to the present, to contemporary theology, that we look for our crucial evidence. Our thesis, or better, our hypothesis, is that for many people at the present time Christian theology functions as a philosophy; that is, it is for at least some adherents a philosophical viewpoint and outlook freely adopted and freely held. Hence, it is in other words, one philosophic option among others—one of the living options of our title. Its opponents may and do castigate it as bad philosophy, but concerning its existence and vitality the very vigor of enemy attack bears testimony.

In many of its current formulations the relation of Christian theology to the institutional church, far from being internal self-understanding, has become radically critical.[3] Running through much of contemporary theology there is what we may characterize as a built-in criticism of religion, some of it as free and often as radical in character as that of the ancient prophets of Israel—or for that matter, of modern critics of religion.[4]

On one frequently recurring issue, current theology makes a counterattack on its philosophic critics. The critics allege, in one set of terms or another, that theology is based upon faith (conceived as belief beyond or against rational test) while philosophy is based upon rational interpretations of experience open to all. The counterattack takes the form of pointing to faith-principles, namely assumptions or presuppositions, hidden in the foundations of philosophies as well as theologies. All systems of thought seem to begin, consciously or unconsciously, with assumptions. What seems important for either theology or philosophy is to keep all such assumptions open to critical inspection.

The task of sketching even some of the main lines of contemporary theology is extremely difficult for several reasons, notably the varieties, often conflicting varieties, of its forms. The range is from Karl Barth and his followers to the death-of-God theologians or to liberation theology, and from existentialism to process theology.[5] It embraces Protestant, Roman Catholic, and Orthodox figures (and sometimes Jews as well) often with puzzling interrelations and alliances. At least one Jewish figure, Martin Buber, has exerted major influence on Christian theology. Recent and current theology features some great names: Barth, Brunner, Bultmann, the Niebuhr brothers, and Tillich among the Protestants; Maritain, Gilson, Rahner, and Kueng among the Catholics; Berdyaev and Bulgakov among the Orthodox, as well as a host of lesser-known men, all of whom have made genuine contributions to theology, and in some cases to philosophy as well. The problem seems to be to find some main threads, some unifying themes or patterns in this vast and various body of writing and study.

It is tempting to undertake our task historically. In this case, the story would begin with Schleiermacher (if not with Kant) who deserves the title of founder of modern theology. From him the line extends through such nineteenth century figures as Ritschl and Herrmann, to Troeltsch and Harnack. Current theology is also giving belated attention to Ludwig Feuerbach's radical criticism of religion. From Germany the lines of influence have extended outward to Great Britain and the United States. In our time it extends to Asia and Africa as well.

In this tradition Karl Barth (1886–1968) must stand as the great revolutionary. For it was he who turned his back on the immanence theologies of his predecessors and asserted the transcendence of God, and the primacy of the Bible with its doctrines of sin, grace, and salvation. The Copernican revolution, which began with Barth's *Commentary on Romans* in 1918, was picked up and developed independently by such figures as Tillich, Bultmann, and the two Niebuhr brothers.[6] Many of the current younger generation of theologians might be characterized as children, or now even grandchildren, of this Barthian revolution.

The metaphor of a Copernican revolution in theology seeks to assert that there has taken place in this field of thought and study a change that is radical, discontinuous, and vast, and that has forcibly transformed the issues for study. One result of this revolution is the large amount of excellent study now going on in theology. To those who might be characterized as twentieth century analogues of Schleiermacher's "cultured despisers," let it be added that here is a field of study comparable in every way to any other academic discipline in the freedom and quality of its thought and the significance of its subject matter.

It will be more useful to approach our subject by means of a series of contemporary themes, rather than historically. To be sure, any choice of themes may well seem arbitrary, and none will fully cover or exhaust the field. However, if we choose well we will be able to trace major patterns of meaning through the subject matter. We shall trace five such themes through contemporary theology: (1) existentialism, (2) the historical character of Christian faith, (3) the social direction and significance of Christian faith, (4) faith and reason, and (5) the relation of sacred to secular in contemporary culture.

Existentialism

Tillich once paraphrased Kant's dictum that mathematics is the good fortune of natural science, saying that existentialism is the good fortune of Christian theology.[7] By this he meant that many important features of Christian faith may be illuminated by exposition in terms of existentialist philosophy in ways analogous to the mathematical forms of expression and thought of the physical sciences. If the main theses of this book are correct, Tillich might well have enlarged his remark to include other forms of religious thought and devotion in addition to Christianity. However, in this chapter our concern is with Christian thought, and hence our immediate question must be: Why is Tillich's assertion so? Indeed, is it true? Looking back to chapter 5 and its discussion of existentialism, what are the features of this philosophy which had led so many theologians to put the case for Christianity in these terms?

In chapter 5 we expounded existentialism as a movement cutting across literature and other arts as well as philosophy and theology, arising in the nineteenth century and coming to fruition in the twentieth, and centering in the question: What is man? What is he actually, really, prior to any philosophical theories or interpretations? More urgently and more personally: Who am I, and why am I living? As we have seen, some writers in this field have distinguished between *existential* and *existentialist* forms of thought. The former approach these questions directly out of the urgency and poignancy of their own experience. Kierkegaard, Dostoyevsky and Nietzsche were such men. The existentialists, who include such names as Heidegger, Jaspers, and Sartre, construct a philosophic ism out of what for the first group is a matter of direct, personal, and often agonized experience.

For both groups, the existential and existentialist, the question, What is man? stands at the center of human thought and experience. Man is the creature who puts this question. His existence entails, and in some sense *is* precisely, this question. As Tillich once remarked, human existence *is* an ontological question mark. As noted in chapter 5, man's active life constitutes in a very direct way his answer to the existential question. The answers to the existential question—if there be such—which existentialist writings have given, vary widely. As we saw in chapter 5, some assert that beyond the defining force of the question there is no answer. Yet, all seem to emphasize the central character of human freedom. Many have also underscored man's alienation in existence from his true nature or essence. In some very basic way man is not actually what he rightly and properly is and ought to be. This quick summary of existentialism is sufficient for our present purpose of showing why theologians have found it a good vehicle for the expression of religious faith, and why existentialism in Tillich's words is the good fortune of Christian theology.

There is also a further, frequently hidden, assumption of the existentialist theologians, generally assumed, but never clearly or explicitly acknowledged in their expositions of religious faith. So pervasive, so generally unacknowledged, and so important is this assumption that it will be worth our while to draw it into the open and look at it. It may be expressed as an assumption about the nature of religious statements and the experience they seek to articulate. What is the primary referent of such statements? What are they about? To what do they refer?

It has been the common assumption of existentialist theology that they are about existence, and that they are not initially or primarily at least, about the universe as a whole or about some remote region beyond the reach of the greatest telescope. That religious faith, Christian and other sorts as well, is primarily a way of understanding human existence—and even more, a way of living it out—is the central affirmation, generally assumed but never explicitly acknowledged by the existentialist theologians. Barth, Bultmann, Tillich, the Niebuhrs, each of these men in his own way focuses attention upon human existence as the primary referent of religious and theological utterances. Clearly this existential (and existentialist) assumption lies at the center of what was termed above as the Copernican revolution of contemporary theology.

Stated thus plainly, it does not seem unreasonable or perverse to say that religious faith is about human existence. Indeed, a good many quotations from the Bible and other primary religious sources come readily to mind to support this view. To be sure, once this primary reference of religious experience to man's existence is established, let it be immediately added that its relation to the wider world can by no means be avoided or ignored. This is for the good reason that man in his actual occurrence is a part of this wider world of reality. So it is that the existentialist theologians have approached these wider questions of philosophy and theology through their bearing on the human situation. As we noted in chapter 5, the way to cosmology and ontology lies through anthropology; the way to the world and God lies through the human situation and not apart from it, as so often has been assumed by traditional theology.

This existentialist way of interpreting and understanding faith and religion has implications not only for theology and philosophy, but for the history of the world's religions as well. These implications may be briefly summarized by recalling our parable at the end of chapter 2 of the little man in the center of the circle. The reader will recall that around the circumference of this circle is gathered a large and various throng of people. As the man in the middle keeps repeating to himself, "Why am I here? What is this all about?," the people around the circumference continue to make their answers to his question. The point of the parable is, once more, that the faiths and philosophies of the world may be approached as proposed answers to the central human question. In terms of their different proposals, the man in the middle, who is Everyman, must make his choice and live his life. Of course, it may turn out that Everyman will ignore them all and listen to some new voice as yet unknown. Or, as the early Sartre suggested, he may make up his own answers as he goes along.

Each of the existentialist theologians has made his own use of this philosophy. Karl Barth in his *Commentary on Romans* made extensive use of Pascal on the grandeur and misery of man, and quoted eloquent and powerful passages from Kierkegaard and Dostoyevsky on the fallen or alienated character of human existence. The fact that Barth later in his *Dogmatics* retracted his existentialism (in order, as he said, to free theology from any and all dependence on philosophy) does not detract from the power of his early work. In fact it might be urged that in spite of himself what Barth did in the *Dogmatics* was to continue a properly baptized Christian version of the same existentialist philosophy under the name of theology.

Reinhold Niebuhr's debt to existentialism is explicit and acknowledged, though developed in his own terms. As the title of his Gifford lectures indicates, his lifelong focus of interest was *The Nature and Destiny of Man* or, as he often expressed the matter, the nature of man in society and history. As a student of social ethics and politics, he sought categories of interpretation adequate to the facts of human existence, encountered in his wide-ranging study and active life. These he believed he found in the Biblical categories of man as image of God and as sinner.[8] Niebuhr interpreted the image of God as man's freedom of self-transcendence, and he viewed sin as human egotism, namely, man's tendency to think of himself more highly than he ought or, in the words of the Bible, to imagine himself "as God."[9] These views have notable antecedents, not only in the Genesis creation story but in such figures as Paul, Augustine, and Calvin. It is this view of the nature of evil as man's egotism or arrogant pride that lies at the foundation of Niebuhr's social philosophy. Niebuhr found this evil element not only in individual life but socially as "collective egotism" in the pride of nations, classes, ethnic groups and, indeed, in all human groups.[10] Such egotism is notably illustrated by rulers who, as Niebuhr wrote in trenchant epigram, "play God and so become the devil to their fellowmen." However, it also finds illustration in man's best and highest qualities as well. Thus, for example, there is a pride of knowledge ("every thinker loves his thought more than he ought"), as well as a pride of morality and of religion. Moral pride is illustrated by the Pharisees, of whom the Bible says they "trusted in themselves and despised the others." Religious pride seeks to put God "on our side," rather than seeking to put man "on God's side."[11]

Rudolph Bultmann is unique among the existentialist theologians in his explicit use of the categories of Heidegger's existentialist philosophy. Bultmann, a New Testament scholar, was fully aware of the problems for twentieth century man in the mythological outlook of the New Testament. It is simply not possible for the thoughtful person in our age to take literally such ideas as the three-story universe of the New Testament. Hence, Bultmann resorted to what he termed the demythologizing (the German word coined by Bultmann is *Entmythologozierung*) or a translation of mythical statements into statements about human existence in Heidegger's philosophy.[12] Thus, for example, the life of faith is rendered as authentic existence, God as Being, and so on.

Most philosophically original of this whole group is Tillich who developed his own version of existentialist philosophy, in which it is the role of philosophy to ask the questions implied in the various aspects of being, and it is theology's role to give Christian answers.[13] Thus, for example, the question implied in Being (or Being-as-such in Tillich's formulation) is answered by the Christian symbol of God, the question implied in existence is answered by Christ, the question implied in philosophy of history and culture is answered by the symbols of Spirit and Holy Spirit. To some of Tillich's critics, such a neat correlation of question and answer constitutes evidence that the show is rigged. Philosophic critics have also argued that philosophy answers questions as well as asking them. Still others of his critics have questioned Tillich's view that existence as such is fallen, such a view being more like a twentieth century version of gnosticism than like orthodox Christianity.[14] Yet beyond all such controversies is the larger fact that Tillich and his fellow existentialists have employed existentialist philosophy for the exposition of Christian faith, and have found it fruitful. They have done so in much the same way that the ancient church fathers used Platonism as a philosophic vehicle for the expression of the same faith.

This alliance between Christianity and existentialism has become considerably less than unanimous in the most recent theological developments. For example, it is clearly not the case with the so-called process theologians, who have sought to use Whitehead's philosophy as a vehicle for the expression of Christian faith.[15] No one could accuse Whitehead of existentialism! He was concerned not so much with the human foreground of experience as with its cosmic background and context. Yet, even here, existentialist insights and concerns have crept into the writings of such process theologians as John Cobb and Shubert Ogden.[16]

Historical Character of Faith

A second important recurring theme in contemporary theology is what we have called the historical and biblical character of Christian faith. These terms, *historical* and *biblical*, call for immediate explanation and clarification. First of all, it is an observable feature of the makers of the contemporary theological revolution that they have returned to the Bible as the primary source of faith, and to such figures as Augustine and Luther as classical expositors of the biblical faith and viewpoint. It must immediately be interjected that this has not meant a return to biblical literalism or fundamentalism. None of these men could possibly be charged with the assertion, "if it is in the Bible, then it must be true." To the contrary, they have fully accepted a critical and scholarly approach to the Bible. Conversely too, under the influence of the new theology a great deal of free, critical biblical scholarship of a high degree of excellence has flourished. The theological revolution has also elicited fresh study of the classic figures of Christian history from the ancient church fathers through the Protestant reformers down to modern theology.

The Bible and the Christian tradition function for contemporary theology as sources of those central and basic images and ideas which, taken together, provide a primary definition of Christian faith. Such, for example, are the images of God, man, sin, Christ, and redemption, which function together to provide a Christian definition of existence. It is the proper business of theology to dig these images and ideas out of the ancient texts in which they first occur, to subject them to systematic and critical study in order to shape them into coherent accounts of man's experience of the world, and then to subject these accounts to rigorous and comprehensive appraisal.

As we have seen, different theologians have been attracted to different images, issues, and emphases: Niebuhr to an Augustinian view of sin as self-love or egotism, Bultmann to the issue of demythologizing, and so on. Yet no feature of the biblical outlook has been more influential than the image of history as linear and dramatic. In chapter 5 we noted the two meanings of history as the events of the human past and as the study of these events. It is primarily the first meaning that is here involved.

In general, two views or images of history seem to occur and recur in the course of human reflection on this subject.[17] According to the first view, history is an endlessly turning cycle or wheel. We have observed this view in cosmic cultures from Greece to China. Frequently associated with the cyclic view has been a devaluation of the whole realm of time and history. For, if history be an ever-turning wheel, then many persons have sought to escape from it to a transhistorical and timeless eternal peace. Reinhold Niebuhr once pungently characterized this view as "putting a ladder up to eternity, climbing the ladder and pulling it up after you." This a-cosmic view of history finds illustration in mystics around the world from Plotinus to Shankara.

In sharpest contrast to both the cosmic and a-cosmic outlooks is the view of the biblical Hebrews that we have termed linear and dramatic. Its defining image is not an ever-turning wheel but a straight line extending from the past through the present into the future. In its fully developed form, it may be compared to a drama of which God is both author and director, and in which humans are called to be participants or actors. It is moreover a drama produced or played through just once. This drama began at Creation, moves to climax with the coming of the Messiah, and to denouement or resolution at Judgment Day.

The beginnings of this way of viewing time and history seem to have been rooted in the early biblical or Hebraic tenet that "God is lord."[18] First, Israel as a people, then later, individuals, were viewed as subjects of this divine sovereign or king. Yet, as people looked abroad, observing the world in which they lived, other gods seemed to be the real rulers or sovereigns of the world. Hence, prophets and seers looked to both past and future to validate and vindicate the hidden sovereignty of Israel's true Lord. They looked to the past, first to their beginnings as a people in the deliverance from Egyptian bondage and to the giving of the Torah on Mt. Sinai, and then subsequently to the origin of things, saying, "In the beginning God . . ." Indeed it was precisely this latter thought that motivated the creation stories. Thus, the central meaning of these stories is not a prescientific theory of origins, but the religious assertion, "In the beginning God . . . ," or "God is lord of first things."

However, ancient Israel's seers and prophets turned to the future as well as the past, saying in effect that in contrast to present appearances to the contrary, one day God's lordship would be vindicated.[19] From this thought came the eschatological outlook of the Bible. Judgment Day means a future time when God's Lordship and Kingship will be clear for all to see. It is in other words the assertion that God is lord of last things as well as first things. Together, these turns of thought to past and future produced the historical outlook so distinctive of the Bible and its people.

It is this historical outlook that pervades every aspect of biblical thinking. To cite a single example, the biblical view of the human self is that of an actor or participant in the divine-human drama. There is a fundamental difference between viewing one's selfhood as a microcosm of the cosmos and as a piece of historical destiny. The biblical view is the latter.

The climax of the drama of history as it developed in the thought of the Bible is the coming of the Messiah, or Anointed One. (*Christos* is simply the Greek translation of the Hebrew, *Messiah* or Anointed One.) The Jewish and Christian versions of the biblical divine-human drama differ at several points, but most notably concerning the Messiah. Judaism teaches that the Messiah is still to come, while Christianity is convinced that the Messiah *has* come in Jesus of Nazareth. In passing, the name, Jesus, is simply the Hellenized form of *Yeshua* or Joshua (meaning "the Lord saves"), hence, the Hebrew formulation is *Yeshua the Messiah*, and the Greek is *Jesus the Christ*. In any language, the fundamental and central conviction of Christian faith is that Jesus is the Christ. This is also the central and primary issue with which Christian theology has wrestled from its beginning to the present.

The first fully developed Christian philosophy of history—and in many ways still its most adequate rendering—is Augustine's *City of God*, in which the plot of the drama of history is conceived as the interaction of the city of God and the city of this world.[20] In Augustine's narrative, the linear-dramatic view of history finds full and explicit expression. Taking Augustine as the paradigmatic model of the biblical view of history, the reader will be able to compare it to other models, such for example as the cyclic view of India, China, and other Asian cultures.

It would be difficult to overstate the influence of the biblical-Augustine view upon subsequent ages of the Western world. The Middle Ages sought to identify Augustine's City of God with the institutional church—and almost succeeded. However, the twelfth century heretical Joachim of Fiori (d. 1202) wrote his own radical version of historical development in his story of the three historical ages of Father, Son, and Holy Spirit.[21] According to Joachim, the first was identified with the history of ancient Israel, the second with the age of official, institutional Christianity in which Joachim lived; but in the third age, still to come, Joachim foresaw such radical developments as the abolition of the church or of institutional religion.

The tradition of a third age, still ahead of us in human history, and of its climactic significance for the whole unfolding drama of history, has haunted the imagination of Western man ever since Joachim's time. For radical Christians of the sixteenth and seventeenth century, it became the millennium which they hoped soon to inherit. For the more secular seers of seventeenth and eighteenth centuries, the third age became the utopia which was the goal of human progress. As Carl Becker convincingly argued, progress was the end result when the eighteenth century philosophers substituted Nature for God, human perfectability for sin, and the human future for heaven.[22] In nineteenth century France, Saint-Simon and Comte gave their own version, at once secular and scientific, but strongly messianic, of this same dream of the third age. In the Comtean interpretation, this vision became a modern philosophy of history and science in which the theological and metaphysical ages are to be followed climactically by the positive or scientific age. Modern positivism in philosophy may be characterized as the somewhat embarrassed inheritor of this legacy of the messianism of science.

In nineteenth century Germany, Hegel gave his own account of the unfolding course of history; but as we said in chapter 7, stemming from Hegel it was Marx whose vision of history was destined to become at once the faith and philosophy of millions of twentieth century men in all parts of the world. Having already examined Marxist philosophy, in present perspective we can look back and better understand its lineage as a secularized and skewed form of the biblical or Augustinian view.

In addition to this pervasive and agelong influence of the biblical view of history on Western thought in all its aspects, it has also specifically become a major subject for contemporary theological reflection. In a variety of ways, theologians continue to wrestle with the radically historical character of Christian faith and thought. The second volume of Niebuhr's *Nature and Destiny of Man* is entitled *Human Destiny*, in which the author approaches such categories as sin, grace, and final fulfillment from the viewpoint of historical faith, that is, faith which takes the idea of history with radical seriousness.[23] Thus, for example, Christ is characterized as the figure who provides the dramatic center for history, and grace is the divine gift that completes and perfects the partial and distorted character of man's historical existence. In a notable paper, Tillich distinguished between the historical and nonhistorical faiths and philosophies in terms of whether the perception of time and history is a primary or a derivative element.[24] In this view the historical religions are those of the Bible, while the nonhistorical faiths, whether cosmic or a-cosmic, are those of East Asia and South Asia. Eliade's *Cosmos and History* makes a similar distinction between those faiths, on the one hand, in which the primary reality is the timeless and harmonious order of the cosmos in which man, gods, and objects of nature are citizens together, and on the other hand, those in which history is the primary reality.[25]

Clearly, this is an issue that goes to the foundations of our present study, distinguishing, once more, between those faiths and philosophies in which reality is primarily and radically historical in character, and those which construe reality as a pattern of timeless order, either cosmic or a-cosmic in character. As we have seen in the chapters on Indian, Chinese, and Japanese thought, these philosophies are not lacking in reflections on the nature of history. However, their views of history show two persistently recurring features. First, history is an ever-turning cycle or wheel, and second, frequently (though not always) there is a devaluation of history. The distinction between this view and the linear-dramatic view of history with its unique or once-for-all quality (in German, *Einmaligkeit*) is of fundamental and pervasive importance. Indeed, it is the most basic and fundamental discontinuity in the history of man's religions.

While the concepts of time and of history are by no means identical, there is a significant overlap between them. Theologians from Augustine to the present have noted that time is a part of God's good creation, and hence in the biblical view it is both real and good. This observation sets the biblical view of time in sharpest contrast to the faiths and philosophies that regard time as either evil or unreal or both. For the latter view, time is something from which man must be rescued. The temporalistic outlook of the Bible—if such we may call it—imparts to Judeo-Christian faith and thought an activism and also a realism that contrast sharply with the contemplative and otherworldly character of the alternative view.

Ethics and Society

Our third main theme, which follows closely upon the second, is the moral and social character of the Christian faith. Secular critics of traditional religion have long tended to assume a priori that all religion is escapist and reactionary in character. Critics from Marx and Freud to Russell and Dewey have assumed for religion an inherently compensatory and illusory nature. This still seems to be the prevailing attitude of the American academic establishment, and it is of course an accurate assessment of much popular religion, both past and present.

To such observers and observations it comes as something of a surprise that the makers of what we have called the theological revolution have invariably been men of profound social concern, and of varying degrees of liberalism or radicalism in social thought and action. While in the Roman Catholic church prior to John XXIII such men and ideas were not notably visible (at least not to the outside world), it now has become clear that this observation holds true also of large sections of this tradition. Contemporary theology, then, is committed to an indefeasibly social conception of Christian faith and to a radical criticism of the world as it is—including the institutional church as it is. Needless to say, these attitudes have aroused not a little anxiety and hostility on the part of the defenders of the status quo, both religious and secular.

No one has had more to do with this shift in the United States and Great Britain than Reinhold Niebuhr, whose biography exemplifies many of these concerns, as his thought expounds them.[26] Coming to maturity in the years just before World War I, he began during that time what was to become a lifelong wrestle with the ethics of war and peace. Taking a pastorate in Detroit in the 1920s, he found material for mordant social criticism in the developing automobile industry, while his own wide reading acquainted him with the social thought of men from Marx to Troeltsch and Barth. Yet more than any outside influence, Niebuhr's social philosophy was his own effort to relate Christian faith, as he knew and experienced it, to the harsh sociopolitical realities of the twentieth century. Assuming the chair in Applied Christianity in Union Theological Seminary in 1929, Niebuhr continued to speak, write, and act on these issues over the next four decades.

He was not alone in this undertaking. The study and practice of the social ethics of Christianity have attracted many of the ablest minds of contemporary theology. Broadly speaking, this study has focused upon two major issues, first the nature of Christian love and its relation to other aspects of the life of faith, and second the social relevance and application of this idea to major issues of social policy. These two subdivisions are frequently formulated as theological ethics and social ethics. We shall consider them briefly in turn.

To the average secular man of the twentieth century, the world, *love*, designates either a somewhat sentimental and romantic attachment of the sexes, located largely in novels and motion pictures, or perhaps an equally sentimental attachment for one's fellowman. In neither case, does he often regard it as worthy of a second thought.

Even for serious students, the ambiguity of the English word, *love*, constitutes a problem demanding extensive clarification.[27] It is a commonplace of theological ethics that the Greek language has no less than four words all translatable by 'love', ranging in meaning from a general gregariousness to sexual love, and from friendship to the sentiment of human brotherhood. This biblical concept of ethical love has been paraphrased by Martin Buber as the fulfillment of an I-Thou relation, or of the relation of persons-in-community.[28] The self or person is the bearer of dignity because he possesses the capacity for self-determination or freedom. Indeed, this last idea seems basic to the very meaning of selfhood or personality. Integrally bound to freedom, love is the attitude of spontaneous respect for, and affirmation of, personhood. Such seems to be the meaning of love in the biblical command, "Thou shalt love thy neighbor as thyself," which may be taken as the primary moral maxim of both Christianity and Judaism. (The New Testament Greek word for ethical love, *agape*, may be taken as a translation of the Hebrew word *ahav*.) The claim of both of these religions is that the command to love neighbor as self is the one fully adequate rendering of the moral law. In neither tradition has it often been construed as an autonomous and isolable command or obligation, but rather as a kind of spontaneous by-product of faith or of the love of God. St. Augustine's two formulations of morality are still pertinent to contemporary theology. Asked for his rule of morality, he replied "Love—and do as you please," and later, "Love God and do as you please." Presumably if a man truly loves, or truly loves God, then he will spontaneously and freely will and do the good. Such at least is the Judeo-Christian contention.[29]

What may perhaps be called the degrees of love has been the subject of much ethical reflection, past and present. It has been construed in terms of the models of a ladder, or of a pyramid.[30] The lowest degree, the bottom of the ladder or the base of the pyramid, is love as that kind of mutual concern among human selves necessary for any group or common life. A step higher is the kind of concern which implies equality and hence, at least by implication, universality. Each person is to count for one and only one. This meaning is an essential ingredient in most conceptions of justice and law. The next higher degree or level is one which, presupposing equality, moves onward to a concern for the special circumstances of particular persons or situations. For example, love for a gifted individual means seeking for him full opportunity to develop his special gifts. The highest degree of all, the top of the ladder, is the kind of sacrificial love exemplified by the Cross of Christ, and expressed in the biblical phrase "greater love has no man than this, that he lay down his life for his friends." While this sacrificial love cannot be made an instrument of social policy in any direct or immediate way, it nevertheless lifts human moral life above prudential calculation, to a level of adventure and grace. Looking at this full and varied reality of ethical love, Niebuhr characteristically remarked that "Love is never a simple possibility," but that it is "always relevant" to the human situation. His social ethics might be characterized as a realistic and pragmatic attempt to spell out this relevance in detail.

The application of ethical love to the main issues of social policy may also be said to constitute the discipline of Christian social ethics. Several main trends or tendencies are discernible in this field of study. First, the Catholic tradition defines this ethical task in dual terms of natural law that can guide man to the natural virtues of prudence, temperance, fortitude, and justice, and of the supernatural virtues of faith, hope, and charity, which, lying beyond reason and nature, are the gifts of God's grace.[31]

By contrast, Niebuhr's thought was formulated in terms of the proximate and pragmatic character of any and all concrete applications for the love ethic.[32] In few if any social decisions, even in the case of the simple face-to-face relation of one human individual to another, is the choice simply and unqualifiedly one of love as against its opposite, self-love. In other words, decision or choice is seldom or never in black and white; rather, it is in shades of gray. In the case of the larger issues of public policy, whether in politics or other regions of society, this becomes notoriously true.

The case of war and peace is a fair illustration of the complexities and ambiguities of moral decision in contemporary society.[33] Seeing the tragic evils
of war, anyone who is committed to human love or brotherhood is tempted
to the complete renunciation of force and violence, that is, to Tolstoian
pacifism. Yet, there are instances, as for example, for many people in World
War II, in which pacifism seems clearly to imply a surrender of justice. The
choice, again, is never the simple one, of love versus its opposite, but rather
of *which* realistic option will most significantly approximate the ideal of love.

Niebuhr once during the 1930s debated the issue of pacifism with the celebrated pacifist, John Haynes Holmes, who declared that under no circumstances would or could he do violence to another person. Niebuhr asked if he
were a sheriff in a southern U.S. town would he shoot to defend his prisoner
from an approaching lynch mob. Holmes replied that he would be morally
unable to be a sheriff in a southern town. Niebuhr's lifelong search was for a
responsible ethic capable of guiding both individual and social action in
difficult decisions of the sort that Holmes rejected.

Such guidance necessitates principles of a sort that several writers have
termed "middle axioms," which is to say, principles of sufficient def-
initeness to mediate between the ideal of love and specific areas of social action. For example, for a modern industrial society full employment is often
asserted to be such a middle axiom. The achievement and maintenance of
political democracy is another. In no case does such a middle axiom provide
full or infallible guidance for moral action, but it does give definite social
shape and guidance of a realistic kind to the love ethic.

In recent decades other Christian ethical thinkers, seeing some of the
shortcomings of such systems of middle axioms, have proposed a different
way of relating the ideal of love to specific situations, namely, in terms of
what they have labeled situationalism or contextualism.[34] These interpretors
have foresworn any absolute or overriding principles that will give specific
application to love in any and all situations. Indeed, they are avowedly opposed to any such rigid rules or principles as contrary to the spirit of love,
claiming that only in specific or concrete contexts does significant moral
thinking take place. What is right in one situation may well be wrong in
another. These ethicists also make considerable use of the social sciences to
provide specific factual guidance for moral decision-making in concrete situations. The contextualists have had considerable difficulty in giving a
defensible and consistent definition or delimitation of the term, context. For
example, if the context of a racial decision be defined as a single southern
U.S. town or state, the decision will be different from one which is made in a
national or global context.

Still another notable recent trend in social ethics has been to concentrate on specific major issues of moral practice. One such issue is America's race problem, another is sex ethics, still another is the ethics of medical practice, including the field of hallucinogenic drugs. On whatever problem they work, the effort of these Christian moralists is to provide adequate and concrete social application for the imperative to love neighbor as self.

Faith and Reason

The fourth theme to be sketched is, in effect, the new formulation of an old, hardy perennial topic, namely, the nature of faith and its relation to reason. Humans have reflected on this issue as long as they have asked themselves what it means to have faith, which is to say, as long as they have been human. Yet, contemporary theologians have succeeded in shedding significant new light on this old problem.

First of all, contemporary theology has redefined, faith or, rather more precisely, it has cut through modern and contemporary misconceptions, and has appealed to the understanding of this crucial concept in the Bible and such classical sources as Augustine and the Reformers. There are perhaps few more widely held misconceptions in the whole field of religious thought and experience than the assertion that faith is "believing what you know is not true," that is, that faith is intellectual assent beyond or against the rational, factual evidence. Whole theologies have been erected on this foundation of sand. While it is by no means the sole conception, this appears as the dominant conception in no less a philosopher-theologian than Thomas Aquinas.[35] A great number of philosophical attacks past and present upon religion proceed from this assumption. In contemporary academic philosophy, there is probably no more widespread and tenaciously held conception or misconception than this. That it continues to exist in much present day philosophy testifies to the mutual contemporary isolation of philosophy and theology.

What then does contemporary theology propose? We shall answer by a threefold analysis of the word *faith*.

(1) The first meaning is achieved by a return to the traditional biblical notion of faith understood as the trust of the heart leading to action. The Hebrew word, *emunah*, is unequivocal in this meaning. It denotes a state of conviction that organizes and unifies a human self, and motivates and guides its action. The Greek term, *pistis*, while somewhat more multivalued, still centrally and basically includes this personal and active meaning. William James once defined faith behaviorally as "a tendency to act." In other

words, it is a phenomenon of the affective life, of the will and not primarily of the intellect; its origin and center is the heart rather than the head.

Tillich, in a classic but controversial phrase, characterized faith as "ultimate concern."[36] Even more neutral and colorless than "concern" would be "interest." Other synonyms are "loyalties," "allegiances," "values," indeed, whatever disposes or inclines a person in one direction rather than another. Personally, this writer's preference is for the term, *value*, for the reason that it establishes relations between the religious experience of faith and the social sciences, and also with a well-established field of philosophic study, namely, value theory or axiology. Faith might in these terms then be defined as ultimate valuation.

Tillich's term, *ultimate*, is a vexing word, concerning which its author was by no means consistent or clear. He moved back and forth between two widely diverging meanings. The first might be characterized as a quality of human attitude or commitment, while the second was roughly synonymous with the Absolute or Ultimate of German idealist philosophy. It will not be far wrong to designate these meanings, respectively, as the subjective and objective ultimates. For the purpose of our analysis of faith it is sufficient to opt for the first characterization or definition. This view of ultimacy may also be specified factually in three fairly definite ways. As we said in the second chapter, an ultimate concern (a) has top priority in the scheme of concerns that make up or constitute a person or a culture; (b) it is deployed in the whole of experience rather than in only part of it; and (c) it is accompanied by a unique affective state or emotion called the holy, which will be discussed below. So conceived and defined, ultimate concern becomes a matter for factual exploration, study, and determination.

In this first meaning of faith as ultimate concern or valuation, all persons may be said to have faith, the atheist and agnostic as well as the theist. But *only* in this meaning of the word is this true. It is faith in this meaning of the word that organizes and unifies personality and guides action, and hence constitutes the foundation of human selfhood.

(2) But if this be so, then what is the relation of faith in this pervasively human sense, on the one hand, to faith in the second and more specifically religious sense on the other hand? Conversely, what is the relation of the historic religions of mankind to the first meaning of faith as defined and described above? To answer briefly, the many religions of mankind may be regarded as symbol-systems which in their respective and distinctive ways seek to express, to communicate, and to transmit faith in this first meaning; and in so doing they constitute the second main meaning of faith. In this second sense of the word we speak of Christian faith, Buddhist faith, and so on.

Religions are the institutions of human society whose distinctive function is to act as vehicles or carriers of ultimate concern or valuation. Yet, here as elsewhere, institutions seldom or never function with full efficiency, and indeed often block the very aims they profess to serve. But again, here as elsewhere, institutionalism is also the price of effectiveness. For without organization, nothing at all gets accomplished in human society and history. It must also be added as a factual observation that in addition to the usual problems of institutionalism, religious organizations frequently show still another of their own making, namely, they seek to hide their problems behind a façade of holiness or sacredness.

One advantage of our present analysis of faith is that is enables us to distinguish between faith in the first and primary sense, and faith in the sense of religion; and in a day when many individuals of unquestionable goodwill and intelligence will have no relation to religion, this seems a considerable advantage. Such people seek secular ways of expressing faith in contrast to the traditional historic religious ways.

(3) Yet a nagging question persists: What are we doing when we are doing faith? What are faith's conditions, its meaning, its implications? To what does it, and does it not, commit us? What will it, and won't it, do for us? In short, how shall we understand faith? Once these questions are raised, faith is on the way to becoming belief, which can be defined as faith become propositional, and which is the third main meaning of the term. It seems to be an aspect of the whole experience of faith, in the first and most general meaning of the word to claim validity or truth for itself. Yet, in what particular sense and meaning is a matter for subsequent analysis and appraisal. The general point seems clear, namely, that faith seeks understanding of itself. *Fides quaerens intellectum* ("faith seeking understanding") defines a general direction or bent of human valuation and thought and not merely a viewpoint of Anselm.[37] It is of great importance to see the way in which this third meaning grows out of the first two meanings.

In the past this aspect of faith has more often than not been badly handled by the traditional religions. For example, it has frequently occurred in the midst of acrimonious controversy, and it has involved appeals to tyrannical authority, to belief or assent beyond or against reasonable evidence, and to innumerable forms of obscurantism. Examples from all the various religious traditions will come readily to mind.

From the exposition of the preceding paragraphs, we are able to see how the misconception of faith as believing beyond or against the evidence has arisen; but we can also see how false and inadequate a view of faith it is and, indeed, how downright unnecessary it is. But what is more important, we are in a position to begin to repair the damage. For, distinguishing the three main meanings from one another, we see the relation of the third to the second and first meanings of faith, and hence we are in a position to pursue the third meaning freely, critically, and reasonably. Far from seeking to protect religious experience from critical inquiry, there are the best of reasons to do just the opposite. Here surely is too important a region of human experience to go unexamined. Let us paraphrase the Socratic maxim that the unexamined life is not worth living, to say that the unexamined faith is not worth holding. An additional advantage of this view of the matter is that in this new reformulation the traditional faith-reason problem acquires new human significance as a rational, critical appraisal of man's ultimate valuations.

Sacred and Secular

The fifth and final theme to be discussed is a cluster of issues centering in the relation of the sacred to the secular elements of culture and personality. As observed in the previous section, the holy may be characterized as the emotive accompaniment of ultimate concern or valuation. Accordingly, it attaches itself readily to the symbols and symbol-systems in which these concerns find expression. Thus, as we noted in chapter 2, the holy provides us with a working definition of religion. As argued there, a religion may be defined as an existing system of holy forms.

To speak more precisely, the holy is an emotive or affective response, while the sacred is volitional or directive in nature. The holy is a unique emotion, which, like all unique entities, can be described or indicated but cannot be defined. The classical description occurs in Rudolph Otto's *Idea of the Holy*, in which this emotion is characterized as being like fear, awe, wonder, mystery, and fascination.[38] In these terms, the sacred may be defined as the unique emotion of holiness plus the concerns or valuations that it accompanies. To summarize this whole issue in the form of an equation, ultimate concern or valuation plus its concomitant emotion of holiness equals the sacred. Hence, conversely, ultimate or sacred value may be said to constitute the human content or substance of all religious experience.

The actual occurrence of such sacred value is widely deployed in both personality and culture, that is, in individual and social experience. The symbolic forms that are its vehicles are innumerably many, and not infrequently seem extreme and bizarre in nature. Nonetheless, some such system of holy forms seems to have been a significant part of every human society of which reliable knowledge exists. Whether it will continue to be true in future is another question. Also, whether it is true not only of societies but of individual human beings is an even more difficult question. Here it must suffice to characterize this as a factual question demanding an answer by specific factual inquiry. Clearly, there are today many individuals throughout the world who claim to have no religion. They are conscious of no religious allegiance, nor of any need or desire for one. The question is whether such attitudes will continue, and prevail in the future.

Discussion of such questions as this brings us to a current issue in theological discussion, namely, the nature and significance of the secular and of secularism. The reader may recall that this subject was broached in chapter 2. Now we must pick up again the main thread of that discussion. Formally, the question seems simple enough. In terms of our definitions of the holy and the sacred, the secular is simply any region of human experience where these affections are absent. The secular is plainly and simply the nonsacred. However, in actual fact, the discussion has been considerably complicated by varying and often conflicting usage of the key concepts, the sacred and the secular.

In chapter 2 we observed that current writing in this area seems to show at least three different uses of such words as *secular, secularity,* and *secularism.* We now return to this threefold division, though in a different order from chapter 2's exposition. First and perhaps most general is Bonhoeffer's use of the term *secular*, to denote an attitude of respect for the rights of secular persons and secular areas of experience.[39] From this it follows that the sacred, particularly in the person of its professional representatives, should claim no special privileges or higher status. The sacred should not intrude where it is not understood or appreciated. There seems to be nothing in this usage that goes beyond well-known attitudes of Martin Luther and other Protestant reformers. It may also be noted in passing that this attitude is to be found in current writing side by side with other passages which argue that religious faith should infuse and guide human practice in all areas of life, secular as well as sacred.

A second meaning of the word, *secular*, derives from those chapters in modern European history in which regions of social life such as art, politics, economics, and education were freed from ecclesiastical domination and control. Having grown to maturity in the household of the faith, during previous ages of history, they have now left home and, as it were, have set up housekeeping on their own. From the Renaissance to the present, this has been the modern history of many major areas of Western society, ranging from art to politics. It has led to the widely popular conception of freedom as autonomy, or freedom from heteronomous control. It is this view of secularization that underlies Bonhoeffer's conception of the "world come of age."[40]

It may also be pointed out in passing that, while the movement of secularization in post-Renaissance Western history is probably more extensive than any other in human history, it is by no means historically unique. Greek society of the sixth and fifth centuries B.C. seems to show a similar movement of secularization. So too, for example, does the Tokugawa period of Japanese history. Still other examples might be cited. The problem posed by such movements is the relation of religion to the newly secularized forms of cultural life.

There is still a third use of the term *secular* in the current literature. This meaning is often designated as "secularism"; and it may be said to range from attitudes of hostile criticism aimed at all institutional forms of the sacred to that form of negative dogmatism which predicts their speedy demise. Perhaps the most forthright presentation of this view occurs in Arend Van Leeuwen's *Christianity in World History* in which, after an inspection of the traditional religions in today's world, the author asserts that the holy forms of religion are dying, and hence that the next age of human history will be wholly secular.[41] Van Leeuwen combines this view with a Barthian theology, which holds that Christian faith will continue to exist as a philosophy or theology of history of the sort characterized in a previous section of this chapter. What the institutional forms of this faith will be he does not say.

Harvey Cox' *Secular City* draws heavily upon Van Leeuwen's predictions of an impending total secularization of society, though Cox is not as forthright as Van Leeuwen in spelling out the implications of this view.[42] Both works are also flawed by their failure to distinguish between (1) secularism as a highly problematical twentieth century ideology and (2) as what these authors assert as a valid theological tenet.

Similar ambiguities are detectable in the "death of God" theologies, and in the controversies that have swirled around them in recent years. These writers do not tell us whether they mean (1) that the holy is no longer a valid and viable human response, or (2) that many modern people believe this to be so. These viewpoints seem to be as different and as incompatible as the following two assertions: (1) God does not exist and we and all of mankind ought to order our lives in the light of this fact, and (2) God *does* exist, but many twentieth century people do not believe this, and hence in fact order their lives as though he did not exist.

Nietzsche, who originated the metaphor of "the death of God" in *Thus Spake Zarathustra*, seems to have meant that the traditional Christian God was dead, in the sense of being incapable of eliciting living religious response in the modern world.[43] However, other religious images, such as that of the ancient Greek god, Dionysius, seem very much alive in Nietzsche's life and writing. Hence, for Nietzsche the slogan might well read: God is dead, long live God; or, Jehovah is dead, long live Dionysius!

For the contemporary theologians who gather under the slogan that God is dead the issue is more ambiguous. Is God dead in the sense of no longer existent? Or is it just some images of God that have died? And if some images are dead, are there others that still live? Once more, in many discussions, the essential contention appears to be that many contemporary people believe that God is dead. These writers seem fundamentally unclear on one, some, or all of these questions, and their plausibility depends upon a similar unclarity in their readers.

However these issues among the theologians may turn out, mankind seems to show little or no lessening of experiences of the holy. While some traditional ecclesiastical forms have retreated before the advance of massive contemporary secular forces, new and sometimes bizarre forms of the holy have erupted with great power in human life. The twentieth century political movements of Nazism and Marxism must be understood not simply as secular social philosophies, but as powerful symbol-systems eliciting religious or quasi-religious responses from their followers. More recently, the new patterns of the holy in the youth culture of the present provide novel and different kinds of verification of this same thesis. Even in so ostensibly secular a region of society as the academic community, the vital forms of human allegiance often show religious overtones and undertones. To such observations as these, man still appears as *homo religiosus*. If one may project the future on the basis of past and present evidence, the question is not sacred versus secular, but rather, which forms of the sacred will elicit and sustain human allegiance in times to come.

SUGGESTIONS FOR FURTHER READING

As many of these works are classics that have appeared in numerous editions, only the most accessible publication is indicated.

Adam, K. *The Spirit of Catholicism*. New York: Macmillan, 1930.

Altizer, T., and Hamilton, W. *Radical Theology and the Death of God*. Indianapolis: Bobbs Merrill, 1966.

Baillie, J. *Our Knowledge of God*. New York: Scribners, 1939.

Barth, K. *The Epistle to Romans*. London: Oxford University Press, 1933.

———. *Evangelical Theology*. Garden City: Doubleday, 1964.

Bettenson, H. *Documents of the Christian Church*. New York: Oxford University Press, 1947.

Brown, R. *The Spirit of Protestantism*. New York: Oxford University Press, 1961.

Brunner, E. *The Divine Human Encounter*. Philadelphia: Westminster Press, 1944.

Buber, M. *I and Thou*. New York: Scribners, 1937.

Bultmann, R. *Kergima and Myth*. London: SPCK, 1957.

Cobb, J. *Living Options in Protestant Theology*. Philadelphia: Westminster Press, 1962.

———. *A Christian Natural Theology*. Philadelphia: Westminster Press, 1965.

Cox, H. *The Secular City*. New York: Macmillan, 1965.

Dillenberger, J., and Welch, C. *Protestant Christianity*. New York: Scribners, 1954.

Ebeling, G. *The Nature of Faith*. Philadelphia: Fortress, 1959.

Farrer, A. *Finite and Infinite*. Westminster: Dacri, 1943.

Fletcher, J. *Situation Ethics*. Philadelphia: Westminster Press, 1966.

Flew, A., and MacIntyre, A., eds. *New Essays in Philosophical Theology*. New York: Macmillan, 1955.

Kueng, H. *The Council in Action*. New York: Sheed & Ward, 1963.

Lehmann, P. *Ethics in a Christian Context*. New York: Harper, 1963.

MacQuarrie, J. *Principles of Christian Theology*. New York: Scribners, 1966.

Mitchell, B., ed. *Faith and Logic*. London: Allen & Unwin, 1957.

Niebuhr, H. R. *The Meaning of Revelation*. New York: Macmillan, 1952.

———. *The Responsible Self*. New York: Harper & Row, 1963.

Niebuhr, R. *The Nature and Destiny of Man*. New York: Scribners, 1943.

———. *Faith and History*. New York: Scribners, 1949.

Rahner, K. *Theological Investigations*. Baltimore: Helicon Press, 1961.

———. *The Spirit in the World*. New York: Herder and Herder, 1968.

Temple, W. *Nature, Man and God*. New York: Macmillan, 1935.

Tillich, P. *Theology of Culture*. New York: Oxford University Press, 1959.

———. *Systematic Theology*. Chicago: University of Chicago Press, 1963.

Walker, W. *A History of the Christian Church*. New York: Scribners, 1959.

Williams, D. *What Present Day Theologians Are Asking*. New York: Harper, 1952.

———. *Spirit and Forms of Love*. New York: Harper & Row, 1968.

XIII
Jewish
Philosophies

PHILOSOPHIES IN THE JEWISH TRADITION claim our attention for several reasons. Judaism is one of the smallest of the world's living faiths, but from its beginning to the present day it has been one of the most creative in all aspects of human culture. We shall want to explore the sources of this creativity, which is nowhere more evident than in philosophy. Philo, Maimonides, Spinoza, Rosenzweig, Buber—these are only a few of the best known names in the great tradition of Jewish philosophy.

Judaism seems also to be in the midst of crisis and renewal today. The vast tragedies of the Hitler period, followed by the founding of the state of Israel, have stirred Judaism to its depths, with results in faith and culture that are only now beginning to take shape. Contemporary Judaism is marked by many significant new directions of thought as well as of feeling and faith.

Another reason for our attention to the Jewish tradition is its combination of likeness and unlikeness to the more widely familiar Christian tradition. Both are founded upon faith in one God, or as the later H. Richard Niebuhr put it, on "radical monotheism."[1] It is all too easy for people familiar only with the Christian tradition to assume axiomatically that its forms alone constitute the natural and normal expression of this faith. The study of Jewish tradition will show us sharply contrasting forms, which is to say significantly diverging ways of devotion and practice, as well as philosophic thought, which also seek to give expression to monotheistic faith in individual and social existence. To be specific, for the Christian, man's primary approach to the one God is through faith in Christ. By contrast, the Jew approaches this same God, as he puts the matter, by "doing the Torah." In other words, Judaism is to Christianity as doing Torah is to faith in Christ. We shall want to see what this difference means, and just how doing the Torah contrasts with faith in Christ.

Moreover, the church fathers of early Christianity, when pressed to interpret and define faith in Christ, produced creed and theology as distinctively Christian forms of interpretive thought and language, even though fabricated largely out of Hellenistic materials. During the same period in which this development was taking place in Christianity, Judaism was drawing apart from the wider life of the Hellenistic world and producing the Talmud as a body of interpretation of the Torah. The Talmud was fabricated largely out of Hebraic rather than Hellenistic materials. Hence, again, Judaism is to Christianity not only as Torah to Christ, but also as Talmud is to creed and theology.

Judaism presents other contrasts as well. We have observed in chapter 2 and in subsequent chapters the general issue of faith's relation to culture. On the one hand, faith provides motivation and direction for cultural action and creation, and conversely culture may be characterized as lived faith. While these relations are generally true, Judaism's small size and minority status during the centuries of dispersion have generated unique emphases and accents. For example, there has been an agelong attrition of individual Jews who for many and varying reasons have renounced or left Judaism. On the other hand, there are many individuals who have specifically avowed Judaism as the religious center of the Jewish culture. Still, again, Jewish culture as a minority or subculture within a larger environing culture has always faced its own distinctive problems. Nowhere is this better illustrated than in the concept of Jewish philosophy.

Among the distinctive features of the Jewish tradition is a cluster of values of very considerable significance for philosophy. This cluster includes an intense desire for learning, skill in argument, and a love of wisdom. All three have grown out of very practical aspects of Jewish life. Learning has long been essential for activities ranging from reading the Torah to participating in the forms of daily work historically open to Jews. Similarly, argument grows out of discussion of issues ranging from the task of interpreting the Torah to making mundane daily decisions; the love of wisdom grows out of admiration for those who excel in learning and argument, along with the corollary realization that these activities can indeed become intrinsic goods. Supremely, it has traditionally been believed that the scholarly study of the Torah and the Talmud can, and, indeed, ought to be pursued as intrinsic goods or ends in themselves. The talmudic admonition is not to make a spade of the Torah, that is, not to treat it as a tool for earning a living. Still another closely related Jewish value has been a love of freedom in all its many aspects, generated, it must be assumed, alike by the moral and religious idealization of this value and the practical lack of freedom during many centuries of Jewish history.

Many of these values found original or initial expression in the Bible, which is the source of the Jewish tradition. The Jewish Bible, be it noted, is not a philosophical text, though in ways which we shall presently observe, it has been the fruitful source of much philosophical activity for Jews, as also for Christians. But first, we must see how the Bible is the source of Jewish faith and life.

Biblical Source

In chapter 5 we were led to define existentialism as the philosophy that places the question, who am I? at the center of philosophic inquiry. We were also led to note the existentialist emphasis upon history (meaning primarily historical *activity* rather than historical *study*). The preceding chapter also noted the ways in which contemporary Christian thought has put existentialism to work in theology. In this chapter we shall be continuing several existentialist categories, notably the idea of history, to interpret Jewish faith and thought.

Like other religious communities of human history, Judaism has been called into being and sustained by history. But there is an additional historical element that is operative in the case of Judaism. What distinguished the biblical Hebrews, who were the founding fathers of this faith, from other ancient Near Eastern peoples was their conscious awareness of the history or historic destiny of which they were a part.[2] This emphasis on history is admirably illustrated by the traditional Seder ritual for the Passover. In this ritual, the youngest child present asks the traditional question, Why is this night different from all other nights? In response, the father tells the story of the deliverance of the Hebrews from Egyptian bondage. It was this awareness of historic destiny under God as the primary form of reality that made the difference between ancient Israel and the cosmic faiths of the environing ancient Near East. In contrast with Egypt, Mesopotamia, and Canaan, with their myths of gods, men, and objects of nature, all as citizens together of the cosmos, ancient Israel told a strangely contrasted story of the one God, who as Lord of history, called Israel into his service. Both the divine call and Israel's response occur in and through specific events of history. This difference between the ancient Near Eastern world and Israel is, as we have had repeated occasion to note, that which Eliade has characterized as between *Cosmos and History*; and it is, in many ways, the deepest and widest discontinuity in all the history of mankind's faiths.

This difference is marked by a radically different style (both of writing and of life), between ancient Israel and her Near Eastern neighbors. That of Mesopotamia might be termed cosmic idealism and is illustrated by such documents as the Babylonian creation story, called the *Enuma Elish*, from its initial words, "when on high. . . ."[3] To see the difference we need only place this document side by side with Genesis 1–3 and compare these texts. The Babylonian story is marked by a plurality of gods who are citizens together, and together with humans and natural objects, of what has been called the city of the cosmos. The biblical story opens with the words, "In the beginning God . . ." and shows a radical discontinuity between God and his creation. In this contrast, Israel's style may be accurately characterized as historical realism. This distinctive style may be observed as an important feature of all the literature of the Old Testament. It is also an integral part of Israel's legacy to the West, and is thus, in general, a significant aspect of such diverse aspects of culture as Western literature and Western philosophy.

This intriguing subject is explored in detail by Erich Auerbach's monumental volume of comparative literary criticism, entitled *Mimesis*.[4] The author introduces his main theme by means of a comparison between what he calls the two great epic styles of the West, namely the Old Testament and Homer. Thus, as samples of these two styles, he contrasts the Genesis chapter 22 account of Abraham's sacrifice of Isaac, and Homer's account in the *Odyssey* of the scar of Odysseus. Homer's style shows such traits as clear and uniform illumination, glorification of the hero, and ornate, intricate detail, which takes many pages to describe such a minor episode as an old nurse's recognition of a scar on the hero's heel. By contrast, the Hebraic style of the Bible is one of vast and contrasting light and shadow, few details, and an unrelenting realism in describing its chief human characters. There are no Homeric heroes in the Bible. Its main characters are depicted as in the sight of God's all-seeing eye. From its biblical source, Auerbach traces the realist style through a continuing tradition of Western literature onward at last to the great realist novels of the nineteenth century.

Another related assumption of the biblical Hebrews of great importance to Western culture is the paradoxical transcendence and immanence of God. If, as philosophers of the ancient cosmos asserted, "the world is full of gods," then a secular society is unthinkable or inconceivable, for these gods are as real and unavoidable as the cosmos of which they are integral parts. In sharpest contrast, the God of the biblical Hebrews was conceived to transcend the world absolutely, thus providing the possibility of a god-free or secular world. On the other hand, according to the ancient Israelites, God also appears to humans in history, setting them tasks to do and purposes to achieve for Him. He is thus not only transcendent but immanent as well. God's purposes define the meaning of history of the people of the Bible and for the traditions which stem from the Bible. Indeed, the historical character

of the biblical outlook seems to bear close relation to the paradoxical doctrine of God's transcendence and immanence.

Ancient Israel thought of herself, then, as drawn into being by the God who spoke through the events of history, calling her to his service. One of the most ancient and briefest accounts of this awareness occurs in Deuteronomy 26:5–9, which has been called Exodus in epitome. In its present context, this passage is the response to be made to the priest by the worshiper at the harvest festival:

> and you shall make response before the LORD your God: A wandering Aramean was my father, and he went down into Egypt and sojourned there few in numbers, and there he became a nation, great, mighty and prosperous. And the Egyptians treated us harshly and afflicted us and laid upon us hard bondage. Then we cried to the LORD the God of our fathers, and the LORD heard our voice and saw our affliction, our toil and our oppression, and the LORD brought us out of Egypt with a mighty hand and an outstretched arm, with great terror, with signs and wonders, and he brought us into this place and gave us the land flowing with milk and honey.

This same story of deliverance from Egyptian slavery and the giving of the Torah on Mt. Sinai is recounted in considerably more detail and with varying emphases in the narratives of Exodus 1–20 and Deuteronomy 1–25. The details of these two renditions need not concern us here, though they did and do concern the people of Israel. All the various accounts tell the story of how the tribes of Israel, sons of Jacob or Israel, found their way to Egypt where, in the course of time, they were subjected to slavery. Deliverance came through the leader Moses who acted as the reluctant instrument or servant of the LORD God. (LORD is the free rendering in the English Bible of the Hebrew tetragrammaton, YHWH, which is the proper name of the Hebrew deity.) The Exodus account of this story (which in the opinion of modern biblical scholarship derives from three writers, designated as J, E, and P) is cast significantly in the form of a dramatic contest of the LORD with Pharaoh as the god-king of Egypt.[5] Moses, the servant of the LORD, challenges Pharaoh who responds with even worse oppression. The conflict deepens with the plagues, culminating in the Hebrew deliverance and the complete rout and annihilation of Pharaoh and his armies in the Red Sea crossing. Under Moses' guidance the Israelites then find their way to Mt. Sinai where, in covenant with the LORD, they are given the Torah, which consists of the LORD's commandments for their common life. Throughout the different biblical versions of this narrative we see as a common element the idea of one God, whose primary requirement of man is a good life in society with his fellowmen. This central aspect of the Torah is, thus, a concrete statement of what philosophically may be termed ethical monotheism.

From Sinai the Hebrew people moved on through the years of wilderness wandering to the conquest of the promised land and then to the monarchy under Saul, David, and Solomon. The ancient Israelite monarchy was not destined to great worldly glory, nor to long life, caught as it was between the upper and the nether millstones of Babylonia and Egypt, and, in the course of a few centuries, ground to pieces. The ten northern tribes were carried into captivity by the Assyrians in 722 B.C. (thus becoming the so-called ten lost tribes) and the southern tribes by Nebuchadnezzar of Babylon in 586 B.C. What is important to see throughout these chapters of history is ancient Israel's conviction that God was speaking through this checkered and tragic history to both Israel and mankind.

Israel's response to this divine initiative was her strong sense of divine vocation and mission, literally and etymologically the sense of being *called* and *sent*. It is these ideas that constituted Israel as a people and nation, and as an enduring community after actual nationhood was destroyed. To be sure, these ideas of vocation and mission are not unique to Israel. Indeed, rather are they strewn through the literature of many nations, ancient and modern. We observed them for example in chapter 10 in the China of Confucius' time. The sense of mission was also strong in ancient Rome. To cite still another example, they are a major theme of American history from earliest Puritan days to Dwight Eisenhower; America too has believed herself *called* and *sent*. From Polk to McKinley, "manifest destiny" has been a powerful conservative form of American nationalism. In more liberal vein, Lincoln spoke of American democracy as the "last great hope of earth."

What is historically unique and creative about Israel's sense of vocation and mission is what it grew into. This development and transformation took place in the minds and lives of the writing prophets from Amos in mid-eighth century to the prophet known to modern scholars as Deutero-Isaiah (Isaiah 40–60) two centuries later. Once again, prophecy is by no means unique to the religion of Israel; oracular figures occur in religions from Greece to China. But ancient Israel's development of prophecy is unique. The prophets conceived of themselves simply as fulfilling or completing the ethical monotheism intended by Moses. Nevertheless, their impact constituted nothing less than a revolutionary transformation of Israel's faith, rendering it consistently ethical, inward, and universal in character. In the prophets is also to be oberved, as we noted in the preceding chapter, what Martin Buber has termed a "turning to the future."[6] Unable to see the LORD's hidden sovereignty over history in the age in which they lived, the prophets appealed to a future time when the divine Kingship and Kingdom would be manifested for all the world to see. It was this turning to the future that created the eschatological aspect of Israel's faith and thought, namely, the vision of history moving toward consummation.

The prophetic impact may also be illustrated by the transformation wrought in Israel's sense of vocation and mission. The earliest biblical occurrences of these ideas were almost entirely in tribal or nationalistic terms. At this time and place in history this was natural and normal. However, the first of the writing prophets, Amos, radically criticized the nationalism of these earlier popular attitudes. He depicted God as standing in judgment over his people. "You only have I known, says the Lord, therefore you will I punish" (Amos 3:2). Again, "Are you not to me as the Ethiopians, O house of Israel?" asks Amos' God of his people, thus clearly implying a universal God of all mankind. The prophets were virtually unanimous in their rejection of the religious nationalism of their contemporaries. Hence, too, they were led onward to a new view of Israel's vocation and mission, which was expressed in the "Servant of the Lord" poems of Deutero-Isaiah. In these poems Israel is construed as God's servant, whose distinctive mission is to be "a light to the nations," to carry the knowledge of God to the ends of the earth.[7] This was a lofty concept that yielded as significant corollaries the momentous ideas of humanity and universal history. The logic of these concepts was, in effect: one God, therefore one world, with Israel as the instrument of God's universal purpose.

Meanwhile, the tumultuous events of Near Eastern history swept on. Their nation destroyed, the Israelites were at first a minuscule community of exiles in Babylonia. Then, under Cyrus the Medo-Persian emperor, some of them returned home to Jerusalem, where they were a subject province first of the Persian, then of the Greek, empire. Then followed the interlude of Israel's independence under the Maccabean rulers, and after that the rule of the Romans until the end of ancient Israel in 135 C.E. (As alternatives to B.C. and A.D., Jewish writers use B.C.E. and C.E., meaning "before the common era" and "common era.")

From 586 B.C.E. onward many Jews lived abroad, and the relation between these Jews of the dispersion and the Palestinian Jews became an important subject for both the thought and life of Judaism.

During these postexilic centuries the argument concerning the nature of Israel's vocation and mission continued between the two parties that we may label the nationalists and the universalists. But, clearly, it was the indefeasible fact of this sense of vocation and mission, however interpreted, that kept Israel alive, against all the probabilities or odds of historical existence.

It was also during these centuries that the Torah was put into final written form. The word, *Torah*, has a primary reference to the first five books of the Jewish Bible, which is also, of course, the Christian Old Testament. The word, *Torah*, means "teaching" and it conveys the image of the LORD as instructing his people with divinely authoritative norms for all of life, individual and social. Accordingly, "to do Torah" means to place all of life under the authority of God, whose will for his people is made clear in these writings.

Traditionally, the Torah was said to have been written by Moses; however, modern scholarship regards these writings as by many authors in a common Mosaic tradition. The ceremony of Israel's acceptance of the Torah as the divinely given norm for all of life is recorded in Nehemiah 8–9, and may be dated ca. 450 B.C.E. Israel was now "the people of the Book." The documents of prophecy and writings were added to the Book or Bible in the immediately succeeding centuries, and the canon or official list of sacred writings was set by an assembly of rabbis at Jabneh in 90 C.E.

Interpreting the Torah

Once it was in existence, the next crucial problem was to interpret the Torah's meaning. If, in these writings, God has made known his will to Israel and to mankind, it is of the greatest importance to know what the writings mean, and to interpret this meaning authoritatively for all the changing circumstances of human life and society. The solution to this problem was of central concern to Israel for approximately the next millennium.

This problem, while equally important to Jews of the dispersion and of the Palestinian homeland, took on widely different meanings for these two groups. For Jews living abroad in the midst of an alien and often hostile gentile culture, the first question was how to understand (and, incidentally, to preserve) the Hebraic words, ideas, and images of the Torah in such an alien context. The social environment of the Mediterranean world was the Hellenistic culture of Greece, itself highly missionary for the Greek way of life and often scornful of other ways, such as those of the biblical Hebrews. Such was the environment of Israel's ancient dispersion in the main cities of the Greco-Roman world.[8]

The Jewish community of Alexandria was particularly large and influential, so it was natural that it should take the lead in interpreting Judaism and its Torah to Hellenistic culture. In the process of this interpretation, the Alexandrian Jews produced two of ancient Judaism's greatest achievements, namely, the Septuagint and the philosophy of Philo Judaeus. The former was a Greek translation of the Old Testament made in late third century B.C.E. under official sponsorship by the ruling Ptolemy family and, according to tradition, done by seventy scholars each working independently and all under divine guidance. To Jews of the ancient dispersion, the Septuagint gave them their Bible in the language they knew and used. Historically, it is also important as the Old Testament most often used and quoted by the early Christian community that grew out of the Jewish dispersion.

Philo Judaeus (20 B.C.E.–40 C.E.) was a leader of the flourishing Alexandrian Jewish community.[9] He was also the first great Jewish philosopher. Philo was impressed by the similarities he observed between Platonic philosophy and Mosaic faith. By Philo's time Plato's thought had become so thoroughly diffused throughout Hellenistic culture as to serve as a general medium of communication in the intellectual world. Philo sought to use Platonism as a means of communicating Mosaic religion. In this latter connection, it is important to distinguish Philo from those self-styled Hellenists among the Jews who gave up their Mosaic heritage, some unwittingly and others deliberately, for Hellenism. By contrast, Philo lived and died a faithful Jew, and apparently thought of his philosophy as a way of making Judaism intelligible and viable in his time and place.

Men have argued for centuries whether he succeeded or failed in this purpose. We shall presently suggest that he succeeded in some respects and failed in others. But in either case he produced a philosophy widely influential in his own time and ever since. It is not necessary to agree with the more controversial aspects of H. W. Wolfson's interpretations of Philo in order to see in Philo's work the Platonic philosophy destined to provide an intellectual framework for three religions—Judaism, Christianity, and Islam—which also extended in continuous philosophic tradition in the West at least as far as Spinoza in the seventeenth century, and perhaps even to the present.[10]

Central in Philo's thought was his notion of God as absolutely transcendent or quality-less (*apoios*). According to Philo, God even transcends the good, an idea which is difficult to reconcile with the strong moral and ethical character of Moses' God. Nevertheless, Philo himself taught that God, through his providence, governs the world for good. Of Philo's transcendent One, mankind may know *that* he is but not *what* he is. This idea seems to be a spelling out of suggestions of transcendence implicit in Plato and the Orphic mysteries before Plato. It was also a clear anticipation of ideas to be made explicit and systematic in Plotinus two centuries after Philo. So far as our present study is concerned, it may be regarded as a statement of the Absolute One we have met under other names in Hindu, Buddhist, and Neo-Confucian traditions. It is indeed the unique and ineffable One of mystical experience and philosophy. In the considered opinion of many students of philosophy and religion, it is difficult to the point of impossibility to reconcile this transcendent One with the living God of Philo's biblical faith; for the former is devoid of concrete content, while the latter is characterized by active goodwill.

So far above the world was Philo's One that an intermediary between God and world was needed. Philo laid hold of the old traditional Greek idea of the *logos* or Reason, and gave it new meaning as the cosmic intermediary between God and world. The Greek word, *logos*, is virtually untranslatable, conveying as it does a great many meanings, ranging from rational conversation to ontological principalities and powers of the world. For Philo it seems clearly to have meant both the creative power and the rational structure of the universe or cosmos. It is, incidentally, this last meaning that Philo bequeathed to the author of the Fourth Gospel of the New Testament. By way of the preface to the Fourth Gospel, Philo's logos entered Christian theology to play a major role in the centuries that followed. Philo's influence was as great or greater on Christianity than on Judaism.

Philo's view of man as well as God showed both Platonic and Mosaic influence. Many of his writings are characterized by a dualism between spirit and flesh that was part of Platonism's legacy to the Hellenistic world. Hence, deliverance from the things of matter and flesh is the chief end of man, a view that clashes with Judaism's strong emphasis on the dignity and worth of the body and of physical things. On the other hand, Philo did maintain a strong belief in free will, against the various forms of determinism, which, in the Hellenistic world, ranged from philosophic materialism to astrology. Indeed, free will must be counted a very significant part of the legacy Philo bequeathed to subsequent Western philosophy.

Another major aspect of Philo's work was his use of the allegorical method of exegesis by which he provided philosophical "explanations" of troublesome anthropomorphic passages of the Bible. For Philo, as for intellectuals in many religious traditions, anthropomorphism was a problem; and he used this method to reduce, if not remove, it. Ingeniously, he allegorized away most of the anthropomorphisms which offended him. If this allegorical method jars the modern intellectual conscience, it must be remembered that Philo was by no means alone in its use (it was a widely current method of interpretation in the ancient Greco-Roman world); and also that, as a result of such allegorical interpretations, the text of the Bible was, in historical fact, preserved. Otherwise, it might well have perished.

Philo's writings of two other general kinds equaled in importance and exceeded in bulk his specifically philosophical writings. First of these were his *apologiae* (the word means "explanation" or "defense," not "apology") for the Jewish people against antisemitic beliefs and actions. He is said to have led an embassy of Alexandrian Jews on such a mission to the emperor Caligula in 40 C.E. The second type of writing was legal and political or, in modern terminology, social philosophy. It stemmed from his interest in the relation of the Torah to social existence, and it places Philo in the long tradition of Jewish thinkers who, through the centuries, have worked at social philosophy in these terms.

While Alexandrian Jews read their Septuagints and Philo pondered the ways of God to man, at home in Palestine different developments were taking shape, though directed to the same goal of interpreting the Torah in the changing scenes of historical existence. As we have seen, assuming the Torah as God's revealed will to his people, the next question was how reasonably and authoritatively to interpret and apply its norms to all the ever-shifting circumstances of human existence. The Sabbath must be hallowed, but how and how not? When does the Sabbath begin and when does it end? What is the precise meaning of the work that is forbidden? First, scribes and then successive generations of rabbis devoted themselves to finding authoritative answers to these questions; and in so doing, in the space of several centuries, they produced the Talmud.[11]

It is significant to observe the emergence of analogous codes of law in all the traditions of monotheistic religion for concrete guidance of human action, in the light of the revealed will of the one God. In Roman Catholicism, canon law was the answer. In the next chapter we shall find Muslim law or *Shar'ia* as still another response to this need. In Calvinistic Protestantism, whether in Geneva, England, or New England, a literal interpretation of Old Testament law served the same purpose of divine law for human life. Religious law and monotheism seem to show a highly significant historical correlation.

The Jewish formulation is the Talmud (the Hebrew word means "teaching" or "learning"). The Talmud is not a book, but a literature, vast and various in extent and character, embracing virtually every aspect of Jewish life, and coming into being, as we have noted, over a period of eight hundred years or more. The written text so clearly reflects an oral tradition that it will not be misleading to call the Talmud the minutes of a centuries-long meeting of the Jewish people.

Following the canonizing of the Torah under Ezra, the scribes of the Great Assembly or Sanhedrin essayed the task of critical interpretation. They were succeeded by the rabbis, reputed to be heads of the Sanhedrin, and later grouped into pairs of contrasting interpretations, the most notable of whom were Hillel and Shammai. During the first century of the Common Era, the work of interpretation continued apace, from Gamaliel (the teacher of St.

Paul) to Johanan ben Zakkai, founder of the house of studies at Jabneh, and the great Rabbi Akiba. Under Judah the Prince, a century later, the first main division of the Talmud, namely the Mishnah, was codified.

Then followed a period of several centuries of further supplemental commentary called the *Gemara*. In contrast to the Hebrew language of the Mishnah, the Gemara was in Aramaic. The final results were assembled as the Jerusalem Talmud of ca. 400 C.E., and the larger and better known Babylonian Talmud of not more than a century later.

To non-Jewish readers the Talmud is a puzzling document. By analogy to Anglo-Saxon common law, we may say that it follows a case method. If the Torah is likened to the American constitution, then the Talmud may be compared to the whole body in constitutional law delineating the constitution's meaning. But in addition to its legal aspects, or *halakah* (from the verb "walk," hence meaning a guide to one's steps) is *haggadah*, or the Talmud's narrative aspects. The whole document is highly contextual in character, hence, the text must always be interpreted in historical and social context.

Whatever the Talmud is or may be, it is not philosophy. Indeed, philosophy was part of the Hellenistic way of life from which Palestinian Judaism sought to turn away. Philosophy was Greek; the Talmud was what the Jewish mind did instead of philosophizing (despite peripheral philosophic influences on the Talmud and its rabbis). Yet, nonphilosophic as it was, the Talmud was a kind of seedbed in which later philosophic attitudes and values might germinate and grow. For example, the decisions of the Talmud were strenuously argued, hence, producing the penchant for dialectical argument that has been an agelong trait of Jewish thought.

More broadly, the Talmud has been called a mirror reflecting the variegated patterns of the Jewish life which it records. Yet, perhaps, it is not so much a mirror as it is a kind of reservoir of Jewish values held under the custodianship of the rabbis, as water to be used when needed. The Jewish historian, Salo Baron, has called it "a bulwark."[12] Perhaps an even better metaphor might be a rudder by which to navigate the stormy seas over which the Jewish people have steered their ship through the centuries of dispersion among the nations. The Talmud's authority is second only to the Torah; and since the latter is understood through the former, the importance of Talmud and its actual influence upon Jewish life has sometimes been greater than that of the Torah itself. As we shall presently note, in the modern centuries of Western Europe and America, the Talmud has been questioned or even rejected by reform Jews, seeking to participate in the non-Jewish culture of their time and place.

Jewish Scholasticism

For most twentieth century people the word *scholasticism* evokes negative images of men who calculate such matters as the number of angels who can dance on the head of a pin. While there is a basis in fact for such negative impressions, they obscure the basic purpose of scholasticism, which may be characterized as the use of philosophy for the exposition and defense of a religious tradition that has been called into question. As we shall soon see, this purpose determined the main issues and problems of scholasticism, such as the relation of faith to reason, rational proofs for faith's object or God, as well as the relation of nature to supernature. While textbooks of Western philosophy tend to associate scholasticism solely with medieval Catholic Christianity, it is, historically, a much more widely diffused phenomenon, extending to many religions and many philosophies. The reader will recall several notable instances of the phenomenon of scholasticism among the philosophies of this volume, as for example in classical India and China. Even if we limit ourselves to medieval Europe (including Spain and the Near East), scholastic philosophy has been involved with three religions, namely, Islam, Judaism, and Christianity. In all three cases the primary philosophical ingredient was the heritage of ancient Greek thought. First Plato and then Aristotle were used as instrumentalities for expounding and defending, and incidentally, criticizing a religious tradition that had come under question.

Ironically enough, scholastic philosophy came to Islam first, to Judaism second, and to Christianity last of all. The Muslim Arabs were the first custodians of the classical Greek heritage of philosophy, hence it was they who first employed Plato and Aristotle for the explication and defense of faith. We shall return to these Muslim scholastics in the next chapter. Meanwhile, the Jews had taken refuge in Muslim lands from the intolerance and antisemitism of Christianity. Jewish scholars who had a taste for philosophy participated freely in Arab philosophy, sometimes, at least, without any consciously Jewish viewpoint or emphasis. It was through such Jewish figures as Maimonides that the classical Aristotelean heritage was transmitted to the medieval Christian philosophers.

The traditional founder of Jewish scholasticism was Saadia ben Joseph (882–942), scholar, translator of the Jewish Bible into Arabic, and opponent of the Karaite sect of Jews, against whom he sought to do battle with weapons of reason.[13] Saadia was much influenced by the Mutazilite theology of Islam which, as we shall see in the next chapter, was an eighth and ninth century Muslim philosophy emphasizing the unity of God and the freedom of man. Against skeptical opponents, Saadia sought to analyze the sources and kinds of knowledge, with a view to showing the rationality of faith. In company with contemporary Muslim philosophers, he also sought to demonstrate rationally the actual temporal creation of the world as a necessary preface to proofs for God.[14]

Saadia was succeeded by a long and numerous tradition of Jewish scholastic philosophers, only a few of the most important of whom can even be mentioned here. Like the Christian scholasticism that it so greatly influenced, early Jewish scholasticism tended to be Platonic in outlook, while later thinkers took their models for thought from Aristotle. The first great Jewish Platonist or Neoplatonist of the middle ages was Ibn Gabirol, Spanish poet-philosopher of the first half of the eleventh century and author of a volume called *The Fountain of Being*. According to this work, being (or all that is) flows forth as from the fountain of primal being or God. From more specifically Hebraic sources, Gabirol drew his notion of the will of God that pervades all existence.

Judah Halevi (1075–1141), also Spanish, drew arguments for the exposition and defense of faith not so much from nature as from Jewish history. His *Book of Proof and Demonstration in Aid of the Despised Religion* is a dialogue concerning the nature of religion. Lines of thought that were opened up by Halevi were followed up by a growing number of later Jewish scholastic philosophers.

By common consent the greatest Jewish scholastic was Moses ben Maimon, known to us in the latinized form of Maimonides (1135–1204). He was born in Cordoba, Spain, but the coming of the fiercely intolerant Almohades sect of Muslims led his family to flee to Africa. There, after many travels, he became a court physician to the Muslim emperor Saladin in Egypt. Physician by profession, he was scholar and philosopher by avocation and commitment. In addition to his best known philosophical work, *A Guide to the Perplexed*, Maimonides produced commentaries on the Talmud, as well as expositions of a great many aspects of Jewish faith and practice.[15] In this respect, Maimonides stands in the tradition of Jewish scholars before and since, for whom the Torah was a main theme for study and critical exposition.

Concerning the *Guide*, Maimonides was aware of the peril involved in this kind of philosophical writing and, hence, sought to keep it within the small and highly selective circle of those able to understand and to cope with its ideas. He sought to conceal his meaning from unwary readers, even at times hiding that meaning under a heavy cloak of contradictory assertions. At least three lines of thought concerning God can be discerned in the *Guide*. First, God is eternal will, not bound by natural laws, and, in his freedom, creating the world and doing other miracles as well. Second, God is the object of the negative theology, the transcendent One whom man can know only by negative attributes. Third is the Aristotelean God, who is by nature pure intellect, and who can thus be known by analogy with the human intellect, particularly through the categories of motion and cause, as Prime Mover and First Cause. While the last is often taken as normative for Maimonides' view of God, the tensions and conflicts between this and the first two views remain still today as problems to be explored in Maimonides' philosophy.

Like other scholastics of both Islam and Judaism, Maimonides held firmly to the freedom of man. The influence of Islamic thought, strong in several aspects of his philosophy, is particularly notable in his rejection of the Aristotelean doctrine of the eternity of the world and the corresponding assertion of the creation of the world in time.

What is of equal or greater importance with his ontological writings, particularly for Jewish tradition, is his writings on law, that is, on the religious commandments of Judaism. His aim in these writings is the exposition and defense of the Torah and the Talmud as the constitutive institutions of Judaism. In this respect Maimonides stands in the long tradition of those wise men or sages who have interpreted the Torah to Israel. The work of Maimonides exemplifies the kind of social philosophy and philosophy of religion we have already seen illustrated in Philo. From Maimonides also stem the so-called traditional Thirteen Principles, which are as close to a creed as Judaism has ever come.[16] These principles, as traditionally formulated, begin with the being, unity, and goodness of the Creator, and move onward through affirmation of Moses and the Torah to the future coming of the Messiah and the resurrection of the dead. Maimonides' influence on the philosophy of both Islam and Christianity has been almost as great as that upon Judaism.

Prominent among later medieval Jewish scholastics is Gersonides (1288–1344). Concerning the divine creation of the world, he sought to oppose alike the Aristotelean doctrine of the eternity of the world and those religious persons who believed in creation out of nothing. God made the world, he taught, but out of a kind of primal matter. He also sought to reconcile man's free will with divine omniscience. A generation later Hasdai Crescas gave Jewish scholasticism a different turn with his general hostility to Aristotelean philosophy and his emphasis on strong volitional factors in his doctrine of man.

The Renaissance, which brought new issues and new vistas to European philosophy, heralding the coming of modernity, brought to Judaism also an additional problem, which though not altogether new, was destined to be greatly increased in modern times. This is, namely, the relation of individual thinkers to the Jewish heritage and community. Two seventeenth century figures, Da Costa (1585–1640) and Spinoza (1632–1677), illustrate and underscore this issue. The former was from a family of Marranos (Jews who converted or simulated conversion to Christianity in order to escape the Spanish Inquisition) who migrated to the relative freedom of Amsterdam, where he wrote and taught such radical doctrines as the mortality of the human soul and the sufficiency of natural moral law. Concerned with such heretical ideas, Da Costa wanted and claimed no relation to Judaism or the Jewish community.

Better known and a greater figure than Da Costa was Baruch Spinoza, who was also of a family of Jewish refugees from Spain who found refuge in the Netherlands. In 1656, Spinoza was excommunicated from the synagogue (a rare phenomenon in the history of Judaism and probably to be explained, in part, by the sensitivity of the Jewish community to the Calvinistic Protestant majority of the Netherlands) for heretical and dangerous ideas. From then until his death Spinoza had virtually no contact with the Jewish community, and his philosophy is in no overt or clear sense Jewish. Accordingly, the question must be raised, ought he then to be considered in any sense a Jewish philosopher?

One answer is that Spinoza's life and thought, superficially so secular and so non-Jewish, were nonetheless nurtured and conditioned in significant ways by this tradition and community. It was through the study of Jewish philosophical texts that Spinoza was first introduced to the study of philosophy. Even more important, the influence of Maimonides, Crescas, and of Jewish mysticism is clearly observable in both the form and substance of his philosophy. In this respect Spinoza might well be called the last Jewish scholastic, as well as one of the first of modern philosophers and modern men. Again, Spinoza devoted considerable time and energy to commenting on matters of religion, ethics, and society. While his doctrine in these matters was novel and radical, his form of thought stands in a tradition going back to Philo. Spinoza was also a harbinger of Jewish modernity, in that the Jewish tradition served as his rootage, while the flower and fruit of his thought bore little substantive relation to historic Judaism. He was, in this respect, the first of a long line of great modern figures including such names as Marx, Freud, Einstein, Bergson, and Husserl.

Jewish Mysticism

In view of its recurrence in so many of the religions and philosophical traditions of the world, it is not surprising to find mysticism in the Jewish tradition. Every age of Jewish history has had its mystics, and, in many instances, they stand essentially as persons possessed with a powerful sense of the immediacy of God in their own individual experience and, hence, impatient with the ponderous scholarship of talmudic rabbis or the equally heavy intellectualism of philosophers like Maimonides. If God is an immediate Reality powerfully present in the human soul, who needs rabbis or philosophers to mediate the Divine Presence to us?

The term *Kabbala* (the word means "tradition") is often applied generically to the great tradition of Jewish mystics and mysticism from ancient days to the present. Like the Talmud, it designates not a book but a library vast and various in its contents. Among its roots, in addition to the Bible, are gnosticism in the Hellenistic world, as well as a variety of primitive mythologies. While the Kabbala shows no single system of doctrine, there are recurring ideas or themes. One is the idea of deity as *En Soph*, the boundless, absolutely transcendent God, emanating through ten *sephiroth*, or regions of being, and, hence, indwelling all things. The relation of this view of deity to the living God of biblical tradition has been a thorny problem, especially since the Boundless has often been conceived as not the creator of the material world. This has been deemed a dubious and defiling task, hence, to be handled by a subordinate or minor deity. Since the Jewish tradition has given central emphasis to a sacred book, the Kabbalists have usually derived and stated their doctrine as the esoteric meaning of the Bible, finding secret meanings in biblical passages, words, and even in the letters of biblical words.

Perhaps the best-known work of the Kabbala is the *Zohar (Book of Splendor)*, now supposed to have been written by the Spanish Kabbalist Moses de Leon (d. 1305) in the latter half of the thirteenth century.[17] It professes to be a commentary on the Pentateuch by a putative ancient Palestinian rabbi named Simon ben Yohei. Its doctrinal contents are characterized by Gershom Scholem as "Jewish theosophy," which is to say, mysticism professing to be a higher and esoteric form of discursive knowledge. The Boundless and its emanations, as well as the ascent of the human soul by means of esoteric knowledge to a state of perfection, are the content of the secret doctrine that rabbi Simon professes to derive from the Pentateuch and to communicate to his readers.

In terms of the distinction made in chapter 1 between mysticism of absorption or union and mysticism of communion, Kabbalism has frequently seemed to favor the former. For this reason it has been the object of suspicion and hostility on the part of more orthodox Jewish minds for whom such union with God constitutes a violation of the first commandment with its clear sharp line between Creator and creation, Lord and world. However, if this charge is true of Kabbalism, it is distinctly not true of another more modern mystical movement generally known as Hasidism.

The Hebrew word, *Hesed* (plural *Hasidim*) means "pious" or "piety," and is sometimes applied generally to movements of mysticism or pietism that have recurred throughout Jewish history. However, the movement under consideration had its origin in eighteenth century Moldavia. It shows some continuity with previous movements of Hasidism and also with Kabbalism, but the decisive source is a figure named Israel of Moldavia (1700–1760) known to his followers as the *Baal Shem Tov* (Master of the Good Name). He seems to have been a kind of illiterate religious genius who, full of love for the Lord, gathered followers about himself and taught them out of his own experience. The Baal Shem saw God in everything in nature and human nature. His was a thoroughly affirmative, spontaneous kind of religious enthusiasm. It soon became a popular movement which spread throughout East European Jewry. Because they challenged the massive authority of talmudic Judaism, Elijah of Vilna, leader of East European Jewry, excommunicated the Hasidic Jews. The Hasidim responded by instituting their own rabbis, called *zaddikim* (meaning "righteous ones"), and their own religious communities.

Gershom Scholem has commented that the great original contribution of Hasidism lay in its fresh interpretation of the values of personal and individual existence, especially ethical values.[18] The truth of this remark may be seen in the impact of Hasidism on the mind of the contemporary Jewish philosopher, Martin Buber, whose conception of I-Thou or person-person relations is drawn largely from Hasidic sources. We shall return to this matter later in this chapter in our discussion of Buber's philosophy. Meanwhile, we note in this connection that Hasidism still lives in twentieth century Judaism. At its best, it adds spontaneity and emotional warmth, as well as moral guidance and emphasis, to Jewish piety. At its worst, it degenerates into eccentric forms of magic and superstition. To philosophy, Jewish and non-Jewish, Hasidism has posed problems of adequately communicating its ethical and metaphysical concerns. The response to these issues continues very much alive to the present moment.

Modern and Contemporary Issues

Modernity came late to Europe's Jews. The Enlightenment, with its promise of freedom and equality for all, did not seem to apply to the Jews. It was not until the nineteenth century that the Jews were granted full participation in

European culture, and then only gradually, fitfully, and grudgingly. Previous to this event, a few individuals had escaped over the ghetto walls and participated in the wider life of European culture. One such was Moses Mendelssohn (1729–1786), who became a friend of Lessing, and about whom *Nathan the Wise* seems to have been written. Mendelssohn used his newly-gained position to make a case for his people and their faith. He translated the Hebrew Bible into German; he wrote one dialogue called *Phaedon* or *Conversations on the Spirituality and Immortality of the Soul*, and another called *Jerusalem*, which was an exposition of Judaism as a faith.

Mendelssohn's philosophy of Judaism is an interesting blend of traditional and modern elements. In content, he retained intact the moral law and substantial sections of Jewish ritual practice. But the forms of his thought were deeply influenced by eighteenth century rationalism. In common with the deism of his age, Mendelssohn believed that universal human reason was capable of proving or establishing such general realities as God, providence, and moral values. The particular or concrete realities of Judaism he regarded as a transaction of God's supernatural grace with Israel. He also made a clear separation in social philosophy between religion and the state. Mendelssohn placed his greatest emphasis upon Israel's moral values, and so opened the way for communication and Jewish participation in the wider, non-Jewish culture of Europe.

A succession of nineteenth century Jewish philosophers, of whom Hermann Cohen (1842–1918) is the best known, pursued the fuller philosophic articulation of these ideas. These philosophic developments also coincided historically with the nineteenth century leveling of ghetto walls and full political Jewish emancipation. These momentous events posed a double problem for Jewish thought and life. Along with every other traditional religion, there was first of all the problem of the Jewish tradition's relation to the modern world. But there was also the additional problem of being a minority religion in the midst of the larger, still nominally Christian society. One widespread response was a religious liberalism similar to that which was gaining ground at the same time in Christianity. In contrast to the radical who seeks to jettison tradition and the reactionary who rejects the modern world, the liberal seeks a mutual accommodation of tradition and modernity. In nineteenth century Judaism, especially in Germany, liberalism found expression in the Reform movement. Followers of this movement attacked the authority of the Talmud, but continued to hold elements of Judaism's tradition of belief and practice which they could meaningfully accept in the modern world. As liberals, the adherents of Reform Judaism sought an accommodation between tradition and modernity. Meanwhile, to the right of Reform, orthodoxy continued on its traditional way, while on the left, many individuals of Jewish background broke completely with their tradition.

While Reform Judaism emerged first in nineteenth century Germany, it soon found its way to America with German immigrants to the new world. The architect of American Reform Judaism was Rabbi Isaac M. Wise (1819–1900), German immigrant and rabbi of congregations in Albany, New York, and Cincinnati, Ohio, and also founder of Hebrew Union College. As Reform Judaism in America moved further away from tradition, the Conservative position arose. Orthodox Judaism in America received its strongest impetus from Eastern European immigrants of the late nineteenth and early twentieth centuries.

Even in the nineteenth century, Judaism was by no means free from the threat of antisemitism, apparently always endemic in Western society, and periodically epidemic. There were notable nineteenth century outbreaks of the disease, but none of the catastrophic proportions of the Hitler period in the twentieth century. The result of Hitler's antisemitism was tragedy unparalleled in the history of Europe's Jewry. Yet out of these catastrophic events has come the state of Israel with its quickening influence as well as its novel problems for every aspect of Jewish faith and culture.

Among the new responses to these tragic and momentous events of the twentieth century is a new direction in Jewish philosophy. It is to be seen in such figures as Franz Rosenzweig (1886–1927) and Martin Buber (1878–1965). The spirit of liberal accommodation and adjustment that characterized Reform Judaism gives way to intense positive affirmations and reaffirmations of Jewish faith and practice. The question is no longer: How much tradition may we rationally retain? Rather, it is the different, opposite one: How, in the midst of the storms of the twentieth century, can we find the meaning of Jewish existence?

Franz Rosenzweig's "road back" to a philosophy of Jewish existence was cut short by his untimely death in 1927, but not before he had produced his *Star of Redemption* and enough other writing for scholars to piece together his suggestive and seminal philosophy.[19] Like many others of his generation he rejected philosophic idealism. His own viewpoint was influenced by Heidegger's existentialist philosophy, by Max Scheler and by nascent Protestant dialectical theology. Rosenzweig drew a sharp distinction between what he termed Greek paganism, with its cosmic philosophic orientation, on the one hand, and the historically oriented biblical faiths, Judaism and Christianity, on the other. He wrestled with such biblical concepts as revelation, which he construed as the encounter of man with God, with faith as trust in God, as well as with the significance of time and redemption. He was also highly critical of the spirit of adjustment and accommodation that characterized liberal or Reform Judaism.

Rosenzweig also distinguished Jewish existence from Christian existence, treating the former as the concrete way of life of the Jewish people, celebrated in its liturgy and lived out in history. In both of these aspects Judaism constitutes an existential statement, in the present tense, of eternal life. His book ends with the aphoristic words: "Into Life." Truly it may be said that the historical period of Jewish philosophy which began with Moses Mendelssohn ended with Franz Rosenzweig. Today's philosophers of Judaism continue to wrestle with the implications of Rosenzweig's ideas for the present and future.

Martin Buber's philosophy may be characterized as his continuing response to the tumultuous age through which his long life extended.[20] Born into a Viennese home where Hasidism as well as the wider heritage of Judaism were known and loved, he received a good Jewish education. To this he added a general humanistic education centering in philosophy and art history. As university professor, journalist, and Jewish educator, he participated fully in the life of his time. In 1920 he joined Rosenzweig to found the *Freies Judisches Lehrhaus* in Frankfort, Germany, devoted to Jewish adult education. From 1924 to 1933 he was professor of Jewish religion and ethics at the University of Frankfort, which, incidentally, was the only such post in a German university. In 1922 he published *Ich und Du (I and Thou)*, the book for which he is best known. In a succession of other books and articles he followed up and developed the implications of the I-Thou relation for many and varied aspects of faith and culture. With the rise of the Hitler movement, he devoted himself to deepening the religious resources of his people. From 1938 until his death in 1965 Buber lived in Jerusalem.

Buber is best known for his concept of I and Thou, or person-person relations. The phrase "I and Thou" he took from Feuerbach; but he gave to it his own highly original and detailed development. For Buber, I-Thou is to be contrasted with I-it, or person-thing experience. The latter, I-it, is often assumed as both logically and epistemologically primary, alike by the philosopher seeking to explain the world, and by the common man in the modern West with its preoccupation with things and its poverty of personal relations. Both are wrong, argued Buber, for not I-it but I-Thou claims an absolute primacy in both thought and action.

For I-it can never be said with the whole self. Only I-Thou can achieve that. So it is that the true primary mode of human experience is person-person meeting. As Buber stated the matter, "all real life is meeting."[21] All of this amounts to a strong and irreducible statement of personalism, a basic attitude which Buber drew from Hasidic and biblical sources, to which he gave strong, clear articulation, and whose implications he traced through all the basic aspects of human culture from art to government. While Buber's voice has not been alone in this message of human personhood, his statement of it has been widely influential, not only among philosophers and theologians, but among social scientists and others who deal with human nature.

For Buber this concept served also as a base of operations from which he moved onward to what he termed the philosophy and life of dialogue. The fulfillment of I-Thou relations or human community is an unsentimental way of expressing the biblical ethic of love; and the achievement and maintenance of human community hence becomes a main moral goal for all who seek human well-being and fulfillment. While the person-person relation is deployed "horizontally" in human ethics and society, the "vertical" assertion of the I-Thou relation constitutes Buber's approach to God, who is simply "the Eternal Thou." As "thou," God cannot be talked *about* but only talked *to*, or directly addressed.[22] In this assertion we see Buber's formulation of what chapter 2 termed the mysticism of communion.

The destiny of selves-in-community, in Buber's view, leads onward to the whole historical dimension of human existence. For history is simply the destiny of selves writ large. Conversely, a self may be characterized as a piece of historic destiny. This in turn led him back to the view of history in the Bible in such books as *The Prophetic Faith*, and *Two Types of Faith*.[23] He also concerned himself with every aspect of human culture, from education to politics or to the arts, and, indeed, to such activities as psychotherapy. He concerned himself with Zionism, opposing the dominant popular formulation of political, nationalistic Zionism, and seeking formulations which he believed to be more consonant with Israel's historic prophetic faith.

While it is still too early to estimate Buber's place in the great tradition of Jewish philosophy, his contributions to contemporary Jewish thought and faith, as well as to the wider human community seem even now both substantial and plain for all to see.

SUGGESTIONS FOR FURTHER READING

As many of these works are classics that have appeared in numerous editions, only the most accessible publication is indicated.

Baeck, L. *Essence of Judaism*. New York: Schocken Books, 1948.

Baron, S. *Social and Religious History of the Jews*. New York: Columbia University Press, 1960.

Baron, S., and Blau, J., eds. *Judaism: Postbiblical and Talmudic*. New York: Liberal Arts, 1954.

Blau, J. *The Story of Jewish Philosphy*. New York: Random House, 1962.

Browne, L., ed. *The Wisdom of Israel*. New York: Modern Library, 1945.

Buber, M. *I and Thou*. New York: Scribners, 1937.

———. *The Writings of Martin Buber*. New York: Meridian Press, 1956.

Diamond, M. *Martin Buber, Jewish Existentialist*. New York: Oxford University Press, 1960.

Glazer, N. *American Judaism*. Chicago: University of Chicago Press, 1957.

Golden, J. *The Living Talmud*. New York: Mentor Books, 1957.

Gutmann, J. *Philosophies of Judaism*. Garden City: Doubleday, 1966.

Herberg, W. *Protestant, Catholic and Jew*. New York: Doubleday, 1955.

———. *Judaism and Modern Man*. New York: Meridian Press, 1960.

Heschel, A. *Man Is Not Alone*. New York: Farrar, Strauss & Young, 1951.

———. *A Philosophy of Judaism*. New York: Farrar, Strauss & Cudahy, 1955.

Moore, G. F. *Judaism*. Cambridge: Harvard University Press, 1927.

Neusner, J. *The Way of the Torah*. Belmont: Dickenson, 1970.

Rotenstreich, N. *Jewish Philosophy in Modern Times*. New York: Holt, Rinehart & Winston, 1960.

Schwarz, L., ed. *Great Ages and Ideas of the Jewish People*. New York: Modern Library, 1956.

XIV
Islamic
Philosophy

AS THESE LINES are written, Jew and Arab are pitted against each other in the Near East in mortal enmity. This seems reason enough to justify a chapter on philosophy in the Islamic tradition. For, as we have seen, philosophy is an excellent port of entry into an understanding of any culture or civilization. But there are many other good reasons as well.

In the preceding chapter we noted the role of classical Arab scholars in transmitting the heritage of Greek philosophy to the medieval, and thence also to the modern, West. In this chapter we must follow up this lead by examining the way in which these Islamic scholars used their Greek heritage. Again, we observed of the Jewish tradition that it has created forms of belief and practice for the expression of monotheistic faith that contrast sharply with the more familiar forms of Christianity. This observation is similarly true of Islam. Islam too has created its own distinctive forms of thought and devotion and of common life, for the expression of monotheistic faith, which contrast with the forms of both Judaism and Christianity, and which make their own distinctive claim for study and understanding.

Islam asserts itself to be monotheism pure and unadulterated.[1] It is a claim that is often made with the implied or expressed suggestion that the Christian doctrines of incarnation and trinity violate monotheism, and constitute a kind of ditheism or tritheism. However this may be, we can see in Islam many of the issues and problems that inhere in pure monotheism. The word, *Islam*, means submission or obedience, that is, to the one absolutely unique God; and a Muslim is, both etymologically and existentially, one who submits or obeys. We have noted as a highly significant characteristic of monotheistic faith the principle of discontinuity, that is, between Creator and creation, God and world; and we have contrasted this with the principles of continuity and consubstantiality that characterize the cosmic religions and cultures. While Judaism and Christianity also exemplify the principle of discontinuity, it is Islam that draws out its implications most clearly, fully, and rigorously. We shall see some of these implications in the Muslim doctrine of *shirk*, which condemns as blasphemous any confusion or comparison of any aspect or object of the creaturely world with the Creator. Yet, surely the best reason of all for a chapter's look at Islamic philosophy is simply and plainly that this is a major philosophic tradition, of which the twentieth century West in characteristic provincialism knows all too little.

Muslim Beginnings

In order to begin to understand Islamic philosophy one must begin to understand Islamic faith and culture. As Muslims like to say, among the religions of the world, Islam began in the full light of history. The founding events center in the life and teachings of the prophet Mohammad (A.D. 570–632). Born in Mecca, the prophet was orphaned while still a small child, and was reared first by his grandfather, and then by an uncle, Abu Talib. His formative years were spent among leading families and figures of his city. Mecca was a city of considerable importance on the trade routes between Byzantium and Asia, and between Iran and Ethiopia. Politically too it was caught during this period of history in the center of a three-sided struggle for power among Byzantium, Abyssinia, and Iran. Mecca also had been for several centuries a place of religious pilgrimage, centering in its even then ancient shrine, the *Kaaba*, with its Black Stone; and this custom had in turn become the source of considerable revenue to the city.

Growing to manhood, Mohammad became a camel driver, and was thus enabled to see many parts of the Near Eastern world. At the age of twenty-five he married his employer, the widow Khadijah who was fifteen years his senior. That the marriage was happy is attested by the fact that during Khadijah's lifetime the Prophet took no other wives. Of their five children, only one, a daughter named Fatima, grew to maturity.

Mohammad became increasingly concerned with religious and ethical issues. Muslim tradition records a milestone in his life in A.D. 610 in what Muslims call the Night of Power and Glory, in which the Archangel Gabriel appeared to him, in effect commissioning him to be Allah's Prophet. As recorded in Surah XCVI of the Qur'an, the Archangel declared:

Read: In the name of thy Lord who createth
          Createth man from a clot

Read: And thy Lord is the most Bounteous
             Who teacheth by the pen
             Teacheth man that which he knew not.[2]

To Mohammad, now the Prophet, the experience was at first shattering, then illuminating, then directive. As more revelations came, he took upon himself the Prophet's role of speaking forth Allah's will to the people of Mecca. They were at first scornful; but as the Prophet's words increasingly conflicted with vested interests, their laughter turned to anger. He made pitifully few converts, and of these several had to seek asylum across the sea in Abyssinia. The climax of ill-fortune was reached in A.D. 619 when both his wife Khadijah and his uncle Abu Talib died. However, later the same year, he was visited by an embassy for the city of Yathrib, asking him to come as their leader. In A.D. 622 in the Hijrah (the Arabic word means "escape"), he made good his escape from Mecca to Yathrib, now renamed Medina (meaning "the city").

In Medina the Prophet moved decisively to reform and reorganize the city's life. As one twentieth century Muslim writer puts the matter, the Prophet's authority in Medina was of "an entirely new and original kind," being at once "absolute and consultative, theocratic and socialist."[3] As such it has served ever since as a paradigm or model for Islamic theology, social theory, and social practice. The Prophet's words, or rather as Muslims would say, those which Allah revealed through the Prophet during the years in Medina, as well as the earlier Meccan years, are now to be found in the Qur'an. The 114 Surahs of the Qur'an supplemented by reliable *hadiths* (which are additional stories of the Prophet's words or deeds) constitute the primary sources for his life and teachings.

The Prophet led the armies of Medina in their defense against attack, and then in sorties against enemies. In the year 630 he led a successful assault against Mecca. He proved in triumph to be a generous and devout conqueror of his former home city, going for worship to the Kaaba with its renowned Black Stone, and insisting only that pagan symbols be purged from this shrine, and that Arabs accept his leadership.

The Prophet then moved toward further unification of all the Arab tribes. However, on the threshold of new developments, in the year 632, he died. The work of leadership was passed to the first caliphs (literally "successors"), in turn: Abu Bekr (632–634), Omar (634–644), Othman (644–656), and the Prophet's son-in-law Ali (656–660). During these crucial years the Surahs of the Qur'an were collected and codified, the institutions of Muslim faith and culture were brought into being; and the Arab people began a process of military and political expansion which in a century's time was to extend their dominion from the gates of India in the east, and to Gibralter, Spain, and North Africa in the west.

The succcessful spread of Islam has often been attributed to the vigor and simplicity of its beliefs and practice as proclaimed and exemplified by the Prophet. The primary or foundational belief of Islam is in the one God, Allah, creator and sovereign of all that is, to whom, and to whom *alone*, man owes the absolute obligation of worship and service. Allah's mercy is revealed in the fact that he has sent messengers to mankind in the persons of angels and prophets. Among these messengers are many of the main figures of the Judeo-Christian scriptures from Adam and Abraham to Jesus. Concerning Jesus, Islam teaches his virgin birth, but denies that he was the incarnation of God. Yet of this succession of prophetic messengers or forthtellers, Mohammad is the culmination, or "seal of the prophets." Hence, he was and is "*the* Prophet." As such, Mohammad has in Muslim interpretation no divine status. He is not son of God or Messiah, but simply man at his paradigmatic human best.

Allah discloses his will for mankind in the words of the Qur'an which are, accordingly, absolute, sacred, infallible, and inerrant. As we shall presently see, this judgment concerning the Qur'an was the end-result of a significant process of theological argument in early Muslim history. Once achieved, the doctrine of literal inerrancy has constituted a continuing problem for Islamic philosophers and mystics who have sought to relate Islamic faith to changing times and circumstances.

Involved in Allah's will is a great deal of what Judaism and Christianity would call prophetic religion and ethics—namely, justice, mercy, and brotherhood as the content of the divine will for mankind. Yet, the crucial doctrinal affirmation of Islam is Judgment Day. While this doctrine includes general and final consummation of the whole world, its primary meaning is for the individual soul and the judgment of this individual soul by Allah for its course of life here below. The corollaries of Judgment Day are Paradise for the faithful, and the fires of Hell for the unfaithful or infidels. The Qur'an has vivid, colorful descriptions of both the delights of Paradise and the miseries of Hell.

Muslim practice as summarized in the traditional Five Pillars is as simple and vigorous as the Muslim creed. The First Pillar is confession, or witness, as man's primary religious obligation. The Muslim witness is to Allah's absolute might and uniqueness. Its classical formulation consists of the well-known words: "There is no god but Allah, and Mohammad is his prophet." The Second Pillar is prayer or worship, traditionally five times a day and in the direction of Mecca. The Third Pillar is fasting as a religious discipline and, following the example of the Prophet, especially during the sacred month of Ramadan. The Fourth Pillar is the religious tax or benevolence, which is given to the religious community to be used for charitable purposes. The Fifth Pillar is climactically the *hajj* or pilgrimage to Mecca, which every Muslim is expected to perform at least once during his lifetime.

The foundations of both faith and culture, begun by the Prophet, were completed by his early followers. The Prophet's words and deeds as recorded in the Qur'an and in hadiths became the paradigmatic models for subsequent Muslim thought and practice. These were eked out by the consensus and practice of the community of followers in the earliest days. Yet, back of all these as their source lay the Muslim perception of the one God and his revealed will for mankind. Truly everything that humans do, feel, and think, both individually and socially, should give expression to this radical monotheistic faith as declared by the Prophet.

Upon these religious foundations men reared the edifice of Islamic civilization, creating the forms and processes by which it lived, working through, and often fighting through, the many controversies and, not least of all, setting out in military conquest in all directions. Out of this military expansion was created an Arab empire and civilization, extending from the Atlantic Ocean on the west to India on the east, and lasting for over half a millennium. In other words, it was an empire, larger and lasting longer than that of Rome. And by the time it crumbled and fell, Islam had spread to still more distant places, now extending from North Africa to India, China, and Indonesia. Here we have space for only the briefest mention of a few of the salient features and issues of this far-flung Muslim community.

(1) One such feature is *Shari'a* or Muslim law. In the previous chapter we noted that monotheistic faith carries within itself the demand for law. If God has disclosed his will for mankind, then it is of paramount importance to apply the divine will to all the many-changing circumstances of individual and social life. In the Jewish tradition this imperative created the Talmud; in Roman Catholic Christianity it created canon law; and in Calvinistic Protestantism it created the Puritan view of Old Testament law.

In Islam the same divine imperative created the Shari'a with its four systems of *fiqh* or jurisprudence. Muslim faith seeks to do the will of Allah in the common life of the community; conversely, the common life of Muslim society is ideally a kind of corporate affirmative response of mankind to the divine will. Yet, what in specific detail is this will in all the varied situations of human life? What does it mean? What are its implications—and what are they not?

Wise men who were also judges and jurists pondered these problems. One way of determining the divine will was conformity to the words of the Qur'an. A second was the authority of those hadiths that had stood the test of critical appraisal. A third test was reasoning by analogy with either or both of the first two sources. The fourth source was the consensus of the Islamic community, used as a means of decision in the earliest days under the first caliphs, then subsequently extended or widened as the community of Islam expanded.

Differing combinations of these four methods of legal reasoning served to create within the first two Muslim centuries, the four main systems of jurisprudence: (1) the Hanifite school originating in Abu-Hanifa (d. 767); (2) the Malikite school originating with Malik ibn Anas (d. 795); (3) the Shafi'ite school founded by Mohammad ibn Idris al Shafi'i (d. 820); and (4) the Hanbalite school founded by Imam Ahmad Ibn Hanbal (d. 855). The first is today found chiefly in India and Pakistan, in countries formerly under the Ottoman Turks, and in China. The Malikite school is found in North Africa and Upper Egypt; and the Shafi'ite interpretation is found in Indonesia, Southern Arabia, Lower Egypt, and parts of Syria. The Hanbalite school, celebrated for its severity and rigor, is influential in Saudi Arabia. The important point is that wherever Islam lives, its law and the interpretations of that law are fundamental aspects of corporate life and thought.

(2) Sectarian controversy, conflict, and division are by no means limited to Islam or indeed to monotheistic faith, but rather seem as general tendencies to grow out of the depth of conviction engendered by any living faith. In all of the world's religious traditions it seems tragically easy for faith to degenerate into fanaticism. Yet, because it is committed actively to doing the will of God, monotheism seems particularly prone to this vice. For the Muslim tradition this has often implied *jihad* or holy war against the enemies of Allah. (Christians who point an accusing finger at this feature of Islam may also be reminded that *crusade* is the analogous Christian term.) For these reasons, and undoubtedly for many more as well, Islam has had its full quota of conflict and of sectarian controversy and division.

The selection of the first three caliphs led directly to the most important single division in Muslim history, namely that of *Shi'ites* from *Sunnis*. The former maintained that the Prophet's son-in-law and cousin, Ali, was his rightful heir and that therefore the first three caliphs were usurpers. The *Shi'a* (literally "followers," that is, of Ali) number some twenty-five million of Islam's total of four hundred million adherents today. The largest single groups of Shi'ites are in Iran and Iraq, while smaller sects, often warring among themselves, are spread over the Muslim world.

Ali was also involved in another kind of sectarian division. Instead of meeting Mu'awiya (who was a rival candidate for caliph, and was also founder of the Abbasid caliphate) on the field of battle, Ali negotiated a settlement. This led to withdrawal and opposition on the part of a group of deeply committed followers called *Kharijites* (meaning "those who withdraw") and subsequently to Ali's assassination by an embittered Kharijite. These fanatical separatists have risen repeatedly in Muslim history, to urge death for all who disagree with them. Opposed to them in early Muslim history were the *Murjites* who proposed in moderation that judgment be deferred until Judgment Day, and also that judgment be executed by God rather than by man.

(3) Still another controversy, equally important and of a different kind, lay at the sources of Muslim theology and philosophy. The argument was between a party called the *Mutazilites*, or Rationalists, and those who came to be known as the *Sunnis* or Traditionalists. The central difference between them was the all-important issue of the nature and attributes of the one God. On this issue the Qur'an appears to secular observation to contain everything from the most literal anthropomorphism to a well-nigh absolute transcendentalism. The Mutazilites had no trouble with the negative attributes of God, but to admit positive attributes seemed to them to conflict with the divine unity. Furthermore, they sought also to maintain the justice or goodness of God, as well as the freedom and responsibility of man. These ancient Muslim rationalists also argued that the Qur'an was created rather than uncreated; in other words, it was on the human side of the line that separates Allah from his creation. For, otherwise, it would have conflicted with Allah's sovereignty.

For a century or more the Mutazilites were the dominant party in Muslim theology. However, in the end they were defeated by the Sunnis, whose most influential thinker was Al Ashari (873–935). His main motivation was an intensely religious concern with the absolute omnipotence of Allah. Ashari argued that only an absolutely all-powerful God can command the absolute allegiance of the human heart. He appears to have been at first a Mutazilite who underwent a conversion experience (the Prophet appeared to him three times in dreams) to become the founder of what was to develop into the Traditionalist or Sunna position. He opposed the doctrine of a created Qur'an with the opposite estimate that the Qur'an was the literal Speech of God. He demanded literal acceptance of such anthropomorphisms as the hand or face of God, and of the contemplation of God by the faithful in Paradise. Against the Mutazilite doctrine of human free will, he staunchly maintained the divine omnipotence, arguing in effect not that man acts, but that God acts in and through man. Such was the uncompromising monotheistic faith that became official Muslim theology. Many of the issues of this early period of theological controversy continued on into the great age of Muslim philosophy. However, before we come to this subject, we must look briefly at Sufism or Islamic mysticism.

Sufism

The word *sufi* means "wool wearer" and probably refers to the coarse wool garment worn as an ascetic exercise; but it has come to designate the whole mystical tradition of Islam. The sources of this tradition are several. First, there are words of the Prophet pointing to the inwardness of the Muslim's relation to Allah ("He is nearer to us than the jugular vein").[4] There is also an influence from the Neoplatonism and gnosticism of the Hellenistic world which bordered the world of Islam. Still again, the turmoil and controversy of early Muslim centuries drove some persons, as in other similar historical situations, to seek refuge within.

Yet, none of these causes, nor all of them taken together, suffice to explain the intensity or magnitude of Sufi mysticism. Rather, it must be asserted, Sufism is a kind of standing protest or rebellion against the extreme rigor and purity of Muslim monotheism, literalism, and legalism. The austere and extreme theology of Al Ashari and his fellow Sunnis or Traditionalists elicited the counterresponse of those who found God as an immediate and loving presence within their own hearts.

However, the Sufi challenge to Muslim tradition and orthodoxy went even further. Many, indeed most, of the Sufis remained what our chapter 2 called mystics of communion. Under various metaphors, principally that of human love (in the full range of this multivalued word) these men sang the praises of Allah's love for man, and man's answering love. As such they provided a warmth, a spontaneity and a joyful emotion frequently lacking in the rigors of traditional Muslim monotheism. The mysticism of communion has played similar roles in other religious traditions as well.

However some bold spirits among the Sufis pressed on from the mysticism of communion to that of absorption or ontological union; and in doing so they challenged the very foundations of Muslim monotheistic faith with its principle of discontinuity. In some notable instances they incurred the charge of shirk or blasphemy, a capital crime in many Muslim lands. It is significant to call attention here once again to the clear sharp difference between such faiths as Buddhism and Hinduism on the one hand, where complete absorption in the religious object is the *summum bonum* and, on the

other hand, the monotheistic faiths where this aim is regarded as blasphe-
mously evil and where the proper goal is the active and loving service of
God.

Notable among the early mystics was the slave girl, Rabia al-Adawiya of
Basra (d. 801), celebrated for her works of devotion and her poems and
preachings of the Divine Love. She has sometimes been called the St.
Theresa of Islam. The following lines are typical:

> I love thee with two loves, love of my happiness
> And perfect love, to love thee as thy due.
> My selfish love is that I do naught
> But think on Thee excluding all beside;
> But that purest love which is thy due
> Is that the veils which hide thee fall and I gaze on Thee.
> No praise to me in either this or that
> May, Thine the praise for both that love and this.[5]

An important step toward the mysticism of union or absorption was taken
by Abu Yasid al Bistami (d. 815) who taught *fana* or the annihilation of individual human consciousness during the mystical experience.[6] Celebrating
the identity of soul and God, he is said to have exclaimed "How great is my
majesty!" He used such metaphors as love and light and wine to proclaim
the mystical experience.

Fuller knowledge exists concerning the unitive mysticism of Al Hallaj (d.
922) and the penalty he paid for it.[7] Born Al Husayn ibn Manson, and called
Al Hallaj, meaning "the wood gatherer," he attained fame as teacher and
practicer of devotion. He was led onward from communion with God to
fana, namely, the extinction of individual consciousness, and thence to complete absorption in God (which, once more, is for many mystics in mankind's history the supreme good and goal, but which in the view of orthodox
Islam is idolatry and blasphemy). "I am the Truth," he cried to the people
of his city, meaning, in effect, "I am God." His last days seem to suggest a
deliberate parallelism with Christ's incarnation of God, hence there is a grim
appropriateness in the penalty of crucifixion that was meted out to him.

A mystic of a very different and more orthodox sort was Al Ghazzali
(1058–1111), by common consent the great theological synthesizer of Islam.
Sufism played a vital role in his synthesis. Appointed a professor at the University of Baghdad while still a young man, he wrote a brilliant polemic
against Neoplatonism called *The Inconsistency of the Philosophers*. Despite
his great outward success, an inner spiritual crisis impelled him to withdraw

from teaching, to leave the university, and assume the role of a simple Sufi saint and seeker. He made the pilgrimage to Mecca, then devoted himself to Sufi austerities and devotions for ten years. Thereafter, he returned briefly to the university, then spent his remaining years at his home in Iran. His great work entitled *The Revivification of the Religious Sciences* may be characterized as a union of Sufism and the Sunna, of mysticism and the tradition, the mystical component being an inwardness that imparted a fresh depth of meaning to Sunni belief and practice.[8]

Other later figures continued the tradition of Sufism. Ibn Arabi (1165–1240), who was born in Spain but taught and wrote in the East, was clearly a mystic of the unitive sort who seems however to have escaped the fate of Al Hallaj. He has frequently been termed a theosophist, inasmuch as his interpretation of mystical experience involved claims to esoteric knowledge of hidden regions of reality. His all-encompassing philosophy of mysticism bears striking similarity to such philosophies in other traditions, from Greece to India and China, in its statement of a single supreme Unity from which all things proceed and to which they return.

In addition to founding the Mevlevi order of dervishes, Jalal al-Din Rumi (1207–1273) wrote mystical poetry and other literature of great excellence. His interpretation of mystical experience accentuates the love metaphor and, like the writings of many Christian and Jewish mystics, treads the borderline between the two types of mysticism, that is, the mysticism of communion and of ontological union. It also explores the emotional depths and the philosophic implications of man's relation to God. The following lines are typical:

> I died as mineral and became a plant
> I died as plant and rose to animal,
> I died as animal and I was man.
> Why should I fear? When was I less by dying?
> Yet once more I shall die as man, to soar
> With angels blest; but even from angelhood
> I must pass on: all except God doth perish.
> When I have sacrificed my angel soul,
> I shall become what no mind e'er conceived
> Oh, let me not exist! for Non-existence
> Proclaims in organ tones, "To Him we shall return."[9]

Islam's mystical tradition continues to the present day; and in the last section of this chapter we shall return to the great mystical and philosophical poet of contemporary Islam, Mohammad Iqbal of Pakistan.

Islamic Scholastic Philosophy

Philosophy began in the Muslim world, as it has in so many other times and places in world history, as an attempt to understand religious faith. Here, as in Christendom and elsewhere, it was a process of "faith seeking understanding," and in this process creating scholastic philosophy. Philosophy grew and flowered in Arabic civilization from the ninth through the twelfth centuries A.D. Islamic philosophy may also be characterized as a secular relative to the Islamic theological studies already noted in the previous section. In origin it was the attempt of Arab scholars to lay hold upon and to reclaim the classical Greek philosophic heritage. It is indeed primarily to these men, from Al-Kindi to Averroes, that the West owes the preservation of Greek philosophy and its transmission to Jewish and Christian scholastics, and thence to the modern Western world.

Beyond their preservation of the Greek texts and ideas, these Arab thinkers broke new ground in attempting a philosophical formulation of what this and the previous two chapters have termed monotheistic faith. What in short they attempted was the use of Greek philosophy, mostly Aristotle filtered through a Neoplatonic Byzantine heritage, for the exposition and defense of Muslim faith. They received hints and suggestions for their task from Christian church fathers such as Origen and Augustine, and from the mystical philosophy of Plotinus, but the basic categories and formulations of scholastic philosophy were their own creation and achievement. Muslim philosophers distinguished themselves from Muslim theology by their reliance upon reason alone, in contrast to theology's reasoning on the basis of faith and within the closed context of the Muslim community.

The founder of Muslim scholasticism was Al-Kindi (800–870), tutor to the son of the caliph of Baghdad, also owner of a large library of Greek science and philosophy, friend and sympathizer with Mutazilite theologians, and himself a Neoplatonist.[10] However, at one point Al-Kindi found Neoplatonism inadequate. In contrast to the Neoplatonic idea of perpetual emanation of the world from the One, he asserted the idea of the creation of the world in time as a necessary implication of Muslim monotheism. In Al-Kindi and his successors, first in Islamic scholasticism, then subsequently in Jewish and Christian scholasticism, this idea of the temporal creation of the world seems to have functioned as a philosophic expression of monotheistic faith. In Al-Kindi's thought, creation and Neoplatonic emanation lay side by side, without serious attempts at reconciliation.

In Al Farabi (875–950) Muslim philosophy achieved maturity. Known to Islamic history as "the Second Teacher" (Aristotle being the "First

Teacher''), he was born in Turkistan and studied philosophy and Greek science in Baghdad.[11] His philosophy was a blend of Aristotle, Plato, and Plotinus. He taught that philosophy rather than theology is the highest knowledge, and is served or assisted by theology and law, rather than vice versa. At the center of his metaphysical system is First Being or absolute One, which in Muslim dogma was understood as equivalent or identical to God. Al Farabi's God was an attempted combination of Plotinus' One and Aristotle's First Cause. From this divine source emanate, in two parallel series, ten successive orders of intellectual and of physical nature, respectively. The last intelligence is Gabriel, who is also characterized as revelation. This last emanation is also what Aristotle termed active intellect. Thus, Al Farabi asserted the equivalence of revelation and active intellect. The parallel physical emanation is the whole sublunary world, whose culminating product is man.

The goal of man according to Al Farabi is to develop his rational faculty by means of his volition or will. Since the end of man is philosophical contemplation, only those with this capacity or power may be said to achieve immortality. Others perish at death. Al Farabi was also interested in social philosophy in ways influenced by Plato's *Republic* and *Laws*. In this field he taught that in the state, as in the universe, there is a head, from whom all authority emanates, and in relation to whom humans find their natural stations or levels of life.

Abu Ali ibn Sina (980–1037), known to the West as Avicenna, was a Persian physician, advisor to rulers, but most of all a student of Greek philosophy and a highly original thinker.[12] Indeed, he was the climactic figure of Muslim scholastic philosophy. He wrote that he had read Aristotle's *Metaphysics* some forty times and knew the text by heart, but was baffled by it until he came upon a small book by Al Farabi. To the Aristotelean categories of matter and form he significantly added a third category, namely, existence; and he made a further distinction, all-important for subsequent scholasticism, between Necessary Being and contingent being. These distinctions enabled him to assert that all existence emanates from Necessary Being or God. He also asserted that in God essence and existence are conjoined, while in contingent beings they are separated.

In these moves of Avicenna we see again an attempt to translate monotheistic faith into the language of scholastic philosophy. Thus, for example, the assertions that God is Necessary Being, in contrast to the contingent being of all else, and that in God essence and existence are joined together, while here below they are sundered, must be understood as philosophical ways of expressing what we have termed the religious principle of discontinuity between Creator and creation, or between God and world. Relative to these issues, Avicenna's thought has had a continuing importance for Western philosophy. For instance, it is interesting to observe the ways in which later Jewish and Christian scholastics used the conceptual equipment that Avicenna constructed, often without acknowledgment, and sometimes blissfully unaware of the source.

Along with Al Farabi before him, Avicenna asserted a kind of parallelism between philosophy and religion, each of which in its own language says the same thing. On the one hand philosophy speaks a language of concepts and arguments, and on the other hand religion speaks in images and symbols whose power is able to hold man's allegiance and move him to action. Once this distinction had been made, scholars were free to choose one or the other language and to make comparative valuations of philosophy and religion. This distinction also opened the way to the doctrine of double truth so that a proposition might be false in philosophy and true in theology, or vice versa, though one must immediately add that Avicenna did not himself draw this conclusion. Most Muslim philosophers were restrained from the doctrine of double truth by their assumption of a harmony between these two regions of experience.

Both Al Farabi and Avicenna addressed themselves to theological issues of great importance to Islamic philosophy and faith. Two such issues were the nature of revelation and of prophethood. Revelation was asserted to be an illumination of the mind by means of religious images and symbols. A capacity for such illumination and for its charismatic communication to other men were asserted as the traits of prophethood. Avicenna also found this quality of illumination at the heart of all intellectual discovery.

We noted in the preceding section the synthetic theology of Al Ghazzali, with its attack on philosophers in *The Inconsistency of the Philosophers*. Al Ghazzali was clearly a theologian and not a philosopher, in that he reasoned and lived within the closed context of Muslim dogma rather than working, as did the philosophers, simply with arguments from self-evident truths of natural reason. One important result of Al Ghazzali's theological achievement was to regain intellectual primacy (in Islam) for theology. After Ghazzali, theology was acknowledged in Islam as queen of the sciences, with results destined to be felt for many centuries.

Muslim philosophy produced one more great figure, important particularly for his influence on Jewish and Christian philosophy, namely, Ibn Rushd (1126–1198) or, as he is known to the West, Averroes.[13] Coming from a family of jurists, he was himself chief judge in Seville and Cordova. He wrote on Malikite jurisprudence as well as on philosophy and theology. He responded to Al Ghazzali's *Inconsistency of the Philosophers* with a po-

lemical tract entitled *The Inconsistency of the Inconsistency*, which was designed to show the capacity of human reason to attain coherent knowledge of the world, including the things of faith.

At the center of his life and thought lay the conviction that philosophy and religion are both true and may therefore be reconciled or harmonized with each other. On this traditional problem of Muslim philosophy he took issue with Avicenna's position. Averroes seems clearly not to have taught what the so-called Latin Averroists of Christianity attributed to him, namely, a theory of double truth. It was through the Aristotelean scholarship of Averroes that medieval Christian Europe had its first fully critical introduction to Aristotle's thought.

After Averroes no philosopher of comparable stature emerged in Islam for several centuries. As we have previously seen, philosophy was transmitted from Islam to Judaism and Christianity in such figures as Maimonides and Thomas Aquinas, finding its way through them into the mainstream of Western culture. The question what happened to Islamic philosophy after the twelfth century has been asked many times by historians of thought. Whatever the reason or reasons, the historical facts are clear, namely, despite occasional individual exceptions, the great flowering of Islamic philosophy was over with Averroes.

Modern and Contemporary Issues

For no other religion of the world has the issue of modernity been as large or as thorny as it has for Islam. At best there has been a kind of armed truce between these combatants, namely, tradition and modernity; at worst there has been a total rejection of the modern world, including modern philosophy. For these attitudes there are doubtless many causes. The *Sunna* or Tradition tied Islam so closely to the Qur'an that philosophers have had little room and little freedom for thought. Again, Islam has been the faith of many traditional peoples either indifferent or hostile to modernity. There are doubtless other contributory causes as well.

Yet, some Muslim thinkers have broken through the barrier and addressed themselves to these issues. Significantly, Indian Islam, where the followers of the Prophet have perforce rubbed elbows with adherents of other faiths, has produced two such notable figures. One was Sir Syed Ahmad Khan (1817–1898), native of Delhi and well-educated in traditional Muslim learning. He was an employee of the British East India Company and sided with the British during the 1857 mutiny. By journalism, education, and scholarship he sought to bridge the gap between Indian Muslims and the modern West. He edited a magazine called the *Improvement of Manners and Morals* devoted to social and religious issues.[14] He wrote widely, including a book of essays on the life of Mohammad, a Qur'an commentary and a wide variety of speeches and essays on topics of the day.

But most important of all he founded Aligarh College in 1875 to impart modern education to Muslim youth. The college became a university in 1921. He wrote widely, in the fashion of a religious liberal, seeking to reconcile Muslim tradition to modern life and thought. His attitude of hostility to the supernatural gained for his followers the label *necharis* (freely translated, "naturalists") as well as the hostile criticism of solidly conservative members of the Indian Muslim community.

The work of philosophic reconciliation begun by Sir Syed Ahmad Khan was carried on by the greater figure of Mohammad Iqbal (1873–1938). Iqbal was born of a pious Muslim family in the Punjab and graduated in 1899 from Government College in Lahore, where he also served as lecturer in philosophy.[15] As a graduate student in philosophy at Cambridge and Munich he came under the influence of European thought, particularly of the philosophies of Nietzsche and Bergson. Returning home he practiced law for a livelihood, but devoted himself to study and writing, gaining recognition both as philosopher and poet. He was knighted by the British in 1921, but he accepted this honor only on the stipulation that it was not regarded as a reward for services rendered to the government.

Like many leading Asians of his generation, his thought was marked by a meeting of East and West. The Western ingredients we have noted. The more important Eastern element was the influence of the Sufi tradition of Islam, particularly of the great mystical poet Jalal al-Din Rumi. Iqbal's own devout Muslim faith was a major factor in his thought and life.

From Western philosophies of life, he acquired a strong aversion to that kind of mystical quietism which he believed to constitute the decadence of faith. Rather, he affirmed that life is action, and that in the strife with evil lies the meaning of human selfhood. God, he taught, does not demand the destruction of the self but rather its fulfillment or realization in obedience to Him, and in fellowship with the community.

While he was a much more conservative figure than Syed Ahmad Khan, Iqbal nonetheless undertook a similar task of reconciling Muslim religious tradition with modern science and philosophy. His volume entitled *The Reconstruction of Religious Thought in Islam* seeks a philosophic justification of traditional religion through the idea of religious experience.[16] In the manner of Western religious liberalism he undertook reformulations of such traditional concepts as God, prayer, and man's freedom and immortality. Out of an intense sense of loyalty to Muslim tradition and culture, he proposed a reformed and reconstructed Islam, dedicated to the service of Allah, and through Allah to mankind.

Iqbal was also a social thinker deeply concerned about the division of mankind into national and racial groups, about colonialism, about the evils of capitalism, and about the problems of injustice generally. Reluctantly, but increasingly, he was drawn into political participation and leadership. As president of the All-India Muslim League in 1930 he first publicly advocated an independent state for Indian Muslims. He is regarded as the father and national poet of Pakistan, though this nation came into existence a full decade after his death in 1938.

Iqbal's poetry stands in the great tradition of Islamic mysticism, and also constitutes his own personal statement of Muslim faith and philosophy. To epitomize both his philosophy and his faith we cannot do better than to quote from his poetry. Excellent English translations exist of two volumes, *Secrets of the Self*, and *Mysteries of Selflessness*, though they are doubtless inadequate to the Urdu and Persian of the original works.[17]

Here are some lines from *The Secrets of the Self*.

The form of existence is an effect of the Self
Whatsoever thou seest is a secret of the Self,
When the Self awoke to consciousness
It revealed the universe of Thought.
A hundred worlds are hidden in its essence:
Self-affirmation brings Not-self to light.

. . . .

Subject, object, means and causes—
All these are forms which it assumes for the purpose of action.
The Self rises, kindles, falls, glows, breathes,
Burns, shines, walks and flies.
The spaciousness of Time is its arena
Heaven is a billow of the dust on its road.
From its rose-planting the world abounds in roses;
Night is born of its sleep, day springs from its waking.
Life is preserved by purpose
Because of the goal its caravan-bell tinkles
Life is latent in seeking
Its origin is hidden in desire,
Keep desire alive in this heart
Lest thy little dust become a tomb.

The luminous point whose name is the Self
Is the life-spark beneath our dust.

By love it is made more lasting.
More living, more burning, more glowing.
From live proceeds the radiance of its being.
And the development of its unknown possibilities.
Its nature gathers fire from love,
Love instructs it to illumine the world.
Love fears neither sword nor dagger,
Love is not born of water and our earth.
Love makes peace and war in the world,
Love is the fountain of life, love is the flashing sword of death
The hardest rocks are shivered by love's glance:
Love of God at last becomes wholly God.

The Mysteries of Selflessness contains the author's statement of Muslim faith and culture.[18]

Our essence is not bound to any place;
The vigor of our wine is not contained
In any bowl; Chinese and Indian
Alike the shard that constitutes our jar,
Turkish and Syrian alike the clay
Forming our body; neither is our heart
Of India, or Syria or Rum
Nor any fatherland do we profess
Except Islam.

Throughout the earth still the Community
Of World Islam maintains its ancient forms.
Love is the universal law of life,
Mingling the fragmentary elements
Of a disordered world. Through our heart's glow
Love lives, irradiated by the spark
There is no god but God.

. . . Love's community is like
The light of God; whatever being we
Possess from its existence is derived.
"None seeketh when or where God's light was born
What need of warp and woof, God's robe to spin?"*
Who suffereth his foot to wear the chains
Of clime and ancestry is unaware
How *He begat not, neither was begot.***

*A quotation from Jalal al-Din Rumi
**An often repeated verse of the Qur'an

SUGGESTIONS FOR FURTHER READING

As many of these works are classics that have appeared in numerous editions, only the most accessible publication is indicated.

Arberry, A. J. *Sufism*. London: Allen & Unwin, 1956.

———. *Revelations and Reason in Islam*. London: Allen & Unwin, 1957.

———. *Arabic Poetry*. Cambridge: Cambridge University Press, 1965.

Arnold, T. W., ed. *The Legacy of Islam*. Oxford: Clarendon Press, 1931.

———. *The Preaching of Islam*. Lahore: Shirkat, 1956.

Coulson, N. J. *A History of Islamic Law*. Edinburgh: University of Edinburgh Press, 1964.

de Bary, W. T., ed. *Sources of the Indian Tradition*. New York: Columbia University Press, 1958.

Gibb, H. A. R. *Mohammedanism*. New York: Mentor Books, 1949.

———. *Studies in the Civilization of Islam*. Boston: Beacon Press, 1962.

Hitti, P. K. *The Arabs, A Short History*. Chicago: Regnery, 1956.

Iqbal, M. *Reconstruction of Religious Thought in Islam*. Lahore: Ashraf, 1944.

———. *Secrets of the Self*. Lahore, Ashraf, 1944.

Jeffry, A., ed. *Islam*. New York: Liberal Arts, 1957.

Kritzeck, J., ed. *Anthology of Islamic Literature*. Harmondsworth: Penguin Books, 1964.

Morgan, K., ed. *Islam: The Straight Path*. New York: Ronald Press, 1958.

Nicholson, R. A. *A Literary History of the Arabs*. Cambridge: Cambridge University Press, 1956.

Pickthall, M. M. *The Meaning of the Glorious Koran*. New York: Mentor Books, 1953.

Rahman, R. *Islam*. New York: Holt, Rinehart & Winston, 1966.

Schacht, J. *An Introduction to Islamic Law*. Oxford: Clarendon Press, 1964.

Watts, M. *Muhammad*. New York: Oxford University Press, 1960.

XV
On Beginning
to Philosophize
in Global
Context

AN OLD ADAGE asserts that to get where you want to go, you have to start from where you are. Accordingly, to move toward global philosophy we must begin from our present situation. It has been the thesis of this book that this means, first of all, an acquaintance with the living options of philosophy as they now exist in the world. This acquaintance is a necessary first step for whatever developments may follow, a first step with which this book has been concerned.

Here again, as in chapter 1, we acknowledge the pioneering work of the University of Hawaii in bringing together philosophers of the West and of Asia, thus beginning the process of mutual acquaintance. The most widely known aspect of this work has been the series of East-West philosophers' conferences from 1939 to 1964. A distillation of these meetings has been brought together in three volumes of papers delivered at these conferences, edited by the late Charles A. Moore and entitled, respectively, *The Indian Mind, The Chinese Mind*, and *The Japanese Mind*.[1] In these volumes the reader may observe the process of mutual acquaintance taking place. However, this same process has included a number of more specialized seminars and consultations. It also includes the journal, *Philosophy East and West*, and surely not least of all the continuing work of classroom and study.

Such mutual acquaintance among the different ways of philosophy is a good in itself, to be sought and cherished by all who believe that philosophy is addressed to one common humanity—to human beings as such. But it also has valuable ulterior consequences, both negative and affirmative. Negatively, it vetoes for all who hear and heed its message, any return to Western parochialism or ethnocentrism. Affirmatively, it serves as an indispensable preparation for whatever future philosophy may have.

As to this future, to speak of a future for philosophy necessarily supposes that mankind has a future. This is an assumption that is today being seriously challenged. Many men of unquestioned intelligence and responsibility assert that this is the time of Last Things for the human race. These grim apocalyptic assessments, while mainly political, economic, and ecological in character, nonetheless take on a philosophic and sometimes a theological quality as well. Hence, they demand philosophic appraisal.

Whether they be judged true, false, or a combination of both, we human beings need to remind ourselves that whatever the hour and whatever the weather, man's central task is to seek his humanity and to resist the dehumanizing forces that assault him. Whatever their disagreements and divergent assessments, all the philosophic options of our study would agree in this. They would also agree that now as always this stance and this task are philosophic in character.

If, on the other hand, we conclude that man's path, however rocky and however hazardous, leads into a future, philosophy will have a significant function along the way. In this book we have argued that men philosophize in particular historical traditions and communities. But if this be true, how can there be global philosophy, either now or in future? Is it realistically possible and is it humanly desirable to hope for or expect, either soon or in the distant future, a single global tradition and community of culture which will supplant the many local traditions and communities that now exist? Indeed, is such a concept even meaningful? Or, contrariwise, will the present plurality of cultural traditions continue for the foreseeable future of mankind? Or, again, ought we to hedge all our predictions with the counsel that in these large issues of the human future we must simply learn to expect the unexpected?

Since no man can really or truly know the answers to these questions, it seems the part of wisdom first to lay out the significant probabilities implicit in present trends and tendencies. Of these, the first is the persistence into the future of the present pluralism of cultural traditions and communities, the second is the emergence of a single global community of culture, and the third may be described as a combination of various elements of the first two.

(1) A strong argument can be made for the persistence into the foreseeable future of the present plurality of human cultures, in much the same way that existing languages show little tendency to melt away before an impending Esperanto. The number of the civilized cultures of mankind may be Toynbee's twenty-one, or there may be more or fewer.[2] But in any case, their plurality expresses the concreteness of particular geographical regions, of particular languages, cultures, and histories. As long as humans remain finite creatures, their lives will be rooted in these particularities.

Universalists and rationalists to the contrary notwithstanding, this plural-

ity of cultures does not constitute simply an inertia to be endured or overcome. Rather, it may be argued, this concrete plurality often adds greatly to
the richness and variety of human existence. Especially is this true in the field
of aesthetic values. Concreteness or particularity refracted through the prism
of the arts yields light of many and varied colors. For example, Shakespeare's
plays are indefeasibly English; Goethe is German; Dostoyevsky is Russian.
While these and other great artists embody values of universal human significance, they do so precisely not by ignoring the concreteness or particularity
of their tradition, but rather in and through it.

Philosophy as mankind has known it to date is as much a part and product of particular cultures as is painting, music, or literature. And it is at
least a distinct possibility that this state of affairs will continue into the foreseeable future. For, as we have observed in the course of our study, philosophy may be characterized in this respect as a culture coming to clear consciousness of itself. In this connection, we note the widespread double usage
of the term, *culture*. People speak of different cultures—American, Chinese,
Eskimo, and others; but they also speak of human culture as a generic fact.
The point to be made here is that philosophy has a significant relation to
both of these uses. In bringing a particular culture to awareness of itself, it
also poses the problem of its relation to human culture as a universal or
generic human fact. If this philosophic function is to continue, it will mean
that philosophy's role in the future will at least include the task of interpreting the world's cultures to each other and to human culture as such, in
much the same way that interpreters or translators today mediate between
people of different languages.

(2) However, on the contrary, it may be argued with great plausibility that
a single global tradition and community are even now taking shape out of
the turmoil and agony of our age. Such a single integral human tradition
and community, if it is to come at all, will grow out of a common history, a
common destiny which mankind has faced and lived through together, and
which will draw them together into a single global human community.
Something like this is the way in which the many local traditions and communities have come into existence. For example, Americans look back to the
formative events of their history, to the colonization of America, to the revolutionary war, the westward migration, the Civil War, and other similar hap-
penings, seeing in the whole pattern of these events the tradition that has
drawn Americans together into a community of people. Hence, analogously,
it may well be that out of the agonized history of the present age a global
human tradition is taking shape, so that mankind of future centuries will
look back on these times as Americans look back on the formative years of

their tradition. Hints of this kind of integrative process may be detected in such organizations as the UN and UNESCO.[3]

If this suggestion has any validity, then such various prospects as global government and global culture (of which global philosophy will be a part) become at least conceivable. However, our present contention is that any or all of these specific activities presuppose the basis of a common life or community. Doubtless, the road to this common human culture, if indeed the future may be said to lie in this direction, will be long, hard, and fraught with vicissitudes beyond our present imagination.

Yet, at the end appears the possibility of a global community whose distinctive values will find expression in culture in ways analogous to the cultures of presently existing societies and peoples. While it is difficult to the point of impossibility to trace out details of such a future human situation, we can at least assert that in this future society man will philosophize as man, as today we philosophize as Indians, Chinese, Westerners, or members of other particular traditions and communities. Such a future global culture will need to be brought to critical self-awareness, and that will still be one of philosophy's tasks.

(3) What is at least as likely as either of these two possibilities is an intermediate state of affairs in which humankind will achieve unity in some ways, but will remain diverse in others.[4] For example, the prospects today are different in the fields, say, of trade and commerce, of politics, of science, of the arts, of religion, and of language. In the opinion of many writers, it is in the material foundations of human life that unity seems alike most necessary, most possible, and most desirable; and conversely, in activities of the human spirit such global unity seems most problematic.

Another formulation of this view asserts that in the sphere of moral values the unity of mankind is imperative, while in the field of aesthetic values, diversity is a continuing good. In this interpretation, intellectual goods or values show a wide range of variety. For example, natural science seems inherently universal in outlook, while the humanities show indefeasible elements of particularity and pluralism. Still other forms of study exhibit significant combinations of universality and particularity.

If this third possibility is the path that humanity is to take into the future, then the most important question will be to distinguish which aspects of man's life can and should move toward unity, and in which aspects unity seems either impossible, undesirable, or both. It hardly needs to be added that this is a philosophical question.

Whatever humankind's path into the future, the role of philosophy will be that of interpreter or guide. The aptness of these metaphors is underscored by the attention they call to the facts that, while interpreters and guides are altogether concrete human beings, they are also committed to the task of interpreting human beings to each other and of guiding them over new and difficult terrain. To this task philosophy is called as never before in its long history.

In the present situation of humanity, religion faces a challenge even more radical than does philosophy. In the course of our study we have been led to several observations concerning the nature and function of mankind's traditional religious faiths. As we have seen, the attitude of the world's philosophies toward religion continues to vary across a wide spectrum, ranging from close alliance in the case of Hindu and Buddhist philosophy, to the secular detachment of modern Western liberal ways, or to the avowedly militant antireligion of Marxism. We have also had occasion to characterize faith as a way of responding to the existential question, why am I alive? This response consists of a cluster of life-values, symbolically expressed, which effectively answer this question, and hence provide mankind with direction and guidance. Hence, too, the various historic religions may be understood as so many paths of life, so many concrete ways of valuation that impart meaning to human existence.

Yet, we have also been forced to note that the historic faiths have been peculiarly susceptible to misuses and vices of several sorts. Faith readily and often hardens into fanaticism. It is also easily misled into unreason and obscurantism. Religion often falls victim to the inertia of tradition, or is trivialized into sentimentality. Many contemporary observers would agree with Gunnar Myrdal's conclusion that in his observation of Asian societies he has not seen a single instance in which religion has helped to facilitate desirable social change. The conclusion of such observations is that religion has no useful function in mankind's future. Hence, it is to be expected that religions will wither and die, and that the human future will be completely secular. Such challenges need to be carefully and candidly evaluated by all who are concerned with religion, as well as by all who are concerned with mankind's future and with the issue of global unity.

As one aspect of this critical appraisal, we repeat what was said in chapter 12 to the effect that, however secular the attitudes of contemporary intellectual elites, there seems to be no corresponding diminution of the sacred for the masses of mankind. To this it may also be added that however high-minded and well-intentioned they may be, such secular attitudes have so far in human history shown little long-time viability. To date at least they have not fared well in the rough and tumble of man's history. Rather, the emergence of such secular attitudes has constituted only a temporary interlude or transition between two systems of sacred forms.

It is of course always possible to argue that the future will be so completely new as to be totally discontinuous with the past, and hence that past evidence is worthless for prediction of the future. But this is a hard case to make, and the burden of proof is on those who seek to make it. Meanwhile, taking our clues from past and present experience, we assert that the real question is not one of a totally secular outlook versus traditional systems of the sacred, but rather *which* system of sacred or holy forms is best or most adequate to human existence and, within it, what relation of sacred to secular concerns seems best or most adequate to the whole of man's existence.

To the traditional religions the challenge is to be what they claim to be, and what they have been in the times of their vitality and power, namely, paths of life, or value systems, which provide stimulus and guidance for individual and social action. If they are functional in this sense, they will live; but if, on the other hand, they make no difference in human behavior, this observation alone will be conclusive evidence that they are in fact already dead. Concerning the future of religion, once more, the biblical maxim is pertinent: by their fruits you shall know them.

The immediate and urgent challenge of the present crisis of humankind to both philosophy and religion is to keep the wide horizon of humanity around human thought and action, against all the forces that divide humankind into warring and suicidal groups. It is also to provide their adherents with the wisdom, the love, and the conviction to walk into the unknown future that lies before us. Among the most important tasks of philosophy, now as always, will continue to be the exposition, clarification, and criticism of faith.

Notes

Chapter I

1. V. G. Childe, *Man Makes Himself* (New York: New American Library, 1951). This book was first published in England under the title *What Happened in History*. See also R. Redfield, *The Primitive World and Its Transformations* (Ithaca: Cornell Univ., 1953).

2. Karl Jaspers, *The Origin and Goal of History* (New Haven: Yale, 1953); John Cobb, *The Structure of Christian Existence* (Philadelphia: Westminster, 1967).

Chapter II

1. G. E. Moore, *Some Main Problems of Philosophy* (London: Allen & Unwin, 1953), pp. 1–2. Reprinted by permission of the publisher.

2. L. Wittgenstein, *Tractatus Logicus Philosophicus*, trans. D. F. Pears and B. F. McGuiness (London: Routledge & Kegan Paul, 1961), ¶2.04, 2.063, pp. 13–14.

3. A. Plantinga, *God, Freedom and Evil* (New York: Harper & Row, 1974); see also by the same author, *God and Other Minds* (Ithaca: Cornell, 1967).

4. Plantinga, *God, Freedom and Evil*, p. 36.

5. Ibid., p. 37.

6. P. Wheelwright, *Metaphor and Reality* (Bloomington and London: Indiana Univ., 1968); P. Ricoeur, "Creativity in Language," *Philosophy Today*, Summer 1973, p. 97f.

7. Stephen Pepper, *World Hypotheses* (Berkeley: Univ. of California, 1966).

8. R. G. Collingwood, *An Essay on Metaphysics* (Oxford: Clarendon, 1940).

9. *Encyclopedia of Philosophy* (New York: Macmillan, 1967), 6 : 446, article on "Presupposing."

10. M. Heidegger, *What Is Philosophy?* (New York: Twayne Publishers, 1958), p. 33f.

11. J. H. Randall, *The Career of Philosophy* (New York: Columbia Univ.), 1 : 4f.

12. A. N. Whitehead, *Science and the Modern World* (New York: Macmillan, 1927), p. 87.

13. J. Hutchison, *Paths of Faith* (New York: McGraw-Hill, 1974), p. 5.

14. J. Hutchison, *Paths of Faith* (New York: McGraw-Hill, second edition, 1975), p. 5.

15. P. Tillich, *The Protestant Era* (Chicago: Univ. of Chicago, 1948), p. xv and passim. The concept of "ultimate concern" also occurs frequently throughout Tillich's other works.

16. H. R. Niebuhr, *The Meaning of Revelation* (New York: Macmillan, 1952), p. 77.

17. E. Bewkes, ed., *The Nature of Religious Experience* (New York: Harper, 1937), R. Niebuhr's essay in this volume is entitled "The Truth in Myths."

18. G. Ryle, *The Concept of Mind* (New York: Barnes & Noble, 1949), p. 8.

19. W. James, *The Varieties of Religious Experience* (New York: New American Library, 1958). See especially lecture 1.

20. W. T. Stace, *Mysticism and Philosophy* (Philadelphia: Lippincott, 1960). See especially chapter 4.

Chapter III

1. C. S. Peirce, see inter alia, *Philosophical Writings of Peirce*, ed. J. Buchler (New York: Dover Press, 1940).

2. W. James, *Pragmatism: A New Name for Some Old Ways of Thinking* (New York: Longmans Green, 1946).

3. P. Bridgman, *The Nature of Physical Theory* (New York: Dover, 1936).

4. J. Dewey, *The Influence of Darwin on Philosophy* (New York: Henry Holt, 1910).

5. A. O. Lovejoy, *The Thirteen Pragmatisms* (Baltimore: Johns Hopkins, 1963).

6. M. Cohen, *Reason and Nature* (Glencoe: Free Press, 1953). The epilogue is entitled "In Dispraise of Life, Experience and Reality."

7. A. N. Whitehead, *The Function of Reason* (Princeton: Princeton Univ., 1929).

8. See inter alia Y. H. Krikorian, ed., *Naturalism and the Human Spirit* (New York: Columbia, 1944). Dewey's essay is entitled "Antinaturalism in Extremis."

9. M. Cohen and E. Nagel, *An Introduction to Logic and the Scientific Method* (New York: Harcourt Brace, 1934). I have this story from A. Kaplan, *The New World of Philosophy* (New York: Random House, 1961).

10. See S. Hook in Y. H. Krikorian, ed., op cit.

11. See "The Humanist" published for the American Humanist Association and the American Ethical Union, Buffalo, New York.

12. See inter alia, J. Dewey, *Theory of Valuation* (Chicago: Univ. of Chicago, 1939).

13. J. Dewey, *Art as Experience* (New York: Capricorn, 1958).

14. W. James. See inter alia *The Moral Equivalent of War and Other Essays*, ed. J. Roth (New York: Harper Torchbooks, 1971).

15. J. Dewey, *The Public and Its Problems* (New York: Holt, 1927).

16. J. Dewey, *Reconstruction in Philosophy* (New York: New American Library, 1950).

17. J. Dewey, *Philosophy and Civilization* (New York: Minton Balch, 1931).

18. See inter alia *The Philosophy of John Dewey*, ed. J. Ratner (New York: Modern Library, 1939), p. 605f.

19. Ibid., p. 343f.

20. J. Dewey, *A Common Faith* (New Haven: Yale Univ., 1934), p. 79f.

Chapter IV

1. A. Ayer and others, *The Revolution in Philosophy* (New York: Macmillan, 1956).

2. *Encyclopedia of Philosophy* (New York: Macmillan, 1967), vol. 5, p. 52f, "Logical Positivism."

3. A. N. Whitehead and B. Russell, *Principia Mathematica* (Cambridge, at the Univ. Press, 1927).

4. B. Russell, *A History of Western Philosophy* (New York: Simon and Schuster, 1945).

5. A. J. Ayer, *Language, Truth and Logic* (New York: Dover, 1952).

6. Karl Popper, *The Logic of Scientific Discovery* (New York: Science Editions, Inc., 1961).

7. O. Neurath, et al., *International Encyclopedia of Unified Science* (Chicago: Univ. of Chicago, 1938 et seq.).

8. G. Bergmann, *The Metaphysics of Logical Positivism* (Madison: Univ. of Wisconsin, 1967).

9. F. Waismann, articles on "Verification" and "Language Strata" in A. Flew, ed., *Logic and Language*, 1st series and 2nd series (Oxford: Blackwell, 1952, 1955).

10. L. Wittgenstein, *Tractatus Logico-Philosophicus* (London: Routledge & Kegan Paul, 1961).

11. Ibid., ¶3.00 et seq.

12. Ibid., ¶2.00 et seq.

13. Ibid., ¶2063.

14. Ibid., ¶6.41.

15. Ibid., ¶7.

16. L. Wittgenstein, *Philosophical Investigations*, tr. G. Anscombe (New York: Macmillan, 1953).

17. Ibid., p. 5f.

18. J. Wisdom, *Philosophy and Psychoanalysis* (New York: Barnes & Noble, 1969).

19. See inter alia A. Flew, ed., *Logic and Language* (Oxford: Blackwell, 1952), p. 187f.

20. J. Findley, ed., *Studies in Philosophy* (London: Oxford Univ., 1966), p. 213f.

21. G. Ryle, *The Concept of Mind* (New York: Barnes & Noble, 1949).

22. See inter alia A. Flew, ed., op cit., p. 11f.

23. Ryle, op cit., Ch. 1.

24. Ibid.

25. Ibid., Ch. 3, p. 62f.

26. Richard Taylor, *Metaphysics* (Englewood Cliffs: Prentice-Hall, 1963), p. 37f.

27. A. I. Melden, *Free Action*. (New York: Humanities Press, 1961)

28. N. Malcolm, "The Conceivability of Mechanism," *Philosophical Review* (January 1968), p. 45f.

29. S. Hampshire, *Thought and Action* (London: Chatto & Windus, 1965).

30. A. Louch, *Explanation and Human Action* (Berkeley: Univ. of California, 1966).

31. J. Austin, *How To Do Things With Words* (Cambridge: Harvard Univ., 1962).

32. Ibid.

33. See inter alia G. Ebeling, *God and Word* (Philadelphia: Fortress Press, 1967).

34. C. Stevenson, *Ethics and Language* (New Haven: Yale Univ., 1944).

35. R. M. Hare, *The Language of Morals* (Oxford: Clarendon Press, 1952).

36. Ibid.

37. See inter alia I. Copi and J. Gould, eds., *Contemporary Readings in Logical Theory* (New York: Macmillan, 1967), p. 165f.

38. W. V. Quine, *Ontological Relativity and Other Essays* (New York: Columbia Univ., 1969).

39. P. Strawson, *Individuals* (New York: Anchor Books, 1959).

40. B. Russell, *A History of Western Philosophy* (New York: Simon and Schuster, 1945).

41. E. Nagel and E. Newman, *Goedel's Proof* (New York: NYU Press, 1958).

42. A. Kaplan, *The New World of Philosophy* (New York: Random House, 1961).

43. See inter alia Morton White, *Pragmatism and The American Mind* (New York: Oxford Univ., 1973), p. 121f.

44. B. Russell, *Introduction to Mathematical Philosophy* (New York: Macmillan, 1920).

45. See inter alia R. Ammerman, ed., *Classics of Analytic Philosophy* (New York: McGraw-Hill, 1965), p. 315f.

46. W. Zuurdeeg, *An Analytic Philosophy of Religion* (New York: Abingdon, 1958).

47. R. B. Braithwaite, *An Empiricist's View of the Nature of Religious Belief* (Folcroft, Pa.: Folcroft Press, 1970).

48. A. Flew and A. Macintyre, eds., *New Essays in Philosophical Theology* (New York: Macmillan, 1955).

49. P. Van Buren, *The Secular Meaning of the Gospel* (New York: Macmillan, 1963).

Chapter V

1. A. Whitehead and B. Russell, *Principia Mathematica* (Cambridge: Cambridge Univ., 1927) vol. 1.

2. J. P. Sartre, *Existentialism* (New York: Philosophical Library, 1947).

3. Vercors, *You Shall Know Them* (Boston: Little Brown, 1953). Vercors is the pen-name of Jean Bruller, and the French title of this novel is *Les Animaux Dénaturés*.

4. Blaise Pascal, *Pensées*, Everyman Edition (London: J. M. Dent, 1908).

5. Martin Heidegger, *Sein und Zeit* (Tübingen: Max Niemeyer, 1929). The English translation is *Being and Time* (New York: Harper & Row, 1962).

6. The late H. R. Niebuhr gave a course at Yale entitled "The Nineteenth Century Underground," dealing with thinkers ranging from Kierkegaard to Marx, and from Darwin to Dostoyevsky.

7. Eric Frank, *Philosophical Understanding and Religious Truth* (New York: Oxford Univ., 1945).

8. See inter alia P. Tillich, "Existential Philosophy" in his *Theology of Culture*. This paper was originally published in the *Journal of the History of Ideas* (January 1944).

9. S. Kierkegaard, *Philosophical Fragments* (London: Oxford Univ., 1936); Kierkegaard, *Concluding Unscientific Postscripts* (Princeton: Princeton Univ., 1941).

10. S. Kierkegaard, *Fear and Trembling* (Princeton: Princeton Univ., 1941); Kierkegaard, *The Sickness Unto Death* (Princeton: Princeton Univ., 1944).

11. See inter alia P. Tillich, *The Courage To Be* (New Haven: Yale Univ., 1952); R. May, *The Meaning of Anxiety* (New York: Ronald Press, 1953).

12. Walter Kaufmann, *Nietzsche: Philosopher, Psychologist, Antichrist* (Princeton: Princeton Univ., 1968).

13. E. Husserl, *Ideas* (New York: Macmillan, 1931). See also H. Spiegelberg, *The Phenomenological Movement* (The Hague: Nijhoff, 1960).

14. M. Heidegger, *Being and Time* (New York: Harper, 1962).

15. P. Sartre, *Being and Nothingness* (New York: Philosophical Library, 1956).

16. M. Merleau Ponty, *The Phenomenology of Perception* (New York: Humanities Press, 1962).

17. P. Tillich, *The Theology of Culture* (New York: Oxford Univ.), p. 76f.

18. G. Ryle, *The Concept of Mind* (New York: Barnes & Noble, 1949), p. 195f.

19. P. Ricoeur, *Fallible Man* (Chicago: Regnery, 1965).

20. J. P. Sartre, *Nausea* (Norfolk, Conn.: New Directions, 1949).

21. Heidegger, *Being and Time*, J. P. Sartre, *L'Être et Le Néant* (Paris: Gallimard, 1947).

22. See Heidegger, op cit., passim.

23. Sartre, *Being and Time* (New York: Philosophical Library, 1956), passim.

24. P. Tillich, *The Courage To Be* (New Haven: Yale Univ., 1952).

25. J. P. Sartre, *No Exit and Three Other Plays* (New York: Vintage, 1955).

26. K. Jaspers, *The Perennial Scope of Philosophy* (New York: Philosophical Library, 1949).

27. See inter alia Gabriel Marcel, *The Existential Background of Human Dignity* (Cambridge: Harvard Univ., 1963).

28. M. Buber, *I and Thou* (New York: Scribners, 1970).

29. M. Friedman, *Martin Buber: The Life of Dialogue* (Chicago: Univ. of Chicago, 1955). The phrases "dialogical philosophical" and "the life of dialogue" occur frequently in the writings of Buber. See W. Herberg, *The Writings of Martin Buber* (New York: New American Library, 1956).

30. M. Buber, op cit.

31. Heidegger, *Being and Time* (New York: Harper & Row, 1962), Division Two, Chapter 5.

32. S. Kierkegaard, *Concluding Unscientific Postscripts* (Princeton: Princeton Univ., 1941).

33. See P. Tillich, "Existential Philosophy," in *Theology of Culture* (New York: Oxford Univ., 1959).

34. I. Kant. *Critique of Practical Reason* (New York: Liberal Arts Press, 1956).

35. See inter alia S. Hook, ed., *Determinism and Freedom* (New York: Collier, 1961).

36. See inter alia R. May, *Existential Psychology* (New York: Random House, 1961).

Chapter VI

1. See inter alia A. A. Brill, ed., *The Basic Writings of Sigmund Freud* (New York: Modern Library, 1938).

2. Ibid., p. 262, 338f.

3. Ibid., p. 528f.

4. Ibid., p. 13, 23f.

5. Ibid., p. 580f.

6. S. Freud, *The Future of an Illusion* (Garden City: Doubleday, 1957).

7. S. Freud, *Civilization and Its Discontents* (New York: Norton, 1962) .

8. Karl Popper, *The Logic of Scientific Discovery* (New York: Science Editions, 1961).

9. S. Hook, ed., *Psychoanalysis Scientific Method and Philosophy* (New York: New York Univ., 1959).

10. John Wisdom, "Gods." See inter alia A. Flew, ed., *Logic and Language First Series* (Oxford: Blackwell, 1951).

11. B. Russell, *Our Knowledge of the External World* (Chicago: Open Court, 1929). See also J. Dewey, *Experience and Nature*; Bergson, *Two Sources of Morality and Religion*.

12. B. Blanshard, *The Nature of Thought* (London: Allen & Unwin), I, p. 313f.

13. See inter alia R. Niebuhr, *The Nature and Destiny of Man*.

14. Gilbert Ryle, *The Concepts of Mind* (New York: Barnes & Noble, 1949), p. 76f.

15. David Bakan, *Sigmund Freud and the Jewish Mystical Tradition* (Princeton: Van Nostrand, 1958).

16. Abraham Kaplan, *The New World of Philosophy*.

17. Philip Rieff, *Freud: The Mind of the Moralist* (Garden City: Doubleday, 1961).

Chapter VII

1. For Marxist humanism see inter alia, E. Bloch, *A Philosophy of the Future* (New York: Herder, 1970); R. Garaudy, *Marxism in the Twentieth Century* (New York: Scribners, 1970); A. Schaff, *Marxism and the Human Individual* (New York: McGraw-Hill, 1970).

2. I. Berlin, *Karl Marx* (New York: Oxford Univ., 1963), p. 23.

3. S. Hook, *From Hegel to Marx* (Ann Arbor: Univ. of Michigan, 1962). See also K. Loewith, *From Hegel to Nietzsche*.

4. J. Loewenberg, *Hegel Selections* (New York: Scribners, 1929), p. 98f.

5. Ibid., p. 443, 450.

6. Ibid., p. 338f.

7. Ibid., p. 443f.

8. L. Feuerbach, *The Essence of Christianity* (New York: Harper, 1957).

9. See inter alia L. Easton and K. Guddat, *Writings of the Young Marx on Philosophy and Society* (Garden City: Doubleday, 1967).

10. K. Marx and F. Engels, *The German Ideology* (New York: International Publishers, 1947).

11. S. Avineri, *The Social and Political Thought of Karl Marx* (Cambridge: Cambridge Univ., 1968).

12. T. Bottomore and M. Ruebel, eds., *Karl Marx* (Harmondsworth: Penguin, 1963), p. 67.

13. Ibid., p. 221f.

14. L. Feuer, ed., *Marx and Engels* (Garden City: Doubleday, 1959), p. 243f.

15. Ibid., p. 7f.

16. Ibid., p. 20.

17. Avineri, op cit., pp. 202–203.

18. See inter alia T. Bottomore and M. Ruebel, eds., op cit., p. 263.

19. Avineri, op cit., pp. 65–66.

20. See inter alia I. Berlin, "Historical Inevitability," in Berlin, *Four Essays on Liberty* (London: Oxford Univ. Press, 1971).

21. See W. Temple, *Nature, Man and God* (New York: Macmillan, 1934), preface. See also R. Niebuhr, *Nature and Destiny of Man* (New York: Scribners, 1941).

22. Niebuhr, op cit.

23. J. Bennett, *Christianity and Communism* (New York: Association Press, 1948).

24. A. Koestler, *Darkness At Noon* (New York: Macmillan, 1946).

Chapter VIII

1. W. T. Jones, *A History of Western Philosophy* (New York: Harcourt Brace, 1969); Bertrand Russell, *A History of Western Philosophy* (New York: Simon and Schuster, 1945).

2. H. Nakamura, *The Ways of Thinking of Eastern Peoples* (Honolulu: East-West Center, 1964).

3. W. Norman Brown, *Man in the Universe* (Berkeley: Univ. of California, 1966).

4. *Rig Veda* X, 129. (The A. A. MacDonell translation is used with permission of Oxford University Press.)

5. R. Thapar, *A History of India*, I (Harmondsworth: Penguin, 1965).

6. See inter alia A. L. Basham, *The Wonder That Was India*.

7. W. T. de Bary, *Sources of the Indian Tradition* (New York: Columbia University Press, 1958).

8. H. Zimmer, *Philosophies of India* (Princeton: Princeton Univ., 1951). See also N. Smart, *Doctrine and Arguments in Indian Philosophy* (New York: Humanities Press, 1964).

9. Smart, op cit.

10. Zimmer, op cit., Ch. 1.

11. Of the numerous translations of the *Bhagavad Gita* I wish to call attention to R. C. Zaehner (London: Oxford Univ., 1966).

12. Zaehner, op cit.

13. Ibid., Ch. 2–4.

14. Ibid., Ch. 2, passim.

15. Ibid., Ch. 10–12.

16. Smart, op cit.

17. Prabhavanavda, *The Crest Jewel of Discrimination* (New York: Mentor, 1970).

18. Nikhilananda, *Self Knowledge* (New York: Ramakrishna-Vivekananda Center, 1970).

19. S. Radhakrishnan and C. Moore, *Sourcebook of Indian Philosophy* (Princeton: Princeton Univ., 1957).

20. G. E. Moore, *Philosophical Studies* (New York: Harcourt Brace, 1922).

21. Radhakrishnan and Moore, op cit.

22. A. Chakravarty, ed., *A Tagore Reader* (Boston: Beacon Press, 1966).

23. S. Radhakrishnan, *Contemporary Indian Philosophy* (London: Allen & Unwin, 1952), Ch. 1.

24. Radhakrishnan and Moore, op cit., Ch. 15. See also Aurobindo, *The Mind of Light*, R. McDermott, ed. (New York: E. P. Dutton, 1971) and *Radhakrishnan*, R. McDermott, ed. (New York: E. P. Dutton, 1970).

25. S. Radhakrishnan, *Indian Philosophy* (New York: Macmillan, 1929–1931).

26. See inter alia, Radhakrishnan, *Recovery of Faith* (New York: Harper).

27. S. Radhakrishnan, *An Idealist View of Life* (London: Allen & Unwin, 1929).

Chapter IX

1. See W. T. de Bary, *Sources of the Indian Tradition* (New York: Columbia Univ., 1958), p. 42f.

2. H. Zimmer, *Philosophies of India* (New York: Meridian, 1957); N. Smart, *Doctrine and Argument in Indian Philosophy* (New York: Humanities Press, 1964).

3. Zimmer, op cit., p. 234, 314.

4. S. Radhakrishnan and C. Moore, *Sourcebook of Indian Philosophy* (Princeton: Princeton Univ.), p. 260.

5. Zimmer, op cit., p. 217f.

6. See inter alia de Bary, op cit., Ch. 4, 5.

7. Radhakrishnan and Moore, op cit., p. 260f.

8. H. C. Warren, *Buddhism in Translations* (Cambridge: Harvard Univ., 1953), Ch. 1. E. B. Seialso Cowell, ed., *Buddhist Mahayana Texts* (New York: Dover, 1969), p. 1f.

9. Kenneth Morgan, ed. *The Path of the Buddha* (New York: The Ronald Press, 1956), p. 8.

10. Quoted from Zimmer, op cit., p. 473.

11. See inter alia C. Hamilton, ed., *Buddhism: A Religion of Infinite Compassion* (New York: Liberal Arts Press, 1952).

12. H. C. Warren, op cit., p. 117.

13. Ibid., pp. 129–137.

14. Ibid., p. 148f.

15. N. Nikan and R. McKeon, *Ashoka: Edicts* (Chicago: Univ. of Chicago, 1958).

16. Richard Robinson, *The Buddhist Religion* (Belmont, CA: Dickenson, 1970).

17. Ibid.

18. Ibid.

19. See inter alia de Bary, ed., op cit., Ch. 6, 7.

20. Warren, op cit., p. 315f.

21. Ibid., p. 202f.

22. Robinson, op cit., p. 51f.

23. Ibid., p. 58f.

24. Ibid., p. 72–73.

25. See F. Streng, *Emptiness: A Study in Religious Meaning* (Nashville: Abingdon, 1967).

26. T. R. V. Murti, *The Central Philosophy of Buddhism* (London: Allen & Unwin, 1968).

27. T. Stcherbatsky, *The Conception of Buddhist Nirvana* (The Hague: Mouton, 1965).

28. Radhakrishnan and Moore, op cit., p. 343, 344.

29. N. Smart, op cit.

30. Zimmer, op cit., p. 520.

31. Ibid., p. 526.

Chapter X

1. M. Eliade, *Cosmos and History*.

2. H. Frankfort et al., *Before Philosophy* (Harmondsworth: Penguin, 1951).

3. E. Reischauer and J. Fairbank, *East Asia: The Great Tradition* (Boston: Houghton Mifflin, 1958), p. 67.

4. Wing-tsit Chan, trans. and comp., *Sourcebook of Chinese Philosophy* (Princeton: Princeton Univ. Press, 1963). Reprinted by permission of Princeton University Press.

5. Y. L. Fung, *A Short History of Chinese Philosophy* (New York: Macmillan, 1948).

6. Y. L. Fung, *A History of Chinese Philosophy* (Princeton: Princeton Univ., 1953).

7. Y. L. Fung, *A Short History of Chinese Philosophy* (New York: Macmillan, 1948).

8. Ibid.

9. W. T. Chan, *Sourcebook*, p. 41 and passim.

10. Ibid., passim.
11. Ibid., p. 28.
12. Ibid., p. 30.
13. Ibid., p. 25.
14. Ibid., p. 35.
15. Ibid., p. 139.
16. Ibid., passim.
17. Ibid., p. 146.
18. Ibid., p. 140f.
19. Ibid., p. 140.
20. Ibid., p. 168.
21. Ibid., p. 183.
22. Ibid., p. 190.
23. W. T. de Bary, ed., *Sources of Chinese Tradition* (New York: Columbia Univ., 1960), p. 79.
24. Chan, op cit., p. 209.
25. Ibid., p. 244f.
26. Ibid., p. 211f.
27. Ibid., p. 232f.
28. Ibid., p. 251f.
29. Ibid., p. 115f.
30. Ibid., p. 49f.
31. de Bary, op cit., p. 251.
32. Ibid., p. 258.
33. Chan, op cit., p. 271f.
34. Ibid., p. 292f.
35. Ibid., p. 314f.
36. Y. L. Fung, *Short History*, p. 231f.
37. Chan, op cit., p. 326f.
38. de Bary, op cit., p. 327f.
39. Ibid.
40. Ibid., p. 330f.
41. Chan, op cit.
42. Ibid., p. 430f.
43. Ibid., p. 430f.
44. Ibid., p. 432.
45. A. Wright, *Buddhism in Chinese History* (Stanford: Stanford Univ., 1959).
46. Chan, op cit., p. 463.
47. Ibid., p. 484.
48. Ibid., p. 497f.
49. Ibid., p. 497.
50. Ibid., pp. 518f., 544f.
51. Ibid., p. 588.
52. Y. L. Fung, *Short History*, p. 281f.
53. Chan, op cit., pp. 638–639.
54. Ibid., p. 654f.

Chapter XI

1. D. Suzuki, *Mysticism: Christian and Buddhist* (New York: Harper, 1957).
2. W. T. de Bary, ed., *Sources of the Japanese Tradition* (New York: Columbia Univ., 1958).

3. Ibid.

4. Ibid.

5. See inter alia H. N. Macfarland, *Rush Hour of the Gods* (New York: Macmillan, 1967). R. Hammer, *Japan's Religious Ferment* (New York: Oxford Univ., 1961). H. Thomsen, *The New Religions of Japan* (Rutland: Tuttle, 1963).

6. H. Nakamura, *The Ways of Thinking of Eastern Peoples* (Honolulu: East-West Center, 1964).

7. J. Kitagawa, *Religion in Japanese History* (New York: Columbia Univ., 1966).

8. de Bary, op cit., p. 106.

9. Ibid., pp. 109–110.

10. Kitagawa, op cit., p. 296.

11. Ibid., p. 296.

12. C. Hamilton, ed., *Buddhism: A Religion of Infinite Compassion* (New York: Liberal Arts Press, 1952).

13. de Bary, op cit., p. 243f.

14. Ibid., p. 237.

15. H. Dumoulin, *A History of Zen* (Boston: Beacon Press, 1969), p. 166f.

16. Ibid., p. 167f.

17. P. Kapleau, *The Three Pillars of Zen* (New York: Harper & Row, 1966).

18. Ibid., p. xvif.

19. Ibid., p. 320.

20. D. T. Suzuki, *Zen Buddhism*, ed. W. Barnett (Garden City: Anchor Books, 1956), p. 111f.

21. Ibid., p. 134f.

22. Ibid., p. 111f.

23. Ibid., p. 134, 140f.

24. Ibid., p. 134.

25. Suzuki, op cit., p. 84f.

26. Moore, C., op cit., p. 288f.

27. Z. Shibayama, *A Flower Does Not Talk* (Rutland: Tuttle, 1970).

Chapter XII

1. K. Barth, *Church Dogmatics* (New York: Scribners, 1936–1969). See esp. Vol. 1, part 2.

2. David Hume, *Dialogues Concerning Natural Religion*, ed. Norman Kemp Smith (New York: T. Nelson, 1947).

3. See inter alia R. Niebuhr, *The Nature and Destiny of Man*, I (New York: Scribners, 1941). See also "Christianity and Crisis," XIV, 1 and XIV, 24 for forceful assertions of Niebuhr's view.

4. Among recent theological critics of religion see H. Gutierrez, *A Theology of Liberation* (Maryknoll: Orbis, 1973); H. Kueng, *Freedom Today* (New York: Sheed, 1966); and H. Cox, *The Seduction of the Spirit* (New York: Simon and Schuster, 1973).

5. For the so-called "death of God" theology see inter alia W. Hamilton and T. Altizer, *Radical Theology and the Death of God* (Indianapolis: Bobbs Merrill, 1966).

6. K. Barth, *The Epistle to the Romans*, E. C. Hoskins, trans. (London: Oxford Univ., 1933).

7. P. Tillich. I have been unable to find this assertion in any published work of Tillich, and therefore cite it as an unpublished remark.

8. R. Niebuhr, *The Nature and Destiny of Man* (New York: Scribners, 1941). See esp. Chapters VI–VIII.

9. Ibid., p. 186f.

10. Ibid., p. 208f.

11. Ibid., p. 188f.

12. R. Bultmann, *Kenygma and Myth* (New York: Harper, 1953). See also by the same author, *Theology of the New Testament* (London: SCM Press, 1952).

13. P. Tillich, *Systematic Theology*, I (Chicago: Univ. of Chicago, 1951).

14. P. Tillich, *Systematic Theology*, II (Chicago: Univ. of Chicago, 1957), passim.

15. See inter alia C. Hartshorn, *The Divine Relativity* (New Haven: Yale Univ., 1948). See also J. Cobb, *A Christian Natural Theology* (Philadelphia: Westminster, 1965).

16. In addition to Cobb, op cit., see inter alia W. Christian, *An Interpretation of Whitehead's Metaphysics* (New Haven: Yale Univ., 1959).

17. P. Tillich, *The Protestant Era* (Chicago: Univ. of Chicago, 1948), Ch. 2, p. 16f. See also R. Niebuhr, *The Nature and Destiny of Man*, II (New York: Scribners, 1943), Ch. 1, esp. p. 15f.

18. G. E. Wright, *God Who Acts* (London: SCM Press, 1952).

19. M. Buber, *The Prophetic Faith* (New York: Macmillan, 1949).

20. Saint Augustine, *The City of God*, M. Dodd, trans. (New York: Modern Library, 1950).

21. M. Reeves, *The Figurae of Joachim* (Oxford: Clarendon, 1972).

22. C. Becker, *The Heavenly City of the Eighteenth Century Philosophers* (New Haven: Yale Univ., 1932).

23. R. Niebuhr, op cit., Vol. II, entitled *Human Destiny* (New York: Scribners, 1942).

24. P. Tillich, *The Protestant Era* (Chicago: Univ. of Chicago, 1948), Ch. II.

25. M. Eliade, *Cosmos and History* (New York: Harper, 1959).

26. R. Niebuhr, *Leaves From the Notebook of a Tamed Cynic* (New York: Meridian Press, 1957).

27. See inter alia M. D'Arcy, *The Mind and Heart of Love* (New York: Meridian, 1956). A. Nygren, *Agape and Eros* (London: SPCK, 1953).

28. M. Buber, *I and Thou* (New York: Scribners, 1970).

29. Augustine, *The City of God*, Book XI, 1.

30. R. Niebuhr, *An Interpretation of Christian Ethics* (New York: Harper, 1935). Note especially Chapters 4 and 5.

31. See inter alia "Natural Law" in *Encyclopedia of Philosophy* (New York: Macmillan, 1966), vol. 5, pp. 450–453. See also *The New Catholic Encyclopedia* (New York: McGraw-Hill, 1967), vol. 10, pp. 251–262.

32. R. Niebuhr, op cit., 4–5.

33. R. Niebuhr, *Christianity and Power Politics* (Hamden, Conn.: Anchor Books, 1969).

34. J. Fletcher, *Situation Ethics* (Philadelphia: Westminster, 1966).

35. Aquinas, *Summa Theologica*, I, 12, 13. See also Ibid., I, 62, 2–4.

36. P. Tillich, see inter alia *The Protestant Era*, XV, 58, 87, 273, *Systematic Theology*, I, passism.

37. Anselm, *Proslogion*, Ch. 2. See inter alia A. Plantinga, *The Ontological Argument* (Garden City: Doubleday, 1965), p. 3f.

38. R. Otto, *The Idea of the Holy* (New York: Oxford Univ., 1958).

39. D. Bonhoeffer, *Letters and Papers from Prison* (New York: Macmillan, 1966).

40. ———, *Ethics* (New York: Macmillan, 1955).

41. A. Van Leeuven, *Christianity in World History* (New York: Scribners, 1964).

42. H. Cox, *The Secular City* (New York: Macmillan, 1966).

43. F. Nietzsche, *Thus Spake Zarathustra* (New York: Modern Library, 1905).

Chapter XIII

1. H. R. Niebuhr, *Radical Monotheism and Western Culture* (New York: Harper, 1960).

2. Frankfort et al., *Before Philosophy* (Harmondsworth: Penguin, 1951). See especially the last chapter, which deals with Israel's historical attitudes.

3. I. Mendelsohn, ed., *Religions of the Ancient Near East* (New York: Liberal Arts Press, 1955).

4. E. Auerbach, *Mimesis* (Princeton: Princeton Univ., 1953). See esp. Chapter 1.

5. B. Anderson, *Understanding the Old Testament* (Englewood Cliffs, N.J.: Prentice Hall, 1957).

6. M. Buber, *The Prophetic Faith* (New York: Macmillan, 1949).

7. The "Servant of the Lord" poems may be found in the OT Book of Isaiah 42:1–4, 49:1–6, 50:4–9, 52:13, 53:2.

8. See inter alia L. Schwarz, ed., *Great Ages and Ideas of the Jewish People* (New York: Random House, 1956).

9. For Philo, see inter alia Lewy et al., eds., *Three Jewish Philosophers* (New York: Atheneum, 1972).

10. H. Wolfson, *Philo: Foundations of Religious Philosophy on Judaism, Christianity and Islam* (Cambridge: Harvard Univ., 1947).

11. J. Blau and S. Baron, *Judaism: Postbiblical and Talmudic* (New York: Liberal Arts Press, 1954).

12. Schwarz, op cit., p. 315f.

13. *Three Jewish Philosophers* (New York: Atheneum, 1972), p. 9f.

14. Ibid., p. 36f.

15. Maimonides, M., *The Guide to the Perplexed*, S. Pines, trans. (Chicago: Univ. of Chicago, 1963).

16. Quoted from J. Hertz, *The Authorized Party Prayer Book* (New York: Block Publishing, 1948).

17. G. Scholem, ed. and trans., *Zohar, The Book of Splendor* (New York: Schocken, 1954).

18. G. Scholem, *Major Trends in Jewish Mysticism* (New York: Schocken, 1954).

19. F. Rosenzweig, *The Star of Redemption* (New York: Holt Rinehart & Winston, 1971).

20. For Buber, see esp. Herberg, ed., *The Writings of Martin Buber* (New York: Meridian, 1956).

21. M. Buber, *I and Thou* (New York: Scribners, 1937), p. 11.

22. Ibid., p. 6f.

23. M. Buber, *The Prophetic Faith* (New York: Macmillan, 1949); *Two Types of Faith* (New York: Harper, 1961).

Chapter XIV

1. See inter alia K. Morgan, *Islam: The Straight Path* (New York: Ronald Press, 1958), passim.

2. Ibid., p. 9, Sura 96.

3. Ibid., p. 13.

4. *Suran*, 50:16. See M. Pickthall, trans., *The Meaning of the Glorious Koran* (New York: Mentor, 1953), p. 370.

5. R. Nicolson, *A Literary History of the Arabs* (Cambridge: Cambridge Univ., 1969), p. 234.

6. R. C. Zaehner, *Hindu and Muslim Mysticism* (London: Athlom Press, 1960).

7. Ibid. See also Hastings, ed., *The Encyclopedia of Religion and Ethics* (New York: Scribners, 1914), VI, p. 480–482.

8. Al Ghazzali, *The Inconsistency of the Philosophers*, Sabih Ahmed Kamali, trans., Lahore, Pakistan Philosophical Congress, 1963. Al Ghazzali, *Our Beginning in Wisdom* (Washington: American Council of Learned Societies, 1953).

9. Quoted from J. Kritzeck, ed., *Anthology of Islamic Literature* (Harmondsworth: Penguin, 1964), p. 258.

10. Al Kindi, *On First Philosophy*, A. L. Ivry, trans. (Albany: State University of New York, 1972).

11. *Al Farabi's Short Commentary on Aristotle's Prior Analytics*, N. Rescher, trans. (Pittsburgh: Univ. of Pittsburgh, 1963).

12. A. J. Arberry, *Revelation and Reason in Islam* (London: Allen & Unwin, 1957).

13. S. Vanden Bergh, trans., *The Inconsistency of the Inconsistency* (London: Oxford, 1954).

14. W. T. de Bary, ed., *Sources of the Indian Tradition,* Ch. 25, p. 740f.

15. Ibid., p. 749f.

16. M. Iqbal, *The Reconstruction of Religious Thought in Islam* (Lahore: Ashraf, 1944).

17. M. Iqbal, *Secrets of the Self* (Lahore: Ashraf, 1940).

18. M. Iqbal, *Mysteries of Selflessness* (New York: Paragon, 1953).

Chapter XV

1. C. A. Moore, ed., *The Indian Mind* (Honolulu: East-West Center, 1967).

2. R. Niebuhr, *Christian Realism and Political Problems* (New York: Scribners, 1953). See especially the essay entitled "The Illusion of World Government."

3. Ibid.

4. W. E. Hocking, *The Coming World Civilization* (New York: Harper, 1956).

Index

About the Author

JOHN A. HUTCHISON describes himself as a philosopher of religion, that is, a philosopher seeking to understand religion, or the religious experience. He is presently Danforth Professor of Philosophy of Religion at Claremont Graduate School. He received his doctorate from Columbia University and has published articles in numerous journals including *The Journal of the History of Philosophy* and *The Journal of Philosophy*. Among his six published books are *The Two Cities* and *Paths of Faith*.

☂ Production Notes

The text of this book has been designed by Roger J. Eggers, and typeset on the Unified Composing System by the design & production staff of The University Press of Hawaii.

The text typeface is Garamond No. 49. The display matter is set in Friz Quadrata.

Offset presswork and binding is the work of The Maple Press Company. Text paper is Glatfelter P & S Offset, basis 55.